BEAR, MAN, AND GOD:

Eight Approaches to William Faulkner's "The Bear"

GO Down Moses

W.F.

N.Y. Random House
1942

EDITED BY

FRANCIS LEE UTLEY *Ohio State University*

LYNN Z. BLOOM *Butler University*

ARTHUR F. KINNEY *University of Massachusetts, Amherst*

BEAR, MAN, AND GOD:

Eight Approaches to William Faulkner's "THE BEAR"

SECOND EDITION

RANDOM HOUSE NEW YORK

Published in the United States by Random House, Inc., New York, and simultaneously in Canada by Random House of Canada Limited, Toronto.

ISBN: 0-394-31546-4

Library of Congress Catalog Card Number: 78-140498

Manufactured in the United States of America
by The Book Press, Brattleboro, Vt.

Second Edition

987

Once again, in honor of William Faulkner

Acknowledgments

To work with the prose of William Faulkner can be a challenging and satisfying experience. Many have helped us in the past, and to that extent share in its rewards. Of these, we should like to extend our gratitude publicly to Professors Richard Altick, Arthur J. Carr, Joe Lee Davis, Hubert M. English, Claude Simpson, and Mark Spilka for their professional counsel; to Charles Pettee of Charles Scribner's Sons, who first suggested the present collaboration; to Philip Lee Utley, who taught one of us how much "The Bear" could mean to an undergraduate; to the staffs of the University of Michigan, Ohio State University, and Clements Libraries for their kind and patient assistance with our research; and to the staff of the University of Michigan Audio-Visual Education Center for their aid. We have also been long indebted to Jane P. Alles, formerly of Random House, who during the first compilation of this work combined the roles of wise advisor, good friend, and communications center.

The present revision was first suggested by David Dushkin of Random House and executed under the wise and patient guidance of James Smith, June Fischbein, and Ricki Anne Sokol. Professors John Hagopian, Jules Chametzky, Sidney Kaplan, Everett Emerson, Mason Lowance, John Muste, and A. W. Plumstead have contributed suggestions for revision; and we are appreciative as well for the helpful assistance of Christopher Diamond and David Williams, who did much of the initial research, and to William Harney and Harry Authelet, who helped in the final stages of editing; to members of the graduate and undergraduate seminars in Faulkner at the University of Massachusetts for a number of proposals; and to the staffs of the New York Public Library; the Education, Peabody, Houghton, and Widener Libraries of Harvard; the Sterling and Beinecke Libraries of Yale; and the Frost Library of Amherst College, the Neilson Library of Smith College, and the Goodell Library of the University of Massachusetts, Amherst. Mrs. Nancy Authelet graciously volunteered to handle all matters dealing with permissions. Throughout our labors, we have been encouraged in a number of ways by Scotty Utley and Martin Bloom.

During our preparations we constantly have benefited from new discoveries we have shared despite our varied backgrounds. We hope our readers have similar experiences.

Contents

Critical Interpretations of "The Bear"

"The Bear" in Relation to Go Down, Moses

Faulkner and the Blacks

The Relation of Style and Form to Meaning in Faulkner's Work

Appendixes

William Faulkner's
"THE BEAR"

Introduction

Despite the central position "The Bear" holds today in the works of William Faulkner and of twentieth-century America, the story remained relatively unknown for several years. Parts of "The Bear" first appeared as magazine stories—one in 1935 and another the day after the final version was published in book form as one of the seven parts of *Go Down, Moses*. The book (Random House, 1942) was concerned with the white McCaslin and the Negro Beauchamp descendants of Lucius Quintus McCaslin, tracing white-black relationships through several generations as observed from several points of view discrete in time and vantage point. Since the publication of the book, "The Bear" has come to take its place with the best works of American fiction.

"The Bear" is comparable in length to *Old Man* and *Spotted Horses*. It is now part of the saga of Faulkner's own imaginative Yoknapatawpha County, now generally held to be a fictional counterpart of Lafayette County, Mississippi. The work is divided into five parts. Parts one, two, three, and five form the central story of the boy Isaac's search for Old Ben and its aftermath; this portion is a traditional *bildungsroman* and one of the great hunting stories in the English language. It is in Faulkner's simplest and most energetic style.

Part four is more difficult. Here Faulkner attempts to extend the meaning of the hunt backward and forward in time, adding significance to each event by mirroring it in the minds of young Ike and his cousin Cass Edmonds so that the story itself comes to serve as history, lesson, program, and ultimately metaphor. This section is Faulkner's comprehensive attempt to express ideas about God, nature, and man coupled with his interpretation of the history of the South; and he has put it into one sentence. Malcolm Cowley (in *The Portable Faulkner*) has pointed out that this sentence runs to sixteen hundred words, each placed rhythmically yet precisely between one capital letter and one period—one of the longest sentences in all literature. Within it, he notes, other sentences roam up to six pages long and, near the center (pp. 48–49), a parenthesis which extends for one and a third pages. Although this section contains some of Faulkner's most challenging thoughts couched in some of his most difficult prose, it nevertheless raises the entire work to a new plane, providing, in the subjective-objective history of the ledgers, in the debate over interpreting the past (particularly as it allows for repudiation), and in the discussion of the Bible and Keats, both a credo of beliefs and a theory of art which go far to locate and to define not only "The Bear" but Faulkner's contribution generally to American letters.

"The Bear"

The events of "The Bear" occur in the northwestern corner of Yoknapatawpha County, well north of Jefferson, its capital city, in a woods along the Tallahatchie River bottom. The land, formerly belonging to a large plantation of a hundred square miles, owned by Thomas Sutpen, was taken over by Major Cassius de Spain through foreclosures. The Major turned a poor white's shack on the land into a hunting cabin and shortly after, each November, began two-week hunting parties into the woods with his old friends General Compson, McCaslin Edmonds, and finally young Isaac McCaslin, the boy of this story. After Major de Spain discovered Old Ben, the bear which was ravaging the countryside, the Major, his friends, and his servants—the Indian guide Sam Fathers, the part-Indian Boon, and the Negro cook Ash—made him the principal quarry of their hunting parties.

1

There was a man and a dog too this time. Two beasts, counting Old Ben, the bear, and two men, counting Boon Hogganbeck, in whom some of the same blood ran which ran in Sam Fathers, even though Boon's was a plebeian strain of it and only Sam and Old Ben and the mongrel Lion were taintless and incorruptible.

He was sixteen. For six years now he had been a man's hunter. For six years now he had heard the best of all talking. It was of the wilderness, the big woods, bigger and older than any recorded document:—of white man fatuous enough to believe he had bought any fragment of it, of Indian ruthless enough to pretend that any fragment of it had been his to convey; bigger than Major de Spain and the scrap he pretended to, knowing better; older than old Thomas Sutpen of whom Major de Spain had had it and who knew better; older even than old Ikkemotubbe, the Chickasaw chief, of whom old Sutpen had had it and who knew better in his turn. It was of the men, not white nor black nor red but men, hunters, with the will and hardihood to endure and the humility and skill to survive, and the dogs and the bear and deer juxtaposed and reliefed against it, ordered and compelled by and within the wilderness in the ancient and unremitting contest according to the ancient and immitigable rules which voided all regrets and brooked no quarter;—the best game of all, the best of all breathing and forever the best of all listening, the voices quiet and weighty and deliberate for retrospection and recollection and exactitude among the concrete trophies—the racked guns and the heads and skins—in the libraries of town houses or the offices of plantation houses or (and best of all) in the camps themselves where the intact and still-warm meat yet hung, the men who had slain it sitting before the burning logs on hearths when there were houses and hearths or about the smoky blazing of piled wood in front of stretched tarpaulins when there were not. There was always a bottle present, so that it would seem to him that those fine fierce instants of heart and brain and courage and wiliness and speed were concentrated and distilled into that brown liquor which not women, not boys and children, but only hunters drank, drinking not of the blood they spilled but some condensation of the wild immortal spirit, drinking it moderately, humbly even, not with the pagan's base and baseless hope of acquiring thereby the virtues of cunning and strength and speed but in salute to them. Thus it seemed to him on this December morning not only natural but actually fitting that this should have begun with whisky.

He realised later that it had begun long before that. It had already begun on that day when he first wrote his age in two ciphers and his cousin McCaslin brought him for the first time to the camp, the big woods, to earn for himself from the wilderness the name and state of hunter provided he in his turn were humble and enduring enough. He had already inherited then, without ever having seen it, the big old bear with one trap-ruined foot that in an area almost a hundred miles square had earned for himself a name, a definite designation like a living man:—the long legend of corn-cribs broken down and rifled, of shoats and grown pigs and even calves carried bodily into the woods and devoured and traps and deadfalls overthrown and dogs mangled and slain and shotgun and even rifle shots delivered at point-blank range yet with no more effect than so many peas blown through a tube by a child—a corridor of wreckage and destruction beginning back before the boy was born, through which sped, not fast but rather with the ruthless and irresistible deliberation of a locomotive, the shaggy tremendous shape. It ran in his knowledge before he ever saw it. It loomed and towered in his dreams before he even saw the unaxed woods where it left its crooked print, shaggy, tremendous, red-eyed, not malevolent but just big, too big for the dogs which tried to bay it, for the horses which tried to ride it down, for the men and the bullets they fired into it; too big for the very country which was its constricting scope. It was as if the boy had already divined what his senses and intellect had not encompassed yet: that doomed wilderness whose edges were being constantly and punily gnawed at by men with plows and axes who feared it because it was wilderness, men myriad and nameless even to one another in the land where the old bear had earned a name, and through which ran not even a mortal beast but an anachronism indomitable and invincible out of an old dead time, a phantom, epitome and apotheosis of the old wild life which the little puny humans swarmed and hacked at in a fury of abhorrence and fear like pygmies about the ankles of a drowsing elephant;—the old bear, solitary, indomitable, and alone; widowered childless and absolved of mortality—old Priam reft of his old wife and outlived all his sons.

Still a child, with three years then two years then one year yet before he too could make one of them, each November he would watch the wagon containing the dogs and the bedding and food and guns and his cousin McCaslin and Tennie's Jim and Sam Fathers too until Sam moved to the camp to live, depart for the Big Bottom, the big woods. To him, they were going not to hunt bear and deer but to keep yearly rendezvous with the bear which they did not even intend to kill. Two weeks later they would return, with no trophy, no skin. He had not expected it. He had not even feared that it might be in the wagon this time with the other skins and heads. He did not even tell himself that in three years or two years or one year more he would be present and that it might even be his gun. He believed that only after he had served his apprenticeship in the woods which would prove him worthy to be a hunter, would he even be permitted to distinguish the crooked print, and that even then for two November weeks he would merely make another minor one, along with his cousin and Major de Spain and General Compson and Walter Ewell and Boon and the dogs which feared to bay it and the shotguns and rifles which failed even to bleed it, in the yearly pageant-rite of the old bear's furious immortality.

His day came at last. In the surrey with his cousin and Major de Spain and General Compson he saw the wilderness through a slow drizzle of November rain just above the ice point as it seemed to him later he always saw it or at least always remembered it—the tall and endless wall of dense November woods under the dissolving afternoon and the year's death, sombre, impenetrable (he could not even discern yet how, at what point they could possibly hope to enter it even though he knew that Sam Fathers was waiting there with the wagon), the surrey moving through the skeleton stalks of cotton and corn in the last of open country, the last trace of man's puny gnawing at the immemorial flank, until, dwarfed by that perspective into an almost ridiculous diminishment, the surrey itself seemed to have ceased to move (this too to be completed later, years later, after he had grown to a man and had seen the sea) as a solitary small boat hangs in lonely immobility, merely tossing up and down, in the infinite waste of the ocean while the water and then the apparently impenetrable land which it nears without appreciable progress, swings slowly and opens the widening inlet which is the anchorage. He entered it. Sam was waiting, wrapped in a quilt on the wagon seat behind the patient and steaming mules. He entered his novitiate to the true wilderness with Sam beside him as he had begun his apprenticeship in miniature to manhood after the rabbits and such with Sam beside him, the two of them wrapped in the damp, warm, negro-rank quilt while the wilderness closed behind his entrance as it had opened momentarily to accept him, opening before his advancement as it closed behind his progress, no fixed path the wagon followed but a channel nonexistent ten yards ahead of it and ceasing to exist ten yards after it had passed, the wagon progressing not by its own volition but by attrition of their intact yet fluid circumambience, drowsing, earless, almost lightless.

It seemed to him that at the age of ten he was witnessing his own birth. It was not even strange to him. He had experienced it all before, and not merely in dreams. He saw the camp—a paintless six-room bungalow set on piles above the spring high-water—and he knew already how it was going to look. He helped in the rapid orderly disorder of their establishment in it and even his motions were familiar to him, foreknown. Then for two weeks he ate the coarse, rapid food—the shapeless sour bread, the wild strange meat, venison and bear and turkey and coon which he had never tasted before—which men ate, cooked by men who were hunters first and cooks afterward; he slept in harsh sheetless blankets as hunters slept. Each morning the gray of dawn found him and Sam Fathers on the stand, the crossing, which had been allotted him. It was the poorest one, the most barren. He had expected that; he had not dared yet to hope even to himself that he would even hear the running dogs this first time. But he did hear them. It was on the third morning—a murmur, sourceless, almost indistinguishable, yet he knew what it was although he had never before heard that many dogs running at once, the murmur swelling into separate and distinct voices until he could call the five dogs which his cousin owned from among the others. "Now," Sam said, "slant your gun up a little and draw back the hammers and then stand still."

But it was not for him, not yet. The humility was there; he had learned that. And he could learn the patience. He was only ten, only one week. The instant had passed. It seemed to him that he could actually see the deer, the buck, smoke-colored, elongated with speed, vanished, the woods, the gray solitude still ringing even when the voices of the dogs had died away; from far away across the sombre woods and the gray half-liquid morning there came two shots. "Now let your hammers down," Sam said.

He did so. "You knew it too," he said.

"Yes," Sam said. "I want you to learn how to do when you didn't shoot. It's after the chance for the bear or the deer has done already come and gone that men and dogs get killed."

"Anyway, it wasn't him," the boy said. "It wasn't even a bear. It was just a deer."

"Yes," Sam said, "it was just a deer."

Then one morning, it was in the second week, he heard the dogs again. This time before Sam even spoke he readied the too-long, too-heavy, man-size gun as Sam had taught him, even though this time he knew the dogs and the deer were coming less close than ever, hardly within hearing even. They didn't sound like any running dogs he had ever heard before even. Then he found that Sam, who had taught him first of all to cock the gun and take position where he could see best in all directions and then never to move again, had himself moved up beside him. "There," he said. "Listen." The boy listened, to no ringing chorus strong and fast on a free scent but a moiling yapping an octave too high and with something more than indecision and even abjectness in it which he could not yet recognise, reluctant, not even moving very fast, taking a long time to pass out of hearing, leaving even then in the air that echo of thin and almost human hysteria, abject, almost humanly grieving, with this time nothing ahead of it, no sense of a fleeing unseen smoke-colored shape. He could hear Sam breathing at his shoulder. He saw the arched curve of the old man's inhaling nostrils.

"It's Old Ben!" he cried, whispering.

Sam didn't move save for the slow gradual turning of his head as the voices faded on and the faint steady rapid arch and collapse of his nostrils. "Hah," he said. "Not even running. Walking."

"But up here!" the boy cried. "Way up here!"

"He do it every year," Sam said. "Once. Ash and Boon say he comes up here to run the other little bears away. Tell them to get to hell out of here and stay out until the hunters are gone. Maybe." The boy no longer heard anything at all, yet still Sam's head continued to turn gradually and steadily until the back of it was toward him. Then it turned back and looked down at him—the same face, grave, familiar, expressionless until it smiled, the same old man's eyes from which as he watched there faded slowly a quality darkly and fiercely lambent, passionate and proud. "He dont care no more for bears than he does for dogs or men neither. He come to see who's here, who's new in camp this year, whether he can shoot or not, can stay or not. Whether we got the dog yet that can bay and hold him until a man gets there with a gun. Because he's the head bear. He's the man." It faded, was gone; again they were the eyes as he had known them all his life. "He'll let them follow him to the river. Then he'll send them home. We might as well go too; see how they look when they get back to camp."

The dogs were there first, ten of them huddled back under the kitchen, himself and Sam squatting to peer back into the obscurity where they crouched, quiet, the eyes rolling and luminous, vanishing, and no sound, only that effluvium which the boy could not quite place yet, of something more than dog, stronger than dog and not just animal, just beast even. Because there had been nothing in front of the abject and painful yapping except the solitude, the wilderness, so that when the eleventh hound got back about mid-afternoon and he and Tennie's Jim held the passive and still trembling bitch while Sam daubed her tattered ear and raked shoulder with turpentine and axle grease, it was still no living creature but only the wilderness which, leaning for a moment, had patted lightly once her temerity. "Just like a man," Sam said. "Just like folks. Put off as long as she could having to be brave, knowing all the time that sooner or later she would have to be brave once so she could keep on calling herself a dog, and knowing beforehand what was going to happen when she done it."

He did not know just when Sam left. He only knew that he was gone. For the next three mornings he rose and ate breakfast and Sam was not waiting for him. He went to his stand alone; he found it without help now and stood on it as Sam had taught him. On the third morning he heard the dogs again, running strong and free on a true scent again, and he readied the gun as he had learned to do and heard the hunt sweep past on since he was not ready yet, had not deserved other yet in just one short period of two weeks as compared to all the long life which he had already dedicated to the wilderness with patience and humility; he heard the shot again, one shot, the single clapping report of Walter Ewell's rifle. By now he could not only find his stand and then return to camp without guidance, by using the compass his cousin had given him he reached Walter waiting beside the buck and the moiling of dogs over the cast entrails before any of the others except Major de Spain and Tennie's Jim on the horses, even before Uncle Ash arrived with the one-eyed wagon-mule which did not mind the smell of blood or even, so they said, of bear.

It was not Uncle Ash on the mule. It was Sam, returned. And Sam was waiting when he finished his dinner and, himself on the one-eyed mule and Sam on the other one of the wagon team, they rode for more than three hours through the rapid shortening sunless afternoon, following no path, no trail even that he could discern, into a section of country he had never seen before. Then he understood why Sam had made him ride the one-eyed mule which would not spook at the smell of blood, of wild animals. The other one, the sound one, stopped short and tried to whirl and bolt even as Sam got down, jerking and wrenching at the rein while Sam held it, coaxing it forward with his voice since he did not dare risk hitching it, drawing it forward while the boy dismounted from the marred one which would stand. Then, standing beside Sam in the thick great gloom of ancient woods and the winter's dying afternoon, he looked quietly down at the rotted log scored and gutted with claw-marks and, in the wet earth beside it, the print of the enormous warped two-toed foot. Now he knew what he had heard in the hounds' voices in the woods that morning and what he had smelled when he peered under the kitchen where they huddled. It was in him too, a little different because they were brute beasts and he was not, but only a little different—an eagerness, passive; an abjectness, a sense of his own fragility and impotence against the timeless woods, yet without doubt or dread; a flavor like brass in the sudden run of saliva in his mouth, a hard sharp constriction either in his brain or his stomach, he could not tell which and it did not matter; he knew only that for the first time he realised that the bear which had run in his listening and loomed in his dreams since before he could remember and which therefore must have existed in the listening and the dreams of his cousin and Major de Spain and even old General Compson before they began to remember in their turn, was a mortal animal and that they had departed for the camp each November with no actual intention of slaying it, not because it could not be slain but because so far they had no actual hope of being able to. "It will be tomorrow," he said.

"You mean we will try tomorrow," Sam said. "We aint got the dog yet."

"We've got eleven," he said. "They ran him Monday."

"And you heard them," Sam said. "Saw them too. We aint got the dog yet. It wont take but one. But he aint there. Maybe he aint nowhere. The only other way will be for him to run by accident over somebody that had a gun and knowed how to shoot it."

"That wouldn't be me," the boy said. "It would be Walter or Major or ——"

"It might," Sam said. "You watch close tomorrow. Because he's smart. That's how come he has lived this long. If he gets hemmed up and has got to pick out somebody to run over, he will pick out you."

"How?" he said. "How will he know. . . ." He ceased. "You mean he already knows me, that I aint never been to the big bottom before, aint had time to find out yet whether I . . ." He ceased again, staring at Sam;

he said humbly, not even amazed: "It was me he was watching. I dont reckon he did need to come but once."

"You watch tomorrow," Sam said. "I reckon we better start back. It'll be long after dark now before we get to camp."

The next morning they started three hours earlier than they had ever done. Even Uncle Ash went, the cook, who called himself by profession a camp cook and who did little else save cook for Major de Spain's hunting and camping parties, yet who had been marked by the wilderness from simple juxtaposition to it until he responded as they all did, even the boy who until two weeks ago had never even seen the wilderness, to a hound's ripped ear and shoulder and the print of a crooked foot in a patch of wet earth. They rode. It was too far to walk: the boy and Sam and Uncle Ash in the wagon with the dogs, his cousin and Major de Spain and General Compson and Boon and Walter and Tennie's Jim riding double on the horses; again the first gray light found him, as on that first morning two weeks ago, on the stand where Sam had placed and left him. With the gun which was too big for him, the breech-loader which did not even belong to him but to Major de Spain and which he had fired only once, at a stump on the first day to learn the recoil and how to reload it with the paper shells, he stood against a big gum tree beside a little bayou whose black still water crept without motion out of a cane-brake, across a small clearing and into the cane again, where, invisible, a bird, the big woodpecker called Lord-to-God by negroes, clattered at a dead trunk. It was a stand like any other stand, dissimilar only in incidentals to the one where he had stood each morning for two weeks; a territory new to him yet no less familiar than that other one which after two weeks he had come to believe he knew a little—the same solitude, the same loneliness through which frail and timorous man had merely passed without altering it, leaving no mark nor scar, which looked exactly as it must have looked when the first ancestor of Sam Fathers' Chickasaw predecessors crept into it and looked about him, club or stone axe or bone arrow drawn and ready, different only because, squatting at the edge of the kitchen, he had smelled the dogs huddled and cringing beneath it and saw the raked ear and side of the bitch that, as Sam had said, had to be brave once in order to keep on calling herself a dog, and saw yesterday in the earth beside the gutted log, the print of the living foot. He heard no dogs at all. He never did certainly hear them. He only heard the drumming of the woodpecker stop short off, and knew that the bear was looking at him. He never saw it. He did not know whether it was facing him from the cane or behind him. He did not move, holding the useless gun which he knew now he would never fire at it, now or ever, tasting in his saliva that taint of brass which he had smelled in the huddled dogs when he peered under the kitchen.

Then it was gone. As abruptly as it had stopped, the woodpecker's dry hammering set up again, and after a while he believed he even heard the dogs—a murmur, scarce a sound even, which he had probably been hearing for a time, perhaps a minute or two, before he remarked it, drifting into hearing and then out again, dying away. They came nowhere near him. If it was dogs he heard, he could not have sworn to it; if it was a bear they ran, it was another bear. It was Sam himself who emerged from the cane and crossed the bayou, the injured bitch following at heel as a bird dog is taught to walk. She came and crouched against his leg, trembling. "I didn't see him," he said. "I didn't, Sam."

"I know it," Sam said. "He done the looking. You didn't hear him neither, did you?"

"No," the boy said. "I ——"

"He's smart," Sam said. "Too smart." Again the boy saw in his eyes that quality of dark and brooding lambence as Sam looked down at the bitch trembling faintly and steadily against the boy's leg. From her raked shoulder a few drops of fresh blood clung like bright berries. "Too big. We aint got the dog yet. But maybe some day."

Because there would be a next time, after and after. He was only ten. It seemed to him that he could see them, the two of them, shadowy in the limbo from which time emerged and became time: the old bear absolved of mortality and himself who shared a little of it. Because he recognised now what he had smelled in the huddled dogs and tasted in his own saliva, recognised fear as a boy, a youth, recognises the existence of love and passion and experience which is his heritage but not yet his patrimony, from entering by chance the presence or perhaps even merely the bedroom of a woman who has loved and been loved by many men. *So I will have to see him,* he thought, without dread or even hope. *I will have to look at him.* So it was in June of the next summer. They were at the camp again, celebrating Major de Spain's and General Compson's birthdays. Although the one had been born in September and the other in the depth of winter and almost thirty years earlier, each June the two of them and McCaslin and Boon and Walter Ewell (and the boy too from now on) spent two weeks at the camp, fishing and shooting squirrels and turkey and running coons and wildcats with the dogs at night. That is, Boon and the negroes (and the boy too now) fished and shot squirrels and ran the coons and cats, because the proven hunters, not only Major de Spain and old General Compson (who spent those two weeks sitting in a rocking chair before a tremendous iron pot of Brunswick stew, stirring and tasting, with Uncle Ash to quarrel with about how he was making it and Tennie's Jim to pour whisky into the tin dipper from which he drank it) but even McCaslin and Walter Ewell who were still young enough, scorned such other than shooting the wild gobblers with pistols for wagers or to test their marksmanship.

That is, his cousin McCaslin and the others thought he was hunting squirrels. Until the third evening he believed that Sam Fathers thought so too. Each morning he would leave the camp right after breakfast. He had his own gun now, a new breech-loader, a Christmas gift; he would own and shoot it for almost seventy years, through two new pairs of barrels and locks and one new stock, until all that remained of the original gun was the silver-inlaid trigger-guard with his and McCaslin's engraved names and the date in 1878. He found the tree beside the little bayou where he had stood that morning. Using the compass he ranged from that point; he was teaching himself to be better than a fair woodsman without even knowing he was doing it. On the third day he even found the gutted log where he had first seen the print. It was almost completely crumbled now, healing with unbelievable speed, a passionate and almost visible relinquishment, back into the earth from which the tree had grown. He ranged the summer woods now, green with gloom, if anything actually dimmer than they had been in November's gray dissolution, where even at noon the sun fell only in windless dappling upon the earth which never completely dried and which crawled with snakes—moccasins and watersnakes and rattlers, themselves the color of the dappled gloom so that he would not always see them until they moved; returning to camp later and later and later, first day, second day, passing in the twilight of the third evening the little log pen enclosing the log barn where Sam was putting up the stock for the night. "You aint looked right yet," Sam said.

He stopped. For a moment he didn't answer. Then he said peacefully, in a peaceful rushing burst, as when a boy's miniature dam in a little brook gives way: "All right. Yes. But how? I went to the bayou. I even found that log again. I ——"

"I reckon that was all right. Likely he's been watching you. You never saw his foot?"

"I . . ." the boy said. "I didn't . . . I never thought . . ."

"It's the gun," Sam said. He stood beside the fence, motionless, the old man, son of a negro slave and a Chickasaw chief, in the battered and faded overalls and the frayed five-cent straw hat which had been the badge of the negro's slavery and was now the regalia of his freedom. The camp—the clearing, the house, the barn and its tiny lot with which Major de Spain in his turn had scratched punily and evanescently at the wilderness—faded in the dusk, back into the immemorial darkness of the woods. *The gun*, the boy thought. *The gun.* "You will have to choose," Sam said.

He left the next morning before light, without breakfast, long before Uncle Ash would wake in his quilts on the kitchen floor and start the fire. He had only the compass and a stick for the snakes. He could go almost a mile before he would need to see the compass. He sat on a log, the invisible compass in his hand, while the secret night-sounds which had ceased at his movements, scurried again and then fell still for good and the owls ceased and gave over to the waking day birds and there was light in the gray wet woods and he could see the compass. He went fast yet still quietly, becoming steadily better and better as a woodsman without yet having time to realise it; he jumped a doe and a fawn, walked them out of the bed, close enough to see them—the crash of undergrowth, the white scut, the fawn scudding along behind her, faster than he had known it could have run. He was hunting right, upwind, as Sam had taught him, but that didn't matter now. He had left the gun; by his own will and relinquishment he had accepted not a gambit, not a choice, but a condition in which not only the bear's heretofore inviolable anonymity but all the ancient rules and balances of hunter and hunted had been abrogated. He would not even be afraid, not even in the moment when the fear would take him completely: blood, skin, bowels, bones, memory from the long time before it even became his memory—all save that thin clear quenchless lucidity which alone differed him from this bear and from all the other bears and bucks he would follow during almost seventy years, to which Sam had said: "Be scared. You cant help that. But dont be afraid. Aint nothing in the woods going to hurt you if you dont corner it or it dont smell that you are afraid. A bear or a deer has got to be scared of a coward the same as a brave man has got to be."

By noon he was far beyond the crossing on the little bayou, farther into the new and alien country than he had ever been, travelling now not only by compass but the old, heavy, biscuit-thick silver watch which had been his father's. He had left the camp nine hours ago; nine hours from now, dark would already have been an hour old. He stopped, for the first time since he had risen from the log when he could see the compass face at last, and looked about, mopping his sweating face on his sleeve. He had already relinquished, of his will, because of his need, in humility and peace and without regret, yet apparently that had not been enough, the leaving of the gun was not enough. He stood for a moment—a child, alien and lost in the green and soaring gloom of the markless wilderness. Then he relinquished completely to it. It was the watch and the compass. He was still tainted. He removed the linked chain of the one and the looped thong of the other from his overalls and hung them on a bush and leaned the stick beside them and entered it.

When he realised he was lost, he did as Sam had coached and drilled him: made a cast to cross his backtrack. He had not been going very fast for the last two or three hours, and he had gone even less fast since he left the compass and watch on the bush. So he went slower still now, since the tree could not be very far; in fact, he found it before he really expected to and turned and went to it. But there was no bush beneath it, no compass nor watch, so he did next as Sam had coached and drilled him: made this next circle in the opposite direction and much larger, so that the pattern of the two of them would bisect his track somewhere, but crossing no trace nor mark anywhere of his feet or any feet, and now he was going faster though still not panicked, his heart beating a little more rapidly but strong and steady enough, and this time it was not even the tree because there was a down log beside it which he had never seen before and beyond the log a little swamp, a seepage of moisture somewhere between earth and water, and he did what Sam had coached and drilled him as the next and the last, seeing as he sat down on the log the crooked print, the warped indentation in the wet ground which while he looked at it continued to fill with water until it was level full and the water began to overflow and the sides of the print began to dissolve away. Even as he looked up he saw the next one, and, moving, the one beyond it; moving, not hurrying, running, but merely keeping pace with them as they appeared before him as though they were being shaped out of thin air just one constant pace short of where he would lose them forever and be lost forever himself, tireless, eager, without doubt or dread, panting a little above the strong rapid little hammer of his heart, emerging suddenly into a little glade and the wilderness coalesced. It rushed, soundless, and solidified—the tree, the bush, the compass and the watch glinting where a ray of sunlight touched them. Then he saw the bear. It did not emerge, appear: it was just there, immobile, fixed in the green and windless noon's hot dappling, not as big as he had dreamed it but as big as he had expected, bigger, dimensionless against the dappled obscurity, looking at him. Then it moved. It crossed the glade without haste, walking for an instant into the sun's full glare and out of it, and stopped again and looked back at him across one shoulder. Then it was gone. It didn't walk into the woods. It faded, sank back into the wilderness without motion as he had watched a fish, a huge old bass, sink back into the dark depths of its pool and vanish without even any movement of its fins.

2

So he should have hated and feared Lion. He was thirteen then. He had killed his buck and Sam Fathers had marked his face with the hot blood, and in the next November he killed a bear. But before that accolade he had become as competent in the woods as many grown men with the same experience. By now he was a better woodsman than most grown men with more. There was no territory within twenty-five miles of the camp that he did not know—bayou, ridge, landmark trees and path; he could have led anyone direct to any spot in it and brought him back. He knew game trails that even Sam Fathers had never seen; in the third fall he found a buck's bedding-place by himself and unbeknown to his cousin he borrowed Walter Ewell's rifle and lay in wait for the buck at dawn and killed it when it walked back to the bed as Sam had told him how the old Chickasaw fathers did.

By now he knew the old bear's footprint better than he did his own, and not only the crooked one. He could see any one of the three sound prints and distinguish it at once from any other, and not only because of its size. There were other bears within that fifty miles which left tracks almost as large, or at least so near that the one would have appeared larger only by juxtaposition. It was more than that. If Sam Fathers had been his mentor and the backyard rabbits and squirrels his kindergarten, then the wilderness the old bear ran was his college and the old male bear itself, so long unwifed and childless as to have become its own ungendered progenitor, was his alma mater.

He could find the crooked print now whenever he wished, ten miles or five miles or sometimes closer than that, to the camp. Twice while on stand during the next three years he heard the dogs strike its trail and once even jump it by chance, the voices high, abject, almost human in their hysteria. Once, still-hunting with Walter Ewell's rifle, he saw it cross a long corridor of down timber where a tornado had passed. It rushed through rather than across the tangle of trunks and branches as a locomotive would, faster than he had ever believed it could have moved, almost as fast as a deer even because the deer would have spent most of that distance in the air; he realised then why it would take a dog not only of abnormal courage but size and speed too ever to bring it to bay. He had a little dog at home, a mongrel, of the sort called fyce by negroes, a ratter, itself not much bigger than a rat and possessing that sort of courage which had long since stopped being bravery and had become foolhardiness. He brought it with him one June and, timing them as if they were meeting an appointment with another human being, himself carrying the fyce with a sack over its head and Sam Fathers with a brace of the hounds on a rope leash, they lay downwind of the trail and actually ambushed the bear. They were so close that it turned at bay although he realised later this might have been from surprise and amazement at the shrill and frantic uproar of the fyce. It turned at bay against the trunk of a big cypress, on its hind feet; it seemed to the boy that it would never stop rising, taller and taller, and even the two hounds seemed to have taken a kind of desperate and despairing courage from the fyce. Then he realised that the fyce was actually not going to stop. He flung the gun down and ran. When he overtook and grasped the shrill, frantically pinwheeeling little dog, it seemed to him that he was directly under the bear. He could smell it, strong and hot and rank. Sprawling, he looked up where it loomed and towered over him like a thunderclap. It was quite familiar, until he remembered: this was the way he had used to dream about it.

Then it was gone. He didn't see it go. He knelt, holding the frantic fyce with both hands, hearing the abased wailing of the two hounds drawing further and further away, until Sam came up, carrying the gun. He laid it quietly down beside the boy and stood looking down at him. "You've done seed him twice now, with a gun in your hands," he said. "This time you couldn't have missed him."

The boy rose. He still held the fyce. Even in his arms it continued to yap frantically, surging and straining toward the fading sound of the hounds like a collection of live-wire springs. The boy was panting a little. "Neither could you," he said. "You had the gun. Why didn't you shoot him?"

Sam didn't seem to have heard. He put out his hand and touched the little dog in the boy's arms which still yapped and strained even though the two hounds were out of hearing now. "He's done gone," Sam said. "You can slack off and rest now, until next time." He stroked the little dog until it began to grow quiet under his hand. "You's almost the one we wants," he said. "You just aint big enough. We aint got that one yet. He will need to be just a little bigger than smart, and a little braver than either." He withdrew his hand from the fyce's head and stood looking into the woods where the bear and the hounds had vanished. "Somebody is going to, some day."

"I know it," the boy said. "That's why it must be one of us. So it wont be until the last day. When even he dont want it to last any longer."

So he should have hated and feared Lion. It was in the fourth summer, the fourth time he had made one in the celebration of Major de Spain's and General Compson's birthday. In the early spring Major de Spain's mare had foaled a horse colt. One evening when Sam brought the horses and mules up to stable them for the night, the colt was missing and it was all he could do to get the frantic mare into the lot. He had thought at first to let the mare lead him back to where she had become separated from the foal. But she would not do it. She would not even feint toward any particular part of the woods or even in any particular direction. She merely ran, as if she couldn't see, still frantic with terror. She whirled and ran at Sam once, as if to attack him in some ultimate desperation, as if she could not for the moment realise that he was a man and a long-familiar one. He got her into the lot at last. It was too dark by that time to back-track her, to unravel the erratic course she had doubtless pursued.

He came to the house and told Major de Spain. It was an animal, of course, a big one, and the colt was dead now, wherever it was. They all knew that. "It's a panther," General Compson said at once. "The same one. That doe and fawn last March." Sam had sent Major de Spain word of it when Boon Hogganbeck came to the camp on a routine visit to see how the stock had wintered—the doe's throat torn out, and the beast had run down the helpless fawn and killed it too.

"Sam never did say that was a panther," Major de Spain said. Sam said nothing now, standing behind Major de Spain where they sat at supper, inscrutable, as if he were just waiting for them to stop talking so he could go home. He didn't even seem to be looking at anything. "A panther might jump a doe, and he wouldn't have much trouble catching the fawn afterward. But no panther would have jumped that colt with the dam right there with it. It was Old Ben," Major de Spain said. "I'm disappointed in him. He has broken the rules. I didn't think he would have done that. He has killed mine and McCaslin's dogs, but that was all right. We gambled the dogs against him; we gave each other warning. But now he has come into my house and destroyed my property, out of season too. He broke the rules. It was Old Ben, Sam." Still Sam said nothing, standing there until Major de Spain should stop talking. "We'll back-track her tomorrow and see," Major de Spain said.

Sam departed. He would not live in the camp; he had built himself a little hut something like Joe Baker's, only stouter, tighter, on the bayou a quarter-mile away, and a stout log crib where he stored a little corn for the shoat he raised each year. The next morning he was waiting when they waked. He had already found the colt. They did not even wait for breakfast. It was not far, not five hundred yards from the stable—the three-months' colt lying on its side, its throat torn out and the entails and one ham partly eaten. It lay not as if it had been dropped but as if it had been struck and hurled, and no cat-mark, no claw-mark where a panther would have gripped it while finding its throat. They read the tracks where the frantic mare had circled and at last rushed in with that same ultimate desperation with which she had whirled on Sam Fathers yesterday evening, and the long tracks of dead and terrified running and those of the beast which had not even rushed at her when she advanced but had merely walked three or four paces toward her until she broke, and General Compson said, "Good God, what a wolf!"

Still Sam said nothing. The boy watched him while the men knelt, measuring the tracks. There was something in Sam's face now. It was neither exultation nor joy nor hope. Later, a man, the boy realised what it had been, and that Sam had known all the time what had made the tracks and what had torn the throat out of the doe in the spring and killed the fawn. It had been foreknowledge in Sam's face that morning. *And he was glad,* he told himself. *He was old. He had no children, no people, none of his blood anywhere above earth that he would ever meet again. And even if he were to, he could not have touched it, spoken to it, because for seventy years now he had had to be a negro. It was almost over now and he was glad.*

They returned to camp and had breakfast and came back with guns and the hounds. Afterward the boy realised that they also should have known then what had killed the colt as well as Sam Fathers did. But that was neither the first nor the last time he had seen men rationalise from and even act upon their misconceptions. After Boon, standing astride the colt, had whipped the dogs away from it with his belt, they snuffed at the tracks. One of them, a young dog hound without judgment yet, bayed once, and they ran for a few feet on what seemed to be a trail. Then they stopped, looking back at the men, eager enough, not baffled, merely questioning, as if they were asking "Now what?" Then they rushed back to the colt, where Boon, still astride it, slashed at them with the belt.

"I never knew a trail to get cold that quick," General Compson said.

"Maybe a single wolf big enough to kill a colt with the damn right there beside it dont leave scent," Major de Spain said.

"Maybe it was a hant," Walter Ewell said. He looked at Tennie's Jim. "Hah, Jim?"

Because the hounds would not run it, Major de Spain had Sam hunt out and find the tracks a hundred yards farther on and they put the dogs on it again and again the young one bayed and not one of them realised then that the hound was not baying like a dog striking game but was merely bellowing like a country dog whose yard has been invaded. General Compson spoke to the boy and Boon and Tennie's Jim: to the squirrel hunters. "You boys keep the dogs with you this morning. He's probably hanging around somewhere, waiting to get his breakfast off the colt. You might strike him."

But they did not. The boy remembered how Sam stood watching them as they went into the woods with the leashed hounds—the Indian face in which he had never seen anything until it smiled, except that faint arching of the nostrils on that first morning when the hounds had found Old Ben. They took the hounds with them on the next day, though when they reached the place where they hoped to strike a fresh trail, the carcass of the colt was gone. Then on the third morning Sam was waiting again, this time until they had finished breakfast. He said, "Come." He led them to his house, his little hut, to the corn-crib beyond it. He had removed the corn and had made a deadfall of the door, baiting it with the colt's carcass; peering between the logs, they saw an animal almost the color of a gun or pistol barrel, what little time they had to examine its color or shape. It was not crouched nor even standing. It was in motion, in the air, coming toward them—a heavy body crashing with tremendous force against the door so that the thick door jumped and clattered in its frame, the animal, whatever it was, hurling itself against the door again seemingly before it could have touched the floor and got a new purchase to spring from. "Come away," Sam said, "fore he break his neck." Even when they retreated the heavy and measured crashes continued, the stout door jumping and clattering each time, and still no sound from the beast itself—no snarl, no cry.

"What in hell's name is it?" Major de Spain said.

"It's a dog," Sam said, his nostrils arching and collapsing faintly and steadily and that faint, fierce milkiness in his eyes again as on that first morning when the hounds had struck the old bear. "It's the dog."

"*The* dog?" Major de Spain said.

"That's gonter hold Old Ben."

"Dog the devil," Major de Spain said. "I'd rather have Old Ben himself in my pack than that brute. Shoot him."

"No," Sam said.

"You'll never tame him. How do you ever expect to make an animal like that afraid of you?"

"I dont want him tame," Sam said; again the boy watched his nostrils and the fierce milky light in his eyes. "But I almost rather he be tame than scared, of me or any man or any thing. But he wont be neither, of nothing."

"Then what are you going to do with it?"

"You can watch," Sam said.

Each morning through the second week they would go to Sam's crib. He had removed a few shingles from the roof and had put a rope on the colt's carcass and had drawn it out when the trap fell. Each morning they would watch him lower a pail of water into the crib while the dog hurled itself tirelessly against the door and dropped back and leaped again. It never made any sound and there was nothing frenzied in the act but only a cold and grim indomitable determination. Toward the end of the week it stopped jumping at the door. Yet it had not weakened appreciably and it was not as if it had rationalised the fact that the door was not going to give. It was as if for that time it simply disdained to jump any longer. It was not down. None of them had ever seen it down. It stood, and they could see it now—part mastiff, something of Airedale and something of a dozen other strains probably, better than thirty inches at the shoulders and weighing as they guessed almost ninety pounds, with cold yellow eyes and a tremendous chest and over all that strange color like a blued gunbarrel.

Then the two weeks were up. They prepared to break camp. The boy begged to remain and his cousin let him. He moved into the little hut with Sam Fathers. Each morning he watched Sam lower the pail of water into the crib. By the end of that week the dog was down. It would rise and half stagger, half crawl to the water and drink and collapse again. One morning it could not even reach the water, could not raise its forequarters even from the floor. Sam took a short stick and prepared to enter the crib. "Wait," the boy said. "Let me get the gun ——"

"No," Sam said. "He cant move now." Nor could it. It lay on its side while Sam touched it, its head and the gaunted body, the dog lying motionless, the yellow eyes open. They were not fierce and there was nothing of petty malevolence in them, but a cold and almost impersonal malignance like some natural force. It was not even looking at Sam nor at the boy peering at it between the logs.

Sam began to feed it again. The first time he had to raise its head so it could lap the broth. That night he left a bowl of broth containing lumps of meat where the dog could reach it. The next morning the bowl was empty and the dog was lying on its belly, its head up, the cold yellow eyes watching the door as Sam entered, no change whatever in the cold yellow eyes and still no sound from it even when it sprang, its aim and co-ordination still bad from weakness so that Sam had time to strike it down with the stick and leap from the crib and slam the door as the dog, still without having had time to get its feet under it to jump again seemingly, hurled itself against the door as if the two weeks of starving had never been.

At noon that day someone came whooping through the woods from the direction of the camp. It was Boon. He came and looked for a while between the logs, at the tremendous dog lying again on its belly, its head up, the yellow eyes blinking sleepily at nothing: the indomitable and unbroken spirit. "What we better do," Boon said, "is to let that son of a bitch go and catch Old Ben and run him on the dog." He turned to the boy his weather-reddened and beetling face. "Get your traps together. Cass says for you to come on home. You been in here fooling with that horse-eating varmint long enough."

Boon had a borrowed mule at the camp; the buggy was waiting at the edge of the bottom. He was at home that night. He told McCaslin about it. "Sam's going to starve him again until he can go in and touch him. Then he will feed him again. Then he will starve him again, if he has to."

"But why?" McCaslin said. "What for? Even Sam will never tame that brute."

"We dont want him tame. We want him like he is. We just want him to find out that the only way he can get out of that crib and stay out of it is to do what Sam or somebody tells him to do. He's the dog that's going to stop Old Ben and hold him. We've already named him. His name is Lion."

Then November came at last. They returned to the camp. With General Compson and Major de Spain and his cousin and Walter and Boon he stood in the yard among the guns and bedding and boxes of food and watched Sam Fathers and Lion come up the lane from the lot—the Indian, the old man in battered overalls and rubber boots and a worn sheepskin coat and a hat which had belonged to the boy's father; the tremendous dog pacing gravely beside him. The hounds rushed out to meet them and stopped, except the young one which still had but little of judgment. It ran up to Lion, fawning. Lion didn't snap at it. He didn't even pause. He struck it rolling and yelping for five or six feet with a blow of one paw as a bear would have done and came on into the yard and stood, blinking sleepily at nothing, looking at no one, while Boon said, "Jesus. Jesus.—Will he let me touch him?"

"You can touch him," Sam said. "He dont care. He dont care about nothing or nobody."

The boy watched that too. He watched it for the next two years from that moment when Boon touched Lion's head and then knelt beside him, feeling the bones and muscles, the power. It was as if Lion were a woman—or perhaps Boon was the woman. That was more like it—the big, grave, sleepy-seeming dog which, as Sam Fathers said, cared about no man and no thing; and the violent, insensitive, hard-faced man with his touch of remote Indian blood and the mind almost of a child. He watched Boon take over Lion's feeding from Sam and Uncle Ash both. He would see Boon squatting in the cold rain beside the kitchen while Lion ate. Because Lion neither slept nor ate with the other dogs though none of them knew where he did sleep until in the second November, thinking until then that Lion slept in his kennel beside Sam Fathers' hut, when the boy's cousin McCaslin said something about it to Sam by sheer chance and Sam told him. And that night the boy and Major de Spain and McCaslin with a lamp entered the back room where Boon slept—the little, tight, airless room rank with the smell of Boon's unwashed body and his wet hunting-clothes—where Boon, snoring on his back, choked and waked and Lion raised his head beside him and looked back at them from his cold, slumbrous yellow eyes.

"Damn it, Boon," McCaslin said. "Get that dog out of here. He's got to run Old Ben tomorrow morning. How in hell do you expect him to smell anything fainter than a skunk after breathing you all night?"

"The way I smell aint hurt my nose none that I ever noticed," Boon said.

"It wouldn't matter if it had," Major de Spain said. "We're not depending on you to trail a bear. Put him outside. Put him under the house with the other dogs."

Boon began to get up. "He'll kill the first one that happens to yawn or sneeze in his face or touches him."

"I reckon not," Major de Spain said. "None of them are going to risk yawning in his face or touching him either, even asleep. Put him outside. I want his nose right tomorrow. Old Ben fooled him last year. I dont think he will do it again."

Boon put on his shoes without lacing them; in his long soiled underwear, his hair still tousled from sleep, he and Lion went out. The others returned to the front room and the poker game where McCaslin's and Major de Spain's hands waited for them on the table. After a while McCaslin said, "Do you want me to go back and look again?"

"No," Major de Spain said. "I call," he said to Walter Ewell. He spoke to McCaslin again. "If you do, dont tell me. I am beginning to see the first sign of my increasing age: I dont like to know that my orders have been disobeyed, even when I knew when I gave them that they would be.—A small pair," he said to Walter Ewell.

"How small?" Walter said.

"Very small," Major de Spain said.

And the boy, lying beneath his piled quilts and blankets waiting for sleep, knew likewise that Lion was already back in Boon's bed, for the rest of that night and the next one and during all the nights of the next November and the next one. He thought then: *I wonder what Sam thinks. He could have Lion with him, even if Boon is a white man. He could ask Major or McCaslin either. And more than that. It was Sam's hand that touched Lion first and Lion knows it.* Then he became a man and he knew that too. It had been all right. That was the way it should have been. Sam was the chief, the prince; Boon, the plebeian, was his huntsman. Boon should have nursed the dogs.

On the first morning that Lion led the pack after Old Ben, seven strangers appeared in the camp. They were swampers: gaunt, malaria-ridden men appearing from nowhere, who ran trap-lines for coons or perhaps farmed little patches of cotton and corn along the edge of the bottom, in clothes but little better than Sam Fathers' and nowhere near as good as Tennie's Jim's, with worn shotguns and rifles, already squatting patiently in the cold drizzle in the side yard when day broke. They had a spokesman; afterward Sam Fathers told Major de Spain how all during the past summer and fall they had drifted into the camp singly or in pairs and threes, to look quietly at Lion for a while and then go away: "Mawnin, Major. We heerd you was aimin to put that ere blue dawg on that old two-toed bear this mawnin. We figgered we'd come up and watch, if you dont mind. We wont do no shooting, lessen he runs over us."

"You are welcome," Major de Spain said. "You are welcome to shoot. He's more your bear than ours."

"I reckon that aint no lie. I done fed him enough cawn to have a sheer in him. Not to mention a shoat three years ago."

"I reckon I got a sheer to," another said. "Only it aint in the bear." Major de Spain looked at him. He was chewing tobacco. He spat. "Hit was a heifer calf. Nice un too. Last year. When I finally found her, I reckon she looked about like that colt of yourn looked last June."

"Oh," Major de Spain said. "Be welcome. If you see game in front of my dogs, shoot it."

Nobody shot old Ben that day. Nobody saw him. The dogs jumped him within a hundred yards of the glade where the boy had seen him that day in the summer of his eleventh year. The boy was less than a quarter-mile away. He heard the jump but he could distinguish no voice among the dogs that he did not know and therefore would be Lion's, and he thought, believed, that Lion was not among them. Even the fact that they were going much faster than he had ever heard them run behind Old Ben before and that the high thin note of hysteria was missing now from their voices was not enough to disabuse him. He didn't comprehend until that night, when Sam told him that Lion would never cry on a trail. "He gonter growl when he catches Old Ben's throat," Sam said. "But he aint gonter never holler, no more than he ever done when he jumping at that two-inch door. It's that blue dog in him What you call it?"

"Airedale," the boy said.

Lion was there; the jump was just too close to the river. When Boon returned with Lion about eleven that night, he swore that Lion had stopped Old Ben once but that the hounds would not go in and Old Ben broke away and took to the river and swam for miles down it and he and Lion went down one bank for about ten miles and crossed and came up the other but it had begun to get dark before they struck any trail where Old Ben had come up out of the water, unless he was still in the water when he passed the ford where they crossed. Then he fell to cursing the hounds and ate the supper Uncle Ash had saved for him and went off to bed and after a while the boy opened the door of the little stale room thunderous with snoring and the great grave dog raised its head from Boon's pillow and blinked at him for a moment and lowered its head again.

When the next November came and the last day, the day on which it was now becoming traditional to save for Old Ben, there were more than a dozen strangers waiting. They were not all swampers this time. Some of them were townsmen, from other county seats like Jefferson, who had heard about Lion and Old Ben and had come to watch the great blue dog keep his yearly rendezvous with the old two-toed bear. Some of them didn't even have guns and the hunting-clothes and boots they wore had been on a store shelf yesterday.

This time Lion jumped Old Ben more than five miles from the river and bayed and held him and this time the hounds went in, in a sort of desperate emulation. The boy heard them; he was that near. He heard Boon whooping; he heard the two shots when General Compson delivered both barrels, one containing five buckshot, the other a single ball, into the bear from as close as he could force his almost unmanageable horse. He heard the dogs when the bear broke free again. He was running now; panting, stumbling, his lungs bursting, he reached the place where General Compson had fired and where Old Ben had killed two of the hounds. He saw the blood from General Compson's shots, but he could go no further. He stopped, leaning against a tree for his breathing to ease and his heart to slow, hearing the sound of the dogs as it faded on and died away.

In camp that night—they had as guests five of the still terrified strangers in new hunting coats and boots who had been lost all day until Sam Fathers went out and got them—he heard the rest of it: how Lion had stopped and held the bear again but only the one-eyed mule which did not mind the smell of wild blood would approach and Boon was riding the mule and Boon had never been known to hit anything. He shot at the bear five times with his pump gun, touching nothing, and Old Ben killed another hound and broke free once more and reached the river and was gone. Again Boon and Lion hunted as far down one bank as they dared. Too far; they crossed in the first of dusk and dark overtook them within a mile. And this time Lion found the broken trail, the blood perhaps, in the darkness where Old Ben had come up out of the water, but Boon had him on a rope, luckily, and he got down from the mule and fought Lion hand-to-hand until he got him back to camp. This time Boon didn't even curse. He stood in the door, muddy, spent, his huge gargoyle's face tragic and still amazed. "I missed him," he said. "I was in twenty-five feet of him and I missed him five times."

"But we have drawn blood," Major de Spain said. "General Compson drew blood. We have never done that before."

"But I missed him," Boon said. "I missed him five times. With Lion looking right at me."

"Never mind," Major de Spain said. "It was a damned fine race. And we drew blood. Next year we'll let General Compson or Walter ride Katie, and we'll get him."

Then McCaslin said, "Where is Lion, Boon?"

"I left him at Sam's," Boon said. He was already turning away. "I aint fit to sleep with him."

So he should have hated and feared Lion. Yet he did not. It seemed to him that there was a fatality in it. It seemed to him that something, he didn't know what, was beginning; had already begun. It was like the last act on a set stage. It was the beginning of the end of something, he didn't know what except that he would not grieve. He would be humble and proud that he had been found worthy to be a part of it too or even just to see it too.

3

It was December. It was the coldest December he had ever remembered. They had been in camp four days over two weeks, waiting for the weather to soften so that Lion and Old Ben could run their yearly race. Then they would break camp and go home. Because of these unforeseen additional days which they had had to pass waiting on the weather, with nothing to do but play poker, the whisky had given out and he and Boon were being sent to Memphis with a suitcase and a note from Major de Spain to Mr Semmes, the distiller, to get more. That is, Major de Spain and McCaslin were sending Boon to get the whisky and sending him to see that Boon got back with it or most of it or at least some of it.

Tennie's Jim waked him at three. He dressed rapidly, shivering, not so much from the cold because a fresh fire already boomed and roared on the hearth, but in that dead winter hour when the blood and the heart are slow and sleep is incomplete. He crossed the gap between house and kitchen, the gap of iron earth beneath the brilliant and rigid night where dawn could not begin for three hours yet, tasting, tongue palate and to the very bottom of his lungs the searing dark, and entered the kitchen, the lamplit warmth where the stove glowed, fogging the windows, and where Boon already sat at the table at breakfast, hunched over his plate, almost in his plate, his working jaws blue with stubble and his face innocent of water and his coarse, horse-mane hair innocent of comb—the quarter Indian, grandson of a Chickasaw squaw, who on occasion resented with his hard and furious fists the intimation of one single drop of alien blood and on others, usually after whisky, affirmed with the same fists and the same fury that his father had been the full-blood Chickasaw and even a chief and that even his mother had been only half white. He was four inches over six feet; he had the mind of a child, the heart of a horse, and little hard shoe-button eyes without depth or meanness or generosity or viciousness or gentleness or anything else, in the ugliest face the boy had ever seen. It looked like somebody had found a walnut a little larger than a football and with a machinist's hammer had shaped features into it and then painted it, mostly red; not Indian red but a fine bright ruddy color which whisky might have had something to do with but which was mostly just happy and violent out-of-doors, the wrinkles in it not the residue of the forty years it had survived but from squinting into the sun or into the gloom of cane-brakes where game had run, baked into it by the camp fires before which he had lain trying to sleep on the cold November or December ground while waiting for daylight so he could rise and hunt again, as though time were merely something he walked through as he did through air, aging him no more than air did. He was brave, faithful, improvident and unreliable; he had neither profession job nor trade and owned one vice and one virtue: whisky, and that absolute and unquestioning fidelity to Major de Spain and the boy's cousin McCaslin. "Sometimes I'd call them both virtues," Major de Spain said once. "Or both vices," McCaslin said.

He ate his breakfast, hearing the dogs under the kitchen, wakened by the smell of frying meat or perhaps by the feet overhead. He heard Lion once, short and peremptory, as the best hunter in any camp has only to speak once to all save the fools, and none other of Major de Spain's and McCaslin's dogs were Lion's equal in size and strength and perhaps even in courage, but they were not fools; Old Ben had killed the last fool among them last year.

Tennie's Jim came in as they finished. The wagon was outside. Ash decided he would drive them over to the log-line where they would flag the outbound log-train and let Tennie's Jim wash the dishes. The boy knew why. It would not be the first time he had listened to old Ash badgering Boon.

It was cold. The wagon wheels banged and clattered on the frozen ground; the sky was fixed and brilliant. He was not shivering, he was shaking, slow and steady and hard, the food he had just eaten still warm and solid inside him while his outside shook slow and steady around it as though his stomach floated loose. "They wont run this morning," he said. "No dog will have any nose today."

"Cep Lion," Ash said. "Lion dont need no nose. All he need is a bear." He had wrapped his feet in towsacks and he had a quilt from his pallet bed on the kitchen floor drawn over his head and wrapped around him until in the thin brilliant starlight he looked like nothing at all that the boy had ever seen before. "He run a bear through a thousand-acre ice-house. Catch him too. Them other dogs dont matter because they aint going to keep up with Lion nohow, long as he got a bear in front of him."

"What's wrong with the other dogs?" Boon said. "What the hell do you know about it anyway? This is the first time you've had your tail out of that kitchen since we got here except to chop a little wood."

"Aint nothing wrong with them," Ash said. "And long as it's left up to them, aint nothing going to be. I just wish I had knowed all my life how to take care of my health good as them hounds knows."

"Well, they aint going to run this morning," Boon said. His voice was harsh and positive. "Major promised they wouldn't until me and Ike get back."

"Weather gonter break today. Gonter soft up. Rain by night." Then Ash laughed, chuckled, somewhere inside the quilt which concealed even his face. "Hum up here, mules!" he said, jerking the reins so that the mules leaped forward and snatched the lurching and banging wagon for several feet before they slowed again into their quick, short-paced, rapid plodding. "Sides, I like to know why Major need to wait on you. It's Lion he aiming to use. I aint never heard tell of you bringing no bear nor no other kind of meat into this camp."

Now Boon's going to curse Ash or maybe even hit him, the boy thought. But Boon never did, never had; the boy knew he never would even though four years ago Boon had shot five times with a borrowed pistol at a negro on the street in Jefferson, with the same result as when he had shot five times at Old Ben last fall. "By God," Boon said, "he aint going to put Lion or no other dog on nothing until I get back tonight. Because he promised me. Whip up them mules and keep them whipped up. Do you want me to freeze to death?"

They reached the log-line and built a fire. After a while the log-train came up out of the woods under the paling east and Boon flagged it. Then in the warm caboose the boy slept again while Boon and the conductor and brakeman talked about Lion and Old Ben as people later would talk about Sullivan and Kilrain and, later still, about Dempsey and Tunney. Dozing, swaying as the springless caboose lurched and clattered, he would hear them still talking, about the shoats and calves Old Ben had killed and the cribs he had rifled and the traps and deadfalls he had wrecked and the lead he probably carried under his hide—Old Ben, the two-toed bear in a land where bears with trap-ruined feet had been called Two-Toe or Three-Toe or Cripple-Foot for fifty years, only Old Ben was an extra bear (the head bear, General Compson called him) and so had earned a name such as a human man could have worn and not been sorry.

They reached Hoke's at sunup. They emerged from the warm caboose in their hunting clothes, the muddy boots and stained khaki and Boon's blue unshaven jowls. But that was all right. Hoke's was a sawmill and commissary and two stores and a loading-chute on a sidetrack from the main line, and all the men in it wore boots and khaki too. Presently the Memphis train came. Boon bought three packages of popcorn-and-molasses and a bottle of beer from the news butch and the boy went to sleep again to the sound of his chewing.

But in Memphis it was not all right. It was as if the high buildings and the hard pavements, the fine carriages and the horse cars and the men in starched collars and neckties made their boots and khaki look a little rougher and a little muddier and made Boon's beard look worse and more unshaven and his face look more and more like he should never have brought it out of the woods at all or at least out of reach of Major de Spain or McCaslin or someone who knew it and could have said, "Dont be afraid. He wont hurt you." He walked through the station, on the slick floor, his face moving as he worked the popcorn out of his teeth with his tongue, his legs spraddled and stiff in the hips as if he were walking on buttered glass, and that blue stubble on his face like the filings from a new gun-barrel. They passed the first saloon. Even through the closed doors the boy could seem to smell the sawdust and the reek of old drink. Boon began to cough. He coughed for something less than a minute. "Damn this cold," he said. "I'd sure like to know where I got it."

"Back there in the station," the boy said.

Boon had started to cough again. He stopped. He looked at the boy. "What?" he said.

"You never had it when we left camp nor on the train either." Boon looked at him, blinking. Then he stopped blinking. He didn't cough again. He said quietly:

"Lend me a dollar. Come on. You've got it. If you ever had one, you've still got it. I dont mean you are tight with your money because you aint. You just dont never seem to ever think of nothing you want. When I was sixteen a dollar bill melted off of me before I even had time to read the name of the bank that issued it." He said quietly: "Let me have a dollar, Ike."

"You promised Major. You promised McCaslin. Not till we get back to camp."

"All right," Boon said in that quiet and patient voice. "What can I do on just one dollar? You aint going to lend me another."

"You're damn right I aint," the boy said, his voice quiet too, cold with rage which was not at Boon, remembering: Boon snoring in a hard chair in the kitchen so he could watch the clock and wake him and McCaslin and drive them the seventeen miles in to Jefferson to catch the train to Memphis; the wild, never-bridled Texas paint pony which he had persuaded McCaslin to let him buy and which he and Boon had bought at auction for four dollars and seventy-five cents and fetched home wired between two gentle old mares with pieces of barbed wire and which had never even seen shelled corn before and didn't even know what it was unless the grains were bugs maybe and at last (he was ten and Boon had been ten all his life) Boon said the pony was gentled and with a towsack over its head and four negroes to hold it they backed it into an old two-wheeled cart and hooked up the gear and he and Boon got up and Boon said, "All right, boys. Let him go" and one of the negroes—it was Tennie's Jim—snatched the towsack off and leaped for his life and they lost the first wheel against a post of the open gate only at that moment Boon caught him by the scruff of the neck and flung him into the roadside ditch so he only saw the rest of it in fragments: the other wheel as it slammed through the side gate and crossed the back yard and leaped up onto the gallery and scraps of the cart here and there along the road and Boon vanishing rapidly on his stomach in the leaping and spurting dust and still holding the reins until they broke too and two days later they finally caught the pony seven miles away still wearing the hames and the headstall of the bridle around its neck like a duchess with two necklaces at one time. He gave Boon the dollar.

"All right," Boon said. "Come on in out of the cold."

"I aint cold," he said.

"You can have some lemonade."

"I dont want any lemonade."

The door closed behind him. The sun was well up now. It was a brilliant day, though Ash had said it would rain before night. Already it was warmer; they could run tomorrow. He felt the old lift of the heart, as pristine as ever, as on the first day; he would never lose it, no matter how old in hunting and pursuit: the best, the best of all breathing, the humility and the pride. He must stop thinking about it. Already it seemed to him that he was running, back to the station, to the tracks themselves: the first train going south; he must stop thinking about it. The street was busy. He watched the big Norman draft horses, the Percherons; the trim carriages from which the men in the fine overcoats and the ladies rosy in furs descended and entered the station. (They were still next door to it but one.) Twenty years ago his father had ridden into Memphis as a member of Colonel Sartoris' horse in Forrest's command, up Main street and (the tale told) into the lobby of the Gayoso Hotel where the Yankee officers sat in the leather chairs spitting into the tall bright cuspidors and then out again, scot-free ——

The door opened behind him. Boon was wiping his mouth on the back of his hand. "All right," he said. "Let's go tend to it and get the hell out of here."

They went and had the suitcase packed. He never knew where or when Boon got the other bottle. Doubtless Mr Semmes gave it to him. When they reached Hoke's again at sundown, it was empty. They could get a return train to Hoke's in two hours, they went straight back to the station as Major de Spain and then McCaslin had told Boon to do and then ordered him to do and had sent the boy along to see that he did. Boon took the first drink from his bottle in the wash room. A man in a uniform cap came to tell him he couldn't drink there and looked at Boon's face once and said nothing. The next time he was pouring into his water glass beneath the edge of a table in the restaurant when the manager (she was a woman) did tell him he couldn't drink there and he went back to the wash-room. He had been telling the negro waiter and all the other people in the restaurant who couldn't help but hear him and who had never heard of Lion and didn't want to, about Lion and Old Ben. Then he happened to think of the zoo. He had found out that there was another train to Hoke's at three oclock and so they would spend the time at the zoo and take the three oclock train until he came back from the wash-room for the third time. Then they would take the first train back to camp, get Lion and come back to the zoo where, he said, the bears were fed on ice cream and lady fingers and he would match Lion against them all.

So they missed the first train, the one they were supposed to take, but he got Boon onto the three oclock train and they were all right again, with Boon not even going to the wash-room now but drinking in the aisle and talking about Lion and the men he buttonholed no more daring to tell Boon he couldn't drink there than the man in the station had dared.

When they reached Hoke's at sundown, Boon was asleep. The boy waked him at last and got him and the suitcase off the train and he even persuaded him to eat some supper at the sawmill commissary. So he was all right when they got in the caboose of the log-train to go back into the woods, with the sun going down red and the sky already overcast and the ground would not freeze tonight. It was the boy who slept now, sitting behind the ruby stove while the springless caboose jumped and clattered and Boon and the brakeman and the conductor talked about Lion and

Old Ben because they knew what Boon was talking about because this was home. "Overcast and already thawing," Boon said. "Lion will get him tomorrow."

It would have to be Lion, or somebody. It would not be Boon. He had never hit anything bigger than a squirrel that anybody ever knew, except the negro woman that day when he was shooting at the negro man. He was a big negro and not ten feet away but Boon shot five times with the pistol he had borrowed from Major de Spain's negro coachman and the negro he was shooting at outed with a dollar-and-a-half mail-order pistol and would have burned Boon down with it only it never went off, it just went snicksnicksnicksnicksnick five times and Boon still blasting away and he broke a plate-glass window that cost McCaslin forty-five dollars and hit a negro woman who happened to be passing in the leg only Major de Spain paid for that; he and McCaslin cut cards, the plate-glass window against the negro woman's leg. And the first day on stand this year, the first morning in camp, the buck ran right over Boon; he heard Boon's old pump gun go whow. whow. whow. whow. whow. and then his voice: "God damn, here he comes! Head him! Head him!" and when he got there the buck's tracks and the five exploded shells were not twenty paces apart.

There were five guests in camp that night, from Jefferson: Mr Bayard Sartoris and his son and General Compson's son and two others. And the next morning he looked out the window, into the gray thin drizzle of daybreak which Ash had predicted, and there they were, standing and squatting beneath the thin rain, almost two dozen of them who had fed Old Ben corn and shoats and even calves for ten years, in their worn hats and hunting coats and overalls which any town negro would have thrown away or burned and only the rubber boots strong and sound, and the worn and blueless guns and some even without guns. While they ate breakfast a dozen more arrived, mounted and on foot: loggers from the camp thirteen miles below and sawmill men from Hoke's and the only gun among them that one which the log-train conductor carried: so that when they went into the woods this morning Major de Spain led a party almost as strong, excepting that some of them were not armed, as some he had led in the last darkening days of '64 and '65. The little yard would not hold them. They overflowed it, into the lane where Major de Spain sat his mare while Ash in his dirty apron thrust the greasy cartridges into his carbine and passed it up to him and the great grave blue dog stood at his stirrup not as a dog stands but as a horse stands, blinking his sleepy topaz eyes at nothing, deaf even to the yelling of the hounds which Boon and Tennie's Jim held on leash.

"We'll put General Compson on Katie this morning," Major de Spain said. "He drew blood last year; if he'd had a mule then that would have stood, he would have ——"

"No," General Compson said. "I'm too old to go helling through the woods on a mule or a horse or anything else any more. Besides, I had my chance last year and missed it. I'm going on a stand this morning. I'm going to let that boy ride Katie."

"No, wait," McCaslin said. "Ike's got the rest of his life to hunt bears in. Let somebody else ——"

"No," General Compson said. "I want Ike to ride Katie. He's already a better woodsman than you or me either and in another ten years he'll be as good as Walter."

At first he couldn't believe it, not until Major de Spain spoke to him. Then he was up, on the one-eyed mule which would not spook at wild blood, looking down at the dog motionless at Major de Spain's stirrup, looking in the gray streaming light bigger than a calf, bigger than he knew it actually was—the big head, the chest almost as big as his own, the blue hide beneath which the muscles flinched or quivered to no touch since the heart which drove blood to them loved no man and no thing, standing as a horse stands yet different from a horse which infers only weight and speed while Lion inferred not only courage and all else that went to make up the will and desire to pursue and kill, but endurance, the will and desire to endure beyond all imaginable limits of flesh in order to overtake and slay. Then the dog looked at him. It moved its head and looked at him across the trivial uproar of the hounds, out of the yellow eyes as depthless as Boon's, as free as Boon's of meanness or generosity or gentleness or viciousness. They were just cold and sleepy. Then it blinked, and he knew it was not looking at him and never had been, without even bothering to turn its head away.

That morning he heard the first cry. Lion had already vanished while Sam and Tennie's Jim were putting saddles on the mule and horse which had drawn the wagon and he watched the hounds as they crossed and cast, snuffing and whimpering, until they too disappeared. Then he and Major de Spain and Sam and Tennie's Jim rode after them and heard the first cry out of the wet and thawing woods not two hundred yards ahead, high, with that abject, almost human quality he had come to know, and the other hounds joining in until the gloomed woods rang and clamored. They rode then. It seemed to him that he could actually see the big blue dog boring on, silent, and the bear too: the thick, locomotive-like shape which he had seen that day four years ago crossing the blow-down, crashing on ahead of the dogs faster than he had believed it could have moved, drawing away even from the running mules. He heard a shotgun, once. The woods had opened, they were going fast, the clamor faint and fading on ahead; they passed the man who had fired—a swamper, a pointing arm, a gaunt face, the small black orifice of his yelling studded with rotten teeth.

He heard the changed note in the hounds' uproar and two hundred yards ahead he saw them. The bear had turned. He saw Lion drive in without pausing and saw the bear strike him aside and lunge into the yelling hounds and kill one of them almost in its tracks and whirl and run again. Then they were in a streaming tide of dogs. He heard Major de Spain and Tennie's Jim shouting and the pistol sound of Tennie's Jim's leather thong as he tried to turn them. Then he and Sam Fathers were riding alone. One of the hounds had kept on with Lion though. He recognised its voice. It was the young hound which even a year ago had had no judgment and which, by the lights of the other hounds anyway, still had none. *Maybe that's what courage is,* he thought. "Right," Sam said behind him. "Right. We got to turn him from the river if we can."

Now they were in cane: a brake. He knew the path through it as well as Sam did. They came out of the undergrowth and struck the entrance almost exactly. It would traverse the brake and come out onto a high open ridge above the river. He heard the flat clap of Walter Ewell's rifle, then two more. "No," Sam said. "I can hear the hound. Go on."

They emerged from the narrow roofless tunnel of snapping and hissing cane, still galloping, onto the open ridge below which the thick yellow river, reflectionless in the gray and streaming light, seemed not to move. Now he could hear the hound too. It was not running. The cry was a high frantic yapping and Boon was running along the edge of the bluff, his old gun leaping and jouncing against his back on its sling made of a piece of cotton plowline. He whirled and ran up to them, wild-faced, and flung himself onto the mule behind the boy. "That damn boat!" he cried. "It's on the other side! He went straight across! Lion was too close to him! That little hound too! Lion was so close I couldn't shoot! Go on!" he cried, beating his heels into the mule's flanks. "Go on!"

They plunged down the bank, slipping and sliding in the thawed earth, crashing through the willows and into the water. He felt no shock, no cold, he on one side of the swimming mule, grasping the pommel with one hand and holding his gun above the water with the other, Boon, opposite him. Sam was behind them somewhere, and then the river, the water above them, was full of dogs. They swam faster than the mules; they were scrabbling up the bank before the mules touched bottom. Major de Spain was whooping from the bank they had just left and, looking back, he saw Tennie's Jim and the horse as they went into the water.

Now the woods ahead of them and the rain-heavy air were one uproar. It rang and clamored; it echoed and broke against the bank behind them and reformed and clamored and rang until it seemed to the boy that all the hounds which had ever bayed game in this land were yelling down at him. He got his leg over the mule as it came up out of the water. Boon didn't try to mount again. He grasped one stirrup as they went up the bank and crashed through the undergrowth which fringed the bluff and saw the bear, on its hind feet, its back against a tree while the bellowing hounds swirled around it and once more Lion drove in, leaping clear of the ground.

This time the bear didn't strike him down. It caught the dog in both arms, almost loverlike, and they both went down. He was off the mule now. He drew back both hammers of the gun but he could see nothing but moiling spotted houndbodies until the bear surged up again. Boon was yelling something, he could not tell what; he could see Lion still clinging to the bear's throat and he saw the bear, half erect, strike one of the hounds with one paw and hurled it five or six feet and then, rising and rising as though it would never stop, stand erect again and begin to rake at Lion's belly with its forepaws. Then Boon was running. The boy saw the gleam of the blade in his hand and watched him leap among the hounds, hurdling them, kicking them aside as he ran, and fling himself astride the bear as he had hurled himself onto the mule, his legs locked around the bear's belly, his left arm under the bear's throat where Lion clung, and the glint of the knife as it rose and fell.

It fell just once. For an instant they almost resembled a piece of statuary: the clinging dog, the bear, the man stride its back, working and probing the buried blade. Then they went down, pulled over backward by Boon's weight, Boon underneath. It was the bear's back which reappeared first but at once Boon was astride it again. He had never released the knife and again the boy saw the almost infinitesimal movement of his arm and shoulder as he probed and sought; then the bear surged erect, raising with it the man and the dog too, and turned and still carrying the man and the dog it took two or three steps toward the woods on its hind feet as a man would have walked and crashed down. It didn't collapse, crumple. It fell all of a piece, as a tree falls, so that all three of them, man dog and bear, seemed to bounce once.

He and Tennie's Jim ran forward. Boon was kneeling at the bear's head. His left ear was shredded, his left coat sleeve was completely gone, his right boot had been ripped from knee to instep; the bright blood thinned in the thin rain down his leg and hand and arm and down the side of his face which was no longer wild but was quite calm. Together they prized Lion's jaws from the bear's thoat. "Easy, goddamn it," Boon said. "Cant you see his guts are all out of him?" He began to remove his coat. He spoke to Tennie's Jim in that calm voice: "Bring the boat up. It's about a hundred yards down the bank there. I saw it." Tennie's Jim rose and went away. Then, and he could not remember if it had been a call or an exclamation from Tennie's Jim or if he had glanced up by chance, he saw Tennie's Jim stooping and saw Sam Fathers lying motionless on his face in the trampled mud.

The mule had not thrown him. He remembered that Sam was down too even before Boon began to run. There was no mark on him whatever and when he and Boon turned him over, his eyes were open and he said something in that tongue which he and Joe Baker had used to speak together. But he couldn't move. Tennie's Jim brought the skiff up; they could hear him shouting to Major de Spain across the river. Boon wrapped Lion in his hunting coat and carried him down to the skiff and they carried Sam down and returned and hitched the bear to the one-eyed mule's saddle-bow with Tennie's Jim's leash-thong and dragged him down to the skiff and got him into it and left Tennie's Jim to swim the horse and the two mules back across. Major de Spain caught the bow of the skiff as Boon jumped out and past him before it touched the bank. He looked at Old Ben and said quietly: "Well." Then he walked into the water and leaned down and touched Sam and Sam looked up at him and said something in that old tongue he and Joe Baker spoke. "You dont know what happened?" Major de Spain said.

"No, sir," the boy said. "It wasn't the mule. It wasn't anything. He was off the mule when Boon ran in on the bear. Then we looked up and he was lying on the ground." Boon was shouting at Tennie's Jim, still in the middle of the river.

"Come on, goddamn it!" he said. "Bring me that mule!"

"What do you want with a mule?" Major de Spain said.

Boon didn't even look at him. "I'm going to Hoke's to get the doctor," he said in that calm voice, his face quite calm beneath the steady thinning of the bright blood.

"You need a doctor yourself," Major de Spain said. "Tennie's Jim ——"

"Damn that," Boon said. He turned on Major de Spain. His face was still calm, only his voice was a pitch higher. "Cant you see his goddamn guts are all out of him?"

"Boon!" Major de Spain said. They looked at one another. Boon was a good head taller than Major de Spain; even the boy was taller now than Major de Spain.

"I've got to get the doctor," Boon said. "His goddamn guts ——"

"All right," Major de Spain said. Tennie's Jim came up out of the water. The horse and the sound mule had already scented Old Ben; they surged and plunged all the way up to the top of the bluff, dragging Tennie's Jim with them, before he could stop them and tie them and come back. Major de Spain unlooped the leather thong of his compass from his buttonhole and gave it to Tennie's Jim. "Go straight to Hoke's," he said. "Bring Doctor Crawford back with you. Tell him there are two men to be looked at. Take my mare. Can you find the road from here?"

"Yes, sir," Tennie's Jim said.

"All right," Major de Spain said. "Go on." He turned to the boy. "Take the mules and the horse and go back and get the wagon. We'll go on down the river in the boat to Coon bridge. Meet us there. Can you find it again?"

"Yes, sir," the boy said.

"All right. Get started."

He went back to the wagon. He realised then how far they had run.

It was already afternoon when he put the mules into the traces and tied the horse's lead-rope to the tail-gate. He reached Coon bridge at dusk. The skiff was already there. Before he could see it and almost before he could see the water he had to leap from the tilting wagon, still holding the reins, and work around to where he could grasp the bit and then the ear of the plunging sound mule and dig his heels and hold it until Boon came up the bank. The rope of the lead horse had already snapped and it had already disappeared up the road toward camp. They turned the wagon around and took the mules out and he led the sound mule a hundred yards up the road and tied it. Boon had already brought Lion up to the wagon and Sam was sitting up in the skiff now and when they raised him he tried to walk, up the bank and to the wagon and he tried to climb into the wagon but Boon did not wait; he picked Sam up bodily and set him on the seat. Then they hitched Old Ben to the one eyed mule's saddle again and dragged him up the bank and set two skid-poles into the open tail-gate and got him into the wagon and he went and got the sound mule and Boon fought it into the traces, striking it across its hard hollow-sounding face until it came into position and stood trembling. Then the rain came down, as though it had held off all day waiting on them.

They returned to camp through it, through the streaming and sightless dark, hearing long before they saw any light the horn and the spaced shots to guide them. When they came to Sam's dark little hut he tried to stand up. He spoke again in the tongue of the old fathers; then he said clearly: "Let me out. Let me out."

"He hasn't got any fire," Major said. "Go on!" he said sharply.

But Sam was struggling now, trying to stand up. "Let me out, master," he said. "Let me go home."

So he stopped the wagon and Boon got down and lifted Sam out. He did not wait to let Sam try to walk this time. He carried him into the hut and Major de Spain got light on a paper spill from the buried embers on the hearth and lit the lamp and Boon put Sam on his bunk and drew off his boots and Major de Spain covered him and the boy was not there, he was holding the mules, the sound one which was trying again to bolt since when the wagon stopped Old Ben's scent drifted forward again along the streaming blackness of air, but Sam's eyes were probably open again on that profound look which saw further than them or the hut, further than the death of a bear and the dying of a dog. Then they went on, toward the long wailing of the horn and the shots which seemed each to linger intact somewhere in the thick streaming air until the next spaced report joined and blended with it, to the lighted house, the bright streaming windows, the quiet faces as Boon entered, bloody and quite calm, carrying the bundled coat. He laid Lion, blood coat and all, on his stale sheetless pallet bed which not even Ash, as deft in the house as a woman, could ever make smooth.

The sawmill doctor from Hoke's was already there. Boon would not let the doctor touch him until he had seen to Lion. He wouldn't risk giving Lion chloroform. He put the entrails back and sewed him up without it while Major de Spain held his head and Boon his feet. But he never tried to move. He lay there, the yellow eyes open upon nothing while the quiet men in the new hunting clothes and in the old ones crowded into the little airless room rank with the smell of Boon's body and garments, and watched. Then the doctor cleaned and disinfected Boon's face and arm and leg and bandaged them and, the boy in front with a lantern and the doctor and McCaslin and Major de Spain and General Compson following, they went to Sam Fathers' hut. Tennie's Jim had built up the fire; he squatted before it, dozing. Sam had not moved since Boon had put him in the bunk and Major de Spain had covered him with the blankets, yet he opened his eyes and looked from one to another of the faces and when McCaslin touched his shoulder and said, "Sam. The doctor wants to look at you," he even drew his hands out of the blanket and began to fumble at his shirt buttons until McCaslin said, "Wait. We'll do it." They undressed him. He lay there—the copper-brown, almost hairless body, the old man's body, the old man, the wild man not even one generation from the woods, childless, kinless, peopleless—motionless, his eyes open but no longer looking at any of them, while the doctor examined him and drew the blankets up and put the stethoscope back into his bag and snapped the bag and only the boy knew that Sam too was going to die.

"Exhaustion," the doctor said. "Shock maybe. A man his age swimming rivers in December. He'll be all right. Just make him stay in bed for a day or two. Will there be somebody here with him?"

"There will be somebody here," Major de Spain said.

They went back to the house, to the rank little room where Boon still sat on the pallet bed with Lion's head under his hand while the men, the ones who had hunted behind Lion and the ones who had never seen him before today, came quietly in to look at him and went away. Then it was dawn and they all went out into the yard to look at Old Ben, with his eyes open too and his lips snarled back from his worn teeth and his mutilated foot and the little hard lumps under his skin which were the old bullets (there were fifty-two of them, buckshot rifle and ball) and the single almost invisible slit under his left shoulder where Boon's blade had finally found his life. Then Ash began to beat on the bottom of the dishpan with a heavy spoon to call them to breakfast and it was the first time he could remember hearing no sound from the dogs under the kitchen while they were eating. It was as if the old bear, even dead there in the yard, was a more potent terror still than they could face without Lion between them.

The rain had stopped during the night. By midmorning the thin sun appeared, rapidly burning away mist and cloud, warming the air and the earth; it would be one of those windless Mississippi December days which are a sort of Indian summer's Indian summer. They moved Lion out to the front gallery, into the sun. It was Boon's idea. "Goddamn it," he said, "he never did want to stay in the house until I made him. You know that." He took a crowbar and loosened the floor boards under his pallet bed so it could be raised, mattress and all, without disturbing Lion's position, and they carried him out to the gallery and put him down facing the woods.

Then he and the doctor and McCaslin and Major de Spain went to Sam's hut. This time Sam didn't open his eyes and his breathing was so quiet, so peaceful that they could hardly see that he breathed. The doctor didn't even take out his stethoscope nor even touch him. "He's all right," the doctor said. "He didn't even catch cold. He just quit."

"Quit?" McCaslin said.

"Yes. Old people do that sometimes. Then they get a good night's sleep or maybe it's just a drink of whisky, and they change their minds."

They returned to the house. And then they began to arrive—the swamp-dwellers, the gaunt men who ran traplines and lived on quinine and coons and river water, the farmers of little corn- and cotton-patches along the bottom's edge whose fields and cribs and pig-pens the old bear had rifled, the loggers from the camp and the sawmill men from Hoke's and the town men from further away than that, whose hounds the old bear had slain and traps and deadfalls he had wrecked and whose lead he carried. They came up mounted and on foot and in wagons, to enter the yard and look at him and then go on to the front where Lion lay, filling the little yard and overflowing it until there were almost a hundred of them squatting and standing in the warm and drowsing sunlight, talking quietly of hunting, of the game and the dogs which ran it, of hounds and bear and deer and men of yesterday vanished from the earth, while from time to time the great blue dog would open his eyes, not as if he were listening to them but as though to look at the woods for a moment before closing his eyes again, to remember the woods or to see that they were still there. He died at sundown.

Major de Spain broke camp that night. They carried Lion into the woods, or Boon carried him that is, wrapped in a quilt from his bed, just as he had refused to let anyone else touch Lion yesterday until the doctor got there; Boon carrying Lion, and the boy and General Compson and Walter and still almost fifty of them following with lanterns and lighted pine-knots—men from Hoke's and even further, who would have to ride out of the bottom in the dark, and swampers and trappers who would have to walk even, scattering toward the little hidden huts where they lived. And Boon would let nobody else dig the grave either and lay Lion in it and cover him and then General Compson stood at the head of it while the blaze and smoke of the pine-knots streamed away among the winter branches and spoke as he would have spoken over a man. Then they returned to camp. Major de Spain and McCaslin and Ash had rolled and tied all the bedding. The mules were hitched to the wagon and pointed out of the bottom and the wagon was already loaded and the stove in the kitchen was cold and the table was set with scraps of cold food and bread and only the coffee was hot when the boy ran into the kitchen where Major de Spain and McCaslin had already eaten. "What?" he cried. "What? I'm not going."

"Yes," McCaslin said, "we're going out tonight. Major wants to get on back home."

"No!" he said. "I'm going to stay."

"You've got to be back in school Monday. You've already missed a week more than I intended. It will take you from now until Monday to catch up. Sam's all right. You heard Doctor Crawford. I'm going to leave Boon and Tennie's Jim both to stay with him until he feels like getting up."

He was panting. The others had come in. He looked rapidly and almost frantically around at the other faces. Boon had a fresh bottle. He upended it and started the cork by striking the bottom of the bottle with the heel of his hand and drew the cork with his teeth and spat it out and drank. "You're damn right you're going back to school," Boon said. "Or I'll burn the tail off of you myself if Cass dont, whether you are sixteen or sixty. Where in hell do you expect to get without education? Where would Cass be? Where in hell would I be if I hadn't never went to school?"

He looked at McCaslin again. He could feel his breath coming shorter and shorter and shallower and shallower, as if there were not enough air in the kitchen for that many to breathe. "This is just Thursday. I'll come home Sunday night on one of the horses. I'll come home Sunday, then. I'll make up the time I lost studying Sunday night. McCaslin," he said, without even despair.

"No, I tell you," McCaslin said. "Sit down here and eat your supper. We're going out to——"

"Hold up, Cass," General Compson said. The boy did not know General Compson had moved until he put his hand on his shoulder. "What is it, bud?" he said.

"I've got to stay," he said. "I've got to."

"All right," General Compson said. "You can stay. If missing an extra week of school is going to throw you so far behind you'll have to sweat to find out what some hired pedagogue put between the covers of a book, you better quit altogether.—And you shut up, Cass," he said, though McCaslin had not spoken. "You've got one foot straddled into a farm and the other foot straddled into a bank; you aint even got a good hand-hold where this boy was already an old man long before you damned Sartorises and Edmondses invented farms and banks to keep yourselves from having to find out what this boy was born knowing and fearing too maybe but without being afraid, that could go ten miles on a compass because he wanted to look at a bear none of us had ever got near enough to put a bullet in and looked at the bear and came the ten miles back on the compass in the dark; maybe by God that's the why and the wherefore of farms and banks.—I reckon you still aint going to tell what it is?"

But still he could not. "I've got to stay," he said.

"All right," General Compson said. "There's plenty of grub left. And you'll come home Sunday, like you promised McCaslin? Not Sunday night: Sunday."

"Yes, sir," he said.

"All right," General Compson said. "Sit down and eat, boys," he said. "Let's get started. It's going to be cold before we get home."

They ate. The wagon was already loaded and ready to depart; all they had to do was to get into it. Boon would drive them out to the road, to the farmer's stable where the surrey had been left. He stood beside the wagon, in silhouette on the sky, turbaned like a Paythan and taller than any there, the bottle tilted. Then he flung the bottle from his lips without even lowering it, spinning and glinting in the faint starlight, empty. "Them that's going," he said, "get in the goddamn wagon. Them that aint, get out of the goddamn way." The others got in. Boon mounted to the seat beside General Compson and the wagon moved, on into the obscurity until the boy could no longer see it, even the moving density of it amid the greater night. But he could still hear it, for a long while: the slow, deliberate banging of the wooden frame as it lurched from rut to rut. And he could hear Boon even when he could no longer hear the wagon. He was singing, harsh, tuneless, loud.

That was Thursday. One Saturday morning Tennie's Jim left on McCaslin's woods-horse which had not been out of the bottom one time now in six years, and late that afternoon rode through the gate on the spent horse and on to the commissary where McCaslin was rationing the tenants and the wage-hands for the coming week, and this time McCaslin forestalled any necessity or risk of having to wait while Major de Spain's surrey was being horsed and harnessed. He took their own, and with Tennie's Jim already asleep in the back seat he drove in to Jefferson and waited while Major de Spain changed to boots and put on his overcoat, and they drove the thirty miles in the dark of that night and at daybreak on Sunday morning they swapped to the waiting mare and mule and as the sun rose they rode out of the jungle and onto the low ridge where they had buried Lion: the low mound of unannealed earth where Boon's spade-marks still showed and beyond the grave the platform of freshly cut saplings bound between four posts and the blanket-wrapped bundle upon the platform and Boon and the boy squatting between the platform and the grave until Boon, the bandage removed, ripped, from his head so that the long scoriations of Old Ben's claws resembled crusted tar in the sunlight, sprang up and threw down upon them with the old gun with which he had never been known to hit anything although McCaslin was already off the mule, kicked both feet free of the irons and vaulted down before the mule had stopped, walking toward Boon.

"Stand back," Boon said. "By God, you wont touch him. Stand back, McCaslin." Still McCaslin came on, fast yet without haste.

"Cass!" Major de Spain said. Then he said "Boon! You, Boon!" and he was down too and the boy rose too, quickly, and still McCaslin came on not fast but steady and walked up to the grave and reached his hand steadily out, quickly yet still not fast, and took hold the gun by the middle so that he and Boon faced one another across Lion's grave, both holding the gun, Boon's spent indomitable amazed and frantic face almost a head higher than McCaslin's beneath the black scoriations of beast's claws and then Boon's chest began to heave as though there were not enough air in all the woods, in all the wilderness, for all of them, for him and anyone else, even for him alone.

"Turn it loose, Boon," McCaslin said.

"You damn little spindling—" Boon said. "Dont you know I can take it away from you? Dont you know I can tie it around your neck like a damn cravat?"

"Yes," McCaslin said. "Turn it loose, Boon."

"This is the way he wanted it. He told us. He told us exactly how to do it. And by God you aint going to move him. So we did it like he said, and I been sitting here ever since to keep the damn wildcats and varmints away from him and by God—" Then McCaslin had the gun, down-slanted while he pumped the slide, the five shells snicking out of it so fast that the last one was almost out before the first one touched the ground and McCaslin dropped the gun behind him without once having taken his eyes from Boon's.

"Did you kill him, Boon?" he said. Then Boon moved. He turned, he moved like he was still drunk and then for a moment blind too, one hand out as he blundered toward the big tree and seemed to stop walking before he reached the tree so that he plunged, fell toward it, flinging up both hands and catching himself against the tree and turning until his back was against it, backing with the tree's trunk his wild spent scoriated face and the tremendous heave and collapse of his chest, McCaslin following, facing him again, never once having moved his eyes from Boon's eyes. "Did you kill him, Boon?"

"No!" Boon said. "No!"

"Tell the truth," McCaslin said. "I would have done it if he had asked me to." Then the boy moved. He was between them, facing Mc-

Caslin; the water felt as if it had burst and sprung not from his eyes alone but from his whole face, like sweat.

"Leave him alone!" he cried. "Goddamn it! Leave him alone!"

4

then he was twenty-one. He could say it, himself and his cousin juxtaposed not against the wilderness but against the tamed land which was to have been his heritage, the land which old Carothers McCaslin his grandfather had bought with white man's money from the wild men whose grandfathers without guns hunted it, and tamed and ordered or believed he had tamed and ordered it for the reason that the human beings he held in bondage and in the power of life and death had removed the forest from it and in their sweat scratched the surface of it to a depth of perhaps fourteen inches in order to grow something out of it which had not been there before and which could be translated back into the money he who believed he had bought it had had to pay to get it and hold it and a reasonable profit too: and for which reason old Carothers McCaslin, knowing better, could raise his children, his descendants and heirs, to believe the land was his to hold and bequeath since the strong and ruthless man has a cynical foreknowledge of his own vanity and pride and strength and a contempt for all his get: just as, knowing better, Major de Spain and his fragment of that wilderness which was bigger and older than any recorded deed: just as, knowing better, old Thomas Sutpen, from whom Major de Spain had had his fragment for money: just as Ikkemotubbe, the Chickasaw chief, from whom Thomas Sutpen had had the fragment for money or rum or whatever it was, knew in his turn that not even a fragment of it had been his to relinquish or sell

not against the wilderness but against the land, not in pursuit and lust but in relinquishment, and in the commissary as it should have been, not the heart perhaps but certainly the solar-plexus of the repudiated and relinquished: the square, galleried, wooden building squatting like a portent above the fields whose laborers it still held in thrall '65 or no and placarded over with advertisements for snuff and cures for chills and slaves and potions manufactured and sold by white men to bleach the pigment and straighten the hair of negroes that they might resemble the very race which for two hundred years had held them in bondage and from which for another hundred years not even a bloody civil war would have set them completely free

himself and his cousin amid the old smells of cheese and salt meat and kerosene and harness, the ranked shelves of tobacco and overalls and bottled medicine and thread and plow-bolts, the barrels and kegs of flour and meal and molasses and nails, the wall pegs dependant with plowlines and plow-collars and hames and trace-chains, and the desk and the shelf above it on which rested the ledgers in which McCaslin recorded the slow outward trickle of food and supplies and equipment which returned each fall as cotton made and ginned and sold (two threads frail as truth and impalpable as equators yet cable-strong to bind for life them who made the cotton to the land their sweat fell on), and the older ledgers clumsy and archaic in size and shape, on the yellowed pages of which were recorded in the faded hand of his father Theophilus and his uncle Amodeus during the two decades before the Civil War, the manumission in title at least of Carothers McCaslin's slaves:

'Relinquish,' McCaslin said. 'Relinquish. You, the direct male descendant of him who saw the opportunity and took it, bought the land, took the land, got the land no matter how, held it to bequeath, no matter how, out of the old grant, the first patent, when it was a wilderness of wild beasts and wilder men, and cleared it, translated it into something to bequeath to his children, worthy of bequeathment for his descendants' ease and security and pride and to perpetuate his name and accomplishments. Not only the male descendant but the only and last descendant in the male line and in the third generation, while I am not only four generations from old Carothers, I derived through a woman and the very McCaslin in my name is mine only by sufferance and courtesy and my grandmother's pride in what that man accomplished whose legacy and monument you think you can repudiate.' and he

'I cant repudiate it. It was never mine to repudiate. It was never Father's and Uncle Buddy's to bequeath to me to repudiate because it was never Grandfather's to bequeath them to bequeath me to repudiate because it was never old Ikkemotubbe's to sell to Grandfather for bequeathment and repudiation. Because it was never Ikkemotubbe's fathers' fathers' to bequeath Ikkemotubbe to sell to Grandfather or any man because on the instant when Ikkemotubbe discovered, realised, that he could sell it for money, on that instant it ceased ever to have been his forever, father to father to father, and the man who bought it bought nothing.'

'Bought nothing?' and he

'Bought nothing. Because He told in the Book how He created the earth, made it and looked at it and said it was all right, and then He made man. He made the earth first and peopled it with dumb creatures, and then He created man to be His overseer on the earth and to hold suzerainty over the earth and the animals on it in His name, not to hold for himself and his descendants inviolable title forever, generation after generation, to the oblongs and squares of the earth, but to hold the earth mutual and intact in the communal anonymity of brotherhood, and all the fee He asked was pity and humility and sufferance and endurance and the sweat of his face for bread. And I know what you are going to say,' he said: 'That nevertheless Grandfather—' and McCaslin

'—did own it. And not the first. Not alone and not the first since, as your Authority states, man was dispossessed of Eden. Nor yet the second and still not alone, on down through the tedious and shabby chronicle of His chosen sprung from Abraham, and of the sons of them who dispossessed Abraham, and of the five hundred years during which half the known world and all it contained was chattel to one city as this plantation and all the life it contained was chattel and revokeless thrall to this commissary store and those ledgers yonder during your grandfather's life, and the next thousand years while men fought over the fragments of that collapse until at last even the fragments were exhausted and men snarled over the gnawed bones of the old world's worthless evening until an accidental egg discovered to them a new hemisphere. So let me say it: That nevertheless and notwithstanding old Carothers did own it. Bought it, got it, no matter; kept it, held it, no matter; bequeathed it: else why do you stand there relinquishing and repudiating? Held it, kept it for fifty years until you could repudiate it, while He—this Arbiter, this Architect, this Umpire—condoned—or did He? looked down and saw—or did He? Or at least did nothing: saw, and could not, or did not see; saw, and would not, or perhaps He would not see—perverse, impotent, or blind: which?' and he

'Dispossessed.' and McCaslin

'What?' and he

'Dispossessed. Not impotent: He didn't condone; not blind, because He watched it. And let me say it. Dispossessed of Eden. Dispossessed of Canaan, and those who dispossessed him dispossessed him dispossessed, and the five hundred years of absentee landlords in the Roman bagnios, and the thousand years of wild men from the northern woods who dispossessed them and devoured their ravished substance ravished in turn again and then snarled in what you call the old world's worthless twilight over the old world's gnawed bones, blasphemous in His name until He used a simple egg to discover to them a new world where a nation of people could be founded in humility and pity and sufferance and pride of one to another. And Grandfather did own the land nevertheless and notwithstanding because He permitted it, not impotent and not condoning and not blind because He ordered and watched it. He saw the land already accursed even as Ikkemotubbe and Ikkemotubbe's father old Issetibbeha and old Issetibbeha's fathers too held it, already tainted even before any white man owned it by what Grandfather and his kind, his fathers, had brought into the new land which He had vouchsafed them out of pity and sufferance, on condition of pity and humility and sufferance and endurance, from that old world's corrupt and worthless twilight as though in the sailfuls of the old world's tainted wind which drove the ships—' and McCaslin

'Ah.'

'—and no hope for the land anywhere so long as Ikkemotubbe and Ikkemotubbe's descendants held it in unbroken succession. Maybe He saw that only by voiding the land for a time of Ikkemotubbe's blood and substituting for it another blood, could He accomplish His purpose. Maybe He knew already what that other blood would be, maybe it was more than justice that only the white man's blood was available and capable to raise the white man's curse, more than vengeance when—' and McCaslin

'Ah.'

'—when He used the blood which had brought in the evil to destroy the evil as doctors use fever to burn up fever, poison to slay poison. Maybe He chose Grandfather out of all of them He might have picked. Maybe He knew that Grandfather himself would not serve His purpose because Grandfather was born too soon too, but that Grandfather would have descendants, the right descendants; maybe He had foreseen already the descendants Grandfather would have, maybe He saw already in Grandfather the seed progenitive of the three generations He saw it would take to set at least some of His lowly people free—' and McCaslin

'The sons of Ham. You quote the Book: the sons of Ham.' and he

'There are some things He said in the Book, and some things reported of Him that He did not say. And I know what you will say now: That if truth is one thing to me and another thing to you, how will we choose which is truth? You dont need to choose. The heart already knows. He didn't have His Book written to be read by what must elect and choose, but by the heart, not by the wise of the earth because maybe they dont need it or maybe the wise no longer have any heart, but by the doomed and lowly of the earth who have nothing else to read with but the heart. Because the men who wrote his Book for Him were writing about truth and there is only one truth and it covers all things that touch the heart.' and McCaslin

'So these men who transcribed His Book for Him were sometime liars.' and he

'Yes. Because they were human men. They were trying to write down the heart's truth out of the heart's driving complexity, for all the complex and troubled hearts which would beat after them. What they were trying to tell, what He wanted said, was too simple. Those for whom they transcribed His words could not have believed them. It had to be expounded in the everyday terms which they were familiar with and could comprehend, not only those who listened but those who told it too, because if they who were that near to Him as to have been elected from among all who breathed and spoke language to transcribe and relay His words, could comprehend truth only through the complexity of passion and lust and hate and fear which drives the heart, what distance back to truth must they traverse whom truth could only reach by word-of-mouth?' and McCaslin

'I might answer that, since you have taken to proving your points and disproving mine by the same text, I dont know. But I dont say that, because you have answered yourself: No time at all if, as you say, the heart knows truth, the infallible and unerring heart. And perhaps you are right, since although you admitted three generations from old Carothers to you, there were not three. There were not even completely two. Uncle Buck and Uncle Buddy. And they not the first and not alone. A thousand other Bucks and Buddies in less than two generations and sometimes less than one in this land which so you claim God created and man himself cursed and tainted. Not to mention 1865.' and he

'Yes. More men than Father and Uncle Buddy,' not even glancing toward the shelf above the desk, nor did McCaslin. They did not need to. To him it was as though the ledgers in their scarred cracked leather bindings were being lifted down one by one in their fading sequence and spread open on the desk or perhaps upon some apocryphal Bench or even Altar or perhaps before the Throne Itself for a last perusal and contemplation and refreshment of the Allknowledgeable before the yellowed pages and the brown thin ink in which was recorded the injustice and a little at least of its amelioration and restitution faded back forever into the anonymous communal original dust

the yellowed pages scrawled in fading ink by the hand first of his grandfather and then of his father and uncle, bachelors up to and past fifty and then sixty, the one who ran the plantation and the farming of it and the other who did the housework and the cooking and continued to do it even after his twin married and the boy himself was born

the two brothers who as soon as their father was buried moved out of the tremendously-conceived, the almost barnlike edifice which he had not even completed, into a one-room log cabin which the two of them built themselves and added other rooms to while they lived in it, refusing to allow any slave to touch any timber of it other than the actual raising into place the logs which two men alone could not handle, and domiciled all the slaves in the big house some of the windows of which were still merely boarded up with odds and ends of plank or with the skins of bear and deer nailed over the empty frames: each sundown the brother who superintended the farming would parade the negroes as a first sergeant dismisses a company, and herd them willynilly, man woman and child, without question protest or recourse, into the tremendous abortive edifice scarcely yet out of embryo, as if even old Carothers McCaslin had paused aghast at the concrete indication of his own vanity's boundless conceiving: he would call his mental roll and herd them in and with a hand-wrought nail as long as a flenching-knife and suspended from a short deer-hide thong attached to the door-jamb for that purpose, he would nail to the door of that house which lacked half its windows and had no hinged back door at all, so that presently and for fifty years afterward, when the boy himself was big to hear and remember it, there was in the land a sort of folk-tale: of the countryside all night long full of skulking McCaslin slaves dodging the moonlit roads and the Patrol-riders to visit other plantations, and of the unspoken gentlemen's agreement between the two white men and the two dozen black ones that, after the white man had counted them and driven the home-made nail into the front door at sundown, neither of the white men would go around behind the house and look at the back door, provided that all the negroes were behind the front one when the brother who drove it drew out the nail again at daybreak

the twins who were identical even in their handwriting, unless you had specimens side by side to compare, and even when both hands appeared on the same page (as often happened, as if, long since past any oral intercourse, they had used the diurnally advancing pages to conduct the unavoidable business of the compulsion which had traversed all the waste wilderness of North Mississippi in 1830 and '40 and singled them out to drive) they both looked as though they had been written by the same perfectly normal ten-year-old boy, even to the spelling, except that the spelling did not improve as one by one the slaves which Carothers McCaslin had inherited and purchased—Roscius and Phoebe and Thucydides and Eunice and their descendants, and Sam Fathers and his mother for both of whom he had swapped an underbred trotting gelding to old Ikkemotubbe, the Chickasaw chief from whom he had likewise bought the land, and Tennie Beauchamp whom the twin Amodeus had won from a neighbor in a poker-game, and the anomaly calling itself Percival Brownlee which the twin Theophilus had purchased, neither he nor his brother ever knew why apparently, from Bedford Forrest while he was still only a slave-dealer and not yet a general (It was a single page, not long and covering less than a year, not seven months in fact, begun in the hand which the boy had learned to distinguish as that of his father:

Percavil Brownly 26yr Old. cleark @ Bookepper. bought from N.B.Forest at Cold Water 3 Mar 1856 $265. dolars

and beneath that, in the same hand:

5 mar 1856 No bookepper any way Cant read. Can write his Name but I already put that down My self Says he can Plough but dont look like it to Me. sent to Feild to day Mar 5 1856

and the same hand:

6 Mar 1856 Cant plough either Says he aims to be a Precher so may be he can lead live stock to Crick to Drink and this time it was the other, the hand which he now recognised as his uncle's when he could see them both on the same page:

Mar 23th 1856 Cant do that either Except one at a Time Get shut of him

then the first again:

24 Mar 1856 Who in hell would buy him

then the second:

19th of Apr 1856 Nobody You put yourself out of Market at Cold Water two months ago I never said sell him Free him

the first:

22 Apr 1856 Ill get it out of him

the second:

June 13th 1856 How $1 per yr 265$ 265 yrs Wholl sign his Free paper

then the first again:

1 Oct 1856 Mule josephine Broke Leg @ shot Wrong stall wrong niger wrong everything $100. dolars

and the same:

2 Oct 1856 Freed Debit McCaslin @ McCaslin $265. dolars

then the second again:

Oct 3th Debit Theophilus McCaslin Niger 265$ Mule 100$ 365$ He hasnt gone yet Father should be here

then the first:

3 Oct 1856 Son of a bitch wont leave What would father done

the second:

29th of Oct 1856 Renamed him

the first:

31 Oct 1856 Renamed him what

the second:

Chrstms 1856 Spintrius

) took substance and even a sort of shadowy life with their passions and complexities too as page followed page and year year; all there, not only the general and condoned injustice and its slow amortization but the specific tragedy which had not been condoned and could never be amortized, the new page and the new ledger, the hand which he could now recognise at first glance as his father's:

Father dide Lucius Quintus Carothers McCaslin, Callina 1772 Missippy 1837. Dide and burid 27 June 1837
Roskus. rased by Granfather in Callina Dont know how old. Freed 27 June 1837 Dont want to leave. Dide and Burid 12 Jan 1841
Fibby Roskus Wife. bought by granfather in Callina says Fifty Freed 27 June 1837 Dont want to leave. Dide and burd 1 Aug 1849
Thucydus Roskus @ Fibby Son born in Callina 1779. Refused 10acre peace fathers Will 28 Jun 1837 Refused Cash offer $200. dolars from A. @ T. McCaslin 28 Jun 1837 Wants to stay and work it out

and beneath this and covering the next five pages and almost that many years, the slow, day-by-day accrument of the wages allowed him and the food and clothing—the molasses and meat and meal, the cheap durable shirts and jeans and shoes and now and then a coat against rain and cold—charged against the slowly yet steadily mounting sum of balance (and it would seem to the boy that he could actually see the black man, the slave whom his white owner had forever manumitted by the very act from which the black man could never be free so long as memory lasted, entering the commissary, asking permission perhaps of the white man's son to see the ledger-page which he could not even read, not even asking for the white man's word, which he would have had to accept for the reason that there was absolutely no way under the sun for him to test it, as to how the account stood, how much longer before he could go and never return, even if only as far as Jefferson seventeen miles away) on to the double pen-stroke closing the final entry:

3 Nov 1841 By Cash to Thucydus McCaslin $200. dolars Set Up blaksmith in J. Dec 1841 Dide and burid in J. 17 feb 1854
Eunice Bought by Father in New Orleans 1807 $650. dolars. Marrid to Thucydus 1809 Drownd in Crick Cristmas Day 1832

and then the other hand appeared, the first time he had seen it in the ledger to distinguish it as his uncle's, the cook and housekeeper whom even McCaslin, who had known him and the boy's father for sixteen years before the boy was born, remembered as sitting all day long in the rocking chair from which he cooked the food, before the kitchen fire on which he cooked it:

June 21th 1833 Drownd herself

and the first:

23 Jun 1833 Who in hell ever heard of a niger drownding him self

and the second, unhurried, with a complete finality; the two identical entries might have been made with a rubber stamp save for the date:

Aug 13th 1833 Drownd herself

and he thought *But why? But why?* He was sixteen then. It was neither the first time he had been alone in the commissary nor the first time he had taken down the old ledgers familiar on their shelf above the desk ever since he could remember. As a child and even after nine and ten and eleven, when he had learned to read, he would look up at the scarred and cracked backs and ends but with no particular desire to open them, and though he intended to examine them someday because he realised that they probably contained a chronological and much more comprehensive though doubtless tedious record than he would ever get from any other source, not alone of his own flesh and blood but of all his people, not only the whites but the black one too, who were as much a part of his ancestry as his white progenitors, and of the land which they had all held and used in common and fed from and on and would continue to use in common without regard to color or titular ownership, it would only be on some idle day when he was old and perhaps even bored a little since what the old books contained would be after all these years fixed immutably, finished, unalterable, harmless. Then he was sixteen. He knew what he was going to find before he found it. He got the commissary key from McCaslin's room after midnight while McCaslin was asleep and with the commissary door shut and locked behind him and the forgotten lantern stinking anew the rank dead icy air, he leaned above the yellowed page and thought not Why drowned herself, but thinking what he believed his father had thought when he found his brother's first comment: Why did Uncle Buddy think she had drowned herself? finding, beginning to find on the next succeeding page what he knew he would find, only this was still not it because he already knew this:

Tomasina called Tomy Daughter of Thucydus @ Eunice Born 1810 dide in Child bed June 1833 and Burd. Yr stars fell

nor the next:

Turl Son of Thucydus @ Eunice Tomy born Jun 1833 yr stars fell Fathers will

and nothing more, no tedious recording filling this page of wages day by day and food and clothing charged against them, no entry of his death and burial because he had outlived his white half-brothers and the books which McCaslin kept did not include obituaries: just *Fathers will* and he had seen that too: old Carothers' bold cramped hand far less legible than his sons' even and not much better in spelling, who while capitalising almost every noun and verb, made no effort to punctuate or construct whatever, just as he made no effort either to explain or obfuscate the thousand-dollar legacy to the son of an unmarried slave-girl, to be paid only at the child's coming-of-age, bearing the consequence of the act of which there was still no definite incontrovertible proof that he acknowledged, not out of his own substance but penalising his sons with it, charging them a cash forfeit on the accident of their own paternity; not even a bribe for silence toward his own fame since his fame would suffer only after he was no longer present to defend it, flinging almost contemptuously, as he might a cast-off hat or pair of shoes, the thousand dollars which could have had no more reality to him under those conditions than it would have to the negro, the slave who would not even see it until he came of age, twenty-one years too late to begin to learn what money was. *So I reckon that was cheaper than saying My son to a nigger* he thought. *Even if My son wasn't but just two words. But there must have been love* he thought. *Some sort of love. Even what he would have called love: not just an afternoon's or a night's spittoon.* There was the old man, old, within five years of his life's end, long a widower and, since his sons were not only bachelors but were approaching middleage, lonely in the house and doubtless even bored since his plantation was established now and functioning and there was enough money now, too much of it probably for a man whose vices even apparently remained below his means; there was the girl, husbandless and young, only twenty-three when the child was born: perhaps he had sent for her at first out of loneliness, to have a young voice and movement in the house, summoned her, bade her mother send her each morning to sweep the floors and make the beds and the mother acquiescing since that was probably already understood, already planned: the only child of a couple who were not field hands and who held themselves something above the other slaves not alone for that reason but because the husband and his father and mother too had been inherited by the white man from his father, and the white man himself had travelled three hundred miles and better to New Orleans in a day when men travelled by horseback or steamboat, and bought the girl's mother as a wife for

and that was all. The old frail pages seemed to turn of their own accord even while he thought *His own daughter His own daughter. No No Not even him* back to that one where the white man (not even a widower then) who never went anywhere any more than his sons in their time ever did and who did not need another slave, had gone all the way to New Orleans and bought one. And Tomey's Terrel was still alive when the boy was ten years old and he knew from his own observation and memory that there had already been some white in Tomey's Terrel's blood before his father gave him the rest of it; and looking down at the yellowed page spread beneath the yellow glow of the lantern smoking and stinking in that rank chill midnight room fifty years later, he seemed to see her actually walking into the icy creek on that Christmas day six months before her daughter's and her lover's (*Her first lover's* he thought. *Her first*) child was born, solitary, inflexible, griefless, ceremonial, in formal and succinct repudiation of grief and despair who had already had to repudiate belief and hope

that was all. He would never need look at the ledgers again nor did he; the yellowed pages in their fading and implacable succession were as much a part of his consciousness and would remain so forever, as the fact of his own nativity:

Tennie Beauchamp 21yrs Won by Amodeus McCaslin from Hubert Beauchamp Esqre Possible Strait against three Treys in sigt Not called 1859 Marrid to Tomys Turl 1859

and no date of freedom because her freedom, as well as that of her first surviving child, derived not from Buck and Buddy McCaslin in the commissary but from a stranger in Washington and no date of death and burial, not only because McCaslin kept no obituaries in his books, but because in this year 1883 she was still alive and would remain so to see a grandson by her last surviving child:

Amodeus McCaslin Beauchamp Son of tomys Turl @ Tennie Beauchamp 1859 dide 1859

then his uncle's hand entire, because his father was now a member of the cavalry command of that man whose name as a slave-dealer he could not even spell: and not even a page and not even a full line:

Dauter Tomes Turl and tenny 1862

and not even a line and not even a sex and no cause given though the boy could guess it because McCaslin was thirteen then and he remembered how there was not always enough to eat in more places than Vicksburg:

Child of tomes Turl and Tenny 1863

and the same hand again and this one lived, as though Tennie's perseverance and the fading and diluted ghost of old Carothers' ruthlessness had at last conquered even starvation: and clearer, fuller, more carefully written and spelled than the boy had yet seen it, as if the old man, who should have been a woman to begin with, trying to run what was left of the plantation in his brother's absence in the intervals of cooking and caring for himself and the fourteen-year-old orphan, had taken as an omen for renewed hope the fact that this nameless inheritor of slaves was at least remaining alive long enough to receive a name:

James Thucydus Beauchamp Son of Tomes Turl and Tenny Beauchamp Born 29th december 1864 and both Well Wanted to call him Theophilus but Tride Amodeus McCaslin and Callina McCaslin and both dide so Disswaded Them Born at Two clock A,m, both Well

but no more, nothing; it would be another two years yet before the boy, almost a man now, would return from the abortive trip into Tennessee with the still-intact third of old Carothers' legacy to his Negro son and his descendants, which as the three surviving children established at last one by one their apparent intention of surviving, their white half-uncles had increased to a thousand dollars each, conditions permitting, as they came of age, and completed the page himself as far as it would even be completed when that day was long passed beyond which a man born in 1864 (or 1867 either, when he himself saw light) could have expected or himself hoped or even wanted to be still alive; his own hand now, queerly enough resembling neither his father's nor his uncle's nor even McCaslin's, but like that of his grandfather's save for the spelling:

Vanished sometime on night of his twenty-first birthday Dec 29 1885. Traced by Isaac McCaslin to Jackson Tenn. and there lost. His third of legacy $1000.00 returned to McCaslin Edmonds Trustee this day Jan 12 1886

but not yet: that would be two years yet, and now his father's again, whose old commander was now quit of soldiering and slave-trading both; once more in the ledger and then not again and more illegible than ever, almost indecipherable at all from the rheumatism which now crippled him and almost completely innocent now even of any sort of spelling as well as punctuation, as if the four years during which he had followed the sword of the only man ever breathing who ever sold him a negro, let alone beat him in a trade, had convinced him not only of the vanity of faith and hope but of orthography too:

Miss sophonsiba b dtr t t @ t 1869

but not of belief and will because it was there, written, as McCaslin had told him, with the left hand, but there in the ledger one time more and then not again, for the boy himself was a year old, and when Lucas was born six years later, his father and uncle had been dead inside the same twelve-months almost five years; his own hand again, who was there and saw it, 1886, she was just seventeen, two years younger than himself, and he was in the commissary when McCaslin entered out of the first of dusk and said, 'He wants to marry Fonsiba,' like that: and he looked past McCaslin and saw the man, the stranger, taller than McCaslin and wearing better clothes than McCaslin and most of the other white men the boy knew habitually wore, who entered the room like a white man and stood in it like a white man, as though he had let McCaslin precede him into it not because McCaslin's skin was white but simply because McCaslin lived there and knew the way, and who talked like a white man too, looking at him past McCaslin's shoulder rapidly and keenly once and then no more, without further interest, as a mature and contained white man not impatient but just pressed for time might have looked. 'Marry Fonsiba?' he cried. 'Marry Fonsiba?' and then no more either, just watching and listening while McCaslin and the Negro talked:

'To live in Arkansas, I believe you said.'

'Yes. I have property there. A farm.'

'Property? A farm? You own it?'

'Yes.'

'You dont say Sir, do you?'

'To my elders, yes.'

'I see. You are from the North.'

'Yes. Since a child.'

'Then your father was a slave.'

'Yes. Once.'

'Then how do you own a farm in Arkansas?'

'I have a grant. It was my father's. From the United States. For military service.'

'I see,' McCaslin said. 'The Yankee army.'

'The United States army,' the stranger said; and then himself again, crying it at McCaslin's back:

'Call aunt Tennie! I'll go get her! I'll—' But McCaslin was not even including him; the stranger did not even glance back toward his voice, the two of them speaking to one another again as if he were not even there:

'Since you seem to have it all settled,' McCaslin said, 'why have you bothered to consult my authority at all?'

'I dont,' the stranger said. 'I acknowledge your authority only so far as you admit your responsibility toward her as a female member of the family of which you are the head. I dont ask your permission. I ——'

'That will do!' McCaslin said. But the stranger did not falter. It was neither as if he were ignoring McCaslin nor as if he had failed to hear him. It was as though he were making, not at all an excuse and not exactly a justification, but simply a statement which the situation absolutely required and demanded should be made in McCaslin's hearing whether McCaslin listened to it or not. It was as if he were talking to himself, for himself to hear the words spoken aloud. They faced one another, not close yet at slightly less than foils' distance, erect, their voices not raised, not impactive, just succinct:

'—I inform you, notify you in advance as chief of her family. No man of honor could do less. Besides, you have, in your way, according to your lights and upbringing ——'

'That's enough, I said,' McCaslin said. 'Be off this place by full dark. Go.' But for another moment the other did not move, contemplating Mc-

Caslin with that detached and heatless look, as if he were watching reflected in McCaslin's pupils the tiny image of the figure he was sustaining.

'Yes,' he said. 'After all, this is your house. And in your fashion you have. . . . But no matter. You are right. This is enough.' He turned back toward the door; he paused again but only for a second, already moving while he spoke: 'Be easy. I will be good to her.' Then he was gone.

'But how did she ever know him?' the boy cried. 'I never even heard of him before! And Fonsiba, that's never been off this place except to go to church since she was born ——'

'Ha,' McCaslin said. 'Even their parents dont know until too late how seventeen-year-old girls ever met the men who marry them too, if they are lucky.' And the next morning they were both gone, Fonsiba too. McCaslin never saw her again, nor did he, because the woman he found at last five months later was no one he had ever known. He carried a third of the three-thousand-dollar fund in gold in a money-belt, as when he had vainly traced Tennie's Jim into Tennessee a year ago. They—the man—had left an address of some sort with Tennie, and three months later a letter came, written by the man although McCaslin's wife Alice had taught Fonsiba to read and write too a little. But it bore a different postmark from the address the man had left with Tennie, and he travelled by rail as far as he could and then by contracted stage and then by a hired livery rig and then by rail again for a distance: an experienced traveller by now and an experienced bloodhound too and a successful one this time because he would have to be; as the slow interminable empty muddy December miles crawled and crawled and night followed night in hotels, in roadside taverns of rough logs and containing little else but a bar, and in the cabins of strangers and the hay of lonely barns, in none of which he dared undress because of his secret golden girdle like that of a disguised one of the Magi travelling incognito and not even hope to draw him but only determination and desperation, he would tell himself: *I will have to find her. I will have to. We have already lost one of them. I will have to find her this time.* He did. Hunched in the slow and icy rain, on a spent hired horse splashed to the chest and higher, he saw it—a single log edifice with a clay chimney which seemed in process of being flattened by the rain to a nameless and valueless rubble of dissolution in that roadless and even pathless waste of unfenced fallow and wilderness jungle—no barn, no stable, not so much as a hen-coop: just a log cabin built by hand and no clever hand either, a meagre pile of clumsily-cut firewood sufficient for about one day and not even a gaunt hound to come bellowing out from under the house when he rode up—a farm only in embryo, perhaps a good farm, maybe even a plantation someday, but not now, not for years yet and only then with labor, hard and enduring and unflagging work and sacrifice; he shoved open the crazy kitchen door in its awry frame and entered an icy gloom where not even a fire for cooking burned and after another moment saw, crouched into the wall's angle behind a crude table, the coffee-colored face which he had known all his life but knew no more, the body which had been born within a hundred yards of the room that he was born in and in which some of his own blood ran but which was now completely inheritor of generation after generation to whom an unannounced white man on a horse was a white man's hired Patroller wearing a pistol sometimes and a blacksnake whip always; he entered the next room, the only other room the cabin owned, and found, sitting in a rocking chair before the hearth, the man himself, reading—sitting there in the only chair in the house, before that miserable fire for which there was not wood sufficient to last twenty-four hours, in the same ministerial clothing in which he had entered the commissary five months ago and a pair of gold-framed spectacles which, when he looked up and then rose to his feet, the boy saw did not even contain lenses, reading a book in the midst of that desolation, that muddy waste fenceless and even pathless and without even a walled shed for stock to stand beneath: and over all, permeant, clinging to the man's very clothing and exuding from his skin itself, that rank stink of baseless and imbecile delusion, that boundless rapacity and folly, of the carpet-bagger followers of victorious armies.

'Dont you see?' he cried. 'Dont you see? This whole land, the whole South, is cursed, and all of us who derive from it, whom it ever suckled, white and black both, lie under the curse? Granted that my people brought the curse onto the land: maybe for that reason their descendants alone can—not resist it, not combat it—maybe just endure and outlast it until the curse is lifted. Then your peoples' turn will come because we have forfeited ours. But not now. Not yet. Dont you see?'

The other stood now, the unfrayed garments still ministerial even if not quite so fine, the book closed upon one finger to keep the place, the lenseless spectacles held like a music master's wand in the other workless hand while the owner of it spoke his measured and sonorous imbecility of the boundless folly and the baseless hope: 'You're wrong. The curse you whites brought into this land has been lifted. It has been voided and discharged. We are seeing a new era, an era dedicated, as our founders intended it, to freedom, liberty and equality for all, to which this country will be the new Canaan ——'

'Freedom from what? From work? Canaan?' He jerked his arm, comprehensive, almost violent: whereupon it all seemed to stand there about them, intact and complete and visible in the drafty, damp, heatless, negro-stale negro-rank sorry room—the empty fields without plow or seed to work them, fenceless against the stock which did not exist within or without the walled stable which likewise was not there. 'What corner of Canaan is this?'

'You are seeing it at a bad time. This is winter. No man farms this time of year.'

'I see. And of course her need for food and clothing will stand still while the land lies fallow.'

'I have a pension,' the other said. He said it as a man might say *I have grace* or *I own a gold mine*. 'I have my father's pension too. It will arrive on the first of the month. What day is this?'

'The eleventh,' he said. 'Twenty days more. And until then?'

'I have a few groceries in the house from my credit account with the merchant in Midnight who banks my pension check for me. I have executed to him a power of attorney to handle it for me as a matter of mutual ——'

'I see. And if the groceries dont last the twenty days?'

'I still have one more hog.'

'Where?'

'Outside,' the other said. 'It is customary in this country to allow stock to range free during the winter for food. It comes up from time to time. But no matter if it doesn't; I can probably trace its footprints when the need ——'

'Yes!' he cried. 'Because no matter: you still have the pension check. And the man in Midnight will cash it and pay himself out of it for what you have already eaten and if there is any left over, it is yours. And the hog will be eaten by then or you still cant catch it, and then what will you do?'

'It will be almost spring then,' the other said. 'I am planning in the spring ——'

'It will be January,' he said. 'And then February. And then more than half of March—' and when he stopped again in the kitchen she had not moved, she did not even seem to breathe or to be alive except her eyes watching him; when he took a step toward her it was still not movement because she could have retreated no further: only the tremendous fathomless ink-colored eyes in the narrow, thin, too thin coffee-colored face watching him without alarm, without recognition, without hope. 'Fonsiba,' he said. 'Fonsiba. Are you all right?'

'I'm free,' she said. Midnight was a tavern, a livery stable, a big store (that would be where the pension check banked itself as a matter of mutual elimination of bother and fret, he thought) and a little one, a saloon and a blacksmith shop. But there was a bank there too. The president (the owner, for all practical purposes) of it was a translated Mississippian who had been one of Forrest's men too: and his body lightened of the golden belt for the first time since he left home eight days ago, with pencil and paper he multiplied three dollars by twelve months and divided it into one thousand dollars; it would stretch that way over almost twenty-eight years and for twenty-eight years at least she would not starve, the banker promising to send the three dollars himself by a trusty messenger on the fifteenth of each month and put it into her actual hand, and he returned home and that was all because in 1874 his father and his uncle were both dead and the old ledgers never again came down from the shelf above the desk to which his father had returned them for the last time that day in 1869. But he could have completed it:

> *Lucas Quintus Carothers McCaslin Beauchamp. Last surviving son and child of Tomey's Terrel and Tennie Beauchamp. March 17, 1874*

except that there was no need: not *Lucius Quintus* @c @c @c, but *Lucas Quintus,* not refusing to be called Lucius, because he simply eliminated that word from the name; not denying, declining the name itself, because he used three quarters of it; but simply taking the name and changing, altering it, making it no longer the white man's but his own, by himself composed, himself self-progenitive and nominate, by himself ancestored, as, for all the old ledgers recorded to the contrary, old Carothers himself was

and that was all: 1874 the boy; 1888 the man, repudiated denied and free; 1895 and husband but no father, unwidowered but without a wife, and found long since that no man is ever free and probably could not bear it if he were; married then and living in Jefferson in the little new jerrybuilt bungalow which his wife's father had given them: and one morning Lucas stood suddenly in the doorway of the room where he was reading the Memphis paper and he looked at the paper's dateline and thought *It's his birthday. He's twenty-one today* and Lucas said: 'Whar's the rest of that money old Carothers left? I wants it. All of it.'

that was all: and McCaslin

'More men than that one Buck and Buddy to fumble-heed that truth so mazed for them that spoke it and so confused for them that heard yet still there was 1865:' and he

'But not enough. Not enough of even Father and Uncle Buddy to fumble-heed in even three generations not even three generations fathered by Grandfather not even if there had been nowhere beneath His sight any but Grandfather and so He would not even have needed to elect and choose. But He tried and I know what you will say. That having Himself created them He could have known no more of hope than He could have pride and grief but He didn't hope He just waited because He had made them: not just because He had set them alive and in motion but because He had already worried with them so long: worried with them so long because He had seen how in individual cases they were capable of anything any height or depth remembered in mazed incomprehension out of heaven where hell was created too and so He must admit them or else admit His equal somewhere and so be no longer God and therefore must accept responsibility for what He Himself had done in order to live with Himself in His lonely and paramount heaven. And He probably knew it was vain but He had created them and knew them capable of all things because He had shaped them out of the primal Absolute which contained all and had watched them since in their individual exaltation and baseness and they themselves not knowing why nor how nor even when: until at last He saw that they were all Grandfather all of them and that even from them the elected and chosen the best the very best He could expect (not hope mind: not hope) would be Bucks and Buddies and not even enough of them and in the third generation not even Bucks and Buddies but—' and McCaslin

'Ah:' and he

'Yes. If He could see Father and Uncle Buddy in Grandfather He must have seen me too.—an Isaac born into a later life than Abraham's and repudiating immolation: fatherless and therefore safe declining the altar because maybe this time the exasperated Hand might not supply the kid—' and McCaslin

'Escape:' and he

'All right. Escape.—Until one day He said what you told Fonsiba's husband that afternoon here in this room: *This will do. This is enough:* not in exasperation or rage or even just sick to death as you were sick that day: just *This is enough* and looked about for one last time, for one time more since He had created them, upon this land this South for which He had done so much with woods for game and streams for fish and deep rich soil for seed and lush springs to sprout it and long summers to mature it and serene falls to harvest it and short mild winters for men and animals and saw no hope anywhere and looked beyond it where hope should have been, where to East North and West lay illimitable that whole hopeful continent dedicated as a refuge and sanctuary of liberty and freedom from what you called the old world's worthless evening and saw the rich descendants of slavers, females of both sexes, to whom the black they shrieked of was another specimen another example like the Brazilian macaw brought home in a cake by a traveller, passing resolutions about horror and outrage in warm and air-proof halls: and the thundering cannonade of politicians earning votes and the medicine-shows of pulpiteers earning Chautauqua fees, to whom the outrage and the injustice were as much abstractions as Tariff or Silver or Immortality and who employed the very shackles of its servitude and the sorry rags of its regalia as they did the other beer and banners and mottoes redfire and brimstone and sleight-of-hand and musical handsaws: and the whirling wheels which manufactured for a profit the pristine replacements of the shackles and shoddy garments as they wore out and spun the cotton and made the gins which ginned it and the cars and ships which hauled it, and the men who ran the wheels for that profit and established and collected the taxes it was taxed with and the rates for hauling it and the commissions for selling it: and He could have repudiated them since they were his creation now and forever more throughout all their generations until not only that old world from which He had rescued them but this new one too which He had revealed and led them to as a sanctuary and refuge were become the same worthless tideless rock cooling in the last crimson evening except that out of all that empty sound and bootless fury one silence, among that loud and moiling all of them just one simple enough to believe that horror and outrage were first and last simply horror and outrage and was crude enough to act upon that, illiterate and had no words for talking or perhaps was just busy not even bothered to inform Him in advance what he was about and had no time to, one out of them all who did not bother Him with cajolery and adjuration then pleading then threat and had so that a lesser than He might have even missed the simple act of lifting the long ancestral musket down from the deerhorns above the door, whereupon He said *My name is Brown too* and the other *So is mine* and He *Then mine or yours cant be because I am against* it and the other *So am I* and He triumphantly *Then where are you going with that gun?* and the other told him in one sentence one word and He: amazed: Who knew neither hope nor pride nor grief *But your Association, your Committee, your Officers. Where are your Minutes, your Motions, your Parliamentary Procedures?* and the other *I aint against them. They are all right I reckon for them that have the time. I am just against the weak because they are niggers being held in bondage by the strong just because they are white.* So He turned once more to this land which He still intended to save because He had done so much for it—' and McCaslin

'What?' and he

'—to these people He was still committed to because they were his creations—' and McCaslin

'Turned back to us? His face to us?' and he

'—whose wives and daughters at least made soups and jellies for them when they were sick and carried the trays through the mud and the winter too into the stinking cabins and sat in the stinking cabins and kept fires going until crises came and passed but that was not enough: and when they were very sick had them carried into the big house itself into the company room itself maybe and nursed them there which the white man would have done too for any other of his cattle that was sick but at least the man who hired one from a livery wouldn't have and still that was not enough: so that He said and not in grief either Who had made them and so could know no more of grief than He could of pride or hope: *Apparently they can learn nothing save through suffering, remember nothing save when underlined in blood*—' and McCaslin

'Ashby on an afternoon's ride, to call on some remote maiden cousins of his mother or maybe just acquaintances of hers, comes by chance upon a minor engagement of outposts and dismounts and with his crimson-lined cloak for target leads a handful of troops he never saw before against an entrenched position of backwoods-trained riflemen. Lee's battle-order, wrapped maybe about a handful of cigars and doubtless thrown away when the last cigar was smoked, found by a Yankee Intelligence officer on the floor of a saloon behind the Yankee lines after Lee had already divided his forces before Sharpsburg. Jackson on the Plank Road, already rolled up the flank which Hooker believed could not be turned and, waiting only for night to pass to continue the brutal and incessant slogging which would fling that whole wing back into Hooker's lap where he sat on a front gallery in Chancellorsville drinking rum toddies and telegraphing Lincoln that he had defeated Lee, is shot from among a whole covey of minor officers and in the blind night by one of his own patrols, leaving as next by seniority Stuart that gallant man born apparently already horsed and sabred and already knowing all there was to know about war except the slogging and brutal stupidity of it: and that same Stuart off raiding Pennsylvania hen-roosts when Lee should have known of all of Meade just where Hancock was on Cemetery Ridge: and Longstreet too at Gettysburg and that same Longstreet shot out of saddle by his own men in the dark by mistake just as Jackson was. His face to us? His face to us?' and he

'How else have made them fight? Who else but Jacksons and Stuarts and Ashbys and Morgans and Forrests?—the farmers of the central and middle-west, holding land by the acre instead of the tens or maybe even the hundreds, farming it themselves and to no single crop of cotton or tobacco or cane, owning no slaves and needing and wanting none and already looking toward the Pacific coast, not always as long as two generations there and having stopped where they did stop only through the fortuitous mischance that an ox died or a wagon-axle broke. And the New England mechanics who didn't even own land and measured all things by the weight of water and the cost of turning wheels and the narrow fringe of traders and ship-owners still looking backward across the Atlantic and attached to the continent only by their counting-houses. And those who should have had the alertness to see: the wildcat manipulators of mythical wilderness townsites; and the astuteness to rationalise: the bankers who held the mortgages on the land which the first were only waiting to abandon and on the railroads and steamboats to carry them still further west, and on the factories and the wheels and the rented tenements those who ran them lived in; and the leisure and scope to comprehend and fear in time and even anticipate: the Boston-bred (even when not born in Boston) spinster descendants of long lines of similarly-bred and likewise spinster aunts and uncles whose hands knew no callus except that of the indicting pen, to whom the wilderness itself began at the top of tide and who looked, if at anything other than Beacon Hill, only toward heaven—not to mention all the loud rabble of the camp-followers of pioneers: the bellowing of politicians, the mellifluous choiring of self-styled men of God, the—' and McCaslin

'Here, here. Wait a minute:' and he

'Let me talk now. I'm trying to explain to the head of my family something which I have got to do which I dont quite understand myself, not in justification of it but to explain it if I can. I could say I dont know why I must do it but that I do know I have got to because I have got myself to have to live with for the rest of my life and all I want is peace to do it in. But you are the head of my family. More. I knew a long time ago that I would never have to miss my father, even if you are just finding out that you have missed your son.—the drawers of bills and the shavers of notes and the schoolmasters and the self-ordained to teach and lead and all that horde of the semiliterate with a white shirt but no change for it, with one eye on themselves and watching each other with the other one. Who else could have made them fight: could have struck them so aghast with fear and dread as to turn shoulder to shoulder and face one way and even stop talking for a while and even after two years of it keep them still so wrung with terror that some among them would seriously propose moving their very capital into a foreign country lest it be ravaged and pillaged by a people whose entire white male population would have little more than filled any one of their larger cities: except Jackson in the Valley and three separate armies trying to catch him and none of them ever knowing whether they were just retreating from a battle or just running into one and Stuart riding his whole command entirely around the biggest single armed force this continent ever saw in order to see what it looked like from behind and Morgan leading a cavalry charge against a stranded man-of-war. Who else could have declared a war against a power with ten times the area and a hundred times the men and a thousand times the resources, except men who could believe that all necessary to conduct a successful war was not acumen nor shrewdness nor politics nor diplomacy nor money nor even integrity and simple arithmetic but just love of land and courage ——'

'And an unblemished and gallant ancestry and the ability to ride a horse,' McCaslin said. 'Dont leave that out.' It was evening now, the tranquil sunset of October mazy with windless woodsmoke. The cotton was long since picked and ginned, and all day now the wagons loaded with gathered corn moved between field and crib, processional across the enduring land. 'Well, maybe that's what He wanted. At least, that's what He got.' This time there was no yellowed procession of fading and harmless ledger-pages. This was chronicled in a harsher book and McCaslin, fourteen and fifteen and sixteen, had seen it and the boy himself had inherited it as Noah's grandchildren had inherited the Flood although they had not been there to see the deluge: that dark corrupt and bloody time while three separate peoples had tried to adjust not only to one another but to the new land which they had created and inherited too and must live in for the reason that those who had lost it were no less free to quit it than those who had gained it were:—those upon whom freedom and equality had been dumped overnight and without warning or preparation or any training in how to employ it or even just endure it and who misused it not as children would nor yet because they had been so long in bondage and then so suddenly freed, but misused it as human beings always misuse freedom, so that he thought *Apparently there is a wisdom beyond even that learned through suffering necessary for a man to distinguish between liberty and license;* those who had fought for four years and lost to preserve a condition under which that franchisement was anomaly and paradox, not because they were opposed to freedom as freedom but for the old reasons for which man (not the generals and politicians but man) has always fought and died in wars: to preserve a status quo or to establish a better future one to endure for his children; and lastly, as if that were not enough for bitterness and hatred and fear, that third race even more alien to the people whom they resembled in pigment and in whom even the same blood ran, than to the people whom they did not,—that race threefold in one and alien even among themselves save for a single fierce will for rapine and pillage, composed of the sons of middleaged Quartermaster lieutenants and Army sutlers and contractors in military blankets and shoes and transport mules, who followed the battles they themselves had not fought and inherited the conquest they themselves had not helped to gain, sanctioned and protected even if not blessed, and left their bones and in another generation would be engaged in a fierce economic competition of small sloven farms with the black men they were supposed to have freed and the white descendants of fathers who had owned no slaves anyway whom they were supposed to have disinherited and in the third generation would be back once more in the little lost county seats as barbers and garage mechanics and deputy sheriffs and mill- and gin-hands and power-plant firemen, leading, first in mufti then later in an actual formalised regalia of hooded sheets and passwords and fiery christian symbols, lynching mobs against the race their ancestors had come to save: and of all that other nameless horde of speculators in human misery, manipulators of money and politics and land, who follow catastrophe and are their own protection as grasshoppers are and need no blessing and sweat no plow or axe-helve and batten and vanish and leave no bones, just as they derived apparently from no ancestry, no mortal flesh, no act even of passion or even of lust: and the Jew who came without protection too since after two thousand years he had got out of the habit of being or needing it, and solitary, without even the solidarity of the locusts and in this a sort of courage since he had come thinking not in terms of simple pillage but in terms of his great-grandchildren, seeking yet some place to establish them to endure even though forever alien: and unblessed: a pariah about the face of the Western earth which twenty centuries later was still taking revenge on him for the fairy tale with which he had conquered it. McCaslin had actually seen it, and the boy even at almost eighty would never be able to distinguish certainly between what he had seen and what had been told him: a lightless and gutted and empty land where women crouched with the huddled children behind locked doors and men armed in sheets and masks rode the silent roads and the bodies of white and black both, victims not so much of hate as of desperation and despair, swung from lonely limbs: and men shot dead in polling-booths with the still wet pen in one hand and the unblotted ballot in the other: and a United States marshal in Jefferson who signed his official papers with a crude cross, an ex slave called Sickymo, not at all because his ex-owner was a doctor and apothecary but because, still a slave, he would steal his master's grain alcohol and dilute it with water and peddle it in pint bottles from a cache beneath the roots of a big sycamore tree behind the drug store, who had attained his high office because his half-white sister was the concubine of the Federal A.P.M.: and this time McCaslin did not even say Look but merely lifted one hand, not even pointing, not even specifically toward the shelf of ledgers but toward the desk, toward the corner where it sat beside the scuffed patch on the floor where two decades of heavy shoes had stood while the white man at the desk added and multiplied and subtracted. And again he did not need to look because he had seen this himself and, twenty-three years after the Surrender and twenty-four after the Proclamation, was still watching it: the ledgers, new ones now and filled rapidly, succeeding one another rapidly and containing more names than old Carothers or even his father and Uncle Buddy had ever dreamed of; new names and new faces to go with them, among which the old names and faces that even his father and uncle would have recognised, were lost, vanished—Tomey's Terrel dead, and even the tragic and miscast Percival Brownlee, who couldn't keep books and couldn't farm either, found his true niche at last, reappeared in 1862 during the boy's father's absence and had apparently been living on the plantation for at least a month before his uncle found out about it, conducting impromptu revival meetings among negroes, preaching and leading the singing also in his high sweet true soprano voice and disappeared again on foot and at top speed, not behind but ahead of a body of raiding Federal horse and reappeared for the third and last time in the entourage of a travelling Army paymaster, the two of them passing through Jefferson in a surrey at the exact moment when the boy's father (it was 1866) also happened to be crossing the Square, the surrey and its occupants traversing rapidly that quiet and bucolic scene and even in the fleeting moment and to others beside the boy's father giving an illusion of flight and illicit holiday like a man on an excursion during his wife's absence with his wife's personal maid, until Brownlee glanced up and saw his late co-master and gave him one defiant female glance and then broke again, leaped from the surrey and disappeared this time for good and it was only by chance that McCaslin, twenty years later, heard of him again, an old man now and quite fat, as the well-to-do proprietor of a select New Orleans brothel; and Tennie's Jim gone, nobody knew where, and Fonsiba in Arkansas with her three dollars each month and the scholar-husband with his lenseless spectacles and frock coat and his plans for the spring; and only Lucas was left, the baby, the last save himself of old Carothers' doomed and fatal blood which in the male derivation seemed to destroy all it touched, and even he was repudiating and at least hoping to escape it;—Lucas, the boy of fourteen whose name would not even appear for six years yet among those rapid pages in the bindings new and dustless too since McCaslin lifted them down daily now to write into them the continuation of that record which two hundred years had not been enough to complete and another hundred would not be enough to discharge; that chronicle which was a whole land in miniature, which multiplied and compounded was the entire South, twenty-three years after surrender and twenty-four from emancipation—that slow trickle of molasses and meal and meat, of shoes and straw hats and overalls, of plowlines and collars and heel-bolts and buckheads and clevises, which returned each fall as cotton—the two threads frail as truth and impalpable as equators yet cable-strong to bind of life them who made the cotton to the land their sweat fell on: and he

'Yes. Binding them for a while yet, a little while yet. Through and beyond that life and maybe through and beyond the life of that life's sons and maybe even through and beyond that of the sons of those sons. But not always, because they will endure. They will outlast us because they are—' it was not a pause, barely a falter even, possibly appreciable only to himself, as if he couldn't speak even to McCaslin, even to explain his repudiation, that which to him too, even in the act of escaping (and maybe this was the reality and the truth of his need to escape) was heresy: so that even in escaping he was taking with him more of that evil and unregenerate old man who could summon, because she was his property, a human being because she was old enough and female, to his widower's house and get a child on her and then dismiss her because she was of an inferior race, and then bequeath a thousand dollars to the infant because he would be dead then and wouldn't have to pay it, than even he had feared. 'Yes. He didn't want to. He had to. Because they will endure. They are better than we are. Stronger than we are. Their vices are vices aped from white men or that white men and bondage have taught them: improvidence and intemperance and evasion—not laziness: evasion: of what white men had set them to, not for their aggrandisement or even comfort but his own—' and McCaslin

'All right. Go on: Promiscuity. Violence. Instability and lack of control. Inability to distinguish between mine and thine—' and he

'How distinguish, when for two hundred years mine did not even exist for them?' and McCaslin

'All right. Go on. And their virtues—' and he

'Yes. Their own. Endurance—' and McCaslin

'So have mules:' and he

'—and pity and tolerance and forbearance and fidelity and love of children—' and McCaslin

'So have dogs:' and he

'—whether their own or not or black or not. And more: what they got not only not from white people but not even despite white people because they had it already from the old free fathers a longer time free than us because we have never been free—' and it was in McCaslin's eyes too, he had only to look at McCaslin's eyes and it was there, that summer twilight seven years ago, almost a week after they had returned from the camp before he discovered that Sam Fathers had told McCaslin: an old bear, fierce and ruthless not just to stay alive but ruthless with the fierce pride of liberty and freedom, jealous and proud enough of liberty and freedom to see it threatened not with fear nor even alarm but almost with joy, seeming deliberately to put it into jeopardy in order to savor it and keep his old strong bones and flesh supple and quick to defend and preserve it; an old man, son of a Negro slave and an Indian king, inheritor on the one hand of the long chronicle of a people who had learned humility through suffering and learned pride through the endurance which survived the suffering, and on the other side the chronicle of a people even longer in the land than the first, yet who now existed there only in the solitary brotherhood of an old and childless Negro's alien blood and the wild and invincible spirit of an old bear; a boy who wished to learn humility and pride in order to become skillful and worthy in the woods but found himself becoming so skillful so fast that he feared he would never become worthy because he had not learned humility and pride though he had tried, until one day an old man who could not have defined either led him as though by the hand to where an old bear and a little mongrel dog showed him that, by possessing one thing other, he would possess them both; and a little dog, nameless and mongrel and many-fathered, grown yet weighing less than six pounds, who couldn't be dangerous because there was nothing anywhere much smaller, not fierce because that would have been called just noise, not humble because it was already too near the ground to genuflect, and not proud because it would not have been close enough for anyone to discern what was casting that shadow and which didn't even know it was not going to heaven since they had already decided it had no immortal soul, so that all it could be was brave even though they would probably call that too just noise. '*And you didn't shoot,' McCaslin said. 'How close were you?'*

'I dont know,' he said. 'There was a big wood tick just inside his off hind leg. I saw that. But I didn't have the gun then.'

'But you didn't shoot when you had the gun,' McCaslin said. 'Why?' But McCaslin didn't wait, rising and crossing the room, across the pelt of the bear he had killed two years ago and the bigger one McCaslin had killed before he was born, to the bookcase beneath the mounted head of his first buck, and returned with the book and sat down again and opened it. 'Listen,' he said. He read the five stanzas aloud and closed the book on his finger and looked up. 'All right,' he said. 'Listen,' and read again, but only one stanza this time and closed the book and laid it on the table. 'She cannot fade, though thou hast not thy bliss,' McCaslin said: 'Forever wilt thou love, and she be fair.'

'He's talking about a girl,' he said.

'He had to talk about something,' McCaslin said. Then he said, 'He was talking about truth. Truth is one. It doesn't change. It covers all things which touch the heart—honor and pride and pity and justice and courage and love. Do you see now?' He didn't know. Somehow it had seemed simpler than that, simpler than somebody talking in a book about a young man and a girl he would never need to grieve over because he could never approach any nearer and would never have to get any further away. He had heard about an old bear and finally got big enough to hunt it and he hunted it four years and at last met it with a gun in his hands and he didn't shoot. Because a little dog—But he could have shot long before the fyce covered the twenty yards to where the bear waited, and Sam Fathers could have shot at any time during the interminable minute while Old Ben stood on his hind legs over them. . . . He ceased. McCaslin watched him, still speaking, the voice, the words as quiet as the twilight itself was: 'Courage and honor and pride, and pity and love of justice and of liberty. They all touch the heart, and what the heart holds to becomes truth, as far as we know truth. Do you see now?' and he could still hear them, intact in this twilight as in that one seven years ago, no louder still because they did not need to be because they would endure: and he had only to look at McCaslin's eyes beyond the thin and bitter smiling, the faint lip-lift which would have had to be called smiling;—his kinsman, his father almost, who had been born too late into the old time and too soon for the new, the two of them juxtaposed and alien now to each other against their ravaged patrimony, the dark and ravaged fatherland still prone and panting from its etherless operation:

'Habet then.—So this land is, indubitably, of and by itself cursed:' and he

'Cursed:' and again McCaslin merely lifted one hand, not even speaking and not even toward the ledgers: so that, as the stereopticon condenses into one instantaneous field the myriad minutia of its scope, so did that slight and rapid gesture establish in the small cramped and cluttered twilit room not only the ledgers but the whole plantation in its mazed and intricate entirety—the land, the fields and what they represented in terms of cotton ginned and sold, the men and women whom they fed and clothed and even paid a little cash money at Christmas-time in return for the labor which planted and raised and picked and ginned the cotton, the machinery and mules and gear with which they raised it and their cost and upkeep and replacement—that whole edifice intricate and complex and founded upon injustice and erected by ruthless rapacity and carried on even yet with at times downright savagery not only to the human beings but the valuable animals too, yet solvent and efficient and, more than that: not only still intact but enlarged, increased; brought still intact by McCaslin, himself little more than a child then, through and out of the debacle and chaos of twenty years ago where hardly one in ten survived, and enlarged and increased and would continue so, solvent and efficient and intact and still increasing so long as McCaslin and his McCaslin successors lasted, even though their surnames might not even be Edmonds then: and he: 'Habet too. Because that's it: not the land, but us. Not only the blood, but the name too; not only its color but its designation: Edmonds, white, but, a female line, could have no other but the name his father bore; Beauchamp, the elder line and the male one, but, black, could have had any name he liked and no man would have cared, except the name his father bore who had no name—' and McCaslin

'And since I know too what you know I will say now, once more let me say it: And one other, and in the third generation too, and the male, the eldest, the direct and sole and white and still McCaslin even, father to son to son—' and he

'I am free:' and this time McCaslin did not ever gesture, no inference of fading pages, no postulation of the stereoptic whole, but the frail and iron thread strong as truth and impervious as evil and longer than life itself and reaching beyond record and patrimony both to join him with the lusts and passions, the hopes and dreams and griefs, of bones whose names while still fleshed and capable even old Carothers' grandfather had never heard: and he: 'And of that too:' and McCaslin

'Chosen, I suppose (I will concede it) out of all your time by Him as you say Buck and Buddy were from theirs. And it took Him a bear and an old man and four years just for you. And it took you fourteen years to reach that point and about that many, maybe more, for Old Ben, and more than seventy for Sam Fathers. And you are just one. How long then? How long?' and he

'It will be long. I have never said otherwise. But it will be all right because they will endure—' and McCaslin

'And anyway, you will be free.—No, not now nor ever, we from them nor they from us. So I repudiate too. I would deny even if I knew it were true. I would have to. Even you can see that I could do no else. I am what I am; I will be always what I was born and have always been. And more than me. More than me, just as there were more than Buck and Buddy in what you called His first plan which failed:' and he

'And more than me:' and McCaslin

'No. Not even you. Because mark. You said how on that instant when Ikkemotubbe realised that he could sell the land to Grandfather, it ceased forever to have been his. All right; go on: Then it belonged to Sam Fathers, old Ikkemotubbe's son. And who inherited from Sam Fathers, if not you? co-heir perhaps with Boon, if not of his life maybe, at least of his quitting it?' and he

'Yes. Sam Fathers set me free.' And Isaac McCaslin, not yet Uncle Ike, a long time yet before he would be uncle to half a county and still father to none, living in one small cramped fireless rented room in a Jefferson boardinghouse where petit juries were domiciled during court terms and itinerant horse- and mule-traders stayed, with his kit of brand-new carpenter's tools and the shotgun McCaslin had given him with his name engraved in silver and old General Compson's compass (and, when the General died, his silver-mounted horn too) and the iron cot and mattress and the blankets which he would take each fall into the woods for more than sixty years and the bright tin coffee-pot

there had been a legacy, from his Uncle Hubert Beauchamp, his godfather, that bluff burly roaring childlike man from whom Uncle Buddy had won Tomey's Terrel's wife Tennie in the poker-game in 1859—'posible strait against three Treys in sigt Not called'—; no pale sentence or paragraph scrawled in cringing fear of death by a weak and trembling hand as a last desperate sop flung backward at retribution, but a Legacy, a Thing, possessing weight to the hand and bulk to the eye and even audible: a silver cup filled with gold pieces and wrapped in burlap and sealed with his godfather's ring in the hot wax, which (intact still) even before his Uncle Hubert's death and long before his own majority, when it would be his, had become not only a legend but one of the family lares. After his father's and his Uncle Hubert's sister's marriage they moved back into the big house, the tremendous cavern which old Carothers had started and never finished, cleared the remaining negroes out of it and with his mother's dowry completed it, at least the rest of the windows and doors and moved into it, all of them save Uncle Buddy who declined to leave the cabin he and his twin had built, the move being the bride's notion and more than just a notion and none ever to know if she really wanted to live in the big house or if she knew before hand that Uncle Buddy would refuse to move: and two weeks after his birth in 1867, the first time he and his mother came down stairs, one night and the silver cup sitting on the cleared dining-room table beneath the bright lamp and while his mother and his father and McCaslin and Tennie (his nurse: carrying him)—all of them again but Uncle Buddy—watched, his Uncle Hubert rang one by one into the cup the bright and glinting mintage and wrapped it into the burlap envelope and heated the wax and sealed it and carried it back home with him where he lived alone now without even his sister either to hold him down as McCaslin said or to try to raise him up as Uncle Buddy said, and (dark times then in Mississippi) Uncle Buddy said most of the niggers gone and the ones that didn't go even Hub Beauchamp could not have wanted: but the dogs remained and Uncle Buddy said Beauchamp fiddled while Nero fox-hunted

they would go and see it there; at last his mother would prevail and they would depart in the surrey, once more all save Uncle Buddy and McCaslin to keep Uncle Buddy company until one winter Uncle Buddy began to fail and from then on it was himself, beginning to remember now, and his mother and Tennie and Tomey's Terrel to drive: the twenty-two miles into the next county, the twin gateposts on one of which McCaslin could remember the half-grown boy blowing a fox-horn at breakfast dinner and supper-time and jumping down to open to any passer who happened to hear it but where there were no gates at all now, the shabby and overgrown entrance to what his mother still insisted that people call Warwick because her brother was if truth but triumphed and justice but prevailed the rightful earl of it, the paintless house which outwardly did not change but which on the inside seemed each time larger because he was too little to realise then that there was less and less in it of the fine furnishings, the rosewood and mahogany and walnut which for him had never existed anywhere anyway save in his mother's tearful lamentations and the occasional piece small enough to be roped somehow onto the rear or the top of the carriage on their return (And he remembered this, he had seen it: an instant, a flash, his mother's soprano 'Even my dress! Even my dress!' loud and outraged in the barren unswept hall; a face young and female and even lighter in color than Tomey's Terrel's for an instant in a closing door; a swirl, a glimpse of the silk gown and the flick and glint of an ear-ring: an apparition rapid and tawdry and illicit yet somehow even to the child, the infant still almost, breathless and exciting and evocative: as though, like two limpid and pellucid streams meeting, the child which he still was had made serene and absolute and perfect rapport and contact through that glimpsed nameless illicit hybrid female flesh with the boy which had existed at that stage of inviolable and immortal adolescence in his uncle for almost sixty years; the dress, the face, the ear-rings gone in that same aghast flash and his uncle's voice: 'She's my cook! She's my new cook! I had to have a cook, didn't I?' then the uncle himself, the face alarmed and aghast too yet still innocently and somehow even indomitably of a boy, they retreating in their turn now, back to the front gallery, and his uncle again, pained and still amazed, in a sort of desperate resurgence if not of courage at least of self-assertion: 'They're free now! They're folks too just like we are!' and his mother: 'That's why! That's why! My mother's house! Defiled! Defiled!' and his uncle: 'Damn it, Sibbey, at least give her time to pack her grip:' then over, finished, the loud uproar and all, himself and Tennie and he remembered Tennie's inscrutable face at the broken shutterless window of the bare room which had once been the parlor while they watched, hurrying down the lane at a stumbling trot, the routed compounder of his uncle's uxory: the back, the nameless face which he had seen only for a moment, the once-hooped dress ballooning and flapping below a man's overcoat, the worn heavy carpet-bag jouncing and banging against her knee, routed and in retreat true enough and in the empty lane solitary young-looking and forlorn yet withal still exciting and evocative and wearing still the silken banner captured inside the very citadel of respectability, and unforgettable.)

the cup, the sealed inscrutable burlap, sitting on the shelf in the locked closet, Uncle Hubert unlocking the door and lifting it down and passing it from hand to hand: his mother, his father, McCaslin and even Tennie, insisting that each take it in turn and heft it for weight and shake it again to prove the sound, Uncle Hubert himself standing spraddled before the cold unswept hearth in which the very bricks themselves were crumbling into a litter of soot and dust and mortar and the droppings of chimney-sweeps, still roaring and still innocent and still indomitable: and for a long time he believed that nobody but himself had noticed that his uncle now put the cup only into his hands, unlocked the door and lifted it down and put it into his hands and stood over him until he had shaken it obediently until it sounded then took it from him and locked it back into the closet before anyone else could have offered to touch it, and even later, when competent not only to remember but to rationalise, he could not say what it was or even if it had been anything because the parcel was still heavy and still rattled, not even when, Uncle Buddy dead and his father, at last and after almost seventy-five years in bed after the sun rose, said: 'Go get that damn cup. Bring that damn Hub Beauchamp too if you have to:' because it still rattled though his uncle no longer put it even into his hands but now carried it himself from one to the other, his mother, McCaslin, Tennie, shaking it before each in turn, saying: 'Hear it? Hear it?' his face still innocent, not quite baffled but only amazed and not very amazed and still indomitable: and, his father and Uncle Buddy both gone now, one day without reason or any warning the almost completely empty house in which his uncle and Tennie's ancient and quarrelsome great-grandfather (who claimed to have seen Lafayette and McCaslin said in another ten years would be remembering God) lived, cooked and slept in one single room, burst into peaceful conflagration, a tranquil instantaneous sourceless unanimity of combustion, walls floors and roof: at sunup it stood where his uncle's father had built it sixty years ago, at sundown the four blackened and smokeless chimneys rose from a light white powder of ashes and a few charred ends of planks which did not even appear to have been very hot: and out of the last of evening, the last one of the twenty-two miles, on the old white mare which was the last of that stable which McCaslin remembered, the two old men riding double up to the sister's door, the one wearing his fox-horn on its braided deerhide thong and the other carrying the burlap parcel wrapped in a shirt, the tawny wax-daubed shapeless lump sitting again and on an almost identical shelf and his uncle holding the half-opened door now, his hand not only on the knob but one foot against it and the key waiting in the other hand, the face urgent and still not baffled but still and even indomitably not very amazed and himself standing in the half-opened door looking quietly up at the burlap shape become almost three times its original height and a good half less than its original thickness and turning away and he would remember not his mother's look this time nor yet Tennie's inscrutable expression but McCaslin's dark and aquiline face grave insufferable and bemused: then one night they waked him and fetched him still half-asleep into the lamp light, the smell of medicine which was familiar by now in that room and the smell of something else which he had not smelled before and knew at once and would never forget, the pillow, the worn and ravaged face from which looked out still the boy innocent and immortal and amazed and urgent, looking at him and trying to tell him until McCaslin moved and leaned over the bed and drew from the top of the night shirt the big iron key on the greasy cord which suspended it, the eyes saying Yes Yes Yes now, and cut the cord and unlocked the closet and brought the parcel to the bed, the eyes still trying to tell him even when he took the parcel so that was still not it, the hands still clinging to the parcel even while relinquishing it, the eyes more urgent than ever trying to tell him but they never did; and he was ten and his mother was dead too and McCaslin said, 'You are almost halfway now. You might as well open it:' and he: 'No. He said twenty-one:' and he was twenty-one and McCaslin shifted the bright lamp to the center of the cleared dining-room table and set the parcel beside it and laid his open knife beside the parcel and stood back with that expression of old grave intolerant and repudiating and he lifted it, the burlap lump which fifteen years ago had changed its shape completely overnight, which shaken gave forth a thin weightless not-quite-musical curiosity muffled clatter, the bright knife-blade hunting amid the mazed intricacy of string, the knobby gouts of wax bearing his uncle's Beauchamp seal rattling onto the table's polished top and, standing amid the collapse of burlap folds, the unstained tin coffee-pot still brand new, the handful of copper coins and now he knew what had given them the muffled sound: a collection of minutely-folded scraps of paper sufficient almost for a rat's nest, of good linen bond, of the crude ruled paper such as negroes use, of raggedly-torn ledger-pages and the margins of newspapers and once the paper label from a pair of overalls, all dated and all signed, beginning with the first one not six months after they had watched him seal the silver cup into the burlap on this same table in this same room by the light even of this same lamp almost twenty-one years ago:

I owe my Nephew Isaac Beauchamp McCaslin five (5) pieces Gold which I.O.U. constitutes My note of hand with Interest at 5 percent.

Hubert Fitz-Hubert Beauchamp
at Warwick 27 Nov 1867

and he: 'Anyway he called it Warwick:' once at least, even if no more. But there was more:

Isaac 24 Dec 1867 I.O.U. 2 pieces Gold H.Fh.B. I.O.U. Issac 1 piece Gold 1Jan 1868 H.Fh.B.

then five again then three then one then one then a long time and what dream, what dreamed splendid recoup, not of any injury or betrayal of trust because it had been merely a loan: nay, a partnership:

I.O.U. Beauchamp McCaslin or his heirs twenty-five (25) pieces Gold This & All preceeding constituing My notes of hand at twenty (20) percentum compounded annually. This date of 19th January 1873

Beauchamp

no location save that in time and signed by the single not name but word as the old proud earl himself might have scrawled Nevile: and that made forty-three and he could not remember himself of course but the legend had it at fifty, which balanced: one: then one: then one: then one and then the last three and then the last chit, dated after he came to live in the house with them and written in the shaky hand not of a beaten old man because he had never been beaten to know it but of a tired old man maybe and even at that tired only on the outside and still indomitable, the simplicity of the last one the simplicity not of resignation but merely of amazement, like a simple comment or remark, and not very much of that:

One silver cup. Hubert Beauchamp

and McCaslin: 'So you have plenty of coppers anyway. But they are still not old enough yet to be either rarities or heirlooms. So you will have to take the money:' except that he didn't hear McCaslin, standing quietly beside the table and looking peacefully at the coffee-pot and the pot sitting one night later on the mantel above what was not even a fireplace in the little cramped icelike room in Jefferson as McCaslin tossed the folded banknotes onto the bed and, still standing (there was nowhere to sit save on the bed) did not even remove his hat and overcoat: and he

'As a loan. From you. This one:' and McCaslin

'You cant. I have no money that I can lend to you. And you will have to go to the bank and get it next month because I wont bring it to you:' and he could not hear McCaslin now either, looking peacefully at McCaslin, his kinsman, his father almost yet no kin now as, at the last, even fathers and sons are no kin: and he

'It's seventeen miles, horseback and in the cold. We could both sleep here:' and McCaslin

'Why should I sleep here in my house when you wont sleep yonder in yours?' and gone, and he looking at the bright rustless unstained tin and thinking and not for the first time how much it takes to compound a man (Isaac McCaslin for instance) and of the devious intricate choosing yet unerring path that man's (Isaac McCaslin's for instance) spirit takes among all that mass to make him at last what he is to be, not only to the astonishment of them (the ones who sired the McCaslin who sired his father and Uncle Buddy and their sister, and the ones who sired the Beauchamp who sired his Uncle Hubert and his Uncle Hubert's sister) who believed they had shaped him, but to Isaac McCaslin too

as a loan and used it though he would not have had to: Major de Spain offered him a room in his house as long as he wanted it and asked nor would ever ask any question, and old General Compson more than that, to take him into his own room, to sleep in half of his own bed and more than Major de Spain because he told him baldly why: 'You sleep with me and before this winter is out, I'll know the reason. You'll tell me. Because I dont believe you just quit. It looks like you just quit but I have watched you in the woods too much and I dont believe you just quit even if it does look damn like it:' using it as a loan, paid his board and rent for a month and bought the tools, not simply because he was good with his hands because he had intended to use his hands and it could have been with horses, and not in mere static and hopeful emulation of the Nazarene as the young gambler buys a spotted shirt because the old gambler won in one yesterday, but (without the arrogance of false humility and without the false humbleness of pride, who intended to earn his bread, didn't especially want to earn it but had to earn it and for more than just bread) because if the Nazarene had found carpentering good for the life and ends He had assumed and elected to serve, it would be all right too for Isaac McCaslin even though Isaac McCaslin's ends, although simple enough in their apparent motivation, were and would be always incomprehensible to him, and his life, invincible enough in its needs, if he could have helped himself, not being the Nazarene, he would not have chosen it: and paid it back. He had forgotten the thirty dollars which McCaslin would put into the bank in his name each month, fetched it in to him and flung it onto the bed that first one time but no more; he had a partner now or rather he was the partner: a blasphemous profane clever old dipsomaniac who had built blockade-runners in Charleston in '62 and '3 and had been a ship's carpenter since and appeared in Jefferson two years ago nobody knew from where nor why and spent a good part of his time since recovering from delirium tremens in the jail; they had put a new roof on the stable of the bank's president and (the old man in jail again still celebrating that job) he went to the bank to collect for it and the president said, 'I should borrow from you instead of paying you:' and it had been seven months now and he remembered for the first time, two-hundred-and-ten dollars, and this was the first job of any size and when he left the bank the account stood at two-twenty, two-forty to balance, only twenty dollars more to go, then it did balance though by then the total had increased to three hundred and thirty and he said, 'I will transfer it now:' and the president said, 'I cant do that. McCaslin told me not to. Haven't you got another initial you could use and open another account?' but that was all right, the coins the silver and the bills as they accumulated knotted into a handkerchief and the coffee-pot wrapped in an old shirt as when Tennie's great-grandfather had fetched it from Warwick eighteen years ago, in the bottom of the iron-bound trunk which old Carothers had brought from Carolina and his landlady said, 'Not even a lock! And you dont even lock your door, not even when you leave!' and himself looking at her as peacefully as he had looked at McCaslin that first night in this same room, no kin to him at all yet more than kin as those who serve you even for pay are your kin and those who injure you are more than brother or wife

and had the wife now, got the old man out of jail and fetched him to the rented room and sobered him by superior strength, did not even remove his own shoes for twenty-four hours, got him up and got food into him and they built the barn this time from the ground up and he married her: an only child, a small girl yet curiously bigger than she seemed at first, solider perhaps, with dark eyes and a passionate heart-shaped face, who had time even on that farm to watch most of the day while he sawed timbers to the old man's measurements: and she: "Papa told me about you. That farm is really yours, isn't it?' and he

'And McCaslin's:' and she

'Was there a will leaving half of it to him?' and he

'There didn't need to be a will. His grandmother was my father's sister. We were the same as brothers:' and she

'You are the same as second cousins and that's all you ever will be. But I dont suppose it matters:' and they were married, they were married and it was the new country, his heritage too as it was the heritage of all, out of the earth, beyond the earth yet of the earth because his too was of the earth's long chronicle, his too because each must share with another in order to come into it and in the sharing they become one: for that while, one: for that little while at least, one: indivisible, that while at least irrevocable and unrecoverable, living in a rented room still but for just a little while and that room wall-less and topless and floorless in glory for him to leave each morning and return to at night; her father already owned the lot in town and furnished the material and he and his partner would build it, her dowry from one: her wedding-present from three, she not to know it until the bungalow was finished and ready to be moved into and he never know who told her, not her father and not his partner and not even in drink though for a while he believed that, himself coming home from work and just time to wash and rest a moment before going down to supper, entering no rented cubicle since it would still partake of glory even after they would have grown old and lost it: and he saw her face then, just before she spoke: 'Sit down:' the two of them sitting on the bed's edge, not even touching yet, her face strained and terrible, her voice a passionate and expiring whisper of immeasurable promise: 'I love you. You know I love you. When are we going to move?' and he

'I didn't—I didn't know—Who told you—' the hot fierce palm clapped over his mouth, crushing his lips into his teeth, the fierce curve of fingers digging into his cheek and only the palm slacked off enough for him to answer:

'The farm. Our farm. Your farm:' and he

'I—' then the hand again, finger and palm, the whole enveloping weight of her although she still was not touching him save the hand, the voice: 'No! No!' and the fingers themselves seeming to follow through the cheek the impulse to speech as it died in his mouth, then the whisper, the breath again, of love and of incredible promise, the palm slackening again to let him answer:

'When?' and he

'I—' then she was gone, the hand too, standing, her back to him and her head bent, the voice so calm now that for an instant it seemed no voice of hers that he ever remembered: 'Stand up and turn your back and shut your eyes:' and repeated before he understood and stood himself with his eyes shut and heard the bell ring for supper below stairs and the calm voice again: 'Lock the door:' and he did so and leaned his forehead against the cold wood, his eyes closed, hearing his heart and the sound he had begun to hear before he moved until it ceased and the bell rang again below stairs and he knew it was for them this time and he heard the bed and turned and he had never seen her naked before, he had asked her to once, and why: that he wanted to see her naked because he loved her and he wanted to see her looking at him naked because he loved her but after that he never mentioned it again, even turning his face when she put the nightgown on over her dress to undress at night and putting the dress on over the gown to remove it in the morning and she would not let him get into bed beside her until the lamp was out and even in the heat of summer she would draw the sheet up over them both before she would let him turn to her: and the landlady came up the stairs up the hall and rapped on the door and then called their names but she didn't move, lying still on the bed outside the covers, her face turned away on the pillow, listening to nothing, thinking of nothing, not of him anyway he thought then the landlady went away and she said, 'Take off your clothes:' her head still turned away, looking at nothing, thinking of nothing, waiting for nothing, not even him, her hand moving as though with volition and vision of its own, catching his wrist at the exact moment when he paused beside the bed so that he never paused but merely changed the direction of moving, downward now, the hand drawing him and she moved at last, shifted, a movement one single complete inherent not practiced and one time older than man, looking at him now, drawing him still downward with the one hand down and down and he neither saw nor felt it shift, palm flat against his chest now and holding him away with the same apparent lack of any effort or any need for strength, and not looking at him now, she didn't need to, the chaste woman, the wife, already looked upon all the men who ever rutted and now her whole body had changed, altered, he had never seen it but once and now it was not even the one he had seen but composite of all woman-flesh since man that ever of its own will reclined on its back and opened, and out of it somewhere, without any movement of lips even, the dying and invincible whisper: 'Promise:' and he

'Promise?'

'The farm.' He moved. He had moved, the hand shifting from his chest once more to his wrist, grasping it, the arm still lax and only the light increasing pressure of the fingers as though arm and hand were a piece of wire cable with one looped end, only the hand tightening as he pulled against it. 'No,' he said. 'No:' and she was not looking at him still but not like the other but still the hand: 'No, I tell you. I wont. I cant. Never:' and still the hand and he said, for the last time, he tried to speak clearly and he knew it was still gently and he thought, *She already knows more than I with all the man-listening in camps where there was nothing to read ever even heard of. They are born already bored with what a boy approaches only at fourteen and fifteen with blundering and aghast trembling:* 'I cant. Not ever. Remember:' and still the steady and invincible hand and he said Yes and he thought, *She is lost. She was born lost. We were all born lost* then he stopped thinking and even saying Yes, it was like nothing he had ever dreamed, let alone heard in mere man-talking until after a no-time he returned and lay spent on the insatiate immemorial beach and again with a movement one time more older than man she turned and freed herself and on their wedding night she had cried and he thought she was crying now at first, into the tossed and wadded pillow, the voice coming from somewhere between the pillow and the cachinnation: 'And that's all. That's all from me. If this dont get you that son you talk about, it wont be mine:' lying on her side, her back to the empty rented room, laughing and laughing

5

He went back to the camp one more time before the lumber company moved in and began to cut the timber. Major de Spain himself never saw it again. But he made them welcome to use the house and hunt the land whenever they liked, and in the winter following the last hunt when Sam Fathers and Lion died, General Compson and Walter Ewell invented a plan to corporate themselves, the old group, into a club and lease the camp and the hunting privileges of the woods—an invention doubtless of the somewhat childish old General but actually worthy of Boon Hogganbeck himself. Even the boy, listening, recognised it for the subterfuge it was: to change the leopard's spots when they could not alter the leopard, a baseless and illusory hope to which even McCaslin seemed to subscribe for a while, that once they had persuaded Major de Spain to return to the camp he might revoke himself, which even the boy knew he would not do. And he did not. The boy never knew what occurred when Major de Spain declined. He was not present when the subject was broached and McCaslin never told him. But when June came and the time for the double birthday celebration there was no mention of it and when November came no one spoke of using Major de Spain's house and he never knew whether or not Major de Spain knew they were going on the hunt though without doubt old Ash probably told him: he and McCaslin and General Compson (and that one was the General's last hunt too) and Walter and Boon and Tennie's Jim and old Ash loaded two wagons and drove two days and almost forty miles beyond any country the boy had ever seen before and lived in tents for the two weeks. And the next spring they heard (not from Major de Spain) that he had sold the timber-rights to a Memphis lumber company and in June the boy came to town with McCaslin one Saturday and went to Major de Spain's office—the big, airy, book-lined second-storey room with windows at one end opening upon the shabby hinder purlieus of stores and at the other a door giving onto the railed balcony above the Square, with its curtained alcove where sat a cedar water-bucket and a sugar-bowl and spoon and tumbler and a wicker-covered demijohn of whiskey, and the bamboo-and-paper punkah swinging back and forth above the desk while old Ash in a tilted chair beside the entrance pulled the cord.

"Of course," Major de Spain said. "Ash will probably like to get off in the woods himself for a while, where he wont have to eat Daisy's cooking. Complain about it, anyway. Are you going to take anybody with you?"

"No sir," he said. "I thought that maybe Boon—" For six months now Boon had been town-marshall at Hoke's; Major de Spain had compounded with the lumber company—or perhaps compromised was closer, since it was the lumber company who had decided that Boon might be better as a town-marshall than head of a logging gang.

"Yes," Major de Spain said. "I'll wire him today. He can meet you at Hoke's. I'll send Ash on by the train and they can take some food in and all you have to do will be to mount your horse and ride over."

"Yes sir," he said. "Thank you." And he heard his voice again. He didn't know he was going to say it yet he did know, he had known it all the time: "Maybe if you . . ." His voice died. It was stopped, he never knew how because Major de Spain did not speak and it was not until his voice ceased that Major de Spain moved, turned back to the desk and the papers spread on it and even that without moving because he was sitting at the desk with a paper in his hand when the boy entered, the boy standing there looking down at the short plumpish grey-haired man in sober fine broadcloth and an immaculate glazed shirt whom he was used to seeing in boots and muddy corduroy, unshaven, sitting the shaggy powerful long-hocked mare with the worn Winchester carbine across the saddlebow and the great blue dog standing motionless as bronze at the stirrup, the two of them in that last year and to the boy anyway coming to resemble one another somehow as two people competent for love or for business who have been in love or in business together for a long time sometimes do. Major de Spain did not look up again.

"No. I will be too busy. But good luck to you. If you have it, you might bring me a young squirrel."

"Yes sir," he said. "I will."

He rode his mare, the three-year-old filly he had bred and raised and broken himself. He left home a little after midnight and six hours later, without even having sweated her, he rode into Hoke's, the tiny log-line junction which he had always thought of as Major de Spain's property too although Major de Spain had merely sold the company (and that many years ago) the land on which the sidetracks and loading-platforms and the commissary store stood, and looked about in shocked and grieved amazement even though he had had forewarning and had believed himself prepared: a new planing-mill already half completed which would cover two or three acres and what looked like miles and miles of stacked steel rails red with the light bright rust of newness and of piled crossties sharp with creosote, and wire corrals and feeding-troughs for two hundred mules at least and the tents for the men who drove them; so that he arranged for the care and stabling of his mare as rapidly as he could and did not look any more, mounted into the log-train caboose with his gun and climbed into the cupola and looked no more save toward the wall of wilderness ahead within which he would be able to hide himself from it once more anyway.

Then the little locomotive shrieked and began to move: a rapid churning of exhaust, a lethargic deliberate clashing of slack couplings traveling backward along the train, the exhaust changing to the deep slow clapping bites of power as the caboose too began to move and from the cupola he watched the train's head complete the first and only curve in the entire line's length and vanish into the wilderness, dragging its length of train behind it so that it resembled a small dingy harmless snake vanishing into weeds, drawing him with it too until soon it ran once more at its maximum clattering speed between the twin walls of unaxed wilderness as of old. It had been harmless once. Not five years ago Walter Ewell had shot a six-point buck from this same moving caboose, and there was the story of the half-grown bear: the train's first trip in to the cutting thirty miles away, the bear between the rails, its rear end elevated like that of a playing puppy while it dug to see what sort of ants or bugs they might contain or perhaps just to examine the curious symmetrical squared barkless logs which had appeared apparently from nowhere in one endless mathematical line overnight, still digging until the driver on the braked engine not fifty feet away blew the whistle at it, whereupon it broke frantically and took the first tree it came to: an ash sapling not much bigger than a man's thigh and climbed as high as it could and clung there, its head ducked between its arms as a man (a woman perhaps) might have done while the brakeman threw chunks of ballast at it, and when the engine returned three hours later with the first load of outbound logs the bear was halfway down the tree and once more scrambled back up as high as it could and clung again while the train passed and was still there when the engine went in again in the afternoon and still there when it came back out at dusk; and Boon had been in Hoke's with the wagon after a barrel of flour that noon when the train-crew told about it and Boon and Ash, both twenty years younger then, sat under the tree all that night to keep anybody from shooting it and the next morning Major de Spain had the log-train held at Hoke's and just before sundown on the second day, with not only Boon and Ash but Major de Spain and General Compson and Walter and McCaslin, twelve then, watching, it came down the tree after almost thirty-six hours without even water and McCaslin told him how for a minute they thought it was going to stop right there at the barrow-pit where they were standing and drink, how it looked at the water and paused and looked at them and at the water again, but did not, gone, running, as bears run, the two sets of feet, front and back, tracking two separate though parallel courses.

It had been harmless then. They would hear the passing log-train sometimes from the camp; sometimes, because nobody bothered to listen for it or not. They would hear it going in, running light and fast, the light clatter of the trucks, the exhaust of the diminutive locomotive and its shrill peanut-parcher whistle flung for one petty moment and absorbed by the brooding and inattentive wilderness without even an echo. They would hear it going out, loaded, not quite so fast now yet giving its frantic and toylike illusion of crawling speed, not whistling now to conserve steam, flinging its bitten laboring miniature puffing into the immemorial woodsface with frantic and bootless vainglory, empty and noisy and puerile, carrying to no destination or purpose sticks which left nowhere any scar or stump as the child's toy loads and transports and unloads its dead sand and rushes back for more, tireless and unceasing and rapid yet never quite so fast as the Hand which plays with it moves the toy burden back to load the toy again. But it was different now. It was the same train, engine cars and caboose, even the same enginemen brakeman and conductor to whom Boon, drunk then sober then drunk again then fairly sober once more all in the space of fourteen hours, had bragged that day two years ago about what they were going to do to Old Ben tomorrow, running with its same illusion of frantic rapidity between the same twin walls of impenetrable and impervious woods, passing the old landmarks, the old game crossings over which he had trailed bucks wounded and not wounded and more than once seen them, anything but wounded, bot out of the woods and up and across the embankment which bore the rails and ties then down and into the woods again as the earth-bound supposedly move but crossing as arrows travel, groundless, elongated, three times its actual length and even paler, different in color, as if there were a point between immobility and absolute motion where even mass chemically altered, changing without pain or agony not only in bulk and shape but in color too, approaching the color of wind, yet this time it was as though the train (and not only the train but himself, not only his vision which had seen it and his memory which remembered it but his clothes too, as garments carry back into the clean edgeless blowing of air the lingering effluvium of a sick-room or of death) had brought with it into the doomed wilderness even before the actual axe the shadow and portent of the new mill not even finished yet and the rails and ties which were not even laid; and he knew now what he had known as soon as he saw Hoke's this morning but had not yet thought into words: why Major de Spain had not come back, and that after this time he himself, who had had to see it one time other, would return no more.

Now they were near. He knew it before the engine-driver whistled to warn him. Then he saw Ash and the wagon, the reins without doubt wrapped once more about the brake-lever as within the boy's own memory Major de Spain had been forbidding him for eight years to do, the train slowing, the slackened couplings jolting and clashing again from car to car, the caboose slowing past the wagon as he swung down with his gun, the conductor leaning out above him to signal the engine, the caboose still slowing, creeping, although the engine's exhaust was already slatting in mounting tempo against the unechoing wilderness, the crashing of drawbars once more travelling backward along the train, the caboose picking up speed at last. Then it was gone. It had not been. He could no longer hear it. The wilderness soared, musing, inattentive, myriad, eternal, green; older than any mill-shed, longer than any spur-line. "Mr Boon here yet?" he said.

"He beat me in," Ash said. "Had the wagon loaded and ready for me at Hoke's yistiddy when I got there and setting on the front steps at camp last night when I got in. He already been in the woods since fo daylight this morning. Said he gwine up to the Gum Tree and for you to hunt up that way and meet him." He knew where that was: a single big sweet-gum just outside the woods, in an old clearing; if you crept up to it very quietly this time of year and then ran suddenly into the clearing, sometimes you caught as many as a dozen squirrels in it, trapped, since there was no other tree near they could jump to. So he didn't get into the wagon at all.

"I will," he said.

"I figured you would," Ash said, "I fotch you a box of shells." He passed the shells down and began to unwrap the lines from the brake-pole.

"How many times up to now do you reckon Major has told you not to do that?" the boy said.

"Do which?" Ash said. Then he said: "And tell Boon Hogganbeck dinner gonter be on the table in a hour and if yawl want any to come on and eat it."

"In an hour?" he said. "It aint nine oclock yet." He drew out his watch and extended it face-toward Ash. "Look." Ash didn't even look at the watch.

"That's town time. You aint in town now. You in the woods."

"Look at the sun then."

"Nemmine the sun too," Ash said. "If you and Boon Hogganbeck want any dinner, you better come on in and get it when I tole you. I aim to get done in that kitchen because I got my wood to chop. And watch your feet. They're crawling.

"I will," he said.

Then he was in the woods, not alone but solitary; the solitude closed about him, green with summer. They did not change, and, timeless, would not, anymore than would the green of summer and the fire and rain of fall and the iron cold and sometimes even snow

the day, the morning when he killed the buck and Sam marked his face with its hot blood, they returned to camp and he remembered old Ash's blinking and disgruntled and even outraged disbelief until at last McCaslin had had to affirm the fact that he had really killed it: and that night Ash sat snarling and unapproachable behind the stove so that Tennie's Jim had to serve the supper and waked them with breakfast already on the table the next morning and it was only half-past one oclock and at last out of Major de Spain's angry cursing and Ash's snarling and sullen rejoinders the fact emerged that Ash not only wanted to go into the woods and shoot a deer also but he intended to and Major de Spain said, 'By God, if we dont let him we will probably have to do the cooking from now on:' and Walter Ewell said, 'Or get up at midnight to eat what Ash cooks:' and since he had already killed his buck for his hunt and was not to shoot again unless they needed meat, he offered his gun to Ash until Major de Spain took command and allotted that gun to Boon for the day and gave Boon's unpredictable pump gun to Ash, with two buckshot shells but Ash said, 'I got shells:' and showed them, four: one buck, one of number three shot for rabbits, two of bird-shot and told one by one their history and their origin and he remembered not Ash's face alone but Major de Spain's and Walter's and General Compson's too, and Ash's voice: 'Shoot? In course they'll shoot! Genl Cawmpson guv me this un'—the buckshot—'right outen the same gun he kilt that big buck with eight years ago. And this un'—it was the rabbit shell: triumphantly—'is oldern thisyer boy!' And that morning he loaded the gun himself, reversing the order: the bird-shot, the rabbit, then the buck so that the buckshot would feed first into the chamber, and himself without a gun, he and Ash walked beside Major de Spain's and Tennie's Jim's horses and the dogs (that was the snow) until they cast and struck, the sweet strong cries ringing away into the muffled falling air and gone almost immediately, as if the constant and unmurmuring flakes had already buried even the unformed echoes beneath their myriad and weightless falling, Major de Spain and Tennie's Jim gone too, whooping on into the woods; and then it was all right, he knew as plainly as if Ash had told him that Ash had now hunted his deer and that even his tender years had been forgiven for having killed one, and they turned back toward home through the falling snow—that is, Ash said, 'Now whut?' and he said, 'This way'—himself in front because, although they were less than a mile from camp, he knew that Ash, who had spent two weeks of his life in the camp each year for the last twenty, had no idea whatever where they were, until quite soon the manner in which Ash carried Boon's gun was making him a good deal more than just nervous and he made Ash walk in front, striding on, talking now, an old man's garrulous monologue beginning with where he was at the moment then of the woods and of camping in the woods and of eating in camps then of eating then of cooking it and of his wife's cooking then briefly of his old wife and almost at once and at length of a new light-colored woman who nursed next door to Major de Spain's and if she didn't watch out who she was switching her tail at he would show her how old was an old man or not if his wife just didn't watch him all the time, the two of them in a game trail through a dense brake of cane and brier which would bring them out within a quarter-mile of camp, approaching a big fallen tree-trunk lying athwart the path and just as Ash, still talking, was about to step over it the bear, the yearling, rose suddenly beyond the log, sitting up, its forearms against its chest and its wrists limply arrested as if it had been surprised in the act of covering its face to pray: and after a certain time Ash's gun yawed jerkily up and he said, 'You haven't got a shell in the barrel yet. Pump it:' but the gun already snicked and he said, 'Pump it. You haven't got a shell in the barrel yet:' and Ash pumped the action and in a certain time the gun steadied again and snicked and he said, 'Pump it:' and watched the buckshot shell jerk, spinning heavily, into the cane. This is the rabbit shot: he thought and the gun snicked and he thought: The next is bird-shot: and he didn't have to say Pump it; he cried, 'Dont shoot! Dont shoot!' but that was already too late too, the light dry vicious snick! before he could speak and the bear turned and dropped to all-fours and then was gone and there was only the log, the cane, the velvet and constant snow and Ash said, 'Now whut?' and he said, 'This way. Come on:' and began to back away down the path and Ash said, 'I got to find my shells:' and he said, 'Goddamn it, goddamn it, come on:' but Ash leaned the gun against the log and returned and stooped and fumbled among the cane roots until he came back and stooped and found the shells and they rose and at that moment the gun, untouched, leaning against the log six feet away and for that while even forgotten by both of them, roared, bellowed and flamed, and ceased: and he carried it now, pumped out the last mummified shell and gave that one also to Ash and, the action still open, himself carried the gun until he stood it in the corner behind Boon's bed at the camp

—; summer, and fall, and snow, and wet and saprife spring in their ordered immortal sequence, the deathless and immemorial phases of the mother who had shaped him if any had toward the man he almost was, mother and father both to the old man born of a Negro slave and a Chickasaw chief who had been his spirit's father if any had, whom he had revered and harkened to and loved and lost and grieved: and he would marry someday and they too would own for their brief while that brief unsubstanced glory which inherently of itself cannot last and hence why glory: and they would, might, carry even the remembrance of it into the time when flesh no longer talks to flesh because memory at least does last: but still the woods would be his mistress and his wife.

He was not going toward the Gum Tree. Actually he was getting farther from it. Time was and not so long ago either when he would not have been allowed here without someone with him, and a little later, when he had begun to learn how much he did not know, he would not have dared be here without someone with him, and later still, beginning to ascertain, even if only dimly, the limits of what he did not know, he could have attempted and carried it through with a compass, not because of any increased belief in himself but because McCaslin and Major de Spain and Walter and General Compson too had taught him at last to believe the compass regardless of what it seemed to state. Now he did not even use the compass but merely the sun and that only subconsciously, yet he could have taken a scaled map and plotted at any time to within a hundred feet of where he actually was; and sure enough, at almost the exact moment when he expected it, the earth began to rise faintly, he passed one of the four concrete markers set down by the lumber company's surveyor to establish the four corners of the plot which Major de Spain had reserved out of the sale, then he stood on the crest of the knoll itself, the four corner-markers all visible now, blanched still even beneath the winter's weathering, lifeless and shockingly alien in that place where dissolution itself was a seething turmoil of ejaculation tumescence conception and birth, and death did not even exist. After two winters' blanketings of leaves and the flood-waters of two springs, there was no trace of the two graves anymore at all. But those who would have come this far to find them would not need headstones but would have found them as Sam Fathers himself had taught him to find such: by bearings on trees: and did, almost the first thrust of the hunting knife finding (but only to see if it was still there) the round tin box manufactured for axelgrease and containing now Old Ben's dried mutilated paw, resting above Lion's bones.

He didn't disturb it. He didn't even look for the other grave where he and McCaslin and Major de Spain and Boon had laid Sam's body, along with his hunting horn and his knife and his tobacco-pipe, that Sunday morning two years ago; he didn't have to. He had stepped over it, perhaps on it. But that was all right. *He probably knew I was in the woods this morning long before I got here*, he thought, going on to the tree which had supported one end of the platform where Sam lay when McCaslin and Major de Spain found them—the tree, the other axelgrease tin nailed to the trunk, but weathered, rusted, alien too yet healed already into the wilderness' concordant generality, raising no tuneless note, and empty, long since empty of the food and tobacco he had put into it that day, as empty of that as it would presently be of this which he drew from his pocket—the twist of tobacco, the new bandanna handkerchief, the small paper sack of the peppermint candy which Sam had used to love; that gone too, almost before he had turned his back, not vanished but merely translated into the myriad life which printed the dark mold of these secret and sunless places with delicate fairy tracks, which, breathing and biding and immobile, watched him from beyond every twig and leaf until he moved, moving again, walking on; he had not stopped, he had only paused, quitting the knoll which was no abode of the dead because there was no death, not Lion and not Sam: not held fast in earth but free in earth and not in earth but of earth, myriad yet undiffused of every myriad part, leaf and twig and particle, air and sun and rain and dew and night, acorn oak and leaf and acorn again, dark and dawn and dark and dawn again in their immutable progression and, being myriad, one: and Old Ben too, Old Ben too; they would give him his paw back even, certainly they would give him his paw back: then the long challenge and the long chase, no heart to be driven and outraged, no flesh to be mauled and bled—Even as he froze himself, he seemed to hear Ash's parting admonition. He could even hear the voice as he froze, immobile, one foot just taking his weight, the toe of the other just lifted behind him, not breathing, feeling again and as always the sharp shocking inrush from when Isaac McCaslin long yet was not, and so it was fear all right but not fright as he looked down at it. It had not coiled yet and the buzzer had not sounded either, only one thick rapid contraction, one loop cast sideways as though merely for purchase from which the raised head might start slightly backward, not in fright either, not in threat quite yet, more than six feet of it, the head raised higher than his knee and less than his knee's length away, and old, the once-bright markings of its youth dulled now to a monotone concordant too with the wilderness it crawled and lurked: the old one, the ancient and accursed about the earth, fatal and solitary and he could smell it now: the thin sick smell of rotting cucumbers and something else which had no name, evocative of all knowledge and an old weariness and of pariah-hood and of death. At last it moved. Not the head. The elevation of the head did not change as it began to glide away from him, moving erect yet off the perpendicular as if the head and that elevated third were complete and all: an entity walking on two feet and free of all laws of mass and balance and should have been because even now he could not quite believe that all that shift and flow of shadow behind that walking head could have been one snake: going and then gone; he put the other foot down at last and didn't know it, standing with one hand raised as Sam had stood that afternoon six years ago when Sam led him into the wilderness and showed him and he ceased to be a child, speaking the old tongue which Sam had spoken that day without premeditation either: "Chief," he said: "Grandfather."

He couldn't tell when he first began to hear the sound, because when he became aware of it, it seemed to him that he had been already hearing it for several seconds—a sound as though someone were hammering a gun-barrel against a piece of railroad iron, a sound loud and heavy and not rapid yet with something frenzied about it, as the hammerer were not only a strong man and an earnest one but a little hysterical too. Yet it couldn't be on the log-line because, although the track lay in that direction, it was at least two miles from him and this sound was not three hundred yards away. But even as he thought that, he realised where the sound must be coming from: whoever the man was and whatever he was doing, he was somewhere near the edge of the clearing where the Gum Tree was and where he was to meet Boon. So far, he had been hunting as he advanced, moving slowly and quietly and watching the ground and the trees both. Now he went on, his gun unloaded and the barrel slanted up and back to facilitate its passage through brier and undergrowth, approaching as it grew louder and louder that steady savage somehow queerly hysterical beating of metal on metal, emerging from the woods, into the old clearing, with the solitary gum tree directly before him. At first glance the tree seemed to be alive with frantic squirrels. There appeared to be forty or fifty of them leaping and darting from branch to branch until the whole tree had become one green maelstrom of mad leaves, while from time to time, singly or in twos and threes, squirrels would dart down the trunk then whirl without stopping and rush back up again as though sucked violently back by the vacuum of their fellows' frenzied vortex. Then he saw Boon, sitting, his back against the trunk, his head bent, hammering furiously at something on his lap. What he hammered with was the barrel of his dismembered gun, what he hammered at was the breech of it. The rest of the gun lay scattered about him in a half-dozen pieces while he bent over the piece on his lap his scarlet and streaming walnut face, hammering the disjointed barrel against the gun-breech with the frantic abandon of a madman. He didn't even look up to see who it was. Still hammering, he merely shouted back at the boy in a hoarse strangled voice:

"Get out of here! Dont touch them! Dont touch a one of them! They're mine!"

Eight Approaches to
"THE BEAR"

Introduction

The measure of an author depends both on his insights into the human condition and on the power and beauty of the language in which he expresses these insights. Throughout Faulkner's fiction his characters and their circumstances function implicitly as metaphors for presenting human nature, admitting varied readings and applications. None of his tales has raised a greater range and frequency of response and analysis than "The Bear."

For some time, Faulkner has been considered a "difficult" writer. This is due, in part, to his comprehensive vision; in writing of Southern men and women he interprets Southern history, economics, sociology, psychology, and cultural attainment. So crowded is the landscape of his imagination that he has founded an entire fictional county to give it range. Faulkner's domain, Yoknapatawpha County, in southern Mississippi, has a diverse population. Its black majority, along with the whites, struggles to maintain a modest, modern economy of farming, crafts, and small businesses. Faulkner's language is as intricate, varied, and individualistic as his microcosm. Frequently he displaces traditional grammar and a traditional narrative ordering of events to reflect the idiosyncratic rhythms of minds in thought. Consequently, the reader can more easily understand Faulkner if he surrenders to the rhythms imposed on words, finding in their repetition and juxtaposition certain patterns which serve as clues to the importance of particular phrases or concepts and implying certain judgments concerning those who voice them. Words as well as Yoknapatawpha become autonomous.

Because Faulkner's mind and art are so original, his works may take longer to understand than the writings of more conventional authors. The rewards of understanding are ample compensation for the task, but the existence of a task and the possibility that guidance might be welcomed are the two reasons for assembling the selections which make up this text. The second part of *Bear, Man, and God* is designed to enrich an understanding of "The Bear" by juxtaposing interpretations made from eight vantage points. However, all these approaches attempt to deal with "The Bear" as an integrated work of art; none tries to divide it artificially into plot, characterization, and setting. Ultimately, each approach becomes a perspective from which the reader may examine "The Bear"; most of them apply to other stories as well.

The first approach, the biographical, explores the role of personal experience in the shaping of Faulkner's fiction. This approach assumes that, whatever else may be true, a work of art is first and last a human product, written by a man who lives in a particular milieu and who has a particular personal and cultural heritage. An informal interview and personal recollections and memoirs reprinted here form a partial portrait of the man and enable one to consider "The Bear" as an expression of an individual who, consciously or not, draws on his own experiences, observations, and interests.

The approach to "The Bear" by way of Faulkner's other fiction is particularly relevant since Faulkner, like Balzac, Hardy, and Zola, usually wrote of a single region. Here are two of his formal statements, upon receipt of the Nobel Prize and of the National Book Award. Here too are excerpts from Faulkner's other fiction which relate to ideas, characters, or events in "The Bear."

The section "Other Versions of 'The Bear' " does not claim to trace the precise genesis of the work, since no one knows where all the versions are, how many there are, or in what order they were written. However, it does include comparisons of the final published text of "The Bear" with other texts.

For some time the cultural approach to "The Bear" was neglected, but publication of the first edition of this book in 1964 helped to remedy this deficiency. Presented in this new edition, following W. J. Cash's definitive analysis of the historical realities of the Southern character prior to 1940, are a number of folk and Southern tall tales and an initiation rite. The section is concluded by an analysis of the Nature myth in "The Bear" and a synthesis of the other materials, in the essay "Pride and Humility."

The interpretive approach tries to answer the most common literary question: "What does it all mean?" Critics may draw on their own research among literary traditions or formulate their own analyses by concentrating on certain ideas implicit or explicit in the story itself. Believing that the discovery of truth arises from the heat of debate, the editors have included here a variety of contradictory interpretations which explore the story from both the main and the less common views.

In his later years Faulkner insisted that *Go Down, Moses,* in which "The Bear" first appeared in the form printed here, was a novel and that the version of "The Bear" which includes Part IV (the dialogue in the commissary) was only a chapter. He did not wish to consider removing "The Bear" as an independent work, although he or his publisher had first titled the book *Go Down, Moses and Other Stories.* The points at issue in the essays included here are whether "The Bear" can stand alone or, if it is integrally related to other stories in the 1942 book, what that relationship is, and how the other stories help readers to understand "The Bear."

During the final decade of his life, Faulkner became increasingly outspoken about public events. Following the 1954 Supreme Court injunction for integrated schools, Faulkner wrote some essays and a number of letters to newspapers and magazines which discussed racial integration in the South. Through his sometimes inconsistent statements Faulkner began making explicit his position on integration, though his views were already imbedded in his fiction, nowhere more centrally than in "The Bear" and "Delta Autumn." It is perhaps a moot point whether Ike's shifting reaction to slavery and the equality of the black race parallels Faulkner's, but Faulkner's own observations do illuminate our understanding of Ike McCaslin's ultimate victory or defeat in his attempt to repudiate his racially mixed kinship.

Finally, the formalistic and stylistic approach, investigating *how* something is said to determine *why,* explores the relation of style and meaning in Faulkner's work. The selections here consider the hallmarks of his writing and demonstrate how expression affects meaning. One critic contends that certain characteristics of Faulkner's style allow his words to take on nuances of their own; another questions whether Faulkner's language is adequate for his purpose. Finally, a parody burlesques Faulkner's themes, characters, settings, and points of view, as well as his rhetoric.

The remaining sections of the second edition of this book have also been considerably revised. The Genealogy, the Chronicle, and the Annotated Bibliography are intended to serve as references rather than as expressions of opinion. Nevertheless, despite their seeming objectivity, the reader should be aware that these, too, represent individual interpretation. These materials, like the rest of the selections in this volume, are designed for judicious consultation. But ultimately the reader must make his own way through the forest and so into the heart of "The Bear." It is hoped that this book will be to him as Sam Fathers, and later Ike McCaslin, was to the hunters in that wilderness.

The Role of Personal Experience in Faulkner's Work

My Brother Bill

JOHN FAULKNER

. . . Dad took us walking in the woods almost every pretty fall Sunday. He loved the woods and hunting and that's where we got our taste for it. It was during these walks that he would remember hunts he had been on and tell us about them. Dad was a good storyteller. We all remembered the stories he told us on those walks, perhaps Bill best of all, for a number of them, or parts of them, appeared in his stories of the woods and hunting in later years. Each time I read those stories the picture comes back to me of Dad walking through the fall woods with three little boys trudging along beside him.

All this had a part in forming Bill's love for the woods and hunting. He was a tenderhearted someone, with a very real feeling for those creatures he killed for food. I never knew him to kill needlessly. One of his outstanding hunting traits was that he would never go off and leave a cripple. I've been with him when he would down a bird, maybe with a broken wing, and we would hunt no more till that bird was found and put out of its misery. One afternoon he crippled a bird not long before dark. We could not find it and the next morning Bill came back to try and find it.

The best hunting story I know of is Bill's "The Bear." He knew the

Big Woods well, for he went there every fall to hunt. But it took a lifetime of training in woodlore to be able to see them as he did and that training started in those autumn walks with Dad.

Dad had mementos of his hunts he kept in a collection at home. There was a panther claw from a big cat he killed in Tippah County, where we all came from, and an eagle feather from the wing of the last eagle ever seen in this part of the country. He shot it at the request of a farmer friend whose flocks and herds were being raided by it. Dad lay in wait and shot it in the air as it came in over a newborn lamb on a spring hillside, and he saved the feather as a souvenir. He also told us about the last wolf ever seen in our own river bottom, Tallahatchie, which was the name given the same river in Bill's Yoknapatawpha County.

The time Dad met the wolf was down at old man Bob Cain's place, down in the bottom. He used to hunt there a lot and this time he was squirrel hunting. He crossed a log over the neck of a slough and just as he stepped up on one end of the log the wolf stepped up on the other. Dad raised his gun as quickly as he could on the slippery log but before he could draw a bead on the wolf it whisked from sight. It was a big gray wolf, the last one ever seen in our bottom.

Our river bottoms were full of virgin timber then, tall soaring gum and oak and cypress, just like in "The Bear." By the time Bill was grown and began deer hunting, our timber had mostly been cut. That's why he had to go to the "Big Bottom" for his story, but he saw its beginnings on the banks of our own Tallahatchie.

The first timber cutters we knew were small bands of Slavic stave cutters who traveled the country for whiskey makers, cutting special hardwoods for whiskey barrels. Dad belonged to a group who had a clubhouse at the mouth of Tippah River where it runs into Tallahatchie and he began taking us down there almost as far back as I can remember. We would see groups of stave cutters camped there in the bottom, cutting staves. They only felled special trees and we hardly missed them.

But then hardwood mills began coming in and after them mills that cut almost anything that would make a board. And our wildlife retreated farther and farther into the Big Woods, the still virgin tracts of timber that cloaked the Mississippi Delta.

The Delta begins thirty miles to the west of us. The bluffs drop a sheer fifty feet to the flat plain that stretches for over fifty miles to the river. It was here, just beyond Batesville at General Stone's cabin, that Bill first went on his deer and bear hunts and wild-turkey shoots.

It was through these woods that the single-line logging road ran. It was here that the half-grown bear, scared by the train's whistle, climbed the tree and stayed up there while the line's only locomotive made the trip to the end of the line and back and was halted to wait until the young bear finally got up nerve to come down. This was the road over which Bill and Mr. Buster Callicot made the first and last part of their journey to Memphis for more whiskey (both incidents appear in "The Bear") when the camp supply ran out, and Mr. Buster got back with the partially wrapped corset he had bought as a present for his wife trailing under his arm. This was the Big Woods that was cut back and back until only the triangle was left that Bill wrote about in "Delta Autumn."

We began our lessons in hunting food for the pot by hunting rabbits. For this Dad bought us beagle hounds. He got us two of them. Bill went hunting with them one day and killed one of them. He dropped his gun and forgot it and brought the dog home in his arms. When he got there he laid the little dog on the porch and went to his room and locked himself in and cried. He was about fourteen then, I think, and did not take up another gun until he was grown and went on the deer hunt below Batesville. . . .

During the time that Bill was living at home [in the early 1930s] and writing short stories, he took up hunting again. He was invited to go on General Stone's deer-and-bear hunt, at his lodge below Batesville in the virgin bottom lands of the Mississippi Delta. Batesville is only thirty miles from Oxford but you had to travel about a hundred and fifty miles and change trains twice to get there by rail. We had no paving then and in winter you couldn't get there in a car.

The hunters went by train and had a wagon meet them in Batesville to take them and the supplies from there to the lodge. They always loaded the wagon and sent it a week ahead of time. Old Add, the cook, and his helper, Curtis, made the trip in the wagon. It would take them most of a week to get from Oxford to the camp, fix it up and then get back to Batesville in time to meet the train with the hunters on it.

Dean [the youngest brother of William and John] always loved hunting more than any of us. Even in high school he'd hurry home in the evenings during quail season and get his gun and dogs to hunt during the hour and a half or two hours left until dusk. I've seen him shoot quail on the wing with a .22. He never shot a squirrel. He simply "barked" him, that is, shot the limb under him to stun the squirrel so he'd fall out of the tree. Then Dean would break his neck with his rifle barrel. That way no meat was spoiled by a bullet.

Of course, Dean was awfully interested in this bear-and-deer hunt that Bill was going on. He pestered Bill about what sort of rifle he'd use. Bill told him which rifle he'd use to kill a deer. When Dean asked him what he'd use to kill a bear, Bill said he didn't intend taking a rifle. He said if he met a bear in the woods he didn't want to have to take the time to throw away a gun before he could start running.

Some of Bill's best short stories came out of those trips. "The Bear" was one. . . .

Bill went on those hunting trips almost every year he was home from then on. He followed the cutting of the big timber and made his last trip down there into the triangle left near Yazoo City, just as Uncle Ike McCaslin did in "Delta Autumn."

Bill served his apprenticeship well. He killed his buck and was blooded, and he also killed a bear. Because he was a writer, the town had already begun to look on him as a little queer, and at first the other hunters didn't know whether they'd get along with him or not. They soon found different.

Bill asked no favors, just to be allowed to hunt with them and be one of them. They assigned him the most remote and least likely stand of all because, as a novice, that was all he rated. He took it without a word and stood fast till they came for him each evening. Before his hunting days were over Bill could find his way around in any woods. He became one of the old men of the hunt and one year was its captain. . . .

Faulkner at West Point

JOSEPH L. FANT III and ROBERT ASHLEY

Q. Mr. Faulkner, I was just wondering if there was any personal experience involved in the inspiration of the events that transpired between the boy and the bear in that story ["The Bear"].

A. Well, that was a part of my youth, my childhood, too. My father and his friends owned leases on the land similar to that. And I was taken there as soon as I was big enough to go into the woods with a gun, and I don't remember now just how much of that might have been actual, how much I invented. The three-toed bear was an actual bear. But I don't know that anyone killed him with a knife. And the dog was an actual dog, but I don't remember that they ever came into juxtaposition. It's difficult to say. That's the case of the three tanks with the collector. The writer's too busy to know whether he is stealing or lying. He's simply telling a story.

Reprinted from Joseph L. Fant, III and Robert Ashley, eds., *Faulkner at West Point*, courtesy of Random House, Inc.

William Faulkner, 1897–1962

ALLEN TATE

I am writing this memoir, or perhaps it had better be called an obituary, in Italy, where it is so difficult to find William Faulkner's books that I have not even tried. But at one time or another I have read them all except *Knight's Gambit* and *The Reivers*, and it is probably better, on this occasion, to rely upon one's memory than to try to read again and "revaluate" the greater books. I am not sure of what I am about to write, but I am thinking of it as recollection and appreciation, not criticism; yet without what amounts to a profound admiration of his works (this is a kind of criticism) I should not have accepted the editor's invitation to write about William Faulkner at all. For in the 31 years of our acquaintance I saw him not more than five or six times, and but for one meeting in Rome about 10 years ago he seemed to me arrogant and ill-mannered in a way that I felt qualified to distinguish as peculiarly "Southern": in company he usually failed to reply when spoken to, or when he spoke there was something grandiose in the profusion with which he sprinkled his remarks with "Sirs" and "Ma'ms." Years ago, when I was editing *The Sewanee Review*, I had some correspondence with him; his letters were signed "Faulkner." I wrote him that English nobility followed this practice and I never heard from him again.

I suppose the main source of my annoyance with him was his affectation of not being a writer, but a farmer; this would have been pretentious even had he been a farmer. But being a "farmer," he did not "associate" with writers—with the consequence that he was usually surrounded by third-rate writers or just plain sycophants. I never heard that he was a friend of anybody who could conceivably have been his peer.

One may leave the man to posterity, but the work must be reread now, and talked about, lest Faulkner, like other writers of immense fame in their lifetime, go into a slump. However great a writer may be, the public gets increasingly tired of him; his death seems to remove the obligation to read him. But if I had read *The Reivers*, I should be willing to say something about the work as a whole, and an essay would make some of the points that I can only suggest in this "obituary" of a man I did not like, but of a writer who since the early Thirties I have thought was the greatest American novelist after Henry James: a novelist of an

Reprinted from Allen Tate, "William Faulkner, 1897–1962," *The Sewanee Review*, LXXI (Winter 1963), 160–164, by permission of Allen Tate and *The Sewanee Review*.

originality and power not equalled by his contemporaries, Hemingway and Fitzgerald.

Leaving aside the two books that I have not read, I should say that he wrote at least five masterpieces (what other American novelist wrote so many, except James?): they are *The Sound and the Fury, As I Lay Dying, Sanctuary, Light in August* and *The Hamlet.* I know people of good judgment who would add to this list *The Wild Palms* and *Absalom, Absalom!*, books that contain some great writing but that in the end are not novels. Of the four first titles, on my list, none appeared after 1932; the fifth, in 1940. *Absalom, Absalom!* and *The Wild Palms* came out in 1936 and 1939. All Faulkner's seven great books were written in a span of about 11 or 12 years. The fine long story "The Bear" was written towards the end of this period. The later books round out the picture of Yoknapatawpha County (Lafayette County, Mississippi), but nobody would know them had the earlier books not been written. William Faulkner wrote only one bad novel, *A Fable,* his version of the Grand Inquisitor, conceived in theological ignorance and placed in a setting that he had not observed.

Observation of scene is the phrase that will take us closer than any other to the mystery of Faulkner's genius. The three plots of *Light in August* are all in synopsis incredible, but we believe them at last, or accept them as probable, because the characters are in the first place credible. The famous violence of William Faulkner is a violence of character, not of action; there are, of course, violent "scenes"; yet these scenes, like the murder of Joe Christmas in *Light in August*, or the Bundren family crossing the swollen river with Addie's coffin, all add up to a powerful "direct impression of life" which Henry James said some 90 years ago would be the province of the novel. I am not indulging myself in paradox when I say that nothing "happens" in *The Sound and the Fury*, just as nothing happens in *Madame Bovary*: in both novels there are famous suicides. Yet Quentin Compson's death, though it comes before the end of the book, is the last brushstroke in the portrait of the Compson family; and likewise the suicide of Emma Bovary rounds out a picture, not an action.

The European reader finds something uniquely American in Faulkner, and obviously no European could have written his books; the few European commentators that I have read seem to me to glorify William Faulkner in a provincial American (or Southern) vacuum. I believe that as his personality fades from view he will be recognized as one of the last great craftsmen of the art of fiction which Ford Madox Ford called the Impressionist Novel. From Stendhal through Flaubert and Joyce there is a direct line to Faulkner, and it is not a mere question of influence. Faulkner's great subject, as it was Flaubert's and Proust's, is passive suffering, the victim being destroyed either by society or by dark forces within himself. Faulkner is one of the great exemplars of the international school of fiction which for more than a century has reversed the Aristotelian doctrine that tragedy is an action, not a quality.

William Faulkner's time and place made it possible for him to extend this European tradition beyond any boundaries that were visible to novelists of New England, the Middle West, or the Far West. The Greco-Trojan myth (Northerners as the upstart Greeks, Southerners as the older, more civilized Trojans) presented Faulkner, before he had written a line, with a large semi-historical background against which even his ignorant characters, like Lena Grove or Dewey Dell Bundren, as well as the more civilized Compsons and Sartorises, could be projected in more than human dimensions. I had occasion some years ago to say in the *New Statesman* that had William Faulkner invented his myth, it could not have been as good as it turned out to be (Sophocles was doubtless in a similarly advantageous position with respect to the Oedipean cycle). Faulkner brought to bear upon the myth greater imaginative powers than any of his contemporaries possessed; but he was not unique; for it is only further evidence of his greatness that he wrote in an age when there were other Southern novelists almost as good: Robert Penn Warren, Caroline Gordon, Andrew Lytle, Stark Young, Eudora Welty, Katherine Anne Porter—and Faulkner would have included Thomas Wolfe, though I did not credit his honesty when he placed Wolfe at the top. (He never mentioned the others.)

Two secondary themes in Faulkner have obscured the critics' awareness of the great theme. These are: the white man's legacy of guilt for slavery and the rape of the land. These themes are almost obsessive, but they are not the main theme. William Faulkner was not a "segregationist." (Whether he was an "integrationist" is a different question.) But how could he not have been a segregationist when he said that he would shoot Negroes in the streets if the Federal Government interfered in Mississippi?[1] Unless the European—or for that matter the Northern—reader understands that for Faulkner, and for thousands of other Southerners of his generation, the separatism and possible autonomy of the South came before all other "problems," he will misread Faulkner because he will not have discerned the great theme. I will repeat it in different language: the destruction of the Old South released native forces of disorder and corruption which were accelerated by the brutal exploitation of the Carpetbaggers and an army of occupation; thus the old order of dignity and principle was replaced by upstarts and cynical materialists. Federal interference in the South had brought this about; and when Faulkner said he would shoot Negroes if that were necessary to keep Federal interference at bay, his response came directly out of

[1] See p. 259—Eds.

the Greco-Trojan myth; and yet it was the response of a man who had depicted Negroes with greater understanding and compassion than any other Southern writer of his time.

He is, I think, with Hawthorne and James, in the United States, and one of the great company in Europe that I have mentioned. "I salute thee, Mantovano." The Tennysonian-Vergilian reference is not inappropriate, for William Faulkner's rhetoric goes back to the Roman oratory of the Old South. He was a great writer. We shall not see his like again in our time.

Faulkner on Faulkner

Many of Faulkner's works and remarks are reflexive and some cast new perspectives on "The Bear." The selections presented here are arranged chronologically. [Page numbers in brackets refer to pages in this volume.]

Sam Fathers

WILLIAM FAULKNER

Quentin Compson describes Sam Fathers, here a carpenter on the Compson farm. Mr. Stokes is the overseer for the Compsons.

He talked like a nigger—that is, he said his words like niggers do, but he didn't say the same words—and his hair was nigger hair. But his skin wasn't quite the color of a light nigger and his nose and his mouth and chin were not nigger nose and mouth and chin. And his shape was not like the shape of a nigger when he gets old. He was straight in the back, not tall, a little broad, and his face was still all the time, like he might be somewhere else all the while he was working or when people, even white people, talked to him, or while he talked to me. It was just the same all the time, like he might be away up on a roof by himself, driving nails. Sometimes he would quit work with something half-finished on the bench, and sit down and smoke. And he wouldn't jump up and go back to work when Mr. Stokes or even Grandfather came along. . . . (1931)

*The Hill Country**

WILLIAM FAULKNER

A mile back he had left the rich, broad, flat river-bottom country and entered the hills—a region which topographically was the final blue and dying echo of the Appalachian mountains. Chickasaw Indians had owned it, but after the Indians it had been cleared where possible for cultivation, and after the Civil War, forgotten save by the small peripatetic sawmills which had vanished too now, their sites marked only by the mounds of rotting sawdust which were not only their gravestones but the monuments of a people's heedless greed. . . . (1940)

Uncle Ike†

WILLIAM FAULKNER

Isaac McCaslin, 'Uncle Ike', past seventy and nearer eighty than he ever corroborated any more, a widower now and uncle to half a county and father to no one

this was not something participated in or even seen by himself, but by his elder cousin, McCaslin Edmonds, grandson of Isaac's father's sister and so descended by the distaff, yet notwithstanding the inheritor, and in his time the bequestor, of that which some had thought then and some still thought should have been Isaac's, since his was the name in which the title to the land had first been granted from the Indian patent and which some of the descendants of his father's slaves still bore in the land. But Isaac was not one of those:—a widower these twenty years, who in all his life had owned but one object more than he could wear and carry in his pockets and his hands at one time, and this was the narrow iron cot and the stained lean mattress which he used camping in the woods for deer and bear or for fishing or simply because he loved the woods; who owned no property and never desired to since the earth

* Reprinted from William Faulkner, *The Hamlet*, by permission of Random House, Inc., the Author's Literary Estate, and Chatto and Windus Ltd. Copyright 1940 by William Faulkner.

† Reprinted from William Faulkner, "Was," *Go Down, Moses*, by permission of Random House, Inc., the Author's Literary Estate, and Chatto and Windus Ltd. Copyright 1942 by William Faulkner.

was no man's but all men's, as light and air and weather were; who lived still in the cheap frame bungalow in Jefferson which his wife's father gave them on their marriage and which his wife had willed to him at her death and which he had pretended to accept, acquiesce to, to humor her, ease her going but which was not his, will or not, chancery dying wishes, mortmain possession or whatever, himself merely holding it for his wife's sister and her children who had lived in it with him since his wife's death, holding himself welcome to live in one room of it as he had during his wife's time or she during her time or the sister-in-law and her children during the rest of his and after

not something he had participated in or even remembered except from the hearing, the listening, come to him through and from his cousin McCaslin born in 1850 and sixteen years his senior and hence, his own father being near seventy when Isaac, an only child, was born, rather his brother than cousin and rather his father than either, out of the old time, the old days (1942)

The Blood Ritual of Isaac McCaslin

WILLIAM FAULKNER

At first there was nothing. There was the faint, cold, steady rain, the gray and constant light of the late November dawn, with the voices of the hounds converging somewhere in it and toward them. Then Sam Fathers, standing just behind the boy as he had been standing when the boy shot his first running rabbit with his first gun and almost with the first load it ever carried, touched his shoulder and he began to shake, not with any cold. Then the buck was there. He did not come into sight; he was just there, looking not like a ghost but as if all of light were condensed in him and he were the source of it, not only moving in it but disseminating it, already running, seen first as you always see the deer, in that split second after he has already seen you, already slanting away in that first soaring bound, the antlers even in that dim light looking like a small rocking-chair balanced on his head.

"Now," Sam Fathers said, "shoot quick, and slow."

The boy did not remember that shot at all. He would live to be eighty, as his father and his father's twin brother and their father in his turn had lived to be, but he would never hear that shot nor remember even the shock of the gun-butt. He didn't even remember what he did with the gun afterward. He was running. Then he was standing over the buck where it lay on the wet earth still in the attitude of speed and not looking at all dead, standing over it shaking and jerking, with Sam Fathers beside him again, extending the knife. "Dont walk up to him in front," Sam said. "If he aint dead, he will cut you all to pieces with his feet. Walk up to him from behind and take him by the horn first, so you can hold his head down until you can jump away. Then slip your other hand down and hook your fingers in his nostrils."

The boy did that—drew the head back and the throat taut and drew Sam Fathers' knife across the throat and Sam stooped and dipped his hands in the hot smoking blood and wiped them back and forth across the boy's face. Then Sam's horn rang in the wet gray woods and again and again; there was a boiling wave of dogs about them, with Tennie's Jim and Boon Hogganbeck whipping them back after each had had a taste of the blood, then the men, the true hunters—Walter Ewell whose rifle never missed, and Major de Spain and old General Compson and the boy's cousin, McCaslin Edmonds, grandson of his father's sister, sixteen years his senior and, since both he and McCaslin were only children and the boy's father had been nearing seventy when he was born, more his brother than his cousin and more his father than either—sitting their horses and looking down at them: at the old man of seventy who had been a negro for two generations now but whose face and bearing were still those of the Chickasaw chief who had been his father; and the white boy of twelve with the prints of the bloody hands on his face, who had nothing to do now but stand straight and not let the trembling show.

"Did he do all right, Sam?" his cousin McCaslin said.

"He done all right," Sam Fathers said.

They were the white boy, marked forever, and the old dark man sired on both sides by savage kings, who had marked him, whose bloody hands had merely formally consecrated him to that which, under the man's tutelage, he had already accepted, humbly and joyfully, with abnegation and with pride too; the hands, the touch, the first worthy blood which he had been found at last worthy to draw, joining him and the man forever, so that the man would continue to live past the boy's seventy years and then eighty years, long after the man himself had entered the earth as chiefs and kings entered it;—the child, not yet a man, whose grandfather had lived in the same country and in almost the same manner as the boy himself would grow up to live, leaving his descendants in the land in his turn as his grandfather had done, and the old man past seventy whose grandfathers had owned the land long before the white men ever saw it and who had vanished from it now with all their kind, what of blood they left behind them running now in another race and for a while even in bondage and now drawing toward the end of its alien and irrevocable course, barren, since Sam Fathers had no children. . . .

That was seventy years ago. The Sam Fathers whom the boy knew was already sixty—a man not tall, squat rather, almost sedentary, flabby-looking though he actually was not, with hair like a horse's mane which even at seventy showed no trace of white and a face which showed no age until he smiled, whose only visible trace of negro blood was a slight dullness of the hair and the fingernails, and something else which you did notice about the eyes, which you noticed because it was not always there, only in repose and not always then—something not in their shape nor pigment but in their expression, and the boy's cousin McCaslin told him what that was: not the heritage of Ham, not the mark of servitude but of bondage; the knowledge that for a while that part of his blood had been the blood of slaves. "Like an old lion or a bear in a cage," McCaslin said. "He was born in the cage and has been in it all his life; he knows nothing else. Then he smells something. It might be anything, any breeze blowing past anything and then into his nostrils. But there for a second was the hot sand or the cane-brake that he never even saw himself, might not even know if he did see it and probably does know he couldn't hold his own with it if he got back to it. But that's not what he smells then. It was the cage he smelled. He hadn't smelled the cage until that minute. Then the hot sand or the brake blew into his nostrils and blew away, and all he could smell was the cage. That's what makes his eyes look like that."

"Then let him go!" the boy cried. "Let him go!"

His cousin laughed shortly. Then he stopped laughing, making the sound that is. It had never been laughing. "His cage aint McCaslins," he said. "He was a wild man. When he was born, all his blood on both sides, except the little white part, knew things that had been tamed out of our blood so long ago that we have not only forgotten them, we have to live together in herds to protect ourselves from our own sources. He was the direct son not only of a warrior but of a chief. Then he grew up and began to learn things, and all of a sudden one day he found out that he had been betrayed, the blood of the warriors and chiefs had been betrayed. Not by his father," he added quickly. "He probably never held it against old Doom for selling him and his mother into slavery, because he probably believed the damage was already done before then and it was the same warriors' and chiefs' blood in him and Doom both that was betrayed through the black blood which his mother gave him. Not betrayed by the black blood and not wilfully betrayed by his mother, but betrayed by her all the same, who had bequeathed him not only the blood of slaves but even a little of the very blood which had enslaved it; himself his own battleground, the scene of his own vanquishment and the mausoleum of his defeat. His cage aint us," McCaslin said. "Did you ever know anybody yet, even your father and Uncle Buddy, that ever told him to do or not do anything that he ever paid any attention to?" . . .

White man's work, when Sam did work. Because he did nothing else: farmed no allotted acres of his own, as the other ex-slaves of old Carothers McCaslin did, performed no field-work for daily wages as the younger and newer negroes did—and the boy never knew just how that had been settled between Sam and old Carothers, or perhaps with old Carothers' twin sons after him. For, although Sam lived among the negroes, in a cabin among the other cabins in the quarters, and consorted with negroes (what of consorting with anyone Sam did after the boy got big enough to walk alone from the house to the blacksmith-shop and then to carry a gun) and dressed like them and talked like them and even went with them to the negro church now and then, he was still the son of that Chickasaw chief and the negroes knew it. And, it seemed to the boy, not only negroes. Boon Hogganbeck's grandmother had been a Chickasaw woman too, and although the blood had run white since and Boon was a white man, it was not chief's blood. To the boy at least, the difference was apparent immediately you saw Boon and Sam together, and even Boon seemed to know it was there—even Boon, to whom in his tradition it had never occurred that anyone might be better born than himself. A man might be smarter, he admitted that, or richer (luckier, he called it) but not better born. Boon was a mastiff, absolutely faithful, dividing his fidelity equally between Major de Spain and the boy's cousin McCaslin, absolutely dependent for his very bread and dividing that impartially too between Major de Spain and McCaslin, hardy, generous, courageous enough, a slave to all the appetites and almost unratiocinative. In the boy's eyes at least it was Sam Fathers, the negro, who bore himself not only toward his cousin McCaslin and Major de Spain but toward all white men, with gravity and dignity and without servility or recourse to that impenetrable wall of ready and easy mirth which negroes sustain between themselves and white men, bearing himself toward his cousin McCaslin not only as one man to another but as an older man to a younger.

. . . But the solitude did not breathe again. It should have suspired again then but it did not. It was still facing, watching, what it had been watching and it was not here, not where he and Sam stood; rigid, not breathing himself, he thought, cried *No! No!*, knowing already that it was too late, thinking with the old despair of two and three years ago: *I'll never get a shot.* Then he heard it—the flat single clap of Walter Ewell's rifle which never missed. Then the mellow sound of the horn came down the ridge and something went out of him and he knew then he had never expected to get the shot at all.

"I reckon that's it," he said. "Walter got him." He had raised the gun slightly without knowing it. He lowered it again and had lowered one of the hammers and was already moving out of the thicket when Sam spoke.

"Wait."

"Wait?" the boy cried. And he would remember that—how he turned upon Sam in the truculence of a boy's grief over the missed opportunity, the missed luck. "What for? Dont you hear that horn?"

And he would remember how Sam was standing. Sam had not moved. He was not tall, squat rather and broad, and the boy had been growing fast for the past year or so and there was not much difference between them in height, yet Sam was looking over the boy's head and up the ridge toward the sound of the horn and the boy knew that Sam did not even see him; that Sam knew he was still there beside him but he did not see the boy. Then the boy saw the buck. It was coming down the ridge, as if it were walking out of the very sound of the horn which related its death. It was not running, it was walking, tremendous, unhurried, slanting and tilting its head to pass the antlers through the undergrowth, and the boy standing with Sam beside him now instead of behind him as Sam always stood, and the gun still partly aimed and one of the hammers still cocked.

Then it saw them. And still it did not begin to run. It just stopped for an instant, taller than any man, looking at them; then its muscles suppled, gathered. It did not even alter its course, not fleeing, not even running, just moving with that winged and effortless ease with which deer move, passing within twenty feet of them, its head high and the eye not proud and not haughty but just full and wild and unafraid, and Sam standing beside the boy now, his right arm raised at full length, palm-outward, speaking in that tongue which the boy had learned from listening to him and Joe Baker in the blacksmith shop, while up the ridge Walter Ewell's horn was still blowing them in to a dead buck.[1]

"Oleh, Chief," Sam said. "Grandfather." (1942)

*Speech of Acceptance Upon the Award of the Nobel Prize for Literature**

William Faulkner

I feel that this award was not made to me as a man, but to my work—a life's work in all the agony and sweat of the human spirit, not for glory and least of all for profit, but to create out of the materials of the human spirit something which did not exist before. So this award is only mine in trust. It will not be difficult to find a dedication for the money part of it

[1] But, we learn, really a spike buck, nearly a fawn, that Ewell thinks is the big buck, because he killed it in the older deer's tracks. Although Sam and young Ike realize the truth, they do not tell Ewell; later, Ike tells his cousin back in Jefferson.—Eds.

* Reprinted from James B. Meriwether, ed., *Essays, Speeches and Public Letters of William Faulkner*, by permission of Random House, Inc., the Author's Literary Estate, and Chatto and Windus Ltd. Copyright © 1965 by Random House, Inc. Delivered in Stockholm, December 10, 1950.

commensurate with the purpose and significance of its origin. But I would like to do the same with the acclaim too, by using this moment as a pinnacle from which I might be listened to by the young men and women already dedicated to the same anguish and travail, among whom is already that one who will some day stand here where I am standing.

Our tragedy today is a general and universal physical fear so long sustained by now that we can even bear it. There are no longer problems of the spirit. There is only the question: When will I be blown up? Because of this, the young man or woman writing today has forgotten the problems of the human heart in conflict with itself which alone can make good writing because only that is worth writing about, worth the agony and the sweat.

He must learn them again. He must teach himself that the basest of all things is to be afraid; and, teaching himself that, forget it forever, leaving no room in his workshop for anything but the old verities and truths of the heart, the old universal truths lacking which any story is ephemeral and doomed—love and honor and pity and pride and compassion and sacrifice. Until he does so, he labors under a curse. He writes not of love but of lust, of defeats in which nobody loses anything of value, of victories without hope and, worst of all, without pity or compassion. His griefs grieve on no universal bones, leaving no scars. He writes not of the heart but of the glands.

Until he relearns these things, he will write as though he stood among and watched the end of man. I decline to accept the end of man. It is easy enough to say that man is immortal simply because he will endure; that when the last ding-dong of doom has clanged and faded from the last worthless rock hanging tideless in the last red and dying evening, that even then there will still be one more sound: that of his puny inexhaustible voice, still talking. I refuse to accept this. I believe that man will not merely endure: he will prevail. He is immortal, not because he alone among creatures has an inexhaustible voice, but because he has a soul, a spirit capable of compassion and sacrifice and endurance. The poet's, the writer's, duty is to write about these things. It is his privilege to help man endure by lifting his heart, by reminding him of the courage and honor and hope and pride and compassion and pity and sacrifice which have been the glory of his past. The poet's voice need not merely be the record of man, it can be one of the props, the pillars to help him endure and prevail. (1950)

Address Upon Receiving the National Book Award for Fiction

William Faulkner

By artist I mean of course everyone who has tried to create something which was not here before him, with no other tools and material than the uncommerciable ones of the human spirit; who has tried to carve, no matter how crudely, on the wall of that final oblivion, in the tongue of the human spirit, "Kilroy was here."

That is primarily, and I think in its essence, all that we ever really tried to do. And I believe we will all agree that we failed. That what we made never quite matched and never will match the shape, the dream of perfection which we inherited and which drove us and will continue to drive us, even after each failure, until anguish frees us and the hand falls still at last.

Maybe it's just as well that we are doomed to fail, since, as long as we do fail and the hand continues to hold blood, we will try again; where, if we ever did attain the dream, match the shape, scale that ultimate peak of perfection, nothing would remain but to jump off the other side of it into suicide. Which would not only deprive us of our American right to existence, not only inalienable but harmless too, since by our standards, in our culture, the pursuit of art is a peaceful hobby like breeding Dalmatians, it would leave refuse in the form of, at best indigence and at worst downright crime resulting from unexhausted energy, to be scavenged and removed and disposed of. While this way, constantly and steadily occupied by, obsessed with, immersed in trying to do the impossible, faced always with the failure which we decline to recognize and accept, we stay out of trouble, keep out of the way of the practical and busy people who carry the burden of America.

So all are happy—the giants of industry and commerce, the manipulators for profit or power of the mass emotions called government, who carry the tremendous load of geopolitical solvency, the two of which conjoined are America; and the harmless breeders of the spotted dogs (unharmed too, protected, immune in the inalienable right to exhibit our dogs to one another for acclaim, and even to the public too; defended in our right to collect from them at the rate of five or ten dollars for the

Reprinted from *The Saturday Review*, by permission of Random House, Inc., the Author's Literary Estate, and Chatto and Windus Ltd. The text of the original typescript of this address appears in James B. Meriwether, ed., *Essays, Speeches and Public Letters of William Faulkner*. For A *Fable* (1954). Delivered in New York City, January 25, 1955.

special signed editions, and even in the thousands to special fanciers named Picasso or Matisse).

Then something like this happens—like this, here, this afternoon; not just once and not even just once a year. Then that anguished breeder discovers that not only his fellow breeders, who must support their mutual vocation in a sort of mutual desperate defensive confederation, but other people, people whom he had considered outsiders, also hold that what he is doing is valid. And not only scattered individuals who hold his doings valid, but enough of them to confederate in their turn, for no mutual benefit of profit or defense but simply because they also believe it is not only valid but important that man should write on that wall "Man was here also A.D. 1953 or '54 or '55," and so go on record like this this afternoon.

To tell not the individual artist but the world, the time itself, that what he did is valid. That even failure is worthwhile and admirable, provided only that the failure is splendid enough, the dream splendid enough, unattainable enough yet forever valuable enough, since it was of perfection.

So when this happens to him (or to one of his fellows; it doesn't matter which one, since all share the validation of the mutual devotion) the thought occurs that perhaps one of the things wrong with our country is success. That there is too much success in it. Success is too easy. In our country a young man can gain it with no more than a little industry. He can gain it so quickly and easily that he has not had time to learn the humility to handle it with, or even to discover, realize that he will need humility. (1955)

The Meaning of the Hunt

William Faulkner

With two others, the narrator, a twelve-year-old boy, has come to hunt in the Big Woods in the same section Uncle Ike McCaslin, Will Legate, Roth Edmonds, and Walter Ewell have come to the day before.

. . . all three of us now turned like one agreement to walk back home, not together in a bunch because we didn't want to worry or tempt one another, because what we had all three spent this morning doing was no play-acting jest for fun, but was serious, and all three of us was still what we was—that old buck that had to run, not because he was skeered, but because running was what he done the best and was proudest at; and Eagle and the dogs that chased him, not because they hated or feared him, but because that was the thing they done the best and was proudest at; and me and Mister Ernest and Dan, that run him not because we wanted his meat, which would be tough to eat anyhow, or his head to hang on a wall, but because now we could go back and work hard for eleven months making a crop, so we would have the right to come back here next November—all three of us going back home now, peaceful and separate, but still side by side, until next year, next time.

. . . all of a sudden I thought about how maybe planting and working and then harvesting oats and cotton and beans and hay wasn't jest something me and Mister Ernest done three hundred and fifty-one days, to fill in the time until we could come back hunting again, but it was something we had to do, and do honest and good during the three hundred and fifty-one days, to have the right to come back into the big woods and hunt for the other fourteen; and the fourteen days that old buck run in front of dogs wasn't jest something to fill his time until the three hundred and fifty-one when he didn't have to, but the running and the risking in front of guns and dogs was something he had to do for fourteen days to have the right not to be bothered for the other three hundred and fifty-one. And so the hunting and the farming wasn't two different things at all—they was jest the other side of each other. . . . (1955)

Faulkner's Commentary on Go Down, Moses

Frederick L. Gwynn and Joseph L. Blotner

Q. I have another question about "The Bear." In the final scene of "The Bear," Boon is sitting under the tree with the squirrels, doing something with his shotgun. It's not clear to me whether he is destroying his shotgun or trying to put it back together.

A. It had jammed. He was trying to get a jammed shell out to make it fire, and he didn't want anybody else to shoot the squirrels. He was under the tree where the squirrels couldn't get out of it and he didn't want anybody else to shoot the squirrels until he could get his gun fixed. . . .

Q. Sir, a fyce plays a minor part in "Was" and in a few more of your stories, I believe. Well, is a fyce just a mongrel or is he an out-of-the-ordinary mongrel that you might equate with the primitive?

A. He is—in our Mississippi jargon, he is any small dog, usually—he was a fox or rat terrier at one time that has gotten mixed up with hound, with bird-dog, everything else, but any small dog in my country is called a fyce.

Reprinted from Frederick L. Gwynn and Joseph L. Blotner, eds., *Faulkner in the University,* by permission of The University Press of Virginia.

Q. Can we look upon him as representing the primitive, such as the bear and the forest?

A. No, he's the—in a way, the antithesis of the bear. The bear represented the obsolete primitive. The fyce represents the creature who has coped with environment and is still on top of it, you might say. That he has—instead of sticking to his breeding and becoming a decadent degenerate creature, he has mixed himself up with the good stock where he picked and chose. And he's quite smart, he's quite brave. All's against him is his size. But I never knew a fyce yet that realized that he wasn't big as anything else he ever saw, even a bear. . . .

Q. Sir, in "Delta Autumn," in the thoughts of Ike McCaslin, when he's talking to the colored girl, you write, "Maybe in a thousand or two thousand years in America, but not now, not now." I was wondering how you might apply that to the present-day conditions that have happened since the writing of the story, with the Supreme Court decision and what not.

A. He used "a thousand or two thousand years" in his despair. He had seen a condition which was intolerable, which shouldn't be but it was, and he was saying in effect that this must be changed, this cannot go on, but I'm too old to do anything about it, that maybe in a thousand years somebody will be young enough and strong enough to do something about it. That was all he meant by the numbers. But I think that he saw, as everybody that thinks, that a condition like that is intolerable, not so much intolerable to man's sense of justice, but maybe intolerable to the condition, that any country has reached the point where if it is to endure, it must have no inner conflicts based on a wrong, a basic human wrong. . . .

Q. Sir, in your story "The Bear," why did Boon kill Sam Fathers?

A. Because Sam asked him to. Sam's life had finished then. He was an old man, he was sick, and Sam at that point represented his whole race. The white man had dispossessed the whole race, they had nothing left, and Sam was old, he was weak and sick. That was the Greek conception, and Sam knew that Boon and this little boy who was too young to have used the knife or whatever it was, would defend Sam's right to die, and would approve of the fact that Boon, the instrument, was willing to kill Sam, but Sam was done with life, and he wanted that done, and Boon was the servant that did it. . . .

Q. Mr. Faulkner, do you look on Ike McCaslin as having fulfilled his destiny, the things that he learned from Sam Fathers and from the other men as in his—when he was twelve to sixteen? Do you feel that they stood him in good stead all the way through his life?

A. I do, yes. They didn't give him success but they gave him something a lot more important, even in this country. They gave him serenity, they gave him what would pass for wisdom—I mean wisdom as contradistinct from the schoolman's wisdom of education. They gave him that.

Q. And was—did he ever have any children? Was he able to pass on this—

A. No, no children.

Q. —that had been transmitted to him?

A. In a way, every little eight- or ten-year-old boy was his son, his child, the ones that he taught how to hunt. He had passed on what he had. He was not trying to tell them how to slay animals, he was trying to teach them what he knew of respect for whatever your lot in life is, that if your lot is to be a hunter, to slay animals, you slay the animals with the nearest approach you can to dignity and to decency. . . .

Q. In "The Bear," Mr. Faulkner, was there a dog, a real Lion?

A. Yes, there was. I can remember that dog—I was about the age of that little boy—and he belonged to our pack of bear and deer dogs, and he was a complete individualist. He didn't love anybody. The other dogs were all afraid of him, he was a savage, but he did love to run the bear. Yes, I remember him quite well. He was mostly airedale, he had some hound and Lord only knows what else might have been in him. He was a tremendous big brute—stood about that high, must have weighed seventy-five or eighty pounds.

Q. In any bear hunt that Lion participated in, did he ever perform a heroic action like the one in the story?

A. No, not really. There's a case of the sorry, shabby world that don't quite please you, so you create one of your own, so you make Lion a little braver than he was, and you make the bear a little more of a bear than he actually was. I am sure that Lion could have done that and would have done it, and it may be at times when I wasn't there to record the action, he did do things like that.

Q. This question is also concerned with "The Bear." In conclusion of the story, Ike McCaslin finds Boon destroying his rifle. Now I was wondering if this incident just showed that Boon could not, shall we say, compete with the mechanical age, or whether this was showing the end of an order, the fact that Lion and old Ben were dead, that the hunters weren't returning to the cabin any more, and the land had been sold to a lumber company.

A. A little of both. It was that Boon, with the mentality of a child, a boy of sixteen or seventeen, couldn't cope not only with the mechanical age but he couldn't cope with any time. Also, to me it underlined the heroic tragedy of the bear and the dog by the last survivor being reduced to the sort of petty comedy of someone trying to patch up a gun in order to shoot a squirrel. That made the tragedy of the dog and the bear a little more poignant to me. That's the sort of *tour de force* that I think the writer's entitled to use. . . .

Q. In "The Bear," Mr. Faulkner, is the possession and destruction of the wilderness a symbolic indication of any sort of corruption in the South, and if this is true, what sort of prognostication does this have for the future and for the South or the country as a whole?

A. Well, of course the destruction of the wilderness is not a phenomenon of the South, you know. That is a change that's going on everywhere, and I think that man progresses mechanically and technically much faster than he does spiritually, that there may be something he could substitute for the ruined wilderness, but he hasn't found that. He spends more time ruining the wilderness than he does finding something to replace it, just like he spends more time producing more people than something good to do with the people or to make better people out of them. That that [?] to me is a sad and tragic thing for the old days, the old times, to go, providing you have the sort of background which a country boy like me had when that was a part of my life. That I don't want it to change, but then that's true of everyone as he grows old. He thinks that the old times were the best times, and he don't want it to change. . . .

Q. Mr. Faulkner, you seem to put so much meaning in the hunt. Could you tell us just why you hunted when you were a little boy, or what meaning the hunt has to you?

A. The hunt was simply a symbol of pursuit. Most of anyone's life is a pursuit of something. That is, the only alternative to life is immobility, which is death. This was a symbolization of the pursuit which is a normal part of anyone's life, while he stays alive, told in terms which were familiar to me and dramatic to me. The protagonist could have been anything else besides that bear. I simply told a story which was a natural, normal part of anyone's life in familiar and to me interesting terms without any deliberate intent to put symbolism in it. I was simply telling something which was in this case the child—the need, the compulsion of the child to adjust to the adult world. It's how he does it, how he survives it, whether he is destroyed by trying to adjust to the adult world or whether despite his small size he does adjust within his capacity. And always to learn something, to learn something of—not only to pursue but to overtake and then to have the compassion not to destroy, to catch, to touch, and then let go because then tomorrow you can pursue again. If you destroy it, what you caught, then it's gone, it's finished. And that to me is sometimes the greater part of valor but always it's the greater part of pleasure, not to destroy what you have pursued. The pursuit is the thing, not the reward, not the gain. . . .

Q. Returning to "The Bear," Mr. Faulkner, why did you put Part V after Part IV?

A. That story was part of a novel. It was—the pursuit of the bear was simply what you might call a dangling clause in the description of that man when he was a young boy. When it was taken from the book and printed as a short story, the publisher, who is very considerate, has a great respect for all work and for mine in particular, he would not have altered one word of that without asking me, and he didn't ask me. If he had told me he was going to print it separately, I would have said, Take this out, this doesn't belong in this as a short story, it's a part of the novel but not part of the story. But rather than to go ahead and do that without asking me—and I wasn't available at that time—he printed it as it was. It doesn't belong with the short story. The way to read that is to skip that when you come to it. . . .

Q. Sir, I'd like some help on understanding what I call the bedroom scene in the fourth section of "The Bear." You made one statement—"She is lost. She was born lost." Could you help me understand what was meant by that?

A. Who does that refer to?

Q. That refers to Ike McCaslin's wife, in that section. . . .

A. Yes, I think I remember now. She—from her background, her tradition, sex was something evil, that it had to be justified by acquiring property. She was ethically a prostitute. Sexually she was frigid. I think what he meant, he knew that there was no warmth that he would ever find from her, no understanding, no chance ever to accept love or return love because she was incapable of it. That's probably what he meant.

Q. And I wondered why she laughed and laughed. . . .

A. She realized then that he was going to give up the land. She married him because she wanted to be chatelaine of a plantation. And then she found he was going to give all that away, and the only revenge she knew was to deny him sexually. That was the only triumph she had. And she was going to make him suffer for that just as much as she could, to get even with him.

Q. So that she intended from the beginning of their marriage to deny him this one thing that he had requested until it was useful in blackmailing—

A. Well, she assumed when they got married that she was going to be chatelaine of a plantation and they would have children. And she was going to be as—according to the rules of the book a good wife to him. She'd still be frigid and cold and a shrew probably but she'd still be a good wife. Then when he was going to throw the plantation away for idealistic folly, all she—the only revenge she had was that. At least he would have no children from her. He'd have no wife from her. And she—

Q. Well, Ike—excuse me.

A. And she hoped that it would make him grieve [?].

Q. Well, Ike says here. . . .

A. Did not mean what?

Q. That he would go back to the land.

A. She must have known that he was not going to retract and take his heritage. Yes, I'm sure she was convinced of that, no matter what he might have said.

Q. Mr. Faulkner, if she had been the kind of wife he needed, and had been able to give him love and companionship and had stuck by him and had children and had a home for him, do you think that his—that he would ever have compromised with his ideals? After all, he had no training, no way of providing for her.

A. I would say, since we are supposing, if she had been that sort of woman, she would have understood his hatred of that condition, she might have been practical enough to say, This is the way we'll do it, we can't abandon these people, but let's do it this way, and he would have said, You're wiser than I, let's try it your way. That's possible, I would like to think that. But he would have stuck to his position, that I will not profit from this which is wrong and sinful.

Q. Sir, one of the most interesting aspects of "The Bear" to me is the conflict between man and the wilderness. I would like to ask you if you intend for the reader to sympathize more with Old Ben in his conflict with the hunters or towards the hunters in their conflict with Old Ben.

A. Well, not "sympathize." I doubt if the writer's asking anyone to sympathize, to choose sides. That is the reader's right. What the writer's asking is compassion, understanding, that change must alter, must happen, and change is going to alter what was. That no matter how fine anything seems, it can't endure, because once it stops, abandons motion, it is dead. It's to have compassion for the anguish that the wilderness itself may have felt by being ruthlessly destroyed by axes, by men who simply wanted to make that earth grow something they could sell for a profit, which brought into it a condition based on an evil like human bondage. It's not to choose sides at all—just to compassionate the good splendid things which change must destroy, the splendid fine things which are a part of man's past too, part of man's heritage too, but they were obsolete and had to go. But that's no need to not feel compassion for them simply because they were obsolete. . . .

Q. Sir, is that what you meant by the ending of this, then—that change must destroy all [goodness]?

A. Change if it is not controlled by wise people destroys sometimes more than it brings. That unless some wise person comes along in the middle of the change and takes charge of it, change can destroy what is irreplaceable. If the reason for the change is base in motive—that is, to clear the wilderness just to make cotton land, to raise cotton on an agrarian economy of peonage, slavery, is base because it's not as good as the wilderness which it replaces. But if in the end that makes more education for more people, and more food for more people, more of the good things of life—I mean by that to give man leisure to use what's up here instead of just leisure to ride around in automobiles, then the—it was worth destroying the wilderness. But if all the destruction of the wilderness does is to give more people more automobiles just to ride around in, then the wilderness was better. . . . (1957–1958)

Boon Hogganbeck

WILLIAM FAULKNER

This account is given by Lucius Priest, a descendant of the McCaslins, who refers to Ike as "Cousin Ike." The actual relationship between Lucius and Ike is unclear.

[Boon's] grandmother had been the daughter of one of old Issetibbeha's Chickasaws who married a white whiskey trader; at times, depending on the depth of his cups, Boon would declare himself to be at least ninety-nine one-hundreths Chickasaw and in fact a lineal royal descendant of old Issetibbeha himself; the next time he would offer to fight any man who dared even intimate that he had one drop of Indian blood in his veins.

He was tough, faithful, brave and completely unreliable; he was six feet four inches tall and weighed two hundred and forty pounds and had the mentality of a child. . . .

In fact, although he was obviously a perfectly normal flesh-and-blood biological result (vide the moments in his cups when he was not merely ready and willing but even eager to fight any man or men either pro or con, depending on how the drink had taken him, for the right to ancestry) and hence he had to have been somewhere during those first nine or ten or eleven years, it was as if Boon had been created whole and already nine or ten or eleven years old, by the three of us, McCaslin-De Spain-Compson, as a solution to a dilemma one day at Major de Spain's hunting camp. . . .

But then, when Boon materialized at the camp one day, full panoplied and already ten or eleven or twelve years old, there were only twenty miles for Major de Spain and General Compson and McCaslin Edmonds and Walter Ewell and old Bob Legate and the half-dozen others who would come and go, to travel. But General Compson, although he had commanded troops not too unsuccessfully as a colonel at Shiloh, and again not too unsuccessfully as a brigadier during Johnston's retreat on Atlanta, was a little short in terrain, topography, and would promptly get lost ten minutes after he left camp (the mule he preferred to ride would have brought him back at any time but, not only a paroled Confederate general but a Compson too, he declined to accept counsel or advice from a mule), so as soon as the last hunter was in from the morning's drive, everyone would take turns blowing a horn until General Compson at last got in. Which was satisfactory, anyway served, until General Compson's hearing began to fail too. Until finally one afternoon Walter Ewell and Sam Fathers, who was half Negro and half Chickasaw Indian, had to track him down and camp in the woods with him all night, facing Major de Spain with the alternative of either forbidding him to leave the tent or expelling him from the club, when lo, there was Boon Hogganbeck, already a giant, even at ten or eleven bigger than General Compson, whose nurse he became—a waif, who seemed to have nothing and know nothing but his name; even Cousin Ike is not sure whether it was McCaslin Edmonds or Major de Spain who found Boon first where whoever bore him had abandoned him. All Ike knows—remembers—is that Boon was already there, about twelve years old, out at old Carothers McCaslin's place, where McCaslin Edmonds was already raising Ike as if he was his father and now and without breaking stride took over Boon too as though he had been Boon's father also, though at that time McCaslin Edmonds himself was only thirty.

Anyway, as soon as Major de Spain realized that he must either expel General Compson from the club, which would be difficult, or forbid him to leave the camp, which would be impossible, and hence he must equip General Compson with something resembling a Boon Hogganbeck, there was the Boon Hogganbeck, produced either by McCaslin Edmonds or perhaps by both of them—Edmonds and De Spain himself—in simultaneous crisis. Ike could remember that: the loading of the bedding and guns and food into the wagon on the fourteenth of November, with Tennie's Jim (grandfather of this Bobo Beauchamp of whom you will hear presently) and Sam Fathers and Boon (he, Ike, was only five or six then; another four or five years before he would be ten and could make one also) and McCaslin himself riding ahead on the horse, to the camp where each morning Boon would follow General Compson on a second mule until by simple force probably, since at twelve Boon was already bigger than his charge, Boon would compel him to the right direction in time to reach camp before dark.

Thus General Compson made a woodsman of Boon despite himself, you might say, in simple self-defense. But even eating at the same table and ranging the same woods and sleeping in the same rain even with Walter Ewell never made a marksman of him; one of the camp's favorite stories was about Boon's shooting, told by Walter Ewell: of being on a stand where he had left Boon (old General Compson had gone to his fathers at last—or to whatever bivouac old soldiers of that war, blue or gray either, probably insisted on going to since probably no place would suit them for anything resembling a permanent stay—and now Boon was a regular hunter like anybody else) and of hearing the hounds and realising that the deer was going to cross at Boon's stand, then of hearing the five shots from Boon's ramshackle pump gun (General Compson had bequeathed it to him; it had never been in the best condition while Compson owned it and Walter said his real surprise was that the gun had fired even twice without jamming, let alone five times) and then Boon's voice across the woods between them: "God damn! Yonder he goes! Head him! Head him!" And how he—Walter—hurried across to Boon's stand and found the five exploded shells on the ground and not ten paces away the prints of the running buck which Boon had not even touched. . . . (1962)

Other Versions of "The Bear"

Criticism based on a close comparison of texts has recently come under attack; often such collation is seen as pedantic and fruitless. But a short time ago an examination of the Mark Twain papers demonstrated that Twain had never composed "The Mysterious Stranger"; rather, an editor had combined selected fragments of his writing after his death to "make" the book. Perhaps in the same spirit of inquiry, critics have examined the various texts of "The Bear" in order to determine through textual changes something of Faulkner's evolving art: such an examination is the closest we can come to seeing Faulkner in his workshop. The two significant earlier versions of "The Bear"—"Lion: A Story" from Harper's Monthly Magazine, *CLXXII (December 1935), 67–77, and "The Bear" from* Saturday Evening Post, *CCXIV (May 9, 1942), 30–31, 74, 76–77—were reprinted in the first edition of this text (New York, 1964), pp. 132–164. [Page numbers in brackets refer to pages in this volume.]*

The Growth of "The Bear"

Edward M. Holmes

. . . The themes of *Go Down, Moses* attain their most explicit statement, regardless of the confusion attendant upon the symbols and allegory, in "The Bear" II,[1] which also, owing to its stemming from two short stories

Reprinted from Edward M. Holmes, *Faulkner's Twice-Told Tales: His Re-Use of His Material*, by permission of Mouton & Co., Publishers.

[1] "The Bear" II is the final version, pp. 5–88 above—Eds.

rather than, as is more usual, one, happens to be one of the more complicated instances in the book of re-used material. The many additions, the entire section Four, for example, and the changes from "Quentin" or "I" to "Ike", and from "father" to "MacCaslin Edmonds", are so obvious as scarcely to require mention in the evolution of a tale from two short stories to one novelette. Yet there are details, or the lack of them, especially in the predecessors to "The Bear" II, that are worth pointing out.

The sharp contrasts of style observed in some of the re-used material already discussed seem not so readily apparent here, despite Mr. O'Connor's feeling that "The Bear" I is told in an idyllic, almost pastoral mood (*The Tangled Fire*, pp. 130, 134). Yet a certain casual quality does enter the first-person telling of "Lion", a tone which is absent from all versions of "The Bear": "So this story might as well begin with whiskey too", says Quentin Compson at the close of the first paragraph.[2] The comparable passage in "The Bear" II reads: "Thus it seemed to him on this December morning not only natural but actually fitting that this should have begun with whiskey" [p. 6].[3] Toward the close of "Lion" we read:

> This is how Lion's death affected the two people who loved him most—if you could have called Boon's feeling for him, for anything, love. And I suppose you could, since they say you always love that which causes you suffering. Or maybe Boon did not consider being clawed by a bear suffering.
>
> Major de Spain never went back again. But we did; he made us welcome to go; it seemed to please him when we went. Father and the others who had been there that time would talk about it, about how maybe if they could just persuade him to go back once. . . . But he would not; he was almost sharp when he refused. (*Harper's*, CLXXII, p. 76)

But "The Bear" II is told in a more formal narrative manner, with that detail that Faulkner almost habitually added, apparently, when he re-used material:

> He went back to camp one more time before the lumber company moved in and began to cut the timber. Major de Spain himself never saw it again. But he made them welcome to use the house and hunt the land whenever they liked, and in the winter following the last hunt when Sam Fathers and Lion died, General Compson and Walter Ewell invented a plan to corporate themselves, the old group, into a club and lease the camp and the hunting privileges of the woods—an invention doubtless of the somewhat childish old General but actually worthy of Boon Hogganbeck himself. Even the boy, listening, recognized it for the subterfuge it was: to change the leopard's spots when they could not alter the leopard, a baseless and illusory hope to which even

[2] "Lion", *Harper's*, CLXXII (December 1935), p. 67.
[3] Page numbers in brackets refer to pages in this volume—Eds.

> McCaslin seemed to subscribe for a while, that once they had persuaded Major de Spain to return to the camp he might revoke himself, which even the boy knew he would not do. And he did not [p. 79].

"The Bear" I, perhaps contrary to expectation, seems at its opening more immediate and more dramatic than does the first-person narrative of "Lion". It begins:

> He was ten. But it had already begun, long before that day when at last he wrote his age in two figures and he saw for the first time the camp where his father and Major de Spain and old General Compson and the others spent two weeks each November and two weeks again each June.[4]

Whereas "Lion" starts with:

> A good part of the lives of dogs—I mean hunting dogs, bear and deer dogs—is whiskey. That is, the men who love them, who hunt hard the hard-hunting and tireless and courageous dogs, drink hard too. (*Harper's*, CLXXII, p.67)

There is, I believe, sound aesthetic reason for these differences, for "Lion" does not attempt to grapple so earnestly, so explicitly, or perhaps so profoundly, with moral themes as do the later stories. But it will not do to emphasize this idea, for "Lion", although more nearly an unadulterated hunting story than the others, does confront us with the death of the heroic hunting dog, the wild and courageous spirit of the hunt, and with the image of the now clearly undisciplined Boon, claiming live squirrels as his private possession. The reader, therefore, tends to think of "Lion" in connection with the destruction-of-the-wilderness theme; of "The Bear" I as dramatizing Ike's initiation into the primitive virtues engendered by the wilderness; of "The Bear" II as merging these and, in section Four, linking them to the theme of the white man's guilt (or if one wishes, the injustice to the Negro) with which much of the rest of *Go Down, Moses* is concerned.

Yet even in "Lion" the reader can find a hint of themes as yet undeveloped which later are treated in *Go Down, Moses*. Boon Hogganbeck, Faulkner writes, has "a bad name among Negroes", but despite this fact, Ad—later to become Ash—talks to Boon when Lion is concerned "just as if Ad were another white man". Furthermore, Boon lets him do so (*Harper's*, CLXXII, 68). By his mere presence Lion, the spirit of the hunt—courageous, amoral, intelligent—paradoxically perhaps enables other hunters, at least in the wilds, to transcend the barriers of race or class. This circumstance or condition of the two men is one of the few elements in "Lion" that help prepare for and make sense of Boon's behavior at the end, long after Lion is dead. In that final scene, which,

[4] "The Bear", *Saturday Evening Post*, May 9, 1942, p. 30; as reprinted in *The Best American Short Stories*, 1943, ed. Martha Foley (Boston, 1943), p. 70.

thanks to more thorough preparation, gains considerable strength later when it re-appears in "The Bear" II, Faulkner writes that

> he [Boon] was living, as always, in the moment; nothing on earth—not Lion, not anything in the past—mattered to him except his helpless fury with his broken gun. (*Harper's*, CLXXII, p.77)

Lion himself is not necessarily beyond being affected by the wilderness, although it is difficult to conceive of its teaching him anything other than the acquired skills of the hunt:

> now and then Lion would open his eyes as if he was listening to the woods for a moment before closing his eyes again, remembering the woods again or seeing that they were still there. Maybe he was, because he waited until dark before he died. (*Harper's*, CLXXII, p. 76)

Through the boy's father, "The Bear" I states so explicitly its theme of the wilds and the activities of the wilds as the teachers of the primitive virtues, and of other virtues besides—"honor and pride and pity and justice and courage and love"—that the fact calls for no discussion here. Possibly it is worth noting, however, that the other portion of the wilderness theme, the destruction of it by man—specifically, now, non-hunting man—also enters "The Bear" I, for Faulkner writes of

> the doomed wilderness whose edges were being constantly worn and punily gnawed at by men with axes and plows who feared it because it was wilderness, man myriad and nameless even to one another . . . (*Best American Short Stories* 1943, p. 71)

And in this story too Faulkner makes a fleeting comment on race and brotherhood that just barely foreshadows what is to come in "The Bear", II: "It [the wilderness] was of the men, not white nor black nor red but men . . ." Then only a few lines later, the boy, who, if he is not Ike McCaslin, will in "The Bear" II become Ike McCaslin, squats "in the blazing firelight as Tennie's Jim [his Negro cousin] squatted, . . ." (*Best American Short Stories* 1943, pp. 83, 84). . . .

The Relationship Between Part IV and the Rest of "The Bear"

Irving Howe

In 1955 William Faulkner printed his final version of "The Bear," without Part IV, in Big Woods. *Irving Howe along with many other critics have found this a weaker text than the base text of 1942.*

. . . In its more successful half, "The Bear" is primarily a story about a group of Southern men and a young boy who go off on a yearly hunt—a story that can hardly be grasped if taken in narrowly realistic terms, but cannot be grasped at all if those terms are dismissed. Symbolic elements pertaining to myth, anthropology, and psychology are surely present in the story, and it needs no more than the usual second-hand acquaintance with *The Golden Bough* to notice that the bear lends itself to totemic uses. That such elements are present in "The Bear" is clear enough, Faulkner himself referring to it as a "pageant-rite." But the sophisticated reader, he more than others, is in danger of neglecting the literal surface of the story, the story as a performance, in behalf of the meanings that can be dredged up from it. He is in danger of forgetting that the bear, like the white whale, is a "real" animal, not a specter of allegory, and in this case an animal with fur and four legs. An important critical issue is at stake here: that the critic should be loyal to the surface of the text, persist in treating it in its own terms as much as he possibly can, and "convert" to other terms only when and if there is no alternative. . . .

If Section IV were omitted, "The Bear" would profit in several ways: the narrative would flow more evenly toward its climax; there would be a more pleasing unity of tone; and the meaning, never reduced to the brittle terms of Isaac's political and moral speculations, would be allowed to rest in a fine implication. Since Section IV is, so to speak, contained in the previous three, it might be desirable for the story to resolve itself on the plane of the implicit, with the ritual in the wilderness suggesting, but no more than suggesting, its relation to the life of Yoknapatawpha. And in fact, this is pretty much the way Faulkner first printed "The Bear" in its magazine version.

The loss, however, would also be considerable. What Section IV now does is to give the story social and historical density, the ceremony in the forest reverberating into the life of the town; it provides an abrasive disruption of the idyllic nostalgia previously accumulated; and it keeps Faulkner's meaning from the confinements of abstract morality. As we now have it, "The Bear" comes to seem a dialectically richer, more troubling work that demands greater energy and attention from its readers than did the earlier version—perhaps a less perfect work but also a more interesting one.

But whatever the justification for the presence of Section IV, there can hardly be any doubt that as a piece of writing it is much inferior to the other parts. The first three sections, a chanted recital of the "pageant-rite" in the wilderness, comprise one of Faulkner's major achievements in style, a style at once richly chromatic and singularly direct. Of Faulkner's more important literary techniques—the stream-of-consciousness in which the character's voice takes over and the stream-of-eloquence in which an anonymous voice assumes control—"The Bear" is second only to "Red Leaves" as a happy example of the latter. The voice in "The Bear" is that of an observer who knows all the actors, Isaac McCaslin and Sam Fathers and Major DeSpain; more important, it is the voice not so much of an individual as of the community itself, the collective conscience of Yoknapatawpha. First heard in *Light in August* it pervades most of Faulkner's later books, its very pitch and inflection conveying moral judgment.

Section IV, by contrast, represents a sharp drop in both composition and content. Its style is also a style of eloquence, but often inflated to Confederate rhetoric. The dialogue between McCaslin and Edmonds, fanciful, flowery and pretentious, is of a kind seldom heard on heaven or earth. As sheer narrative, the section breaks down several times, forcing the reader to fumble his way through cryptic references and opaque prose. It may be urged that similar demands are made by other works of literature, and this is true; the only question, here as elsewhere, is whether the reward is worth the labor. Whenever Faulkner troubles to dramatize Section IV, as in Isaac's visit to the freed slave Fonsiba, the writing is unforgettably strong; but the bulk of the section is merely an exchange of sentiments, frequently interesting but slowed and stopped by passages of turgidity. The hunt sections present an image and the commissary section records a discourse. The two are related somewhat like poem and paraphrase; and while there is no need to suppose that in literature discourse is always inferior to image, for Faulkner something of the sort is usually true.

At the end "The Bear" returns to its opening style: "He went back to the camp once more . . ." Just as the story began with a glimpse of the bear prowling through the wilderness, so it ends with an equally powerful vignette: Boon Hogganbeck, the man who killed the bear, sitting beneath a tree, his gun dismembered and his mind shriveled by hysteria. Nothing in Section IV—neither the entries in the family record-book nor the eloquence of Isaac McCaslin as he castigates the sins of the South and praises the virtues of the Negroes—nothing can equal these images: the bear in the forest, the man beneath the tree. Perhaps it is the point and purpose of the story to show that nothing can.

The Cultural Roots of "The Bear"

Dimensions of folklore, myth, and anthropology are all apparent in "The Bear" and may provide, directly or indirectly, the soil from which it grew. Cash gives here an overview of the Southern culture, followed by experiences of initiation, hunting stories and tall tales, and the use of myths endemic to American culture and art. Some synthesis of primary attitudes and materials as they relate to "The Bear" is attempted in each of the final two selections.

The Mind and Character of the South

W. J. Cash

The Southerner, however, was primarily a direct product of the soil, as the peasant of Europe is the direct product of the soil. His way of life was his, not—John Crowe Ransom to the contrary notwithstanding—as one "considered and authorized," not because he himself or his ancestors or his class had deliberately chosen it as against something else, not even because it had been tested through centuries and found to be good, but because, given his origins, it was the most natural outcome of the conditions in which he found himself.

The whole difference can be summed up in this: that, though he galloped to hounds in pursuit of the fox precisely as the squire did, it was for quite other reasons. It was not that hoary and sophisticated class tradition dictated it as the proper sport for gentlemen. It was not even, in the first place, that he knew that English squires so behaved, and hungered to identify himself with them by imitation, though this of course was to play a great part in confirming and fixing the pattern. It was simply and primarily for the same reason that, in his youth and often into late manhood, he ran spontaneous and unpremeditated foot-races, wrestled, drank Gargantuan quantities of raw whisky, let off wild yells, and hunted the possum:—because the thing was already in his mores when he emerged from the backwoods, because on the frontier it was the obvious thing to do, because he was a hot, stout fellow, full of blood and reared to outdoor activity, because of a primitive and naïve zest for the pursuit in hand.

I do not forget the Virginians and their artificializing influence. I shall have, indeed, presently to report our Southerner as developing a striking self-consciousness and as growing somewhat more complex. But this is what he almost invariably was in the beginning, and what he remained at bottom right down to the end. This simple, rustic figure is the true center from which the Old South proceeded—the frame about which the conditions of the plantation threw up the whole structure of the Southern mind.

Inevitably, then, the dominant trait of this mind was an intense individualism—in its way, perhaps the most intense individualism the world has seen since the Italian Renaissance and its men of "terrible fury." The simple man in general invariably tends to be an individualist. Everywhere and invariably his fundamental attitude is purely personal—and purely self-asserting. . . .

And what is true of the planter is true also, *mutatis mutandis*, for the poorer whites under this plantation order. The farmers and the crackers were in their own way self-sufficient too—as fiercely careful of their prerogatives of ownership, as jealous of their sway over their puny domains, as the grandest lord. No man felt or acknowledged any primary dependence on his fellows, save perhaps in the matter of human sympathy and entertainment—always a pressing one in a wide and lonely land. . . .

And when to that was added the natural effect on the planters of virtually unlimited sway over their bondsmen, and the natural effect on the common whites of the example of these planters, it eventuated in this: that the individualism of the plantation world would be one which, like that of the backcountry before it, would be far too much concerned with bald, immediate, unsupported assertion of the ego, which placed too great stress on the inviolability of personal whim, and which was full of the chip-on-the-shoulder swagger and brag of a boy—one, in brief, of which the essence was the boast, voiced or not, on the part of every Southerner, that he would knock hell out of whoever dared to cross him.

This character is of the utmost significance. For its corollary was the perpetuation and acceleration of the tendency to violence which had grown up in the Southern backwoods as it naturally grows up on all frontiers. Other factors, some of which we shall glance at later on, played their part in perpetuating and elaborating this pattern, too. But none was more decisive than this one. However careful they might be to walk softly, such men as these of the South were bound to come often into conflict. And being what they were—simple, direct, and immensely personal—and their world being what it was—conflict with them could only mean immediate physical clashing, could only mean fisticuffs, the gouging ring, and knife and gun play.

Nor was it only private violence that was thus perpetuated. The Southerner's fundamental approach carried over into the realm of public offenses as well. What the direct willfulness of his individualism demanded, when confronted by a crime that aroused his anger, was immediate satisfaction for itself—catharsis for personal passion in the spectacle of a body dancing at the end of a rope or writhing in the fire—now, within the hour—and not some ponderous abstract justice in a problematic tomorrow. And so, in this world of ineffective social control, the tradition of vigilante action, which normally lives and dies with the frontier, not only survived but grew so steadily that already long before the Civil War and long before hatred for the black man had begun to play any direct part in the pattern (of more than three hundred persons said to have been hanged or burned by mobs between 1840 and 1860, less than ten per cent were Negroes) the South had become peculiarly the home of lynching.

But if I show you Southern individualism as eventuating in violence, if I imply that the pride which was its root was in some sense puerile, I am very far from suggesting that it ought to be held in contempt. For it reached its ultimate incarnation in the Confederate soldier.

To the end of his service this soldier could not be disciplined. He slouched. He would never learn to salute in the brisk fashion so dear to the hearts of the professors of mass murder. His "Cap'n" and his "Gin'ral" were likely to pass his lips with a grin—were charged always with easy, unstudied familiarity. He could and did find it in himself to jeer openly and unabashed in the face of Stonewall Jackson when that austere Presbyterian captain rode along his lines. And down to the final day at Appomattox his officers knew that the way to get him to execute an order without malingering was to flatter and to jest, never to command too brusquely and forthrightly. And yet—and yet—and by virtue of precisely these unsoldierly qualities, he was, as no one will care to deny, one of the world's very finest fighting men.

Allow what you will for *esprit de corps*, for this or for that, the thing that sent him swinging up the slope at Gettysburg on that celebrated, gallant afternoon was before all else nothing more or less than the thing which elsewhere accounted for his violence—was nothing more or less than his conviction, the conviction of every farmer among what was essentially only a band of farmers, that nothing living could cross him and get away with it.

But already, by implication, I have been taking you deep into the territory of a second great Southern characteristic which deserves to be examined thoroughly in its own right. I mean the tendency toward unreality, toward romanticism, and, in intimate relation with that, toward hedonism. And rightly to understand this tendency, we cannot begin better than by returning upon the simple figure which I have posed as the center about which the Southern pattern would be built.

A common impression to the contrary notwithstanding, the simple man in general rarely has any considerable capacity for the real. What is ordinarily taken for realism in him is in fact only a sort of biological pragmatism—an intuitive faculty of the practical, like that exhibited by those astounding wasps and bees celebrated by Jean-Henri Fabre—born of the circumstance that he has nearly everywhere and always been the driven slave of the belly, and confined to the narrow sphere of interests and activities marked out by the struggle for mere animal existence.

Relax that drive a little, let him escape a little from this struggle, and the true tenor of his nature promptly appears: he stands before us, has always stood before us in such circumstances, as a romantic and a hedonist. And this, indeed, inheres in the very terms of the equation. To say that he is simple is to say in effect that he necessarily lacks the complexity of mind, the knowledge, and, above all, the habit of skepticism essential to any generally realistic attitude. It is to say that he is inevitably driven back upon imagination, that his world-construction is bound to be mainly a product of fantasy, and that his credulity is limited only by his capacity for conjuring up the unbelievable. And it is to say also that he is the child-man, that the primitive stuff of humanity lies very close to the surface in him, that he likes naïvely to play, to expand his ego, his senses, his emotions, that he will accept what pleases him and reject what does not, and that in general he will prefer the extravagant, the flashing, and the brightly colored—in a word, that he displays the whole catalogue of qualities we mean by romanticism and hedonism. . . .

Such is the primary picture. But I must not leave the theme without calling your attention specifically to the stimulation of the tendency to violence which these things obviously involved. Nor must I leave it without pointing to two significant patterns which grew up in the closest association with this romanticism and hedonism and served it as channels of discharge.

The first of these is the Southern fondness for rhetoric. A gorgeous, primitive art, addressed to the autonomic system and not to the encephalon, rhetoric is of course dear to the heart of the simple man everywhere. In its purest and most natural form, oratory, it flourishes wherever he for-gathers—and particularly in every new land where bonds are loosed and imagination is vaulting. It flourished over the whole American country in these days of continental expansion, as it has rarely flourished elsewhere at any time.

But in the South, to recapitulate, there was the rising flood of romanticism and hedonism clamoring for expression, and in the South there was the daily impact upon the white man of the example of the Negro, concerning whom nothing is so certain as his remarkable tendency to seize on lovely words, to roll them in his throat, to heap them in redundant profusion one upon another until meaning vanishes and there is nothing left but the sweet, canorous drunkenness of sound, nothing but the play of primitive rhythm upon the secret springs of emotion. Thus rhetoric flourished here far beyond even its American average; it early became a passion—and not only a passion but a primary standard of judgment, the *sine qua non* of leadership. The greatest man would be the man who could best wield it.

But to speak of the love of rhetoric, of oratory, is at once to suggest the love of politics. The two, in fact, were inseparable. Hand in hand they emerged from the frontier tradition, flourished over the swelling territory of the young Republic of the West, and grew into romantic Southern passions. . . .

. . . running counter, as we have seen, to the stream of its time, and, above all, running counter to the moral notions of that time in embracing slavery at the hour when the rest of the West was decisively giving it up, [the South] had to stand against the whole weight of the world's question and even of the world's frown.

And, worst of all, there was the fact that the South itself definitely shared in these moral notions—in its secret heart always carried a powerful and uneasy sense of the essential rightness of the nineteenth century's position on slavery. The evangelical religious sects had all begun by denouncing it, and were still muttering over it as late as the early 1830's. Of the 130 abolition societies established before 1827 by Lundy, the forerunner of Garrison, more than a hundred, with four-fifths of the total membership, were in the South. And in the days of their sway the old colonial gentry had been so disturbed by the institution that numbers of them had followed the lead of Christopher Gadsden of South Carolina and Thomas Jefferson in pronouncing it an insufferable crime. In the State of Virginia itself, as is well known, they had twice come close to abolishing it.

This Old South, in short, was a society beset by the specters of defeat, of shame, of guilt—a society driven by the need to bolster its morale, to nerve its arm against waxing odds, to justify itself in its own eyes and in those of the world. Hence a large part—in a way, the very largest part—of its history from the day that Garrison began to thunder in Boston is the history of its efforts to achieve that end, and characteristically by means of romantic fictions.

And of all these fictions, the most inevitable and obviously indicated was just that one which we know today as the legend of the Old South—the legend of which the backbone is, of course, precisely the assumption that every planter was in the most rigid sense of the word a gentleman.

Enabling the South to wrap itself in contemptuous superiority, to sneer down the Yankee as low-bred, crass, and money-grubbing, and even to beget in his bourgeois soul a kind of secret and envious awe, it was a nearly perfect defense-mechanism. And the stage was magnificently set for its acceptance. For the Yankee, accustomed by long habit and the myopia usual in such cases to thinking of the South purely in terms of its nearest and for so many years most important part, Virginia, had the association of plantation and aristocrat fixed in his mind with axiomatic force; he invariably assumed the second term of the equation when he thought of the first. And what was true of the Yankee was equally true of the world in general, which received the body of its impressions of the South directly from him.

Nor was this all. It was for the principal Western nations, as is commonly known, an age of nostalgia. An age in which, underneath all the optimistic trumpeting for the Future, all the solemn self-congratulation on Progress, there was an intense revulsion against the ugliness of the new industrialism and the drab monotony of the new rule of money-bags miscalled democracy, and a yearning back toward the colorfulness and the more or less imaginary glory of the aristocratic and purely agricultural past. An age which, producing such various phenomena of dissatisfaction as the reaction which began with Chateaubriand and flowered in Joseph de Maistre, the romanticism of Byron and the Blue Flower, the bitter tirades of John Ruskin, and the transcendental outpourings of Coleridge, Carlyle, and Emerson, found perhaps the most perfect expression for this part of its spirit in the cardboard medievalism of the Scotch novels. It was an age, in other words, of which it may be truthfully said, I think (and however paradoxical it may seem, I include Yankeedom in the allegation), that it was not only ready but eager to believe in the Southern legend—that it fell with a certain distinct gladness on this last purely agricultural land of the West as a sort of projection ground for its own dreams of a vanished golden time. . . .

Just as plain was the fact that the institution [of slavery] was brutalizing—to white men. Virtually unlimited power acted inevitably to call up, in the coarser sort of master, that sadism which lies concealed in the depths of universal human nature—bred angry impatience and a taste for cruelty for its own sake, with a strength that neither the kindliness I have so often referred to (it continued frequently to exist unimpaired side by side, and in the same man, with this other) nor notions of honor could effectually restrain. And in the common whites it bred a savage and ignoble hate for the Negro, which required only opportunity to break forth in relentless ferocity; for all their rage against the "white-trash" epithet concentrated itself on him rather than on the planters.

There it stood, then—terrible, revolting, serving as the very school of violence, and lending mordant point to the most hysterical outcries of the Yankee.

But the South could not and must not admit it, of course. It must prettify the institution and its own reactions, must begin to boast of its own Great Heart. To have heard them talk, indeed, you would have thought that the sole reason some of these planters held to slavery was love and duty to the black man, the earnest, devoted will not only to get him into heaven but also to make him happy in this world. He was a child whom somebody had to look after. More, he was in general, and despite an occasional spoiled Nat Turner, a grateful child—a contented, glad, loving child. Between the owner and the owned there was everywhere the most tender and beautiful relationship.

Mrs. Stowe did not invent the figure of Uncle Tom, nor did Christy invent that of Jim Crow—the banjo-picking, heel-flinging, hi-yi-ing happy jack of the levees and the cotton fields. All they did was to modify them a little for their purposes. In essentials, both were creations of the South—defense-mechanisms, answers to the Yankee and its own doubts, projections from its own mawkish tears and its own mawkish laughter over the black man, incarnations of its sentimentalized version of slavery. And what is worth observing also is that the Negro, with his quick, intuitive understanding of what is required of him, and his remarkable talents as a mime, caught them up and bodied them forth so convincingly that his masters were insulated against all question as to their reality—were enabled to believe in them as honestly as they believed in so many other doubtful things.

But there was another factor which was perhaps even more important for the growth of sentimentality than this: the influence of the presence of the Negro in increasing the value attaching to Southern woman. For, as perpetuator of white superiority in legitimate line, and as a creature absolutely inaccessible to the males of the inferior group, she inevitably became the focal center of the fundamental pattern of Proto-Dorian pride.

Nor, in this connection, must we overlook the specific role played by the Negro woman. Torn from her tribal restraints and taught an easy complaisance for commercial reasons, she was to be had for the taking. Boys on and about the plantation inevitably learned to use her, and having acquired the habit, often continued it into manhood and even after marriage. For she was natural, and could give herself up to passion in a way impossible to wives inhibited by Puritanical training. And efforts to build up a taboo against miscegenation made little real progress. I do not mean to imply, certainly, that it was universal. There were many men in the South who rigidly abstained from such liaisons, and scorned those who indulged....

The South's perpetual need for justifying its career, and the will to shut away more effectually the vision of its mounting hate and brutality toward the black man, entered into the equation also and bore these people yet further into the cult of the Great Southern Heart. The Old South must be made not only the happy country but the happy country especially for the Negro. The lash? A lie, sir; it had never existed. The only bonds were those of tender understanding, trust, and loyalty. And to prove it, here about us in this very hour of new freedom and bitter strife are hundreds of worn-out Uncle Toms and black mammies still clinging stubbornly to the old masters who can no longer feed them, ten thousand Jim Crows still kicking their heels and whooping for the smile of a white man. Such is the Negro, sir, when he is not corrupted by meddling fools. Hate him? My good friend, we love him dearly—and we alone, for we alone know him.

Do I again seem to satirize them for sniveling hypocrites? Then I must assure you once more that they were not. They believed in their professions here more fully than they had ever done. And they did love the thing, compounded of one part fact and three parts fiction and the black man's miming, which subsisted in their minds under the denomination of the Good Negro.

Lastly, the increased centrality of woman, added up with the fact that miscegenation, though more terrifying than it had been even in the Old South, showed little tendency to fall off despite efforts to build up standards against it, served to intensify the old interest in gyneolatry, and to produce yet more florid notions about Southern Womanhood and Southern Virtue, and so to foster yet more precious notions of modesty and decorous behavior for the Southern female to live up to. . . .

This analysis might be carried much farther. But the book is already too long, and so I think I shall leave it at this. The basic picture of the South is here, I believe. And it was that I started out to set down.

Proud, brave, honorable by its lights, courteous, personally generous, loyal, swift to act, often too swift, but signally effective, sometimes terrible, in its action—such was the South at its best. And such at its best it remains today, despite the great falling away in some of its virtues. Violence, intolerance, aversion and suspicion toward new ideas, an incapacity for analysis, an inclination to act from feeling rather than from thought, an exaggerated individualism and a too narrow concept of social responsibility, attachment to fictions and false values, above all too great attachment to racial values and a tendency to justify cruelty and injustice in the name of those values, sentimentality and a lack of realism—these have been its characteristic vices in the past. And, despite changes for the better, they remain its characteristic vices today.

In the coming days, and probably soon, it is likely to have to prove its capacity for adjustment far beyond what has been true in the past. And in that time I shall hope, as its loyal son, that its virtues will tower over and conquer its faults and have the making of the Southern world to come. But of the future I shall venture no definite prophecies. It would be a brave man who would venture them in any case. It would be a madman who would venture them in face of the forces sweeping over the world in the fateful year of 1940.

The Pattern of Initiation

MIRCEA ELIADE

Everywhere one meets with mysteries of initiation, and everywhere, even in the most archaic societies, they include the symbolism of a death and a new birth. We cannot here undertake a historical analysis of initiation —such as might enable us to elucidate the relations between this and that cultural structure and the types of initiation—but let us retain at least certain characteristic features that are common to the majority of these secret ceremonies.

(1) Everywhere the mystery begins with the separation of the neophyte from his family, and a "retreat" into the forest. In this there is already a symbolisation of death; the forest, the jungle and the darkness symbolise "the beyond," the Shades. In certain places it is believed that a tiger comes and carries the candidates into the jungle on its back; the wild animal incarnates the mythical Ancestor, the Master of the initiation who conducts the adolescents to the Shades. In other places the neophyte is supposed to be swallowed by a monster—an initiatory motif that will claim our attention later on: for the moment we are concerned with the symbolism of darkness. In the belly of the monster it is cosmic Night; this is the embryonic mode of existence, both upon the plane of the cosmos and on the plane of human life.

(2) In many regions, there is a hut for initiations in the bush. It is there that young candidates undergo a part of their ordeals and are instructed in the secret traditions of the tribe. And the initiation-cabin symbolises the maternal womb.[1] The death of the neophyte signifies a

[1] R. Thurnwald, "Primitive Initiations- und Wiedergeburtsriten," p. 393. See also Frazer, *Spirits of the Corn,* I, pp. 225ff.

regression to the embryonic state, but this must not be understood only in terms of human physiology but also, and chiefly, in cosmological terms; the fœtal condition is equivalent to a temporary regression into the *virtual,* or precosmic mode of being before "the dawn of the first day" as the Karadjeri say. We shall have an opportunity to return to this multivalent symbol of a new birth expressed in terms of gestation. For the present, let us add this: the candidate's regression to the prenatal stage is meant to render him contemporary with the creation of the world. He now lives no longer in the maternal womb as he did before his biological birth, but in the cosmic Night and in expectation of the "dawn"—that is, of the Creation. To become a new man, he has to relive the cosmology.

(3) Other rituals throw light upon the symbolism of the initiatory death. Among certain peoples, the candidates are buried or laid out in newly dug graves. They are either covered with branches, and remain motionless like the dead; or they are rubbed with a white powder to make them look like ghosts. The neophytes also imitate the behaviour of ghosts: they do not use their fingers in eating, but pick up the food directly with the teeth as the souls of the dead are believed to do. Finally, the tortures that they undergo, and which of course have a multitude of meanings, have this one among others: the tortured and mutilated neophyte is supposed to be tortured, dismembered, boiled or grilled by the demon-masters of initiation—that is by the mythic Ancestors. His physical sufferings correspond to the situation of the man who is "eaten" by the demonic wild animal, is cut to pieces between the jaws of that initiatory monster and is digested in his belly. The initiates' mutilations, too, are charged with a symbolism of death. The majority of those mutilations come under the lunar deities. Now, the Moon disappears—that is, dies—periodically, to be born again three nights later; and this lunar symbolism stresses the idea that death is the first condition of all mystical regeneration.

(4) Besides specific operations—such as circumcision and subincision—and apart from initiatory mutilations (extractions of teeth, amputations of fingers, etc.), there are other external marks of death and resurrection, such as tattooings and scarifications. As for the symbolism of the mystical rebirth, it presents itself in many forms. The candidates are given new names which for the future are to be their real names. In certain tribes, the young initiates are deemed to have forgotten all their previous lives; immediately after initiation they are fed like little children, led by the hand and taught how to behave in every way, as though they were babies. In the bush, they generally learn a new language, or at least a secret vocabulary known only to the initiates. Thus, we see, at an initiation everything begins anew. *Incipit vita nova.* Sometimes the symbolism of the "second birth" is expressed in concrete gestures. Among

some Bantu peoples the boy who is to be circumcised is the object of a ceremony known explicitly as "being born anew."[2] The father sacrifices a ram; and three days later he envelops the child in the animal's stomach-membrane and in its skin. Before being thus attired, the child has to climb into the bed beside his mother and cry like a new-born infant. He remains in the ram's skin for three days and, on the fourth, the father cohabits with his wife. Among these same people, the dead are buried in rams' skins and in the embryonic position. We will say no more here about the symbolism of the mystical rebirth for which one is ritually dressed in the skin of an animal—a symbolism that is attested both in ancient Egypt and in India.[3]

(5) Finally, we must say a few words about another motif which appears in a great many initiations, and not always in the most primitive societies. It concerns the injunction to kill a man. Here, for instance, is what happens among the Papuan Koko.[4] The candidate has first to undergo ordeals analogous to those of any other initiation—prolonged fasting, solitude, tortures, the revelation of the bull-roarer and traditional instruction. But in the end they say to him: "Now you have seen the Spirit, and you are a real man. In order to prove that in your own eyes, you must slay a man." Head-hunting, and certain forms of cannibalism, are parts of the same initiatory schema. Before pronouncing a moral judgment upon these customs, one should remember this—that to kill a man, and eat him or preserve his head as a trophy, is to imitate the behaviour of the Spirits, or of the gods. Thus, replaced in its own context, the act is a religious one, a ritual. The neophyte must kill a man because the god did so before him; furthermore he, the neophyte, has just been killed by the god during initiation; he has known death. He has to repeat what has been revealed to him: the mystery instituted by the gods in mythic times.

We have alluded to this type of ritual because it has played a very great part in military initiations, above all in proto-historical Europe. The warrior hero is not only a killer of dragons and other monsters; he is also a killer of men. The heroic duel is a sacrifice: war is a decadent ritual in which a holocaust of innumerable victims is offered up to the gods of victory.

[2] M. Canney, "The Skin of Rebirth," in *Man*, July, 1939, No. 91, pp. 104–105; *cf.* C. W. Hobley, *Bantu Beliefs and Magic*, London, 1922, pp. 78ff. and 98ff.

[3] *Cf.* E. A. Wallis Budge, *From Fetish to God in Ancient Egypt*, Oxford, 1934, p. 494; S. Stevenson, *The Rites of the Twice-born*, London, 1920, pp. 33, 40, etc.

[4] E. W. P. Chinnery and W. N. Beaver, "Notes on the Initiation Ceremony of the Koko; Papua" in *Journal of the Royal Anthropological Institute*, No. 45, 1915 (pp. 69–78), especially pp. 76ff.

An Indian Boy's Initiation into Manhood in the Omaha Tribe

A. C. Fletcher and F. LaFlesche

In the ceremony of cutting the hair the priest in charge gathered a tuft from the crown of the boy's head, tied it, then cut it off and laid it away in a parfleche case, which was kept as a sacred repository, singing as he cut the lock a ritual song explanatory of the action. The severing of the lock was an act that implied the consecration of the life of the boy to Thunder, the symbol of the power that controlled the life and death of the warrior—for every man had to be a warrior in order to defend the home and the tribe. The ritual song which followed the cutting of the lock indicated the acceptance of the offering made; that is, the life of the warrior henceforth was under the control of the Thunder to prolong or to cut short at will. . . .

From this ritual song we learn that the lock laid away in the sacred case in care of the Thunder priest symbolically was sent to the Thunder god dwelling "far above on high," who was ceremonially addressed as "Grandfather"—the term of highest respect in the language. The hair of a person was popularly believed to have a vital connection with the life of the body, so that anyone becoming possessed of a lock of hair might work his will on the individual from whom it came. In ceremonial expressions of grief the throwing of locks of hair upon the dead was indicative of the vital loss sustained. In the light of customs that obtained among the people, the hair, under certain conditions, might be said to typify life. Because of the belief in the continuity of life a part could stand for the whole, so in this rite by the cutting off of a lock of the boy's hair and giving it to the Thunder the life of the child was given into the keeping of the god. It is to be noted that later, when the hair was suffered to grow on the boy's head, a lock on the crown of the head was parted in a circle from the rest of the hair and kept constantly distinct and neatly braided. Upon this lock the war honors of the warrior were worn, and it was this lock that was cut from the head of a slain enemy and formed the central object in the triumph ceremonies, for the reason that it preeminently represented the life of the man who had been slain in battle. . . .

The next stage in the life of the Omaha youth was marked by the rite known by the name of No^{n}'zhi^{n}zho^{n}. The literal meaning of the

Reprinted from A. C. Fletcher and F. LaFlesche, *The Omaha Tribe*, by permission of the United States Government Printing Office.

word is "to stand sleeping"; it here implies that during the rite the person stands as if oblivious of the outward world and conscious only of what transpires within himself, his own mind. This rite took place at puberty, when the mind of the child had "become white." This characterization was drawn from the passing of night into day. It should be remembered that in native symbolism night is the mother of day; so the mind of the new-born child is dark, like the night of its birth; gradually it begins to discern and remember things as objects seen in the early dawn; finally it is able to remember and observe discriminatingly; then its mind is said to be "white," as with the clear light of day. At the period when the youth is at the verge of his conscious individual life, is "old enough to know sorrow," it was considered time that through the rite No^{n}′zhi^{n}zho^{n} he should enter into personal relations with the mysterious power that permeates and controls all nature as well as his own existence. . . .

Four days and nights the youth was to fast and pray provided he was physically able to bear so long a strain. No matter how hungry he became, he was forbidden to use the bow and arrows put into his hands by his father when he left his home for this solitary test of endurance. When he fell into a sleep or a trance, if he saw or heard anything, that thing was to become a special medium through which the youth could receive supernatural aid. . . .

When going forth to fast, the youth went silently and unobserved. No one accosted him or gave him counsel or direction. He passed through his experience alone, and alone he returned to his father's lodge. No one asked him of his absence, or even mentioned the fact that he had been away. For four days he must rest, eat little, and speak little. After that period he might go to an old and worthy man who was known to have had a similar vision. After eating and smoking with the old man, when they were quite alone it was permitted the youth to mention that he had had a vision like that of his host, of beast, or bird, or whatever it might have been. Should he speak of his vision before the expiration of the four days, it would be the same as lost to him. After the youth had spoken to the old man it became his duty to travel until he should meet the animal or bird seen in his vision, when he had to slay it, and preserve either the whole or a part of its body. This trophy became the visible sign of his vision and the most sacred of his possessions. He might wear it on his scalp lock or elsewhere on his person during sacred festivals, when going to war, or on some other important occasions. This article has been spoken of by some writers as the man's "personal totem." When the vision came in the form of a cloud or the sound of the thunder, these were symbolized by certain objects or were typified in designs painted on the man or on his belongings.

Some visions were regarded as "lucky," as giving special and helpful advantages to the man. Hawks were "lucky"—they helped to success and prowess in war. Bears, being slow and clumsy, were "not so good," although possessing great recuperative power. The elk was fleet. Snakes were "not good," etc.

How to Catch Bears (Twenyucis's Dream)

FRANK G. SPECK and JESSE MOSES

This "dream" is from a text composed by Nekatcit or Nicodemus Peters, "an Indian sage of the Delaware Nation," and represents his memory of the Bear Sacrifice Ceremony of the Munsee-Mahican branches of the Eastern Woodlands people. It was collected along with other traditions in the Hudson Valley in 1932–1938.

Twenyucis had a dream. Then she told the chief, about the time of the new moon when we celebrate the feast, "I know where the bear is living. So you call these young men to go and bring the bear." The chief went and brought Maxkok. The chief told Maxkok, "Twelve men will go with you. All twelve men of the Big House." Then Twenyucis told Maxkok, "Very near daybreak you will reach there. Then you will see a little creek which runs by. And the tree standing there is an oak. A little hole will be visible. Then the bear's nose will appear as though it comes out of the hole pushed through, his nose icy about the edge. Do not bring him. That is not a good one, it is a smooth bear. You will go on, down past him. Then you will see an elm tree leaning toward the east. Then you will look up. You will see a hole. That is the bear's home. Thence you cannot come back. There, accordingly, you stay all night. And then standing by that tree there, you are all standing around. Then you hit that tree standing up with your bow on that tree. Three times you will hit that tree. You tell the bear, 'I find you.' Then nothing will be heard. Then also you hit that tree three times. Tell the bear, 'I find you.'"

Then they heard him moving about. Once more the tree was hit. He told him. "You we have found." All these men look upward. All saw the bear's head sticking out. Then Maxkok told the bear, "Come down! The chief wants your body." Then that bear climbed down. Then that bear came down on the ground. Then that bear let his head hang down on the ground. "Surely like a dog he was ashamed of something." Maxkok told the bear, "The chief wants your body." Then he told the bear to turn around. Then that bear turned around. Maxkok told this bear, "That's enough." He told him, "Now you go and take the lead." The bear went on ahead. Then these men all came behind him. Then they

Reprinted from Frank G. Speck and Jesse Moses, *The Celestial Bear Comes Down to Earth*, by permission of the Reading Public Museum and Art Gallery.

reached the little creek here. Then that bear lay down. Maxkok told him, "What is wrong? Get up!" Truly that bear did not move. Then Maxkok told these men, "The bear will come to the Big House." Then Maxkok appointed one man. He told him, "So, you will tell the chief that the bear refuses to come. You will go there yourself." Then the chief came there. Then Maxkok told him, "The bear will not come to the Big House. So no more will there be a feast dance. Therefore you will have to kill the bear right here." Then the chief told the bear, "Right here we will have to kill you. We want your body for the Big House." Then that bear got up. His head was still hanging down on the ground, his eyes were closed. The chief hit him. Then he died. He never kicked. Then these men skinned him. Then that Maxkok picked up the bear skin. He gave it to the chief. Then the chief told these men, "Now will we go to the Big House. You men carry the bear. We, with the dead bear, will take the lead. You will come behind."

Then they reached the Big House. Then they went into the Big House, to the middle of the building. Then they lowered that bear on the ground.

Then that chief untied the old bear hide and put the old bear hide down on the ground. Then he wrapped the new hide around the center post, a little below where these False Faces were hanging. Then that chief told the woman and one appointed man, "You cut up that bear. Help these women in the cooking."

Then that chief stood in the center of the house. "Therefore indeed we are thankful, all of us, that God should help us. All of us people, we should help one another, that we do not steal, not to steal your brother's wife."

Then all of us people came into the Big House. A new moon elevated as high as the tree tops sets and goes down. Then the chief stands right in the middle of the floor of the Big House and talks to these people. He tells them, "All be good to one another, do not cheat one's living companions." Then the moon goes down. Then the chief tells them, "Go home, don't be trifling, be good to one another."

Bear Ceremonialism in the Eastern Woodlands Area

A. Irving Hallowell

When a bear is discovered in its winter retreat, or attacked in the woods, it is customary among the Algonkian tribes to dispatch the animal by means of a spear or an axe. Although one might expect that upon the

Reprinted from A. Irving Hallowell, *Bear Ceremonialism in the Northern Hemisphere,* by permission of the author.

introduction of firearms and steel traps, such methods would have fallen into almost immediate decadence, such was not actually the case. Contemporary practice, as well as traditional testimony indicates the use of the more primitive weapons in many instances, even when guns are available. This appears to be due to an inhibition which, although difficult to define except in rather vague terms, seems, nevertheless, to be connected with the whole ideology of which the bear is the focus. It is simply the feeling, conserved from a remote past, perhaps, that in killing a bear the most appropriate weapon for the task must be one of an aboriginal type. The Montagnais-Naskapi as well as the Penobscot, for example, consider it proper to strike the animal with an axe as it emerges from its den. In the old days the latter people say that sometimes the bear would be attacked in the open by three or four hunters, armed only with their knives lashed on canoe poles or staves. After the animal was brought to bay and surrounded, one of them would throw a freshly cut balsam branch into the beast's clutches. This served to confuse the bear who would start to maul it, giving the hunters time to run him through. If the animal turned in one direction a man from the opposite side would attack, and so on until the bear was overcome.

Among the northern Saulteaux there is a specific prohibition upon shooting bears in their winter lairs. Custom prescribes that the animal be killed by a blow on the head with a club as it emerges from its refuge. Among the Cree, "in the old days, the hunters engaged the bear in hand to hand conflicts and clubbed it to death, for the bow and arrows were not considered strong enough weapons." "Even at present," Skinner says, "bears caught in steel traps are sometimes killed by striking them over the head with an axe, although they are usually shot." For the central Algonkian generally, there is traditional information, so Mr. Skinner tells me, to the effect that good sportsmanship dictated that the bear should be attacked only with weapons such as the spear or axe. There was no taboo upon other instruments of the chase, but, because the bear was considered such an unusual sort of animal, it was thought that the use of these weapons was the manly way of attacking the beast. One met it on more common ground, as it were, by this manner of combat. . . .

The account which Curtis gives of the Kwakiutl is also worth quoting. The procedure closely parallels that given by Jewitt, although several details of interest are added. It is to be noted that he states that the ceremony follows the killing of the *first* bear of the season. "The hunter," he says, "would bring it to the village, and while yet a short distance away he would call, 'I have a visitor!' Then all of the people very solemnly and quietly would assemble in his house. The bear was placed in a sitting posture in the place of honor at the middle of the back part of the room, with a ring of cedar bark about its neck and eagle down on its head.

Food was then given to each person and a portion was placed before the bear. Great solemnity prevailed. The bear was treated as an honored guest, and was so addressed in the speeches. The people, one by one, would advance and take its paws in their hands as if uttering a supplication. After the ceremonial meal was over, the bear was skinned and prepared for food." Another Kwakiutl procedure is described as follows: "When a black bear is killed, the hunter steps up to it and says: 'Thank you, friend, for meeting me. I did not do any harm to you. You came to meet me sent by our creator that I should shoot you that I may eat together with my wife and friend.' Thus he says and after he has said this he turns the bear over and places the blade of the knife at the chin of the bear and pretends to cut it. This is repeated three times. The fourth time he really cuts. He takes off the skin. Then he takes the skin with the right hand at the head and with the left hand at the small of the back, holds up the skin, and if it is a female bear he will say, 'Now, friend, call your husband to come to me also.' Then he throws down the skin on the body of the bear. He takes it up again and says, 'Now call your father to come here also.' Again he throws down the skin and says, holding it up, 'Oh friend, call your mother to come here also.' Then he throws down the skin on the body. He holds up the skin and says, 'Now call your children to come here also,' and throws down the skin on the body. Then the hunter himself answers his prayer saying, 'I am going to do so.' "

The Bear and the Baby

This was in Mississippi too, out at Baldwin, where there used to be bears in the big woods. This woman was visiting some of her sick neighbors. A man was low sick, and she would go sit up there with his wife, to help wait on him. Then on the way back her own husband would meet her, to take the baby over the fence at night—it was a tall rail fence. She had to take the baby with her 'cause he hadn't got home from work. This night she got to the crook in the fence and handed it to him, and then started to climb over. She handed it to a bear. When she said, "Here, Sam, take the baby," the bear just reached out and taken the baby. (They call a bear Sam, you know.) By the time she got over the fence the bear had gone off follering the fence road, and she went straight on home, trying to catch up. She found the door shut; so she asked her husband, "Sam, why did you shut the door?" He said, "I

Reprinted from Richard M. Dorson, ed., *Negro Folktales in Michigan*, by permission of Richard M. Dorson. Collected from Mrs. E. L. Smith.

didn't shut the door, because I been asleep." She said, "What did you do with the baby?" He said, "I never took the baby, I slept too late to meet you."

They were afraid to go out that night, but early next morning they told the neighbors and went out to search for the baby, and found the bear at the end of the fence road lying on his back in a pile of leaves playing with the baby. He hadn't eaten him—wasn't hongry—a bear won't harm a baby unless he's hongry.

So one man took an ax and hit him in the head. They didn't know much about a gun then. (It was over fifty years ago; I was eight or nine years old.)

Bears stand up on their hind legs just like a man. And if one peeps in here, he can tell if you're goodhearted. He'll let a woman get close to him, he knows she's scary, but he won't let a man come close.

A Bear Hunter Who Lost His Nerve

No matter how brave a man is, he'll lose his nerve if you catch him wrong.

John Hugens was about six foot four inches, a light brown skin, weighed about a hundred and ninety, a mixed breed—Indian and white too. He lived out from Indianola, and was known as a great hunter, and used to run a ball team.

He had a lot of sharecroppers and farmers and day laborers, had about two hundred acres from Billy McCleod, and subrented. He had a gambling house in Sunflower City, another in Indianola, and one on the river where he was at—a big sport. Teddy Roosevelt used to come down and go bear hunting with him. (He appointed Wayne Cox's wife postmaster of Indianaola, a colored woman, and got to know Hugens through him. Wayne Cox owned three to four thousand acres of land, was a thirty-second degree Mason. Had a bank of his own, was a mail clerk on the Southern.)

One day they were hunting over on Quiver River, and jumped a big bear. The men were all on stands, waiting for the bear. John took his in the fork of a tree that had fell down, so he'd have a place to sit. So the dogs was running right to him, and he was looking for the bear. Then he looked around, the bear had turned off to his left and was coming right behind him. John said when he looked over he was about fifteen feet from him, walking on his hind legs over the bresh. John said if it wasn't for the bresh the bear would have had him before he seen him. And when he seen him his bristles was raised up over his head (like a dog's only bigger), and his teeth were shining. The bear come in a different direction, that's what threw John off and excited him. Well he had a trained dog Bulger, old Bulger, said when he heard John's gun shoot he'd know it from any gun there was, and he'd make for him. John shot at the bear sixteen times.

So we was off, we heard the shots. Sam Johnson (white fellow) said, "Listen to that old John." He knowed that was his rifle popping over there. Said,

"Fry some, stew some, brile some."
[*Hummed softly*]

John was a crack shot, never knowed him to shoot that many times. The bear weighed about five hundred, and he was within two feet of the bear when he fired the last shot, and then he missed him. So he grabbed the barrel—he'd emptied the Winchester—and he was going to hit him with it; he couldn't run because he was between the fork. That time he seen old Bulger leap right on the bear's back. So the bear was trying to reach behind and get him. So John dropped his gun and pulled his dirk—his Bowie knife, long hunting knife, a dirk they usually call it—and stabbed the bear right in his heart.

(In switch cane that's the way they kill bear all the time, when the bear gets hot and sits down and swipes at the dogs. John sneaks up behind and stabs him. He'd never use no steel arm either, would rather depend on old Bulger.)

The Bear Hunt [1846]

Abraham Lincoln

Alluded to in a letter from Lincoln to Andrew Johnston from Springfield, Ohio, on September 6, 1846, this poem by Lincoln is probably based on an actual experience which may have taken place during Lincoln's boyhood in Indiana.

A wild bear chase, didst never see?
Then hast thou lived in vain.
Thy richest lump of glorious glee,
Lies desert in thy brain.

Reprinted from Philip Van Doren Stern, ed., *The Life and Writings of Abraham Lincoln.*

When first my father settled here,
'Twas then the frontier line;
The panther's scream, filled night with fear
And bears preyed on the swine.

But wo for Bruin's short lived fun,
When rose the squealing cry;
Now man and horse, with dog and gun,
For vengeance, at him fly.

A sound of danger strikes his ear;
He gives the breeze a snuff;
Away he bounds, with little fear,
And seeks the tangled rough.

On press his foes, and reach the ground,
Where's left his half munched meal;
The dogs, in circles, scent around,
And find his fresh made trail.

With instant cry, away they dash,
And men as fast pursue;
O'er logs they leap, through water splash,
And shout the brisk halloo.

Now to elude the eager pack,
Bear shuns the open ground;
Through matted vines, he shapes his track
And runs it, round and round.

The tall fleet cur, with deep-mouthed voice,
Now speeds him, as the wind;
While half-grown pup, and short-legged fice,
Are yelping far behind.

And fresh recruits are dropping in
To join the merry corps:
With yelp and yell—a mingled din—
The woods are in a roar.

And round, and round the chase now goes,
The world's alive with fun;
Nick Carter's horse, his rider throws,
And Mose' Hill drops his gun.

Now sorely pressed, bear glances back,
And lolls his tired tongue;
When is, to force him from his track,
An ambush on him sprung.

Across the glade he sweeps for flight,
And fully is in view.
The dogs, new-fired, by the sight,
Their cry, and speed, renew.

The foremost ones, now reach his rear,
He turns, they dash away;
And circling now, the wrathful bear,
They have him full at bay.

At top of speed, the horsemen come,
All screaming in a row.
"Whoop! Take him Tiger—Seize him Drum"—
Bang—bang—the rifles go.

And furious now, the dogs he tears,
And crushes in his ire.
Wheels right and left, and upward rears,
With eyes of burning fire.

But leaden death is at his heart,
Vain all the strength he plies,
And, spouting blood from every part,
He reels, and sinks and dies.

And now a dinsome clamor rose,
'Bout who should have his skin.
Who first draws blood, each hunter knows,
This prize must always win.

But who did this, and how to trace
What's true from what's a lie,
Like lawyers, in a murder case
They stoutly argufy.

Aforesaid fice, of blustering mood,
Behind, and quite forgot,
Just now emerging from the wood,
Arrives upon the spot.

With grinning teeth, and up-turned hair—
Brim full of spunk and wrath,
He growls, and seizes on dead bear,
And shakes for life and death.

And swells as if his skin would tear,
And growls, and shakes again;
And swears, as plain as dog can swear,
That he has won the skin.

Conceited whelp! we laugh at thee—
Now mind, that not a few
Of pompous, two-legged dogs there be,
Conceited quite as you.

He Run Over the Dog[1]

A fellow come along with a big heavy wagon, and he run over a fine foxhound. So he went up to the house and told the woman about it. She says her man is working in the field, and he'll raise hell when he hears about his best dog being run over. "You better break it kind of easy," she says. "Tell him first it was one of the kids you run over, and lead up to old Bulger kind of gradual." Everybody had plenty of children in them days, but a good dog wasn't so easy to get.

The Big Bear of Arkansas

THOMAS BANGS THORPE

This story, one of the finest of the Southwest tall tales, first appeared in the periodical The Spirit of the Times *(March 27, 1841). William T. Porter, editor of* The Spirit, *reprinted it often in a volume* The Big Bear of Arkansas and Other Sketches *(1845, 1846, 1850, 1851, 1855, and possibly 1858). The author, however, was Thomas Bangs Thorpe, and he included it in his* The Hive of "The Bee-Hunter," A Repository of Sketches *(New York: D. Appleton & Co., 1854). Blair's edition appears to be based on one of the later editions of Porter, since it varies from the first edition slightly, but lacks the auctorial revisions of* The Hive, *most of which are improvements. One, perhaps, is not: the self-conscious substitution of "bear" for "bar" in the first edition. Professor Utley has collated the last auctorial edition of Thorpe with the periodical version, using a copy of* The Hive *in the Ohio State University Library, and a photograph of* The Spirit *provided through the courtesy of Lawrence*

[1] Told by Ed Wall, Pineville, Mo., July, 1925. He heard it near Elk Springs, Mo., about 1900.

Johnson, Sheridan and Lawrence (*The Laughter Library*, 1936, p. 175) tell the same story, and observe that the dog's owner is "an Ozark mountaineer." Williams (*Master Book of Humorous Illustrations*, 1938, pp. 280–281) says it happened in the Ozarks.

Roberts of the University of Kentucky Library. A few variants in the original edition deserve mention: it is headed "(Written for the 'Spirit of the Times.')" and "BY THE AUTHOR OF TOM OWEN, THE BEE HUNTER." *and at the end appear the initials* "T.B.T." *and the postscript* "Louisiana, Feb., 1841." *There are fewer commas in Thorpe's version, and many more paragraph separations. The game "checkers and roulette" of our text was "chickens and roulette" in the original print: the editor changed some dialect words into their standard forms: "tuck" became "took," "diggins" became "diggings," and so forth. Thorpe's later version contains "pre-emption" for "land," and this may well have been an auctorial revision, for the* Dictionary of Americanisms *cites the word for the first time in 1844 as applied to "A piece of land obtained or to be obtained by pre-emption"; what readers of Westerns would call a* homestead *or a* claim. *These and several other major changes indicate that the best text is Thorpe's own supervised text, which is reproduced here.*

The quotation from Carvel Collins in Professor Utley's essay "Pride and Humility," the final selection in this section, indicates the striking major agreements between Thorpe and Faulkner. Many others might be cited: Jim Doggett's "greenness" in New Orleans resembles that of Boon in Memphis; there is a remarkable dog, Bowieknife, who participates in the climactic hunt; and a brave but foolhardy little pup whom the Big Bar destroys; the Bar is hunted for several years before the climax; the hunter is the hunted for the Big Bar like a devil "hunted me"; Jim's gun fails and he helps his dog with a knife, as Boon does; the Big Bar tends to exchange his identity with the hunter. Perhaps the most striking agreement is Jim's boast about predicting an earlier bear's length by marks on the trees. Comically he says, "I swelled up considerably—I've been a prouder man ever since. So I went on, larning something every day, until I was reckoned a buster, and allowed to be decidedly the best bear hunter in my district." Here, one might argue, is the germ of the initiation theme, of the "pride and humility" paradox of Faulkner's story.

A steamboat on the Mississippi, frequently, in making her regular trips, carries between places varying from one to two thousand miles apart; and, as these boats advertise to land passengers and freight at "all intermediate landings," the heterogeneous character of the passengers of one of these up-country boats can scarcely be imagined by one who has never seen it with his own eyes.

Starting from New Orleans in one of these boats, you will find yourself associated with men from every State in the Union, and from every portion of the globe; and a man of observation need not lack for amusement or instruction in such a crowd, if he will take the trouble to read the great book of character so favorably opened before him.

Here may be seen, jostling together, the wealthy Southern planter and the pedler of tin-ware from New England—the Northern merchant and the Southern jockey—a venerable bishop, and a desperate gambler—the land speculator, and the honest farmer—professional men of all creeds and characters—Wolvereens, Suckers, Hoosiers, Buckeyes, and Corncrackers, beside a "plentiful sprinkling" of the half-horse and half-alligator species of men, who are peculiar to "old Mississippi," and who appear to gain a livelihood by simply going up and down the river. In the pursuit of pleasure or business, I have frequently found myself in such a crowd.

On one occasion, when in New Orleans, I had occasion to take a trip of a few miles up the Mississippi, and I hurried on board the well-known "high-pressure-and-beat-every-thing" steamboat "Invincible," just as the last note of the last bell was sounding; and when the confusion and bustle that is natural to a boat's getting under way had subsided, I discovered that I was associated in as heterogeneous a crowd as was ever got together. As my trip was to be of a few hours' duration only, I made no endeavors to become acquainted with my fellow-passengers, most of whom would be together many days. Instead of this, I took out of my pocket the "latest paper," and more critically than usual examined its contents; my fellow-passengers, at the same time, disposed of themselves in little groups.

While I was thus busily employed in reading, and my companions were more busily still employed, in discussing such subjects as suited their humors best, we were most unexpectedly startled by a loud Indian whoop, uttered in the "social hall," that part of the cabin fitted off for a bar; then was to be heard a loud crowing, which would not have continued to interest us—such sounds being quite common in that *place of spirits*—had not the hero of these windy accomplishments stuck his head into the cabin, and hallooed out, "Hurra for the Big Bear of Arkansaw!"

Then might be heard a confused hum of voices, unintelligible, save in such broken sentences as "horse," "screamer," "lightning is slow," &c.

As might have been expected, this continued interruption, attracted the attention of every one in the cabin; all conversation ceased, and in the midst of this surprise, the "Big Bear" walked into the cabin, took a chair, put his feet on the stove, and looking back over his shoulder, passed the general and familiar salute—"Strangers, how are you?"

He then expressed himself as much at home as if he had been at "the Forks of Cypress," and "prehaps a little more so."

Some of the company at this familiarity looked a little angry, and some astonished; but in a moment every face was wreathed in a smile. There was something about the intruder that won the heart on sight. He appeared to be a man enjoying perfect health and contentment; his eyes were as sparkling as diamonds, and good-natured to simplicity. Then his perfect confidence in himself was irresistibly droll.

"Prehaps," said he, "gentlemen," running on without a person interrupting, "prehaps you have been to New Orleans often; I never made *the first visit before,* and I don't intend to make another in a crow's life. I am thrown away in that ar place, and useless, that ar a fact. Some of the gentlemen thar called me *green*—well, prehaps I am, said I, *but I arn't so at home;* and if I aint off my trail much, the heads of them perlite chaps themselves wern't much the hardest; for according to my notion, they were *real know-nothings,* green as a pumpkin-vine—couldn't, in farming, I'll bet, raise a crop of turnips; and as for shooting, they'd miss a barn if the door was swinging, and that, too, with the best rifle in the country. And then they talked to me 'bout hunting, and laughed at my calling the principal game in Arkansaw poker, and high-low-jack.

" 'Prehaps,' said I, 'you prefer checkers and roulette;' at this they laughed harder than ever, and asked me if I lived in the woods, and didn't know what *game* was?

"At this, I rather think *I* laughed.

" 'Yes,' I roared, and says, I, 'Strangers, if you'd asked me *how we got our meat* in Arkansaw, I'd a told you at once, and given you a list of varmints that would make a caravan, beginning with the bar, and ending off with the cat; that's *meat* though, not game.

"Game, indeed,—that's what city folks call it; and with them it means chippen-birds and shite-pokes; may be such trash live in my diggins, but I arn't noticed them yet: a bird anyway is too trifling. I never did shoot at but one, and I'd never forgiven myself for that, had it weighed less than forty pounds. I wouldn't draw a rifle on any thing less heavy than that; and when I meet with another wild turkey of the same size, I will drap him."

"A wild turkey weighing forty pounds!" exclaimed twenty voices in the cabin at once.

"Yes, strangers, and wasn't it a whopper? You see, the thing was so fat that it couldn't fly far; and when he fell out of the tree, after I shot him, on striking the ground he bust open behind, and the way the pound gobs of tallow rolled out of the opening was perfectly beautiful."

"Where did all that happen?" asked a cynical-looking Hoosier.

"Happen! happened in Arkansaw: where else could it have happened, but in the creation State, the finishing-up country—a State where the *sile* runs down to the centre of the 'arth, and government gives you a title to every inch of it? Then its airs—just breathe them, and they will make you snort like a horse. It's a State without a fault, it is."

"Excepting mosquitoes," cried the Hoosier.

"Well, stranger, except them; for it ar a fact that they are rather *enormous,* and do push themselves in somewhat troublesome. But, stranger, they never stick twice in the same place; and give them a fair chance for a few months, and you will get as much above noticing them as an alligator. They can't hurt my feelings, for they lay under the skin;

and I never knew but one case of injury resulting from them, and that was to a Yankee: and they take worse to foreigners, any how, than they do to natives. But the way they used that fellow up! first they punched him until he swelled up and busted; then he sup-per-a-ted, as the doctor called it, until he was as raw as beef; then, owing to the warm weather, he tuck the ager, and finally he tuck a steamboat and left the country. He was the only man that ever tuck mosquitoes at heart that I knowd of.

"But mosquitoes is natur, and I never find fault with her. If they ar large, Arkansaw is large, her varmints ar large, her trees ar large, her rivers ar large, and a small mosquito would be of no more use in Arkansaw than preaching in a cane-brake."

This knock-down argument in favor of big mosquitoes used the Hoosier up, and the logician started on a new track, to explain how numerous bear were in his "diggins," where he represented them to be "about as plenty as blackberries, and a little plentifuller."

Upon the utterance of this assertion, a timid little man near me inquired, if the bear in Arkansaw ever attacked the settlers in numbers?

"No," said our hero, warming with the subject, "no, stranger, for you see it ain't the natur of bear to go in droves; but the way they squander about in pairs and single ones is edifying.

"And then the way I hunt them—the old black rascals know the crack of my gun as well as they know a pig's squealing. They grow thin in our parts, it frightens them so, and they do take the noise dreadfully, poor things. That gun of mine is a perfect *epidemic among bear:* if not watched closely, it will go off as quick on a warm scent as my dog Bowieknife will: and then that dog—whew! why the fellow thinks that the world is full of bear, he finds them so easy. It's lucky he don't talk as well as think; for with his natural modesty, if he should suddenly learn how much he is acknowledged to be ahead of all other dogs in the universe, he would be astonished to death in two minutes.

"Strangers, that dog knows a bear's way as well as a horse-jockey knows a woman's: he always barks at the right time, bites at the exact place, and whips without getting a scratch.

"I never could tell whether he was made expressly to hunt bear, or whether bear was made expressly for him to hunt; any way, I believe they were ordained to go together as naturally as Squire Jones says a man and woman is, when he moralizes in marrying a couple. In fact, Jones once said, said he, 'Marriage according to law is a civil contract of divine origin; it's common to all countries as well as Arkansaw, and people take to it as naturally as Jim Doggett's Bowieknife takes to bear.' "

"What season of the year do your hunts take place?" inquired a gentlemanly foreigner, who, from some peculiarities of his baggage, I suspected to be an Englishman, on some hunting expedition, probably at the foot of the Rocky Mountains.

"The season for bear hunting, stranger," said the man of Arkansaw, "is generally all the year round, and the hunts take place about as regular. I read in history that varmints have their fat season, and their lean season. That is not the case in Arkansaw, feeding as they do upon the *spontenacious* productions of the sile, they have one continued fat season the year round; though in winter things in this way is rather more greasy than in summer, I must admit. For that reason bear with us run in warm weather, but in winter they only waddle.

"Fat, fat! its an enemy to speed; it tames every thing that has plenty of it. I have seen wild turkeys, from its influence, as gentle as chickens. Run a bear in this fat condition, and the way it improves the critter for eating is amazing; it sort of mixes the ile up with the meat, until you can't tell t'other from which. I've done this often.

"I recollect one perty morning in particular, of putting an old he fellow on the stretch, and considering the weight he carried, he run well. But the dogs soon tired him down, and when I came up with him wasn't he in a beautiful sweat—I might say fever; and then to see his tongue sticking out of his mouth a feet, and his sides sinking and opening like a bellows, and his cheeks so fat that he couldn't look cross. In this fix I blazed at him, and pitch me naked into a briar patch, if the steam didn't come out of the bullet-hole ten foot in a straight line. The fellow, I reckon, was made on the high-pressure system, and the lead sort of bust his biler."

"That column of steam was rather curious, or else the bear must have been very *warm*," observed the foreigner, with a laugh.

"Stranger, as you observe, that bear was WARM, and the blowing off of the steam show'd it, and also how hard the varmint had been run. I have no doubt if he had kept on two miles farther his insides would have been stewed; and I expect to meet with a varmint yet of extra bottom, that will run himself into a skinfull of bear's grease: it is possible; much onlikelier things have happened."

"Whereabouts are these bears so abundant?" inquired the foreigner, with increasing interest.

"Why, stranger, they inhabit the neighborhood of my settlement, one of the prettiest places on old Mississipp—a perfect location, and no mistake; a place that had some defects until the river made the 'cut-off' at 'Shirt-tail bend,' and that remedied the evil, as it brought my cabin on the edge of the river—a great advantage in wet weather, I assure you, as you can now roll a barrel of whiskey into my yard in high water from a boat, as easy as falling off a log. It's a great improvement, as toting it by land in a jug, as I used to do, *evaporated* it too fast, and it became expensive.

"Just stop with me, stranger, a month or two, or a year, if you like, and you will appreciate my place. I can give you plenty to eat; for beside hog and hominy, you can have bear-ham, and bear-sausages, and a mattrass of bear-skins to sleep on, and a wildcat-skin, pulled off hull, stuffed with corn-shucks, for a pillow. That bed would put you to sleep if you had the rheumatics in every joint in your body. I call that ar bed, a *quietus.*

"Then look at my 'pre-emption'—the government aint got another like it to dispose of. Such timber, and such bottom land,—why you can't preserve any thing natural you plant in it unless you pick it young, things thar will grow out of shape so quick.

"I once planted in those diggins a few potatoes and beets; they took a fine start, and after that, an ox team couldn't have kept them from growing. About that time I went off to old Kaintuck on business, and did not hear from them things in three months, when I accidentally stumbled on a fellow who had drapped in at my place, with an idea of buying me out.

" 'How did you like things?' said I.

" 'Pretty well,' said he, 'the cabin is convenient, and the timber land is good; but that bottom land aint worth the first red cent.' "

" 'Why?' said I.

" ' 'Cause,' said he.

" ' 'Cause what?' said I.

" ' 'Cause it's full of cedar stumps and Indian mounds, and *can't be cleared.*'

" 'Lord,' said I, 'them ar "cedar stumps" is beets, and them ar "Indian mounds" tater hills.'

"As I had expected, the crop was overgrown and useless: the sile is too rich, *and planting in Arkansaw is dangerous.*

"I had a good-sized sow killed in that same bottom land. The old thief stole an ear of corn, and took it down to eat where she slept at night. Well, she left a grain or two on the ground, and lay down on them: before morning the corn shot up, and the percussion killed her dead. I don't plant any more: natur intended Arkansaw for a hunting ground, and I go according to natur."

The questioner, who had thus elicited the description of our hero's settlement, seemed to be perfectly satisfied, and said no more; but the "Big Bear of Arkansaw" rambled on from one thing to another with a volubility perfectly astonishing, occasionally disputing with those around him, particularly with a "live Sucker" from Illinois, who had the daring to say that our Arkansaw friend's stories "smelt rather tall."

The evening was nearly spent by the incidents we have detailed; and conscious that my own association with so singular a personage would probably end before morning, I asked him if he would not give me a description of some particular bear hunt; adding, that I took great interest in such things, though I was no sportsman. The desire seemed to please him, and he squared himself round towards me, saying, that he could give me an idea of a bear hunt that was never beat in this world, or in any other. His manner was so singular, that half of his story consisted in his excellent way of telling it, the great peculiarity of which was, the happy manner he had of emphasizing the prominent parts of his conversation. As near as I can recollect, I have italicized the words, and given the story in his own way.

"Stranger," he said, "in bear hunts *I am numerous,* and which particular one, as you say, I shall tell, puzzles me.

"There was the old she devil I shot at the Hurricane last fall—then there was the old hog thief I popped over at the Bloody Crossing, and then—Yes, I have it! I will give you an idea of a hunt, in which the greatest bear was killed that ever lived, *none excepted;* about an old fellow that I hunted, more or less, for two or three years; and if that aint a *particular bear hunt,* I ain't got one to tell.

"But in the first place, stranger, let me say, I am pleased with you, because you aint ashamed to gain information by asking and listening; and that's what I say to Countess's pups every day when I'm home; and I have got great hopes of them ar pups, because they are continually *nosing* about; and though they stick it sometimes in the wrong place, they gain experience any how, and may learn something useful to boot.

"Well, as I was saying about this big bear, you see when I and some more first settled in our region, we were drivin to hunting naturally; we soon liked it, and after that we found it an easy matter to make the thing our business. One old chap who had pioneered 'afore us, gave us to understand that we had settled in the right place. He dwelt upon its merits until it was affecting, and showed us, to prove his assertions, more scratches on the bark of the sassafras trees, than I ever saw chalk marks on a tavern door 'lection time.

" 'Who keeps that ar reckoning?" said I.

" 'The bear,' said he.

" 'What for?' said I.

" 'Can't tell,' said he; 'but so it is: the bear bite the bark and wood too, at the highest point from the ground they can reach, and you can tell, by the marks,' said he, 'the length of the bear to an inch.'

" 'Enough,' said I; 'I've learned something here a'ready, and I'll put it in practice.'

"Well, stranger, just one month from that time I killed a bar, and told its exact length before I measured it, by those very marks; and when I did that, I swelled up considerably—I've been a prouder man ever since.

"So I went on, larning something every day, until I was reckoned a buster, and allowed to be decidedly the best bear hunter in my district; and that is a reputation as much harder to earn than to be reckoned first man in Congress, as an iron ramrod is harder than a toadstool.

"Do the varmints grow over-cunning by being fooled with by greenhorn hunters, and by this means get troublesome, they send for me, as a matter of course; and thus I do my own hunting, and most of my neighbors'. I walk into the varmints though, and it has become about as much the same to me as drinking. It is told in two sentences—

"A bear is started, and he is killed.

"The thing is somewhat monotonous now—I know just how much they will run, where they will tire, how much they will growl, and what a thundering time I will have in getting their meat home. I could give you the history of the chase with all the particulars at the commencement, I know the signs so well—*Stranger, I'm certain.* Once I met with a match, though, and I will tell you about it; for a common hunt would not be worth relating.

"On a fine fall day, long time ago, I was trailing about for bear, and what should I see but fresh marks on the sassafras trees, about eight inches above any in the forests that I knew of. Says I, 'Them marks is a hoax, or it indicates the d——t bear that was ever grown.' In fact, stranger, I couldn't believe it was real, and I went on. Again I saw the same marks, at the same height, and *I knew the thing lived.* That conviction came home to my soul like an earthquake.

"Says I, 'Here is something a-purpose for me: that bear is mine, or I give up the hunting business.' The very next morning, what should I see but a number of buzzards hovering over my corn-field. 'The rascal has been there,' said I, 'for that sign is certain:' and, sure enough, on examining, I found the bones of what had been as beautiful a hog the day before, as was ever raised by a Buckeye. Then I tracked the critter out of the field to the woods, and all the marks he left behind, showed me that he was *the bear.*

"Well, stranger, the first fair chase I ever had with that big critter, I saw him no less than three distinct times at a distance: the dogs run him over eighteen miles and broke down, my horse gave out, and I was as nearly used up as a man can be, made on *my* principle, *which is patent.*

"Before this adventure, such things were unknown to me as possible; but, strange as it was, that bear got me used to it before I was done with him; for he got so at last, that he would leave me on a long chase *quite easy.* How he did it, I never could understand.

"That a bear runs at all, is puzzling; but how this one could tire down and bust up a pack of hounds and a horse, that were used to overhauling every thing they started after in no time, was past my understanding. Well, stranger, that bear finally got so sassy, that he used to help himself to a hog off my premises whenever he wanted one; the buzzards followed after what he left, and so, between *bear and buzzard,* I rather think I got *out of pork.*

"Well, missing that bear so often took hold of my vitals, and I wasted away. The thing had been carried too far, and it reduced me in flesh faster than an ager. I would see that bear in every thing I did: *he hunted me*, and that, too, like a devil, which I began to think he was.

"While in this shaky fix, I made preparations to give him a last brush, and be done with it. Having completed every thing to my satisfaction, I started at sunrise, and to my great joy, I discovered from the way the dogs run, that they were near him. Finding his trail was nothing, for that had become as plain to the pack as a turnpike road.

"On we went, and coming to an open country, what should I see but the bear very leisurely ascending a hill, and the dogs close at his heels, either a match for him this time in speed, or else he did not care to get out of their way—I don't know which. But wasn't he a beauty, though! I loved him like a brother.

"On he went, until he came to a tree, the limbs of which formed a crotch about six feet from the ground. Into this crotch he got and seated himself, the dogs yelling all around it; and there he sat eyeing them as quiet as a pond in low water.

"A greenhorn friend of mine, in company, reached shooting distance before me, and blazed away, hitting the critter in the centre of his forehead. The bear shook his head as the ball struck it, and then walked down from that tree, as gently as a lady would from a carriage.

" 'Twas a beautiful sight to see him do that—he was in such a rage, that he seemed to be as little afraid of the dogs as if they had been sucking pigs; and the dogs warn't slow in making a ring around him at a respectful distance, I tell you; even Bowieknife himself, stood off. Then the way his eyes flashed!—why the fire of them would have singed a cat's hair; in fact, that bear was in a *wrath all over*. Only one pup came near him, and he was brushed out so totally with the bear's left paw, that he entirely disappeared; and that made the old dogs more cautious still. In the mean time, I came up, and taking deliberate aim, as a man should do, at his side, just back of his foreleg, *if my gun did not snap*, call me a coward, and I won't take it personal.

"Yes, stranger, *it snapped*, and I could not find a cap about my person. While in this predicament, I turned round to my fool friend—'Bill,' says I, 'you're an ass—you're a fool—you might as well have tried to kill that bear by barking the tree under his belly, as to have done it by hitting him in the head. Your shot has made a tiger of him; and blast me, if a dog gets killed or wounded when they come to blows, I will stick my knife into your liver, I will ——.' My wrath was up. I had lost my caps, my gun had snapped, the fellow with me had fired at the bear's head, and I expected every moment to see him close in with the dogs and kill a dozen of them at least. In this thing I was mistaken; for the bear leaped over the ring formed by the dogs, and giving a fierce growl, was off—the pack, of course, in full cry after him. The run this time was short, for coming to the edge of a lake, the varmint jumped in, and swam to a little island in the lake, which it reached, just a moment before the dogs.

" 'I'll have him now,' said I, for I had found my caps in the *lining of my coat*—so, rolling a log into the lake, I paddled myself across to the island, just as the dogs had cornered the bear in a thicket. I rushed up and fired—at the same time the critter leaped over the dogs and came within three feet of me, running like mad; he jumped into the lake, and tried to mount the log I had just deserted, but every time he got half his body on it, it would roll over and send him under; the dogs, too, got around him, and pulled him about, and finally Bowieknife clenched with him, and they sunk into the lake together.

"Stranger, about this time I was excited, and I stripped off my coat, drew my knife, and intended to have taken a part with Bowieknife myself, when the bear rose to the surface. But the varmint staid under—Bowieknife came up alone, more dead than alive, and with the pack came ashore.

" 'Thank God!' said I, 'the old villain has got his deserts at last.'

"Determined to have the body, I cut a grape-vine for a rope, and dove down where I could see the bear in the water, fastened my rope to his leg, and fished him, with great difficulty, ashore. Stranger, may I be chawed to death by young alligators, if the thing I looked at wasn't a *she bear, and not the old critter after all.*

"The way matters got mixed on that island was onaccountably curious, and thinking of it made me more than ever convinced that I was hunting the devil himself. I went home that night and took to my bed—the thing was killing me. The entire team of Arkansaw in bear-hunting acknowledged himself used up, and the fact sunk into my feelings as a snagged boat will in the Mississippi. I grew as cross as a bear with two cubs and a sore tail. The thing got out 'mong my neighbors, and I was asked how come on that individ-u-al that never lost a bear when once started? and if that same individ-u-al didn't wear telescopes when he turned a she-bear, of ordinary size, into an old he one, a little larger than a horse?

" 'Prehaps,' said I, 'friends'—getting wrathy—'prehaps you want to call somebody a liar?'

" 'Oh, no,' said they, 'we only heard of such things being *rather common* of late, but we don't believe one word of it; oh, no,'—and then they would ride off, and laugh like so many hyenas over a dead nigger.

"It was too much, and I determined to catch that bear, go to Texas, or die—and I made my preparations accordin'.

"I had the pack shut up and rested. I took my rifle to pieces, and iled it.

"I put caps in every pocket about my person, *for fear of the lining.*

"I then told my neighbors, that on Monday morning—naming the day—I would start THAT B(E)AR, and bring him home with me, or they might divide my settlement among them, the owner having disappeared.

"Well, stranger, on the morning previous to the great day of my hunting expedition, I went into the woods near my house, taking my gun and Bowieknife along, just *from habit*, and there sitting down, also from habit, what should I see, getting over my fence, but *the bear!* Yes, the old varmint was within a hundred yards of me, and the way he walked *over that fence*—stranger; he loomed up like a *black mist*, he seemed so large, and he walked right towards me.

"I raised myself, took deliberate aim, and fired. Instantly the varmint wheeled, gave a yell, and *walked through the fence,* as easy as a falling tree would through a cobweb.

"I started after, but was tripped up by my inexpressibles, which, either from habit or the excitement of the moment, were about my heels, and before I had really gathered myself up, I heard the old varmint groaning, like a thousand sinners, in a thicket near by, and, by the time I reached him, he was a corpse.

"Stranger, it took five niggers and myself to put that carcass on a mule's back, and old long-ears waddled under his load, as if he was foundered in every leg of his body; and with a common whopper of a bear, he would have trotted off, and enjoyed himself.

" 'Twould astonish you to know how big his was; I made a *bed-spread of his skin,* and the way it used to cover my bear mattress, and leave several feet on each side to tuck up, would have delighted you. It was, in fact, a creation bear, and if it had lived in Samson's time, and had met him in a fair fight, he would have licked him in the twinkling of a dice-box.

"But, stranger, I never liked the way I hunted him, *and missed him.* There is something curious about it, that I never could understand,—and I never was satisfied at his giving in so *easy at last.* Prehaps he had heard of my preparations to hunt him the next day, so he jist guv up, like Captain Scott's coon, to save his wind to grunt with in dying; but that ain't likely. My private opinion is, that that bear was an *unhuntable bear, and died when his time come.*"

When this story was ended, our hero sat some minutes with his auditors, in a grave silence; I saw there was a mystery to him connected with the bear whose death he had just related, that had evidently made a strong impression on his mind. It was also evident that there was some superstitious awe connected with the affair,—a feeling common with all "children of the wood," when they meet with any thing out of their everyday experience.

He was the first one, however, to break the silence, and, jumping up, he asked all present to "liquor" before going to bed,—a thing which he did, with a number of companions, evidently to his heart's content.

Long before day, I was put ashore at my place of destination, and I can only follow with the reader, in imagination, our Arkansas friend, in his adventures at the "Forks of Cypress," on the Mississippi.

Nature Myth in Faulkner's The Bear

John Lydenberg

. . . But of course [Faulkner's] stories are not merely about the South; they are about men, or Man. Here appears the other type of myth [which is different from the myth of a Southern society]: the primitive nature myth. Perhaps one should not say "appears," for the myth lies imbedded in Faulkner's feeling about human actions and seldom appears as a readily visible outcropping, as does his conception of the mythical kingdom. Faulkner feels man acting in an eternity, in a timeless confusion of past and future, acting not as a rational Deweyan creature but as a natural, unthinking (but always moral) animal. These men do not "understand" themselves, and neither Faulkner nor the reader fully understands them in any naturalistic sense. Sometimes these creatures driven by instinct become simply grotesques; sometimes the inflated rhetoric gives the characters the specious portentousness of a gigantic gray balloon. But often the aura of something-moreness casts a spell upon the reader, makes him sense where he does not exactly comprehend the eternal human significance of the ritual activities carried out by these suprahuman beings. They are acting out magical tales that portray man's plight in a world he cannot understand or control. They are Man, the primordial and immortal, the creator and protagonist of myth.

This dual myth-making can best be demonstrated in the short story "The Bear." "The Bear" is by general agreement one of Faulkner's most exciting and rewarding stories. . . . beneath its other layers of meaning, the story is essentially a nature myth.

. . . On one level the story is a symbolic representation of man's relation to the land, and particularly the Southerner's conquest of his native land. In attempting to kill Old Ben, the men are contending with the wilderness itself. In one sense, as men, they have a perfect right to do this, as long as they act with dignity and propriety, maintaining their humility while they demonstrate the ability of human beings to master the brute forces of nature. The hunters from Jefferson are gentlemen and sportsmen, representing the ideals of the old order at its best, the honor, dignity, and courage of the South. In their rapport with nature and their contest with Old Ben, they regain the purity they have lost in their workaday world, and abjure the petty conventions with which they ordinarily mar

Reprinted from John Lydenberg, "Nature Myth in Faulkner's *The Bear*," *American Literature*, XXIV (March 1952), 62–72, by permission of Duke University Press and the author.

their lives. But as Southerners they are part of "that whole edifice intricate and complex and founded upon injustice"; they are part of that South that has bought and sold land and has held men as slaves. Their original sins have alienated them irrevocably from nature. Thus their conquest of Old Ben becomes a rape. What might in other circumstances have been right, is now a violation of the wilderness and the Southern land.

Part IV makes explicit the social comment implied in the drama of Old Ben. It consists of a long and complicated account of the McCaslin family, white and mulatto, and a series of pronunciamentos by Ike upon the South, the land, truth, man's frailties and God's will. It is in effect Ike's spiritual autobiography given as explanation of his reasons for relinquishing and repudiating, for refusing to own land or participate actively in the life of the South. Ike discovers that he can do nothing to lift or lighten the curse the Southerners have brought on themselves, the monstrous offspring of their God-given free will. The price of purity, Ike finds, is noninvolvement, and he chooses purity.

Thus Part IV carries us far beyond the confines of the story of the hunt. It creates a McCaslin myth that fits into the broad saga of Faulkner's mythical kingdom, and it includes in nondramatic form a good deal of direct social comment. The rest of "The Bear" cannot be regarded as *simply* a dramatic symbolization of Ike's conscientious repudiation. Its symbolism cannot fully be interpreted in terms of this social myth. One responds emotionally to the bear hunt as to a separate unit, an indivisible and self-sufficient whole. Part IV and Old Ben's story resemble the components of a binary star. They revolve about each other and even cast light upon each other. But each contains the source of its own light.[1]

II

It is the mythical quality of the bear hunt proper that gives the story its haunting power. Beneath its other meanings and symbolisms lies the magical tale enacted by superhuman characters. Here religion and magic are combined in a ritual demonstration of the eternal struggle between Man and Nature. A statement of the legend recounting their partial reconciliation would run somewhat as follows:

Every fall members of the tribe make a pilgrimage to the domain of the Great Beast, the bear that is more than a bear, the preternatural animal that symbolizes for them their relation to Nature and thus to life. They maintain, of course, the forms of routine hunts. But beneath the conventional ritual lies the religious rite: the hunting of the tribal god, whom they dare not, and cannot, touch, but whom they are impelled to challenge. In this rite the established social relations dissolve; the artificial

[1] Two early versions of "The Bear" appeared in magazines; little of Part IV is to be found in either version.

ranks of Jefferson give way to more natural relations as Sam Fathers is automatically given the lead. The bear and Sam are both taboo. Like a totem animal, Old Ben is at the same time sacred, and dangerous or forbidden (though in no sense unclean). Also he is truly animistic, possessing a soul of his own, initiating action, not inert like other creatures of nature. And Sam, the high priest, although alone admitted to the arcana and trusted with the tutelage of the young neophyte, is yet outside the pale, living by himself, irrevocably differentiated from the others by his Negro blood, and yet kept pure and attuned to nature by his royal Indian blood.

This particular legend of man and the Nature God relates the induction of Ike, the natural and pure boy, into the mysteries of manhood. Guided by Sam Fathers, Ike learns how to retain his purity and bring himself into harmony with the forces of Nature. He learns human woodlore and the human codes and techniques of the hunt. And he learns their limitations. Old Ben, always concerned with the doings of his mortals, comes to gaze upon Ike as he stands alone and unprepared in a clearing. Ike "knew that the bear was looking at him. He never saw it. He did not know whether it was facing him from the cane or behind him." His apprehension does not depend on human senses. Awareness of his coming relation to the bear grows not from rational processes, but from intuition: "he knew now that he would never fire at it."

Yet he must see, must meet, Old Ben. He will be vouchsafed the vision, but only when he divests himself of man-made signs of fear and vanity. "*The gun*, the boy thought. *The gun*. 'You will have to choose,' Sam said." So one day, before light, he starts out unarmed on his pilgrimage, alone and helpless, with courage and humility, guided by his newly acquired woodlore, and by compass and watch, traveling till past noon, past the time at which he should have turned back to regain camp in safety. He has not yet found the bear. Then he realizes that divesting himself of the gun, necessary as that is, will not suffice if he wishes to come into the presence. "He stood for a moment—a child, alien and lost in the green and soaring gloom of the markless wilderness. Then he relinquished completely to it. It was the watch and the compass. He was still tainted."

He takes off the two artifacts, hangs them from a bush, and continues farther into the woods. Now he is at last pure—and lost. Then the footprints, huge, misshapen, and unmistakable, appear, one by one, leading him back to the spot he could no longer have found unaided, to the watch and the compass in the sunlight of the glade.

> Then he saw the bear. It did not emerge, appear; it was just there, immobile . . .

Ike has seen the vision. That is his goal, but it is not the goal for the tribe, nor for Sam Fathers who as priest must prepare the kill for them. They are under a compulsion to carry out their annual ritual at the time of "the year's death," to strive to conquer the Nature God whose very presence challenges them and raises doubts as to their power.

The priest has first to make the proper medicine; he has to find the right dog. Out of the wilds it comes, as if sent by higher powers, untamable, silent, like no other dog. Then Sam, magician as well as priest, shapes him into the force, the instrument, that alone can master Old Ben. Lion is almost literally bewitched—broken maybe, but not tamed or civilized or "humanized." He is removed from the order of nature, but not allowed to partake of the order of civilization or humanity.

Sam Fathers fashions the instrument; that is his duty as it has been his duty to train the neophyte, to induct him into the mysteries, and thus to prepare, in effect, his own successor. But it is not for the priest to perform the impious and necessary deed. Because he belongs to the order of nature as well as of man—as Ike does now—neither of them can do more than assist at the rites. Nor can Major de Spain or General Compson or other human hunters pair with Lion. That is for Boon, who has never hit any animal bigger than a squirrel with his shotgun, who is like Lion in his imperturbable nonhumanity. Boon is part Indian; "he had neither profession job nor trade"; he has "the mind of a child, the heart of a horse, and little hard shoe-button eyes without depth or meanness or generosity or viciousness or gentleness or anything else." So he takes Lion into his bed, makes Lion a part of him. Divorced from nature and from man—"the big, grave, sleepy-seeming dog which, as Sam Fathers said, cared about no man and no thing; and the violent, insensitive, hard-faced man with his touch of remote Indian blood and the mind almost of a child"—the two mavericks live their own lives, dedicated and fated.

The "yearly pageant-rite" continues for six years. Then out of the swamps come the rest of the tribe, knowing the climax is approaching, accepted by the Jefferson aristocrats as proper participants in the final rites. Ike, the young priest, is given the post of honor on the one-eyed mule which alone among the mules and horses will not shy at the smell of blood. Beside him stands the dog who "loved no man and no thing." . . .

The final hunt is short, for Old Ben can be downed only when his time has come, not by the contrived machinations of men, but by the destined ordering of events and his own free will. The hounds run the bear; a swamper fires; Walter Ewell fires;[2] Boon cannot fire.[3] Then the bear turns and Lion drives in, is caught in the bear's two arms and falls

[2] In "The Old People," the story preceding "The Bear" in *Go Down, Moses,* Faulkner says that Walter Ewell never misses. Thus mention of his shooting and missing at this particular time takes on added significance.

[3] Boon explained that he could not fire because Lion was too close. That was, of course, not the "real" reason; Boon could not kill Ben with a civilized gun (to say nothing of the fact that he couldn't hit anything with his gun anyway).

with him. Ike draws back the hammers of his gun. And Boon, like Lion, drives in, jumps on Ben's back and thrusts his knife into the bear's throat. Again they fall. Then "the bear surged erect, raising with it the man and the dog too, and turned and still carrying the man and the dog it took two or three steps towards the woods on its hind feet as a man would have walked and crashed down. It didn't collapse, crumple. It fell all of a piece, as a tree falls, so that all three of them, man dog and bear, seemed to bounce once."

The tribe comes up, with wagon and mules, to carry back to camp the dead bear, Lion with his guts raked out, Boon bleeding, and Sam Fathers who dropped, unscathed but paralyzed, at the moment that Ben received his death wound. The doctor from the near-by sawmill pushes back Lion's entrails and sews him up. Sam lies quiet in his hut after talking in his old unknown tongue, and then pleading, "Let me out, master. Let me go home."

Next day the swampers and trappers gather again, sitting around Lion in the front yard, "talking quietly of hunting, of the game and the dogs which ran it, of hounds and bear and deer and men of yesterday vanished from the earth, while from time to time the great blue dog would open his eyes, not as if he were listening to them but as though to look at the woods for a moment before closing his eyes again, to remember the woods or to see that they were still there. He died at sundown." And in his hut Sam quietly goes after the bear whose death he was destined to prepare and upon whose life his own depended, leaving behind the de Spains and Compsons who will no longer hunt in this wilderness and the new priest who will keep himself pure to observe, always from the outside, the impious destruction of the remaining Nature by men who can no longer be taught the saving virtues of pride and humility. They have succeeded in doing what they felt they had to do, what they thought they wanted to do. But their act was essentially sacrilegious, however necessary and glorious it may have seemed. They have not gained the power and strength of their feared and reverenced god by conquering him. Indeed, as human beings will, they have mistaken their true relation to him. They tried to possess what they could not possess, and now they can no longer even share in it.

Boon remains, but he has violated the fundamental taboo. Permitted to do this by virtue of his nonhumanity, he is yet in part human. He has broken the law, killed with his own hand the bear, taken upon himself the mastery of that which was no man's to master. So when the chiefs withdraw, and the sawmills grind their way into the forests, Boon polices the new desecrations. When Ike returns to gaze once more upon the remnants of the wilderness, he finds Boon alone in the clearing where the squirrels can be trapped in the isolated tree. Boon, with the gun he could never aim successfully, frenziedly hammers the barrel against the breech of the dismembered weapon, shouting at the intruder, any intruder, "Get out of here! Don't touch them! Don't touch a one of them! They're mine!" Having killed the bear, he now possesses all the creatures of nature, and will snarl jealously at the innocent who walks peacefully through the woods. The result of his impiety is, literally, madness.

III

That, of course, is not exactly Faulkner's "Bear." But it is part of it, an essential part. If a reading of the story as myth results in suppressions and distortions, as it does, any other reading leaves us unsatisfied. Only thus can we answer certain crucial questions that otherwise baffle us. The most important ones relate to the four central characters: Why can Ike or Sam not kill the bear? Why can Boon? Why are Boon and Lion drawn precisely so? And why does Sam Fathers die along with Old Ben?

Ike has developed and retained the requisite purity. He has learned to face nature with pride and humility. He is not tainted like de Spain and Compson by having owned slaves. According to Faulkner's version of the huntsman's code, Ike should be the one who has the right to kill Old Ben, as General Compson feels when he assigns him the one mule that can approach the bear. Or it might be argued that Sam Fathers, with his unsurpassed knowledge, instinct, and dignity, rightly deserves the honor. If Old Ben is merely the greatest of bears, it would seem fitting for either Ike or Sam to demonstrate his impeccable relationship to nature by accomplishing the task. But Faulkner rules differently.

Lion and Boon do it. At first glance that may seem explicable if we consider Old Ben's death as symbolizing man's destruction of the wilderness. Then the deed cannot be performed by Ike or Sam, for it would be essentially vicious, done in violation of the rules by men ignorant or disrespectful of the rules. Thus one may think it could be assigned to Boon, "the plebeian," and that strange, wild dog. But actually neither of them is "bad," neither belongs to a mean order of hunters. Boon and Lion are creatures set apart, dehumanized, possessing neither virtues nor vices. In their actions and in his words describing them, Faulkner takes great pains to link them together and to remove from them all human traits.[4]

Thus the killing of the bear cannot be explained by a naturalistic interpretation of the symbolism. Old Ben is not merely an extraordinary bear representing the wilderness and impervious to all but the most skillful or improper attacks. He is the totem animal, the god who can never be bested by men with their hounds and guns, but only by a nonhuman Boon with Lion, the instrument fashioned by the priest.

Sam Fathers' death can likewise be explained only by the nature myth. If the conquest of Old Ben is the triumphant culmination of the boy's induction into the hunting clan, Sam, his mentor, would presumably be

[4] In "The Old People," Boon is referred to as "a mastiff."

allowed a share in the triumph. If the bear's death symbolizes the destruction of the wild, Sam's demise can be seen as paralleling that of the nature of which he is so completely a part. But then the whole affair would be immoral, and Sam could not manage and lead the chase so willingly, nor would he die placid and satisfied. Only as part of a nature rite does his death become fully understandable. It is as if the priest and the god are possessed of the same soul. The priest fulfills his function; his magic makes the god vulnerable to the men. He has to do it; and according to human standards he wins a victory for his tribe. But it is a victory for which the only fit reward is the death he is content to accept. The actors act out their ordained roles. And in the end the deed brings neither jubilation nor mourning—only retribution, tragic in the high sense, right as the things which are inevitable are right.

A further paradox, a seeming contradiction, appears in the conjunction of the two words which are repeated so often that they clearly constitute a major theme. Pride and humility. Here conjoined are two apparently polar concepts: the quintessence of Christianity in the virtue of humility; and the greatest of sins, the sin of Satan. Though at first the words puzzle one, or else slip by as merely a pleasant conceit, they soon gather up into themselves the entire "meaning" of the story. This meaning can be read in purely naturalistic terms: Faulkner gives these two qualities as the huntsman's necessary virtues. But they take on additional connotations. Humility becomes the proper attitude to the nature gods, with whom man can merely bring himself into harmony as Sam teaches Ike to do. The pride arises out of the individual's realization of his manhood: his acquisition of the self-control which permits him to perform the rituals as he should. Actually it is humanly impossible to possess these two qualities fully at the same time. Sam alone truly has them, and as the priest he has partly escaped from his humanity. Ike apparently believes he has developed them, finally; and Faulkner seems to agree with him. But Ike cannot quite become Sam's successor, for in acquiring the necessary humility—and insight—he loses the ability to act with the full pride of a man, and can only be an onlooker, indeed in his later life, as told in Part IV and "Delta Autumn," a sort of Ishmael.

In conclusion, then, "The Bear" is first of all a magnificent story. The inclusion of Part IV gives us specific insights into Faulkner's attitude toward his Southern society and adds another legend to the saga of his mythical kingdom. The tale of Old Ben by itself has a different sort of effect. Our response is not intellectual but emotional. The relatively simple story of the hunting of a wise old bear suggests the mysteries of life, which we feel subconsciously and cannot consider in the rationalistic terms we use to analyze the "how" of ordinary life. Thus it appears as a nature myth, embodying the ambivalences that lie at the heart of primitive taboos, rituals, and religions, and the awe we feel toward that which we are unable to comprehend or master. From strata buried deep under our rationalistic understanding, it dredges up our feeling that the simple and the primitive—the stolid dignity and the superstitions of Sam Fathers—are the true. It evokes our terrible and fatal attraction toward the imperturbable, the powerful, the great—as symbolized in the immortal Old Ben. And it expresses our knowledge that as men we have to conquer and overcome, and our knowledge that it is beyond our human power to do so—that it is necessary and sacrilegious.

Pride and Humility: The Cultural Roots of Ike McCaslin

FRANCIS LEE UTLEY

I

Out of the "driving complexity" of Faulkner's *The Bear* many strands may be unwoven; like *Don Quixote* or *Hamlet*, the story allows an infinity of readings. Here we shall seek one which recognizes the culture from which Ike derives and which he represents and transcends. It is the tall tale of an epic hunt for an immortal Hunted Bear who like God is also mortal, the realistic tale of how one boy is initiated into pride and humility, and the romantic tale of how that boy is prepared by his culture for one massive and courageous act of repudiation of a land tainted by slavery and miscegenation. Ike's rejection of his inheritance makes him momentarily like the Carpenter who repudiated (and perpetuated) the Law; since he was but mortal, it left him drained, a no-'count poor white hunter despite his high-born ancestry, a sterile sacrifice to truth and humanity. The temptation to narrow such a tale to the religious, the social, the local is great; we shall try to view it in its breadth without reduction.

A good hunting story has a wide appeal; New England has its great cosmic yarn of a hunt—Ahab's pursuit of Moby Dick. But the hunting culture of America is found at its most intense in the Old South, with its wilderness old and new. What W. J. Cash has called the "romantic and hedonistic" character of his native region[1] finds some of its most natural expression in the hunt, exclusively male, or as Faulkner puts it "the best game of all, the best of all breathing and forever the best of all listening." Many Northern boys know a hobby called hunting; most Southern boys know hunting as a way of life. Hunting is a masculine

This essay, first published in the first edition of this text, was independently anticipated in part by Alexander Kern, "Myth and Symbol in Criticism of Faulkner's 'The Bear' " in *Myth and Symbol: Critical Approaches and Applications*, ed. Bernice Slote (Lincoln: University of Nebraska Press, 1963), pp. 152–161; and the anonymous "The Bear and Huckleberry Finn: Heroic Quests for Moral Liberation," *Mark Twain Journal*, XII:1 (Spring 1963), pp. 12–13, 21.

1 W. J. Cash, *The Mind of the South* (New York: Vintage Books, 1954), pp. 46–49.

democracy: the gentry like Major de Spain and General Compson drink, play poker and hunt with or beside Sam Fathers and Tennie's Jim, both of whom have Negro blood; the poor whites, swampers and farmers and loggers, collect to witness the climactic battle between their own Boon Hogganbeck, the dog Lion, and the bear Old Ben.

Faulkner, it is rumored, had to be assured of good hunting in Virginia before he could settle down as a writer in residence at Jefferson's University. He has often insisted that *The Bear,* if printed out of the historical context of the "novel" *Go Down, Moses,* should drop its lengthy and surrealistic fourth part, which demonstrates how Ike renounced his plantation heritage.[2] Some of this conviction, which is rarely shared by critics[3] (who would as soon lose the last chapter of Joyce's *Ulysses* because it likewise violated the norms of English punctuation), comes from Faulkner's knowledge that he had several times written an earlier form of the story, of which "Lion," a pure hunting yarn, is perhaps the most successful example. Faulkner knows that the story of the Last Great Hunt in the dying Wilderness will appeal directly to his people, who may be distracted by the revolutionary repudiation of Part IV. The distraction is less in the full setting of *Go Down, Moses,* which puts Ike himself in perspective, strengthens the element of initiation in the story, shows us the heroism of the Old South, white and black, and the pride and humility of the New South, white and black. But above all one assumes that Faulkner's fellow-Southerners love the hunt so intensely that they will take a good deal from a tale which celebrates it. If we, following the lead of other critics, remove the tale from its literary context, we must grant the tale its cultural context as reparation.

Now that we have a hunt, what of the quarry? Clearly there is a closeness between hunter and hunted, of the kind missed by the American in England who was rebuked by the Master of the Hunt for a breach of etiquette. When he saw the fox he did not shout "Tally-ho!" as he should, but "There goes the little son of a bitch!" Hunting, one of the most ancient of sports, breeds ceremony, and the center of the ceremony must be respected. Old Ben is a monster like Beowulf's Grendel, ageless, "a phantom, epitome and apotheosis of the old, wild life which the little puny humans swarmed and hacked at in a fury of abhorrence and fear, like pygmies about the ankles of a drowsing elephant;—the old bear, solitary, indomitable, and alone; widowered, childless, and absolved of mortality—old Priam reft of his old wife and outlived all his sons." He

[2] Frederick L. Gwynn and Joseph L. Blotner, eds., *Faulkner in the University* (Charlottesville: University of Virginia Press, 1959), pp. 3–4, 273.

[3] One exception is Richard J. Stonsifer, "Faulkner's 'The Bear': A Note on Structure," *College English,* XXIII (1961), pp. 219–223. Stonsifer's search for sevens to equate with Ishtar's descent into the underworld is an example of mythical legerdemain of the kind I hope this essay does not sponsor, despite its use of ritual metaphors.

appears to Ike in a series of ritual epiphanies—eight of them in all. At ten Ike only hears him, in the company of his priest and tutor, Sam Fathers. Here the Bear is not the hunted but the hunter. " 'He come to see who's here, who's new in camp this year, whether he can shoot or not, can stay or not. . . . Because he's the head bear. He's the man.' " The Man, like Sam's own ancestor Doom or "du Homme," an Indian adventurer whose acquisition of these lands by questionable means but with no lack of force and leadership, sets the whole sequence of *Go Down, Moses* in motion. Two weeks later Ike merely senses that Ben looks at him; the Bear is still the Hunter. The third time Ike, courageously alone and ritually naked of gun, watch and compass, confronts Old Ben directly; a mystic link between them is riveted. The fourth and fifth meetings occur in Part II when Ike is thirteen; a new source of *mana* or spirit power, the dog Lion, has joined the destined hunters. Once, "still hunting with Walter Ewell's rifle," Ike sees the Bear from a distance Later, in the company of his "frantic fyce," a little dog who is the essence of courage because he cannot aspire to Lion's strength, Ike sees Old Ben once more; he fails to shoot him because he would kill the absurd fyce, who is surrounding Ben on all sides. But he comes close enough to smell the Bear, "strong and hot and rank." The sixth time Lion, the destined antagonist of Ben, is present, but Ben escapes the dog and the hunters by covering his trail with the river. Next November Lion jumps Ben and General Compson draws blood; Boon shoots five times but misses him, and nearly dies of shame. A year later (Part III), when Ike is sixteen, the yearly ritual of pursuit continues, but this time Old Ben comes to his fated end, bringing down with him Lion and Sam Fathers, the ancient Chief and Hunter.

This climactic ladder of pursuits and escapes is obviously, among other things, a repeated ritual dealing with the destinies of gods and men. Master of the rite is Sam Fathers, who knows the destinies and teaches craft and wisdom to Ike, his fosterling. He foresees that if Ben "gets hemmed up and has got to pick out somebody to run over, he will pick out you," a prophecy of the fifth epiphany, when Ben looms above Ike and the fyce. Sam knows that one particular dog (not yet chosen) will be Old Ben's Nemesis, and Ike, who is learning second sight from Sam, echoes him with "So it won't be until the last day. When even he don't want it to last any longer." Sam's foreknowledge, against the rationalizations of his social "betters," leads him to lure Lion out of the wilderness and to tame him for the fated task, which coincides with the death of Ben, Lion, and Sam himself. On the "last day," only Ike knows that Sam is going to die: "Sam's eyes were probably open again on that profound look which saw further than them or the hut, further than the death of a bear and the dying of a dog." As in all rituals, in which man follows the ways of the gods in order to control them, the borderline between man's choice and man's fate becomes blurred. Sam directs Boon, his acolyte, to the last rites, including those of his own funeral.

Similarly, in a Munsee-Mahican Bear Sacrifice ceremony related by Nicodemus Peters, an Indian sage of the Delaware Nation,[4] the twelve male participants seek the very real bear they want to sacrifice. They come upon a bear in an oak tree, his nose showing through a little hole, and they reject him. Then they find an elm tree containing the right bear, and knock four times on the tree, crying out "You we have found." The bear comes out, acts ashamed, like a dog. The hero Maxkok orders the bear to come and to take the lead towards the Big House where the sacrifice is to take place. The bear lies down and makes further difficulties. Maxkok says "The bear will not come to the Big House. So no more will there be a feast dance. Therefore you will have to kill the bear right here." Courteously they order the bear to get up, he does, and they kill him, skin him, and complete the ceremony.

Here also, then, we have a fated bear, a "right" one, whose cooperation in his own death is demanded, since as the god he will want to share in all parts of the sacrifice which honors him with death. The bridge from the mythical to the real bear is crossed pragmatically by anticipation of some apparent lack of cooperation: if he runs away he is leading them; if he lies down he is ritually refusing to come; if, threatened by death, he rises to run again he is making it possible for the hunters to kill him. Folk wisdom has caught up the humor of this kind of situation in the proverbial dialogue: "I have caught a bear. —Bring it here. —It won't come. —Then come yourself. —It won't let me go." Catching a bear is like catching a Tartar.[5] The Hunted and the Hunter, as in Francis Thompson's *Hound of Heaven*, are one and the same.

Like Sam and the Munsee bear, Old Ben knows his fatal day. Here we find Faulkner reflecting[6] one of the greatest tall tales of the American Southwest, Thomas B. Thorpe's *The Big Bear of Arkansas*, of which Carvel Collins says:

> In Thorpe as in Faulkner the hunted animal is extraordinarily large, competent, and mysterious. Its hunters, with varying intensity, see it as

[4] Frank G. Speck and Jesse Moses, *The Celestial Bear Comes Down to Earth* (Reading, Pa., 1945), pp. 61–62. [See pp. 140–141 above.]

[5] Archer Taylor, *The Proverb* (Cambridge: Harvard University Press, 1931), p. 156.

[6] Faulkner's warnings about research find special appropriateness when we seek for examples of ritual parallels among the Choctaw and Chickasaw aborigines of Yoknapatawpha County. A. I. Hallowell, *Bear Ceremonialism in the Northern Hemisphere* (Philadelphia, 1926), p. 72, notes that "no rites accompanying the killing or eating of a bear have been reported for the peoples of" the Southeastern region or the related Iroquois. John R. Swanton's definitive *The Indians of the Southeastern United States* (Bureau of American Ethnology Bulletin 137, Washington, D.C., 1946) offers little or nothing on the "universal" custom of initiation (see the *huskanaw* on p. 712); only a little on the bear hunt with less on ceremonial (pp. 321–324); and something on burial customs as reflected in Sam Fathers' platform (p. 728).

supernatural and an embodiment of large principles. Even in minor matters the two works are parallel with each other and with the basic folktale: these details include a plunge through water at a climax of the hunt, the temporary substitution of an inferior for the real quarry, and the inability of the hunters to confront the bear when they are conventionally prepared for the hunt.[7]

Conventional preparation is of the real world; ritual demands special conditions, and any small omission may destroy the efficacy of the ceremony. So Ike must abandon watch, compass, gun and stick even to have a view of the god; and Boon must finish him off with a woodsman's knife, since guns will not work,[8] being tainted with novelty.

Thorpe's hero, Jim Doggett, hunted his quarry many times without success until one day, in an embarrassing posture while answering a call of nature, he saw the bear who, in his words:

"loomed up like a *black mist*, he seemed so large, and he walked right towards me. I raised myself, took deliberate aim, and fired. Instantly the varmint wheeled, gave a yell, and *walked through the fence*, as easy as a falling tree would through a cobweb. I started after, but was tripped up by my inexpressibles, which, either from habit or the excitement of the moment, were about my heels, and before I had really gathered myself up, I heard the old varmint groaning, like a thousand sinners, in a thicket near by, and, by the time I reached him, he was a corpse. . . . It was, in fact, a creation bear, and if it had lived in Samson's time, and had met him in a fair fight, he would have licked him in the twinkling of a dice-box.

But, stranger, I never liked the way I hunted him, *and missed him*. There is something curious about it, that I never could understand,—and I never was satisfied at his giving in *so easy at last*. Prehaps he had heard of my preparations to hunt him the next day, so he jist guv up, like Captain Scott's coon, to save his wind to grunt with in dying; but that ain't likely. My private opinion is, that that bear was *an unhuntable bear, and died when his time come*."[9]

The dying god, in short, knows his destiny. One need not regard these parallels from Thorpe and the Munsee-Mahicans as "sources," but rather

[7] Carvel Collins, "Faulkner and Certain Earlier Southern Fiction," *College English*, XVI (1954), 96.

[8] Faulkner did not make it a *flint* knife, which it must be in many hypothetical rites which antedate the age of iron. See James G. Frazer, *The Golden Bough* (New York: Macmillan, 1935), III, 225–236; Hallowell, pp. 33–35. The pioneer iron knife of Daniel "Boon" is enough to show the conservative nature of ritual. LaBudde, *American Quarterly*, II (1950), 324, interprets the stabbing with the knife as "reverence" for the quarry; ritual conservatism is a better explanation to serve both his purposes and those of this essay.

[9] In Wright Morris's *Ceremony in Lone Tree* (New York: Atheneum, 1960), p. 66, the grandfather of a Nebraska family, aged ninety, remarks: "One thing nobody in the world knows is when his time is come. That is God's secret."

as cultural roots, as evidence of the closeness of Faulkner's story to the land from which it is taken. Faulkner at Virginia elaborately disclaimed direct sources:

> As far as I know I have never done one page of research. Also, I doubt if I've ever forgotten anything I ever read too. . . . That what research I read, I read exactly as I do fiction because it's people, man, in motion, and the writer, as I say, never forgets that, he stores it away.[10]

At the same time he admits indirect or unconscious sources, and it is unlikely that the author of *The Bear* and *Spotted Horses,* the latter with its tell-tale teller Ratliff, did not know Davy Crockett, Thorpe, James Baldwin, Sut Lovingood and other Münchhausens of flush times in Mississippi, Georgia, Tennessee, and Arkansas Travellers. The Munsee-Mahican Bear Ceremony was published by Speck after *The Bear* was written; yet if Old Ben could foresee his own end and die "when his time come," he could surely anticipate a collector of traditions like Speck.[11]

Old Ben, like Thorpe's Big Bear, has cosmic dimensions; he is the God of the Wilderness. At his death the Wilderness dies, or at least shrinks to a tiny plot of hunting land surrounding the graves of the ritual dead: Lion, Old Ben, Sam Fathers. Ike, fleeing a Snopesian civilization and the raucous planing-mill which is its symbol, revisits the "dead." Like gods they never die. "It was as if the old bear, even dead there in the yard, was a more potent terror still than they could face without Lion between them." Death and life are earth's cycles. The graves are gone:

> He passed one of the four concrete markers set down by the lumber company's surveyor to establish the four corners of the plot which Major de Spain had reserved out of the sale, then he stood on the crest of the knoll itself, the four corner-markers all visible now, blanched still even beneath the winter's weathering, lifeless and shockingly alien in that place where dissolution itself was a seething turmoil of ejaculation tumescence conception and birth, and death did not even exist. . . . he had not stopped, he had only paused, quitting the knoll which was no abode of the dead because there was no death, not Lion and not Sam: not held fast in earth but free in earth and not in earth but of earth, myriad yet undiffused of every myriad part . . . dark and dawn and dark and dawn again in their immutable progression and, being myriad, one: and Old Ben too, Old Ben too; they would give him his paw back even.

Ike's recollections of the seasonal myths and the resurrection of the god are interrupted by the sight of a rattlesnake, the snake of this diminished

[10] Gwynn and Blotner, p. 251.

[11] Speck (p. xii) collected the ritual from Nekatcit in 1938; his informant died in 1939. The first version of *The Bear* (*Lion*) appeared in *Harper's Magazine* in 1935; the final magazine version in *The Saturday Evening Post* in 1942. *Go Down, Moses* was also published in 1942. See LaBudde, *American Quarterly,* II (1950), 322.

Eden—the immortal snake who stole life from man and who is the prototype of the logging train which devours the wilderness.

II

Gods do not exist without their cults or without their priests. The hunt, as in many cultures, is blended in the story with initiation or puberty ritual. For if this is the story of a Bear, it is also the story of a Boy who achieves pride and humility through a lengthy testing in the woods. The unprecedented appeal of this story to young and old alike is partly the result of Faulkner's meticulous account of Ike's precocious growth as a "man's hunter." Mircea Eliade's classic definition of initiation as Birth and Rebirth might have been written with Ike specifically in mind:

> In philosophical terms, initiation is equivalent to a basic change in existential condition; the novice emerges from his ordeal endowed with a totally different being from that which he possessed before his initiation; he has become *another*. . . . Initiation introduces the candidate into the human community and into the world of spiritual and cultural values. . . . he learns the mystical relations between the tribe and the Supernatural Beings as those relations were established at the beginning of Time. . . . Initiatory death is indispensable for the beginning of spiritual life. Its function must be understood in relation to what it prepares: birth to a higher mode of being. As we shall see farther on, initiatory death is often symbolized, for example, by darkness, by cosmic night, by the telluric womb, the hut, the belly of a monster.[12]

So Ike "entered his novitiate to the true wilderness with Sam beside him as he had begun his apprenticeship in miniature to manhood after the rabbits and such with Sam beside him, the two of them wrapped in the damp, warm, Negro-rank quilt, while the wilderness closed behind his entrance as it had opened momentarily to accept him, opening before his advancement as it closed behind his progress. . . . It seemed to him that at the age of ten he was witnessing his own birth."[13]

The subtle steps by which Ike approaches the god, never close enough to be hurt by him as Lion was in body and Boon in mind, are the vicarious

[12] Mircea Eliade, *Birth and Rebirth* (New York: Harper and Brothers, 1958), pp. x–xiv. [See pp. 135–137 above.]

[13] Mordecai Marcus, who is skeptical of the too extensive use of the word "initiation" to characterize a host of modern stories, gives *The Bear* a clean bill. The marking of Ike's forehead with the blood of his first slain deer and the abandonment of watch, gun and compass "combine psychological compulsion and the sense of a half-intuited myth, the feeling that nature demands a certain rite. More distinctly psychological are the ritualistic intensity with which Ike pores over his grandfather's ledgers . . . and Ike's decision to renounce the land. . . . Faulkner's primitive and psychological rituals are always convincing." See "What Is an Initiation Story?" *Journal of Aesthetics and Art Criticism*, XIX (1960), 226–227. I would think the decision to renounce the land is ritually strengthened historical action, rather than ritual itself.

paths a good society (the hunter's society, not the world of the present) provides for its adolescents to make them men. The rites coincide with "the yearly pageant-rite of the old bear's furious immortality," but they are not identical with it; except for one close call as he saves the frantic fyce, Ike never comes really in contact with the Godhead. But he grows in hunting wisdom and also in spiritual perception; he abandons the tainted weapons of civilization; he progresses until General Compson can decry the conventional schoolhouse from which Ike wants to play hookey so that he may tend the dying Sam:

> "And you shut up, Cass . . . You've got one foot straddled into a farm and the other foot straddled into a bank; you aint even got a good hand-hold where this boy was already an old man . . . that could go ten miles on a compass because he wanted to look at a bear none of us had ever got near enough to put a bullet in and looked at the bear and came the ten miles back on the compass in the dark."

Ike then is the responsive initiate, like young Marlow in Conrad's *Youth*, Nick Adams in Hemingway's *Big Two-Hearted River*, or the boy soldier in Stephen Crane's *Red Badge of Courage*. Sam is the priest and Boon the acolyte, and Boon, who completes the killing of the Bear, goes mad, while Sam loses his life as part of the sacrifice. "Sam was the chief, the prince; Boon, the plebeian, was his huntsman." In keeping with the return to nature, to Eliade's "telluric womb," the various animals of the story closely parallel the three human ritual actors. They share in the rite like the totemic ancestors, ancestral beasts, or culture heroes; they are shadows of the men and the boy, or rather the doubles, for it is uncertain here just who is shadow and who is substance. Spiritually speaking Sam is Ike's "Chief, Grandfather"; his father, Uncle Buck, has died long ago, and his grandfather Carothers is the compulsive villain of the story, archetypal slaveowner and seducer of his Negro women, one of them his own daughter. Sam, like the priest of Nemi, is identical with the god he must kill and be killed by. By juxtaposition Faulkner makes the equation clear: "an old bear, fierce and ruthless with the fierce pride of liberty and freedom . . . an old man, son of a Negro slave and an Indian king, inheritor on the one hand of the long chronicle of a people who had learned humility through suffering and learned pride through the endurance which survived the suffering, and on the other side the chronicle of a people even longer in the land than the first, yet who now existed there only in the solitary brotherhood of an old and childless Negro's alien blood and the wild and invincible spirit of an old bear." To them comes "a boy who wished to learn humility and pride in order to become skillful and worthy in the woods but found himself becoming so skillful so fast that he feared he would never become worthy, because he had not learned humility and pride though he had tried, until one day an old man, who could not have defined either, led him as though by the hand to where an old bear and a little mongrel dog showed him that, by possessing one thing other, he would possess them both." The one thing other is bravery; the fyce, who is as clearly Ike as Old Ben is Sam, is neither humble nor proud but only brave, although the world would "probably call that too just noise."

And if these equations hold, there is no trouble with the last one, Boon's identity with Lion. One of the magnificent things of this story is the love affair between the giant poor white Boon and "the great grave blue dog" who helps him kill Old Ben. Their relationship comes directly out of Southern culture.[14] Faulkner knows his Southern songs: the "Go Down, Moses" of the novel; "That Evening Sun," from "St. Louis Blues," with its tragic implications for Dilsey's daughter Nancy; Dilsey's own endurance, which owes much to various spirituals; and the widely-known song "Old Blue," which mingles rite with humor. A Mississippi version of the last, which Faulkner may have known, begins:

> I had an old dog, his name was Blue;
> I tell you boys, he was a rounder too.

Blue catches a possum, but dies of the exertion.

> Old Blue died; I laid him in the shade,
> I dug his grave with a silver spade.
> CHORUS: Come on, Blue, Come on Blue,
> You old rascal you.
>
> I let him down with a golden chain;
> Link by link slipped through my hand.
>
> There is only one thing that bothers my mind;
> Blue went to heaven and left me behind.
>
> When I get there, the first thing I'll do,
> Grab me a horn and blow for Old Blue.[15]

Like the singer of this song, Boon is a whiskey-drinking rounder; Lion is a savage mongrel, not from the pack but out of the wilderness. Lion's use is confined to his obsessive desire to kill Old Ben, but he has the power which the brave little fyce lacked; he dies with Old Ben, his mortal enemy, and Boon cares for him like a human being. Boon defies Major de

[14] The clearest mark of poor-white or hillfolk status is the hound-dog, according to James West (pseud. for George Withers), *Plainsville U.S.A.* (New York: Columbia University Press, 1961), pp. 20, 132, 138. See also William H. Nicholls, *Southern Tradition and Regional Progress* (Chapel Hill: University of North Carolina Press, 1960), pp. 37, 39, 125.

[15] Arthur P. Hudson, *Folksongs of Mississippi and Their Background* (Chapel Hill: University of North Carolina Press, 1936), pp. 201–202; see also Henry M. Belden and Arthur P. Hudson, *Folk Songs from North Carolina* (Durham: Duke University Press, 1952), pp. 252–253; Vance Randolph, *Ozark Folksongs* (State Historical Society of Missouri, 1946–50), II, 383, and my forthcoming book on *Folksongs of the Flood*.

Spain and demands a doctor, not for himself or for Sam Fathers, as one might think, but for the great blue dog. He digs his grave, and no doubt expects to meet him in heaven. As Ike had refrained from shooting Ben for the fyce's sake, Boon refrains for Lion's sake. Boon fed Lion, slept with him, and lived for him; they were as one. At the beginning of the climactic hunt, the final epiphany, Lion "moved its head and looked at" Ike "across the trivial uproar of the hounds, out of the yellow eyes as depthless as Boon's, as free as Boon's of meanness or generosity or gentleness or viciousness. They were just cold and sleepy."

Thus the initiate Ike viewed a ritual drama which made a man of him, which taught him finally the "pride and humility" he needed. These paradoxical words move like a *leitmotif* throughout the story; I count at least twenty occurrences of them separate or combined. Though they are as hard for us to define as they were for Sam Fathers, they are in a sense the key to the story. Hunters need "humility and skill" to survive; Ike learns humility on his first hunting trip—how to prepare his gun when he doesn't shoot; his mentor Sam is "passionate and proud"; Ike at ten has dedicated his life "to the wilderness with patience and humility"; his eagerness for hunting is tempered with "an abjectness, a sense of his own fragility and impotence against the timeless woods"; he is too humble to know that he will be the first to come near to the bear, be "run over" by him; he relinquishes his gun "in humility and peace and without regret"; he approaches Old Ben with beating heart but with steadiness.

In Part II the keywords strangely vanish until one significant paragraph at the end. It is because this section is in a measure an exemplum of pride and independence, and of the fixing of the fates which consists in the finding of the proper instruments for the climactic ceremony. The words are not needed, for the action is enough. In Part I Ike had learned humility as well as skill, but the skill, too personal, had not yet become pride to balance the humility. In Part II we have the episode of the fyce which ambushed the Bear, which bayed on the hounds and ran to Old Ben with insane courage, forcing Ike to do the same until "it seemed to him that he was directly under the bear. He could smell it, strong and hot and rank. Sprawling, he looked up where it loomed and towered over him like a thunderclap."

Neither Ike nor the fyce, though brave even to foolhardiness, are the proper instruments. Those instruments are Boon and Lion, and the section is devoted to showing how Lion's independence is tamed by Sam and Boon, but tamed only insofar as to make him obsessed with a need to kill Old Ben. Here humility is not made into pride, but pride is tempered. Boon becomes so much Lion's double that he defies his employer Major de Spain, who had ordered Lion outside so that his scent would not be ruined by "the smell of Boon's unwashed body and his wet hunting-clothes." The next night he is back with Boon. With humor the Major admits that he is outsmarted. And Boon is right—the powerful odor of Old Ben, which had come so close to Ike, was not likely to be obscured by Boon and Lion's common bed. On Old Ben's seventh appearance, just before the climactic kill, Boon fails, to his utter shame, to shoot him. He laments, concerned only with Lion's reaction: "I ain't fit to sleep with him." The section closes with Ike's meditation: "So he should have hated and feared Lion. Yet he did not. It seemed to him that there was a fatality in it. It seemed to him that something, he didn't know what, was beginning; had already begun. It was like the last act on a set stage. It was the beginning of the end of something, he didn't know what except that he would not grieve. He would be humble and proud that he had been found worthy to be a part of it too or even just to see it too." Ike has learned that the pride comes from sharing the rite, from collective rather than individual action. He must not hate Lion, who replaces his double the fyce as major actor just as Boon replaces Ike. Boon's apparent independence and pride is a part of the sense of collective destiny; he must not be separated from Lion, for their *mana* or spirit power is reciprocal. Boon's "humility" when he fails Lion is the other side of the coin; to us it is almost absurd sensitivity, but Boon knows that he has not yet performed his task rightly, and that Lion knows it.

By Part III, Ike possesses the pair of virtues. In Memphis with Boon, the Major has put him in charge of the money, with orders to give Boon nothing for whiskey. But Ike is loyal to Boon, who had once saved him from a wild, unbroken horse, and he disobeys the Major and gives Boon a dollar. Waiting outside the saloon, Ike "felt the old lift of the heart, as pristine as ever, as on the first day; he would never lose it, no matter how old in hunting and pursuit: the best, the best of all breathing, the humility and the pride." The episode is not mere comedy; Boon's drinking, while it demonstrates his warfare with the town, has no ill effects. It is a necessary communion with the wine which will strengthen him for his final role. Ike remains true to his basic ties with Boon, as the keywords illustrate. Once more Boon exemplifies pride and valor; working in partnership with Lion he kills Old Ben and now, more openly, defies the Major:

> "Boon!" Major de Spain said. They looked at one another. Boon was a good head taller than Major de Spain; even the boy was taller now than Major de Spain.
>
> "I've got to get the doctor," Boon said. "His goddam guts——"
>
> "All right," Major de Spain said.

The whiskey-soaked, no-'count half-breed, who can do nothing but drink in town because he is so alien there, and who must through his feeling of inferiority brag through liquor of Lion and the chase of Old Ben, rises finally to the greatest height of physical valor and pride of any character in the story, as he confronts the great Bear and kills him. After the kill, disregarding his own injuries and those of Sam Fathers, he tends the disembowelled Lion like the lover that he is. It is pride overcoming humility; through great, rash heedless acts, compelled by destiny and by love, Boon will pay for his excess of virtue; by the last act Boon, mad with contact with the God and the loss of his beloved Wilderness and his beloved Lion, is a mass of shivering hysteria. Part V is merely a coda to Part III; Ike pays humble tribute to the graves of Sam and Lion and Old Ben; Boon smashes his gun while the squirrels leap about—ostensibly because it had jammed, actually because it is a tainted weapon, unlike the primitive woodsman's knife[16] with which he had killed Old Ben. His final cry is ironic:

"Get out of here! Don't touch them! Don't touch a one of them! They're mine!" On the surface he means the squirrels, the last vestige of the wild beings to whom his life had been devoted. But the mad cry is of greed, directed to his best human friend Ike; the craving is for the pride of possession, the vice which has destroyed the wilderness. Ike has learned the humility of pride; Boon has never learned the humility; he is in imbalance, out of *mesure*, mad.

III

So far we have said nothing of Part IV and its treatment of pride and humility; we have reserved it for an assault on our final problem—how the apparently incoherent flashback fits the story as a whole. Pride and humility, learned from initiation and climactic Hunt, lead Ike to transcend his culture and to do it by strength gained from the culture itself. In no section, except the first, are the keywords more significantly used.

The narrative now moves out of its hunting context, from the protecting womb of the wilderness, to the stages of history and of the cosmos, to a real and not a vicarious testing of Isaac McCaslin. Ike declares that his repudiation of the land is no repudiation because the earlier owners had never owned it. God had given it to men; He had allowed them "to hold the earth mutual and intact in the communal anonymity of brotherhood, and all the fee He asked was pity and humility and sufferance and endurance and the sweat of his face for bread." God, though blind and dispossessed of Eden, suffered through the corruptions of Roman bagnios and Germanic hordes "until He used a simple egg to discover to them a new world where a nation of people could be founded in humility and pity and sufferance and pride of one to another."

[16] See note 8.

It becomes clear that the true pride and endurance lies in the humblest of status—in the Northern Negro who defies Cass and marries Fonsiba, Ike's first cousin by Carothers's miscegenation, who proudly dotes on the white man's weapon, the book, at the risk of losing his livelihood on the farm which he cannot run; even more so in the Southern Negro Lucas, Fonsiba's youngest brother, biggety and defiant and proud, who on his twenty-first birthday demands his heritage from Cass.

The destinies are working themselves out; even God must await them. Having created man, "He could have known no more of hope than He could of pride and grief, but He didn't hope He just waited because He had made them." Humility is of the Godhead itself. But "He had seen how in individual cases" men "were capable of anything." There were Buck and Buddy, Lucas, Sam and Ike, all of whom learned both pride and humility, not through reason but, like the frantic fyce, through an irrational bravery. Keats's eternal truth and beauty "covers all things which touch the heart—honor and pride and pity and justice and courage and love. . . . what the heart holds to becomes truth, as far as we know truth." With this discovery that one must rest one's mortal case not on reason or conformity or the social pressures, or even on the marked-out destinies, Ike learns that he is free to repudiate his heritage. Cass, a lesser soul though a worthy one, who half understands Ike as he tries to dissuade him, denies the freedom of choice. Negro and White shall never be free, "we from them nor they from us . . . I am what I am; I will be always what I was born and have always been." Not so, says Ike, "Sam Fathers set me free." And he adopts the mystic role of the Carpenter[17] who had also repudiated the World, the Flesh, and the Devil. Ike gives up his land, and tries to live a life free from the obsessions of property and the taint of slavery. But he makes his great gesture "not in mere static and hopeful emulation of the Nazarene . . . (without the arrogance of false humility and without the false humbleness of pride, who intended to earn his bread, didn't especially want to earn it but had to earn his bread . . .) because if the Nazarene had found carpentering good for the life and ends He had assumed and elected to serve, it would be all right too for Isaac McCaslin."

Ike's exact ends are unclear; like Sam Fathers he could have defined completely neither pride nor humility. Though it is plain that the paradoxical words mean much to Faulkner, critics have said little about them. Perhaps there has been some fear that the author is a mere slave to the verbal fashions of a time when Eliot and Empson have encouraged literary ambivalences. Yet it is easy to show that the linking of pride and hu-

[17] My colleague, John Muste, has prepared a study underlining the irony which lies in Ike's choice of a profession—timber, the product of the logger and the sawmill, is the raw material of the carpenter's craft. Hence the destruction of the wilderness is essential for Ike's act of repudiation.

mility is much older than the Freudian present. Macarius, a saint of the Egyptian desert in the early days of Christian asceticism, forces the devil, ancient symbol of pride, to complain:

> "In only one thing dost thou overmaster me." And when the saint asked what that might be, he answered "In thy humility." And the saint fell on his knees—it may be to repel this last and subtlest temptation—and the devil vanished into the air.[18]

We will recall the fourth and final temptation which assailed Eliot's Becket in *Murder in the Cathedral*. The deadliest sin of all may be pride in one's own humility. So Christianity: it was the essence of the Renaissance to penetrate to a juncture between the two. Erwin Panofsky tells us:

> It is from this ambivalent conception of *humanitas* that humanism was born. It is not so much a movement as an attitude which can be defined as the conviction of the dignity of man, based on both the insistence on human values (rationality and freedom) and the acceptance of human limitations (fallibility and frailty); from this two postulates result—responsibility and tolerance.[19]

Is there a better statement of the forces which strengthened Ike to his great repudiation—the responsibility of pride and the tolerance of humility?

The validity of the ambivalence is shown in two great antagonistic eighteenth-century figures, the hedonistic mystic William Blake and the stern moralist Immanuel Kant. Blake reverses, in his fragmentary *The Everlasting Gospel*, the usual meaning of the words:

> I was standing by when Jesus died;
> What I call'd humility, they call'd pride.
> He who loves his enemies betrays his friends.
> This is surely not what Jesus intends;
> But the sneaking pride of heroic schools,
> And the Scribes' and Pharisees' virtuous rules,
> For He acts with honest, triumphant pride,
> And this is the cause that Jesus died.
> He did not die with Christian ease,
> Asking pardon of His enemies:
> If He had, Caiaphas would forgive;
> Sneaking submission can always live. . . .
> God wants not man to humble himself:
> That is the trick of the Ancient Elf.
> This is the race that Jesus ran:
> Humble to God, haughty to man. . . .

[18] Helen Waddell, *The Desert Fathers* (Ann Arbor Paperbacks, 1960), pp. 12–13.
[19] Erwin Panofsky, *Meaning in the Visual Arts* (New York: Anchor Books, 1955), p. 2.

"Thou art a Man: God is no more:
Thy own Humanity learn to adore,
For that is My spirit of life." . . .
But when Jesus was crucified,
Then was perfected His galling pride.[20]

Blake does not expect his transvaluation of values to gain immediate acceptance:

I am sure this Jesus will not do,
Either for Englishman or Jew.

But Blake, though perhaps much akin to the mature and transcending Ike McCaslin, is scarcely a respectable authority for the joining of pride and humility. Hence we may turn to Immanuel Kant, the moral giant of Königsberg, and ancestor of modern philosophy:

> The moral law is holy (unyielding) and demands holiness of morals, although all moral perfection to which man can attain is only virtue . . . consequently, man can achieve only a self-esteem combined with humility. . . . Fontanelle says, "I bow to a great man, but my mind does not bow." I can add; to a humble plain man, in whom I perceive righteousness in a higher degree than I am conscious of in myself, *my mind bows* whether I choose or not, and however high I carry my head that me may not forget my superior position. Why? His example holds a law before me which strikes down my self-conceit when I compare my own conduct with it. . . . Nevertheless . . . when once we renounce our self-conceit and respect has established its practical influence, we cannot ever satisfy ourselves in contemplating the majesty of this law, and the soul believes itself to be elevated in proportion as it sees the holy law as elevated over it and its frail nature.[21]

Humility and the pride of perfection, in other words, are closely allied: in Saint Macarius, Renaissance humanism, Kant's man, and Blake's and Faulkner's Nazarene.

IV

Being a modern man Ike does not seek celibacy, as Christ and His followers had done, but marries a woman who soon betrays that her eye is on the land which he had repudiated but could, she believes, have back again if he wished. Basically frigid by nature, she tries to seduce

[20] John Sampson, ed., *The Poetical Works of William Blake* (New York: Oxford University Press, 1958), pp. 150–151, 157. See Milton O. Percival, *William Blake's Circle of Destiny* (New York: Columbia University Press, 1938), pp. 188, 195.

[21] Lewis W. Beck, ed., *The Critique of Practical Reason* (Chicago: The University of Chicago Press, 1949), copyright 1949 by The University of Chicago, pp. 184–185, 231; see also pp. 39, 41, 181; see also *Critique of Pure Reason* (London: J. M. Dent, 1942), p. 468 (pride or humility depends on a subjective or objective view of belief in God).

him with her body and the promise of a son and heir, but Ike refuses the temptation and the marriage breaks up with a hysterical laughter on her possessive part which is repeated in the hysteria of Boon, also dispossessed, at the end of the story. Ike himself is repudiated by the nameless woman who for a brief time shared his bed.

This passage means many things, and it is not certain just which of them Faulkner wishes to keep uppermost. In his public comments he has interpreted the episode wholly in a particular vein, without universal significance: a good woman might have helped Ike in his battle with the results of Negro slavery and miscegenation.[22] But we might predict that Ike's initiation and skill in the hunt, won in exclusively masculine company, could not be transferred to a world which included woman. As many a man has found, woman is a hostage to fortune: the commitment to dynastic aims rather than to the "pure" aims of the individual; the commitment to property because the freedom to choose repudiation becomes complex when one has a wife and child to support. Woman, moreover, meant miscegenation; the crimes of Carothers which forced Ike to his gesture are bound up in the lusts of the flesh and the pride of life.

Woman thus has no place in Ike's world of values; he refuses the rationalization which exalts the white woman at the expense of her black sister, and to the peril of her black brother. As W. J. Cash puts it:

> We strike back to the fact that this Southern woman's place in the Southern mind proceeded primarily from the natural tendency of the great basic pattern of pride in superiority of race to center upon her as the perpetuity of that superiority in legitimate line, and attached itself precisely, and before anything else, to her enormous remoteness from the males of the inferior group, to the absolute taboo on any sexual approach to her by the Negro. . . . What Southerners felt, therefore, was that any assertion of any kind on the part of the Negro constituted in a perfectly real manner an attack on the Southern woman . . . a condition for which the term "rape" stood as truly as for the *de facto* deed.[23]

Ike's renunciation of the world of woman goes back at least one generation to Uncle Buck, who was forced into marriage with Miss Sophonsiba by a card game and an intriguing brother. The gesture of Uncle Buck and Uncle Buddy, which had consisted of manumitting the Negroes and of building a house with their own hands (they are carpenters before Isaac) and the herding of the Negroes into the Big House of their father Carothers McCaslin, had to take place before the marriage. After Miss Sophonsiba, mother of Ike, has died, Uncle Buddy takes on the shaman's role of cook. Miss Sophonsiba does not share men's guilt; she drives her brother Hubert's black concubine away; if women had been masters there

[22] Gwynn and Blotner, pp. 275–276.
[23] Cash, pp. 118–119.

would have been no taint, and thus women cannot understand man's obsession with guilt and repentance.

But the guilt leads to powerful action in Ike's case, and he is sure that from time to time some, like the Nazarene, Uncle Buck and Uncle Buddy, and himself, will be able to transcend the cultural environment into which they are born, and make the gesture which casts off the tainted heritage, the original sin. In this he is like Huck Finn, torn between his cultural and his private values: "it hit me all of a sudden that here was the plain hand of Providence slapping me in the face and letting me know my wickedness was being watched all the time from up there in heaven, whilst I was stealing a poor old woman's nigger that hadn't ever done me no harm. . . ." The training of his society tells Huck clearly that he must give back his friend Nigger Jim, and he writes a letter to Jim's owner, Miss Watson. But observe the ambiguity in the illiterate boy's misplaced modifier. It was not only Miss Watson, but Jim as well, that "hadn't ever done me no harm." So Huck, like Ike, repudiates—here the letter and the heavenly climate: " 'All right, then, I'll *go* to hell'—and tore it up." He had tried to pray to God for what seemed to be help, but "the words wouldn't come," for, as he realized, "You can't pray a lie—I found that out." He was holding on to what seemed to be the greatest sin of all, before God Himself—the refusal to follow his culture's fiat and to give Jim up. But again the ambivalence—what, after all, is the lie?

These "transcendences" of two Southern boys in the face of the great problem of the Negro appear like heroism to one born in the North. And so they are; any man who learns to probe to the center of the unsolved problems of his community and to try, even as lonely individual, to once make the right gesture, is a hero, like Thoreau with his Civil Disobedience, or Antigone with her obeisance to the gods in the burial of her brothers and her defiance of Creon. But we must come up short before we end in regional condescension—a major obstacle to helping the South to solve its problem or the North to solve its kindred ones. The heroism is nothing without the ambivalence, without the genuine struggle between old cultural and newly emerging values. Can anyone but the Southern boy be involved in this particular kind of heroic defiance? Can he achieve it without the aid of the values his culture has provided for him? It was the pride and humility gained in the wilderness, surrounded by a simple world of masculine values, and demonstrating the worth of every creature—the half-breed Negro and Indian Sam Fathers; the drunken no-'count Boon; Major de Spain and Cass, gentle in breeding and will but as yet unwilling to forego the more obvious values of their culture; the furious fyce and the calculating ominous Lion and the savage, cunning and god-like Old Ben; the poor white swampers who are in the main spectators but yet passionate followers of the Hunt—all of these lie behind this Southern boy who makes a quixotic gesture to erase, he hopes, the miscegenation of his fathers, and condemns his own line to sterility and his own life to a compulsive repetition of the patterns of his childhood initiation, the endless, seasonal hunt. Such a chivalric gesture was only made possible by the nature of the South itself, with its individualism learned in the Edenic wilderness and its romanticism learned from Sir Walter Scott.[24] The South provided the hunting culture, with Ike's long training and testing in the hands of Sam Fathers, true heir, if there was one, to the land—descendant of Doom and double of the Bear that walked like a Man. While an initiation is a rebirth into the culture which surrounds one, it paradoxically may give one the strength to rise above the culture's own ostensible values. To transcend one's culture one must learn from it, one must lean upon it for the upward leap; if there is no agony in the cutting of the ties it may be presumed that there are no ties of importance to cut.

Kenneth LaBudde, in his study of "Cultural Primitivism in William Faulkner's 'The Bear' "[25] shares with this essay of mine an interest in the anthropological parallels to Ike's story. I cannot agree with him, however, in reducing Faulkner's "driving complexity" to a Rousseauistic myth. His conclusion that "Wisdom is achieved by intuition schooled by nature rather than by reason fashioned according to the ways of men" is only part of the truth. The Bear is as ambiguous as Moby Dick; if he is the doomed integral Wilderness he is also the creator of "a corridor of wreckage and destruction beginning back before the boy was born . . . a phantom, epitome and apotheosis of the old, wild life which the little puny humans swarmed and hacked at in a fury of abhorrence and fear." There is similar irony in the Major's charge that Old Ben must now be hunted because he has threatened sacred "property" by killing the colt. Our radical instincts are aroused by this; it would seem that puny man puts property above heroism and excellence. Yet, radical or conservative, we are human beings, and we find it hard to divorce ourselves from the championing of mankind, collective or individual, against the destructive forces of nature, whether they are in the wilderness, the sea, or in outer space. Faulkner essentially justifies our position in his comments external to the text.[26] Discussing the destruction of Old Ben and the wilderness he says:

> change can destroy what is irreplaceable. . . . But if in the end that makes more education for more people, and more food for more people, more of the good things of life. . . . it is worth destroying the wilderness. But if all the destruction of the wilderness does is to give more people more automobiles just to ride around in, then the wilderness was better.

[24] Cash, pp. 127–135 above.
[25] LaBudde, pp. 322–328.
[26] Gwynn and Blotner, p. 277.

It is interesting to note that another Southern novelist also saw the lumber companies as a destructive force. Planning a novel about the decay of an aristocratic family just after the Civil War, Thomas Wolfe projected the following element in the plot: "Against Eugene's and his mother's protest that to sell their land at next to nothing is criminal, the Colonel hard-pressed for money, and unwilling to work or have his boys work, sells his 500,000 acres for 25 cents an acre to a New Eng. lumber firm."[27] The coincidence shows that there is a real as well as a symbolic basis for the wilderness theme; it is no mere noble savagery.

A simple primitivism is not borne out by other figures in the story besides Old Ben. Boon is the rugged hero of the hunt, who fights Old Ben face to face with knife rather than with gun and risks his own life to save Lion, yet in town he is a self-conscious yokel, forced to drink whiskey to hide his embarrassments and to build his ego, and at the end of the story he goes mad, incapable of coping with civilization. His drunkenness and his fidelity to the Major are both virtues (the Major) or both vices (Cass). General Compson exalts the Hunt above school as a means to education; yet it is clear that Ike has learned the tale of human history both broad and narrow, both from Eden on to the major present and in the pages of the family ledgers. One must *read* to do this, and reading is not an accomplishment of noble savages. The Negro's freedom and honor is the subject of *The Bear* and even more of "Delta Autumn"; yet the one Negro in the hunting story (eliminating the symbolic half-breed Sam Fathers) is Ash, the cook, who has never learned to hunt, and who through his jealousy of Ike's baptism of blood becomes the subject of a comic hunting story about a gun which went off by itself.

The poetic justices of primitivism are cancelled out by the tragic spirit. God looks "upon this land this South for which he had done so much with woods for game and streams for fish and deep rich soil for seed and lush springs to sprout it and long summers to mature it and serene falls to harvest it and short mild winters for men and animals, and saw no hope anywhere and looked beyond it where hope should have been, where to East North and West lay illimitable that whole hopeful continent dedicated as a refuge and sanctuary of liberty and freedom from what you called the old world's worthless evening, and saw the rich descendants of slavers, females of both sexes . . . passing resolutions about horror and outrage in warm and air-proof halls." Only John Brown transcended this universal depravity. The Negro, despite his role as Noble Savage, his potential for endurance and his primitive strength, is human enough to share original sin: "those upon whom freedom and equality had been dumped overnight and without warning or preparation or any training in how to employ it or even just endure it and who misused it, not as children would

[27] *Thomas Wolfe's Letters to His Mother*, ed., John K. Terry (New York: Charles Scribner's Sons, 1946), pp. 16, 26.

nor yet because they had been so long in bondage and then so suddenly freed, but misused it as human beings always misuse freedom." Faulkner, in short, pays the Negro his tribute as a man, but with it must come man's human weaknesses.

Ike's freedom, patterned upon the initiation or not, is an achieved success, a progress rather than a nostalgic regression, a dynamism of the future rather than a return to the past, however much it has its roots in the culture and hence in the history of the race. As Cass, envious of Ike's release but aware of his own lack of it, says, the great hunt of the story proper is linked to the gesture of repudiation. "Chosen, I suppose (I will concede it) out of all your time by Him, as you say Buck and Buddy were from theirs. And it took Him a bear and an old man and four years just for you. And it took you fourteen years to reach that point and about that many, maybe more, for Old Ben, and more than seventy for Sam Fathers. And you just one. How long then? How long?" This is tragedy, a tragic conflict aided by God between man and his own society, the slow inching upward of evolution, and not the regression of primitivism. Redemptive tragedy, for the individual falls by the wayside as he saves us all. The primitive provides strength for those who would make civilization civilized, not a haven for those merely weary of civilization. Ike's gesture, as we can see, was dynamic and redemptive, a step in the salvation of the oppressed, the primitive; his later life was a regression, as we shall see in "Delta Autumn," for he was himself caught in the static back-eddies of "repudiation." There is, after all, a snake in Eden, and it has been there from the beginning.

Fortified, then, by the long developed ceremonial of the hunt and by the individualism and romanticism of his Southern culture. Ike has the courage to make the initial repudiation, and to sustain it in spite of the demonic temptation offered by his greedy and hysterical wife. He has emulated the Nazarene, and he is one therefore of those many characters of Faulkner, like Joe Christmas in *Light in August* and the Corporal in *The Fable,* who seem to repeat among proud and humble men, the meek who shall inherit the earth, the story of the Passion. Faulkner's attitude towards such symbolic readings has always been cavalier and oblique:

> And that Christ story is one of the best stories that man has invented, assuming that he did invent that story, and of course it will recur. Everyone that has had the story of Christ and the Passion as part of his Christian background will in time draw from that. There was no deliberate attempt to repeat it. That the people to me come first. The symbolism comes second. . . . Well, one symbol was the bear represented the vanishing wilderness. The little dog that wasn't scared of the bear represented the indomitable spirit of man. I'll have to dig back and get up some more of these symbols, because I have learned around an even dozen that I put into that story without knowing it.[28]

[28] Gwynn and Blotner, pp. 117, 280.

Some of this is chaff, of course, the protective coloration of an author besieged by brash young students and persistent old women to tell the inmost secrets of his craft, which are either in his eyes inferrable from his text or else not worth pursuing. But it allows us the identification of Ike with the Nazarene; Ike is at least a diminished Christ.

Elsewhere Faulkner has said that Ike is really a "no-'count," a man who is anything but the hero of history. Here he would seem to accept the doubts of Major de Spain, who fears that Ike, in renouncing his heritage, has "just quit." The Major modifies his remark by saying "I have watched you in the woods too much and I don't believe you just quit even if it does look damn like it." Perhaps this is mere persuasion, calculated to cause Ike to change his course once again, though a comparison to the Nazarene follows. But Ike does, to all respectable people, become a no-'count, who gives up his farm and becomes a poor menial and spends his life passing on the lore of Sam Fathers, second-hand, to youngsters.

Faulkner has been careful not to endow him with omniscience. His renunciation of the world of woman's love, which surely means the natural world of society, may not be as wise as it seems. Perhaps there is some deficiency in this hunter, initiated into a man's world.

He triumphs, surely, in *The Bear*. But *The Bear* must be read along with "Delta Autumn," in which a young Negro girl, seduced by his kinsman Roth Edmonds, turns out to be a daughter of his black cousin Tennie's Jim. Ike, who has the sensitivity and judgment to give her the horn which is a symbol of their mutual heritage, nevertheless urges her to go back North and to marry a man of her own race (as Fonsiba, without notable success, had done). The girl's proud words force a large salient of doubt into the assumption that Ike has really cut loose from his culture:

> "Old man," she said, "have you lived so long and forgotten so much that you don't remember anything you ever knew or felt or even heard about love?"

If Ike is a Christ-figure, he is a much diminished one; he may in his youth have cast off Agape as well as Eros. Yet in his age he can still learn something: though the wall between the races is still thick and high, and its vanishing may be far in the future, it may, given some centuries, vanish completely. From a woman he learns of his deficiency, and with that knowledge he transcends not only the values of his people, his culture, but also those of the Hunt itself. The values of the Hunt had aided him to surmount the flaws of his immediate society, the South and the wider world of men's greed; the values of Love, learned from a Negro girl, may help him at last to surmount the limits of the cloistered Hunt.

> "It was a doe," he said.

Critical Interpretations of "The Bear"

Brief remarks by two distinguished critics of Faulkner follow longer critical essays; together they represent the wide range of interpretation evoked by "The Bear."

The Hero in the New World: William Faulkner's The Bear

R. W. B. Lewis

If, as several of Faulkner's most enlightened observers have suggested, the novels and stories preceding *Go Down, Moses* possess an atmosphere like that of the Old Testament, then *The Bear* may be regarded as Faulkner's first sustained venture towards the more hopeful and liberated world after the Incarnation. It is also of course a story about the South in the 1880's, when the frontier was rapidly disappearing. And it is another American *bildungsroman*, another tale of a boy growing up in America, with all the special obstacles to moral maturity which our culture has erected and which comprise the drama for many another sad or lucky protagonist of fiction. We must not forget that *The Bear* is grounded in these historic and locally traditional elements. But we should say at the outset that in it

Reprinted from R. W. B. Lewis, "The Hero in the New World: William Faulkner's *The Bear*," *Kenyon Review*, XIII: 4 (Autumn 1951), 641–660, by permission of Kenyon College and the author.

we meet Faulkner's first full-fledged hero—and that he is a young man who quite deliberately takes up carpentering because

> if the Nazarene had found carpentering good for the life and ends He had assumed and elected to serve, it would be all right too for Isaac McCaslin.

The Bear is a canticle or chant relating the birth, the baptism and the early trials of Isaac McCaslin; it is ceremonious in style, and it is not lacking in dimly seen miraculous events. We get moreover *an* incarnation, if not *the* Incarnation: or at least we get a reincarnation; and we witness an act of atonement which may conceivably flower into a redemption.

Consequently *The Bear* is a pivotal work. Change is of its essence. Our notion about it is reinforced when we encounter the same reanimated human will at work and a still larger conviction of human freedom in the novel which followed it, *Intruder in the Dust*. In both stories, but much more spectacularly and indeed much more visibly in *The Bear*, what is positive in human nature and in the moral structure of the world envelops and surrounds what is evil; which is to say, more significantly, that the corrupting and the destructive and the desperate in human experience become known to us in their opposition and even their subordination to the creative and the soul-preserving. This presents us with just the sort of dramatic clarity that seems otherwise denied to writers for almost a century. The highest reaches of modern literature, in fact, have taken the form of an ultimate and vibrant duplicity, the best account of our times that honest genius has been empowered to construct—with every virtue and every value rendered instantly suspect by the ironic co-existence of its opposite: Ahab and Starbuck, and all their fellows, in a never-ending exchange of the reader's allegiance. We have known these splendid discords and artful confusions in the early novels of William Faulkner: which is why *The Bear* appears as pivotal; although it is as likely to appear merely old-fashioned, and to be regretted—the way *Billy Budd* is sometimes regretted—as a regression to lucidity.

It is true, and worth pausing over for a moment, that in those earlier novels as well a not entirely dissimilar ethical distribution can be alleged. *As I Lay Dying*, for example, and *Light in August* have been compared to Jacobean drama; presumably with the thought that they are projections of worlds wherein what is human or decent or pure flickers uncertainly in a darkness charged with violence and horror; the horror and the darkness being the norm, and the measure of such pitiful virtue as stirs feebly to combat them. But even there, something more ancient and enduring, something more substantial than the central tragic characters and their wicked propensities flows through them and reaffirms itself at the end as it flows on into the future. And this is what, with a wry face, we have to call life itself. The grimace is due to the form in which life re-exerts itself:

a new set of false teeth, in *As I Lay Dying,* a new wife for Anse Bundren: "a kind of duck-shaped woman all dressed up, with them kind of hard-looking pop eyes like she was daring ere a man to say nothing"; an illegitimate child, which Dewey Dell has not found the medical means to get rid of. Life in *Light in August* is personified on the first and the last pages by Lena Grove, moving calmly and with animal obstinacy across a stage littered elsewhere with depravity and death, carrying in her womb her own bastard child, to be born on the other side of town. But it would scarcely be honest to describe either novel as a drama of the triumph of life: the design in each case is, if anything, a tension between creative and destructive possibilities.

In *The Bear,* however, the balance is tipped. What we discover first, along with young Ike McCaslin, and what determines his and our subsequent judgments is an archetypal or ideal human personality. It is something composed of a cluster of virtues unambiguously present from the beginning, as qualities to be striven for, prizes to be won: proving their efficacy in the mastery of self and the conquest of temptation—pity and humility and courage and pride and the will to endure and the rest. Their names recur with musical regularity, like the burden of a song. And together they are what we may call the honorable: something Roman and a trifle stiff, but independent of the fluctuation of moral fashions in the city. It is the honorable which permeates the wilderness, scene of the main action and home of the main actors in the story. And like Old Ben, the bear, patriarch of the wilderness, embodying the virtues in some undefined and magical way, the honorable exists as an ethical reality before the story opens, "before the boy was born": as a glimpse of immortality. It is an ideal prior to civilization, but it is not an uncivilized ideal and has nothing to do with noble savagery; it is prior exactly insofar as it is ideal, not so much older as timeless; and taking the humanly recognizable shape of a ritual pattern of behavior. The narrative image of that pattern is "the yearly rendez-vous," "the yearly pageant-rite of the old bear's furious immortality": the annual duel between the skilled hunters and the shaggy, tremendous, indomitable Old Ben. It is a duel enacted within a solid set of conventions and rules, faultlessly observed on both sides. This is the ritual by participation in which the young hero, Isaac McCaslin, becomes reborn and baptized, receives the sacramental blessing and accomplishes his moral liberation. It is the substance of the first half of the story; in a sense I will suggest later, it is the whole of the story; the rest of the book tells us how a properly baptized and educated hero may act when confronted with evil.

But it is evident that in order to explain these remarks and to see more deeply into the total experience, we must examine the experience in its only exact and living form. We must, that is, look more closely at the story's structure.

II

The difficulty of any Faulkner story lies in the order of its telling. He has always provided us with lots of action; and if his unconventional arrangement of incidents sometimes suggests an antic shuffle through a fateful crazy-house, it does at least avoid the other extreme in modern fiction: it never dissolves into atmosphere and "situation." What *happens* in a Faulkner story is more important than anything else; but it is the last thing we understand—we are let in on it gradually, from many different viewpoints and at different times. *The Bear* has a plot relatively simpler than, say, *The Sound and the Fury:* but here also Faulkner has played weird tricks with chronology. In particular, he has concluded his narrative with an episode that occurs at a moment earlier in conventional time than one of the chief episodes which precede it in the telling. If we follow the events in the life of Isaac McCaslin rather than the numerical sequence of the sections, we discover this personal history:

(Sections One, Two, Three) A boy named Ike McCaslin grows up in Mississippi, during the years after the Civil War. Every year from the time he is ten, he goes bear-hunting in the still untracked wilderness north of the town, along with his cousin Cass and some of the town's leading citizens—all highly skilled hunters. He gradually acquires some of the skill of the older men, and the virtues that are the product of so severe and masculine a life. There is one bear, greater and older than any of the others, who engages the hunters in an annual duel. He is called Old Ben. When the boy is sixteen, Old Ben is killed by one of the men and a huge mongrel dog.

(Section Five) After Old Ben's death, the boy, now eighteen, comes back once to the wilderness, but the old hunting-lodge is gone, the group of hunters broken up, and tourists have begun to invade and transform the forest. He encounters Boon Hogganbeck, the man who had killed Old Ben, and finds him reduced to hysteria.

(Section Four) At the age of twenty-one, Ike inherits the land and money that have been passed down through his father (known as Uncle Buck) from his grandfather, Carothers McCaslin. Ike decides to give up this inheritance, since he had previously discovered that it is tainted at the source by the misdeeds of his grandfather. The latter had seduced and had a child by a negress slave, Tomasina, who may well have been his own daughter also. Such a combination of incest and miscegenation represents for Ike an image of the evil condition of the South—and of humanity in general from the beginning of time. Ike determines not to compromise with this condition. He continues to live a simple, somewhat Christ-like existence. He takes up carpentering and marries the daughter of his partner. He has no children.

Thus the "real life" equivalent of the career of Ike McCaslin; but we must keep in mind, during the remarks that follow, that we come upon the incidents of his twenty-first year and of his later years *before* we are told about the return to the woods, at eighteen, in the fifth section.

André Gide, when he was writing *The Counterfeiters,* confided to his journal an ambition to render the events of his novel *légèrement déformés,* so that the reader's interest might be aroused in the effort to restore the originals: the reader becoming thereby the author's collaborator. Faulkner's motive may be much the same; his so-called contempt for the reader (and others have made the point) has the effect anyhow of involving the reader nearly to the extent of devouring him. Certainly no other American writer engages his readers so strenuously; and there is no doubt that, except for those who fear and resent him on quite other grounds, the readers of Faulkner do or can derive immense aesthetic pleasure in that participation with him that verges on the creative. Homer and Virgil (not to mention Conrad, or the Russians) ask no less of us. *The Odyssey,* for example, indicates importance by the chronological order of presentation, and we can only assess the famous wanderings of Odysseus when we notice that they are not given us directly but as they issue much later from the memory of a gifted liar: much, though Ike is no liar, as the revelations of evil exist primarily in the young man's memory. And in the *Aeneid* of Virgil (a poet much closer to Faulkner), the last event in the poem occurs many centuries before some of the events already described in it. Here of course the grandiose history of the ages to come appears explicitly as a prophecy, and almost as a dream: but I am willing to suggest that such may also be the nature of the fourth section in *The Bear.*

Before we get that far, however, a few mechanical observations may be helpful. It is worth seeing that the fourth section has the same purely formal organization and is roughly the same in length as the first three combined: this suggests, rightly, that it has the function of counter-weight. Both of these two large parts begin at a certain moment in Ike's life (16 and 21 respectively), retreat to an earlier period and circle back through their starting-points. The recurring insistence of Faulkner upon his hero's age is too striking to be overlooked: a whispering connivance, like a plea: "He was sixteen then . . . then he was sixteen." Ike's age is the chief structural element; and his sixteenth year was the *annus mirabilis:* the story flows through that year on three distinct occasions, as though only by this means could the contradictory richness of its experience be made apparent.

This aspect of the structure can be presented graphically, while not forgetting the many warnings against draining away Faulkner's vitality in cold schemas. [See the figure on page 193.] The graph suggests, at least, the very considerable artfulness that governs Faulkner's temporal rearrangements; if we have survived the shock of the initial disorder, we can admire the elegance and symmetry in the redistribution. The solid lines

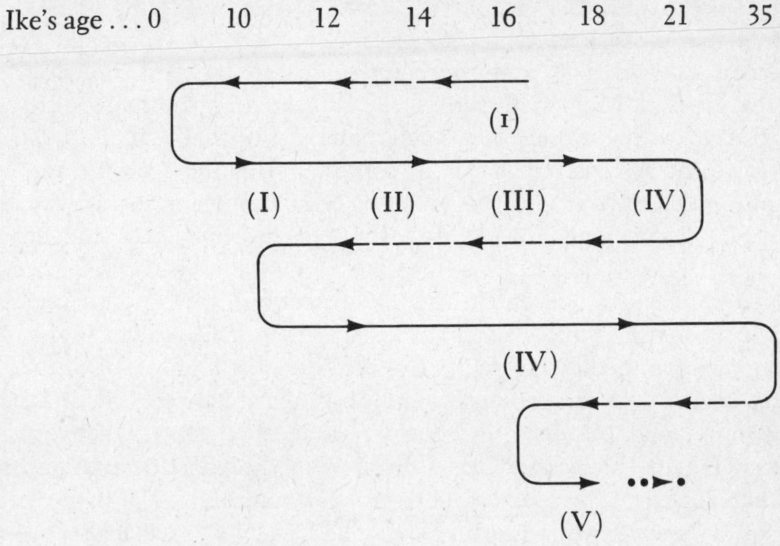

are of course the sustained narrative, and the broken lines the more rapid shifts in time: even these, however, not so much sudden leaps across the years as a fading backward of memory or a surge forward of imagination. But while we are aware of strong currents carrying us forward and backward in *The Bear,* we must also acknowledge the corollary impression that time is motionless, and everything is occurring simultaneously. This effect Faulkner achieves by bringing in past events as they are returned to in present memory: by parentheses, and by parentheses within those parentheses, like one memory jogging another. He achieves it too, in his narrative order, by the triple journey through the sixteenth year. *The Bear* thus constitutes (as the graph may dimly show) a unique conjunction of time and eternity: if we accept the word of Boethius, who distinguished between them as between a flowing-away and a standing-still.

The story begins in Ike's sixteenth year. It would have to, because it is Ike's story, and it is only then that his history ceases to be mysterious; it is only then that he completes the ritual of his initiation. Till that moment he had grasped the importance but not fully the meaning of the experience.

> It seemed to him there was a fatality in it. It seemed to him that something, he didn't know what, was beginning; had already begun. It was like the last act on a set stage. It was the beginning of the end of something, he didn't know what except that he would not grieve. He would be humble and proud that he had been found worthy to be a part of it or even just to see it too.

The drama he is engaged in is the drama of death and birth, and this is what he is disciplined to perceive as the story returns, in part three, to the great year: the death of Old Ben, of Sam Fathers, of Lion—and of the wilderness as wilderness and the companionship Ike had known there; and the birth of Isaac McCaslin as the reincarnation of those dead and the witness of that world. We might almost say that Old Ben dies in child-birth; he has many features in common with the "terrible mother" of many heroic myths; and the name of Sam Fathers is in no way accidental. It requires only the slightest twist of the tongue to convert the story's title into "The Birth."

Then, finally, we find out in the fourth section, if we submit ourselves to its spell, that it is in his sixteenth year also, on a December night after the last bear-hunt, that Ike solves the riddle of his family's history. That section begins with the sentence, ominously uncapitalized: "then he was twenty-one"; and the defining occasion of most of it is a conversation between Ike and his cousin Cass Edmonds in the plantation commissary on what appears to be Ike's twenty-first birthday; but, while the entire span of Ike's eighty-year-long life is touched on, it is specifically the discoveries of his sixteenth year that account for the intensity of Ike's speech and the resoluteness of his decision to give up his inheritance. With the conversation as foreground, those discoveries pass through Ike's memory like shadows on the wall behind—shadows themselves engaged in ghostly conversation; for they appear as remembered entries in the commissary ledgers, written in a question-and-answer manner. The very language of the entries—made several decades earlier by Ike's uncle and father, and agonizingly pieced together by Ike five years before the present moment—has the sparseness and the foreshortened quality of a memory.

> Uncle Buck: "Eunice Bought by Father in New Orleans 1807 650 dolars. Marrid to Thucydus 1809 Drowned in Crick Cristmas Day 1832."
>
> Uncle Buddy: "June 21th 1833 Drowned herself."
>
> Uncle Buck: "23 Jun 1833 Who in hell ever heard of a niger drownding herself."
>
> Uncle Buddy: "Aug. 13th Drownd herself."

The motivation for Eunice's suicide is revealed to us through its implications, in the shape it assumes in Ike's oddly mythopoetic imagination. It is up to us, participants in the hunt, to discover that Eunice had been the mistress of the grandfather, Carothers McCaslin, and bought by him and married to "Thucydus" when she was pregnant with the child Tomasina; and that Eunice drowned herself when she realized that her daughter was pregnant by her lover. For Ike, the tragic event has the fixed formality of legend:

> He seemed to see her actually walking into the icy creek on that Christmas day six months before her daughter's and her lover's (*Her first lover's,* he thought. *Her first*) child was born, solitary, inflexible, griefless, ceremonial, in formal and succinct repudiation of grief and despair, who had already had to repudiate belief and hope.

The first essential link between the first three and the fourth sections is the literal near-simultaneity of the death of Old Ben and the discovery of mixed blood in the McCaslin clan. But the relationship is a good deal more organic than that; the fourth section of *The Bear* ought not to be taken (as I am afraid it sometimes is taken) as merely the further adventures of Isaac McCaslin. We appreciate the harmony of the parts when we begin to describe the two different moments in ancient formulae: the birth into virtue and the vision of evil. For only a person adequately baptized is capable of having the vision at all; and only the grace bestowed at the baptism enables the initiate to withstand the evil when it is encountered. The action in Section Four is made possible by the experience preceding it: the ritual in the wilderness *contains* the decision in the commissary.

And this leads us into a somewhat more complex view of the relationship. For it is quite exact to say that the whole of the fourth section is contained within the sections which have the wilderness as their setting: this is the unmistakable effect accomplished when Faulkner concludes the story with a short section which returns to the forest, returns to the life of Ike before he is twenty-one, returns to the atmosphere and the rhythms of the hunting world. The fifth section reverts too to the style—relatively straightforward, though highly orchestrated and charged with autumnal splendor—of the first, second and third: picking up that style where it had been left almost sixty pages before, and so enveloping and containing the style in between. The difference is shown by quoting the last lines of Section Four and the first of Section Five—breaking in anywhere on the endlessly flowing sentence of the former:

> and on their wedding night she had cried and he thought she was crying now at first, into the tossed and wadded pillow, the voice coming from somewhere between the pillow and the cachinnation: 'And that's all. That's all from me. If this don't get you that son you talk about, it won't be mine': lying on her side, her back to the empty rented room, laughing and laughing
>
> He went back to the camp one more time before the lumber company moved in and began to cut the timber. Major de Spain himself never saw it again.

Faulkner has even gone to the extreme of employing the single inverted comma in the conversations of the fourth section: the conventional sign of the speech contained within the speech—as against the double comma elsewhere. It is the sort of device that is peculiarly trying for those not already persuaded by Faulkner; but it is another instance of his anxiety that we should recognize the mode of existence of this moment in the experience.

For what we are given in the fourth section is essentially not a narrative of past events, but a vision of the future. We can justify its appearance between the third and the fifth sections—between, that is, episodes of Ike's sixteenth and his eighteenth years—by thinking of it as a dream; perhaps, though this is not necessary, a dream in the year between. It is a true dream to be sure, issuing securely from the gate of horn, but passing before our eyes events which, at this moment of perception, exist only in a state of possibility. A condition of potentiality, as of something not yet fully realized, is carried in the prose itself. We are struck at once by the decrease in visibility: on an immeasurably vast setting, actions and dialogue have curiously hazy outlines; sentences spray out in all directions, rarely reaching (within our hearing) their probable periods. Everything is unfinished, incomplete. But the experience is not a *mere* possibility, in the sense that its opposite is equally possible; for we have to reckon here with Faulkner's implicit theories of time and destiny, according to which all events are predetermined and so can be said to exist and to be seen as taking place simultaneously. To see them this way is to assume the divine viewpoint, as Mme. Magny has observed; divine also, as she does not go on to say, because Faulkner manages—in *The Bear* anyhow—to detect a modicum of human liberty within the grand design: as though not discontent with the ancient and irresolvable paradox of fixity and freedom. Thus the events are certain, but they are not yet; and so they are not clearly to be distinguished by a human perception fully competent only with the past.

Something like this fourth section is probably as close as contemporary fiction can come to that moment in the traditional career of the hero when he descends into the dark underworld, encounters his ancestry and has a vision of the future. We have become skeptical of prophecy; we no longer project spiritual darkness in such simple geographic terms. But here, as Ike sees his inevitable moral decision and its determination in the vast sweep of human history, we partake again of that transfiguring moment narrated already by Homer in *Odyssey* XI and by Virgil in *Aeneid* VI.

III

It is a very long way from Mississippi to ancient Rome and Greece, and no doubt it is time now to remember the national and provincial boundaries within which Ike's initiation is undertaken. For like *Moby Dick, The Bear* is most in tune with primary and perennial rhythms of experience when it is most explicitly American. The content of its story is drawn from that imaginary world inhabited also by many of the heroes of Hawthorne and Melville, and much more recently of F. Scott Fitzgerald. And if we close in more sharply on the particular portion of America that provides the image for its dramatic scene (as, in *The Divine Comedy,* we must remember Florence as well as Italy in general), we recognize the most significant prototype of *The Bear* in *Huckleberry Finn.* Both are narratives of boys growing up in the 19th Century southwest; but the essence of the analogy lies, of course, in their common sense of the kinship between white and black, in their common identification of slavery as a kind of original sin, in their common reversal of the conventional morality that legitimizes social injustice. Faulkner, characteristically, carries the inter-racial kinship literally into the blood streams: Ike and Tennie's Jim are cousins in fact as well as brothers in the spirit of humanity; and also characteristically, Faulkner intrudes a lecture on social legislation, with a warning to the national government up north to keep its hands off the problems of the south—while Mark Twain never exposes Huck Finn to the danger of a pretentious awareness of his own virtue. But both novelists, while telling again the most familiar of stories, confront their heroes with the trials peculiar to the southerner before and just after the Civil War: especially, the challenge of negro slavery.

The central poetic insight, however, which Faulkner shares with Mark Twain and many another American writer is something larger: it is an insight into the fertile and ambiguous possibility of moral freedom in the new world. In the Mississippi wilderness of the eighteen-seventies and -eighties, Faulkner has projected another compelling image, so striking elsewhere in American fiction, of the ethically undefined: undefined, that is—like the river in *Huckleberry Finn* and the sea in *Moby Dick*—only in the sense of not yet fixed in the implicitly hypocritical conventions of "civilized" life. The frontier, as Turner and Constance Rourke were the first to make clear, was the major physical source of this uniquely American idea: the idea, I mean, of a new, unspoiled area in which a genuine and radical moral freedom could once again be exercised—as once, long ago, it had been, in the garden of Eden; and Faulkner locates his image in time at the very moment when the frontier was disappearing. Insofar as *The Bear* is a story about death, it is about the death of the frontier-world; and to a very limited degree it may be regarded as a narrative enactment of the historic development elaborated in Turner's famous essay. But to say so without qualification would be to ascribe to Faulkner a view of innocence quite the opposite of that finally revealed in *The Bear;* and it would be to forget how often Faulkner, like Hawthorne and Melville, has engaged in the ritual slaughter of the animal innocent.

A part of the history Ike McCaslin rehearses for Cass Edmonds seems to echo the comfortable story optimistic Americans were telling each other a century ago.

> [God] made the earth first and peopled it with dumb creatures, and then He created man to be His overseer on the earth and to hold suzerainty over the earth and the animals on it in His name, not to hold for himself and his descendants inviolable title forever. . . . and all the fee He asked was pity and humility and endurance. . . . He watched it. And let me say it. Dispossessed of Eden. Dispossessed of Canaan and those who . . . devoured their ravished substance ravished in turn again and then snarled in what you call the old world's worthless twilight over the old world's gnawed bones, blasphemous in His name until He used a simple egg to discover to them a new world where a nation of people could be founded in humility and pity and sufferance and pride of one to another.

Such an identification of the new world as a divinely offered second chance for humanity, after the first opportunity had been so thoroughly muffed, can be matched in countless editorials and orations: especially during the generation before the Civil War. But Faulkner's hero is examining the myth to see where it went wrong; and he concludes, not that the new world is devoid of evil, but that evil was brought into it with the first settlers, "as though in the sailfuls of the old world's tainted wind which drove the ships." It was the evil of slavery; and beneath it and responsible for it, the sin of spiritual pride. Ike McCaslin is the first of Faulkner's characters to understand American history.

He can do so because he is free—or rather, because he has achieved freedom. He is even, we may say, innocent: but in a crucially new sense. For the quality of innocence undergoes a profound dialectical transformation in *The Bear*. The nature of the dialectic is indicated very forcefully in the opening sentences:

> There was a man and a dog too this time. Two beasts counting Old Ben, the bear, and two men, counting Boon Hogganbeck, in whom some of the same blood ran which ran in Sam Fathers, even though Boon's was a plebeian strain of it and only Sam and Old Ben and the mongrel Lion were taintless and incorruptible.

Taintless, in a new sense, for Lion is a mongrel and Sam (we know this also from "A Justice") is the half-bred offspring of a negress slave and a Chickasaw Indian. But in the moral world of *The Bear* a primary purity, fundamentally materialistic and suggested by the physical purity of the land, is transcended as a dangerous illusion; and for it there is substituted a purity and a freedom much tougher and far more durable. This innocence is an achievement, not merely a gift; it is gained through discipline and submission, it is announced in a ritual. This innocence is nothing else than conscience itself.

Now conscience is the mark of maturity; and, exactly because of the historical illusion so tenaciously clung to, conscience has been something not often reached without the intervention of tragedy, in the American literature of education: consider Donatello and Billy Budd and Jay Gatsby. Isaac's achievement is the achievement of his creator, working an astonishing alchemical change on specifically American materials: converting not only history into art, but illusion into reality, and converting qualities like innocence from a lower to a higher order of value. In order to see the magnitude of this change—of the transmutation of values on which the story rests—we must move into a somewhat more expansive vocabulary than we have employed so far.

Faulkner himself is most willing, too willing perhaps, that we should recognize the universal design into which his southern saga fits; he plants, if anything, too many clues to his wider ranges of meaning. Nonetheless *The Bear* is his masterpiece in this respect: it is his most successful attempt to accommodate to each other in a single narrative the various accounts of themselves that the world and man can give. The fusion has been strained and uneven heretofore; but now it is as though Faulkner, the artist, had like his hero Ike discovered the unity of meaning. And so, while grounded historically and built out of the moral dilemmas which the history gave rise to, *The Bear* no less impressively reflects a timeless psychic drama. It is indeed a treasure-chest for psychologists in criticism (among whom I do not very warmly count myself), for object after object that are known to be recurring symbols in the dream legends of the unconscious are scattered throughout the story: the forest, the tree, the rifle, the bear, and a score of others. The great adventure in which these objects play such a prominent part is quite plainly that transformation of character which is like a second birth, and which some psychologists refer to as the return to the womb; as Faulkner is careful we should see: "It seemed to [Ike] that at the age of ten he was witnessing his own birth." "The birth of the hero," Carl Jung concludes from his survey of world-mythology, "is not that of an ordinary mortal, but is a rebirth from the mother-spouse . . . because only through her does he share in immortality." The second mother is often an animal, Jung assures us, and may be one normally thought of as male: like Hiawatha's mother who first appeared as the Great Bear of the Mountains. Ike first shares in Old Ben's "furious immortality" during that extraordinary episode, like a dream in color, when he penetrates the heart of the forest, finds the (sacred) tree, manifests his submission by abandoning first his gun and then his watch and his compass: until, stripped of hostility and outside of time, he stands in the presence of the wilderness god. It is a liberating experience, as the return to the womb (or any well-organized education) is supposed to be. But final freedom comes only with the death of the parents: for Ike, of Sam Fathers and Old Ben; and then he is prepared to meet the challenge of maturity. Traditionally in this phase of the psychic journey, the hero moves, in the words of Joseph Campbell, "in a dream landscape of curiously fluid, ambiguous forms, where he must survive a succession of trials." It is an apt description of the fourth section.

Yet if Old Ben does have some of the qualities of the "terrible mother" in the myth of the hero, he is at the same time the embodiment of the courage and chivalry and the will to endure which are shaping elements in the honorable. He is "not malevolent, just big"; and if in one of the most extraordinary verbal achievements in modern literature we hear of "the legend" about him: "corncribs broken . . . shoats and grown pigs and even calves carried bodily into the woods and devoured . . . dogs mangled and slain . . . a corridor of wreckage and destruction" —still, Old Ben emerges from this epic portrait by way of a comparison with Priam, King of Troy. Priam, we remember, was the ruler of the old citadel and was destroyed with it; but one warrior survived him, Aeneas, his nephew and we may say his foster-child, who after many trials established a new kingdom in a new country. I do not say that all this is packed into Faulkner's single allusion; but I suggest that we are closer to the archetypal image reproduced in *The Bear* if we think of it as a pattern of redemption in terms of the ultimate forces in the world (like the *Aeneid*), rather than a dream projection mirroring interior psychic conflicts. And in identifying the pattern, we do well to look carefully at the nature and use of *power* within it.

Power is often symbolized, in the heroic myth, by the character of the hero's "magic weapon," and the use to which he puts it: and we can contemplate a significant range from the great bow of Odysseus, with which he ruthlessly slays a houseful of political and domestic rivals, to St. Martin of Tours, telling the pagan Emperor that "Armed only with the Cross, in the forefront of the enemy, I will fear no evil." Aeneas enters his supreme battle wearing a shield on which is engraved the histories and the triumphs to come of the Roman people; it is a recorded destiny which renders him invulnerable to the mightiest of the Latins. In *Moby Dick*, Ahab forges a tremendous harpoon for the final hunt (in a scene consciously modelled on similar moments in Homer and Virgil), and he baptizes it "Not in the name of the father, but in the name of the devil"—the book's secret motto, Melville said later: the secret source of Ahab's strength; and the harpoon is the instrument of his own violent death. For Isaac McCaslin there is the rifle, and much is made of it. First, a rifle too large for him, a man's weapon in a boy's hands, which he can no more handle than can Telemachus his father's bow; and then at ten years, the year of his first communion with Old Ben, he receives "his own gun . . . a new breech-loader, a Christmas gift." "He would own it and shoot it for almost seventy years." The imagery of the gun is diffused through the story; it becomes one of the central unifying symbols. Ike has two occasions on which he might use his rifle against Old Ben: the first time, he abandons it in order to present himself in evident humility to the bear; the second time, he throws it away and risks his life in the charitable act of rescuing the little fyce.

This, I believe, is the essential symbolic movement of the story (it was the conclusion, in the original short version of *The Bear*), and it is not surprising that this, of all incidents, is remembered and re-examined in the fourth section when Ike is expressing his insight into history and his own historic role. For what we comprehend at last in *The Bear* is the transmutation of power into charity. No loss of power is effected; but it suffers a rich sea-change, it comes under the control of moral understanding; grace enters into it. More concretely: Ike does not give up his gun altogether; on the contrary, we have swift previews of him in later years as the greatest hunter in Yoknapatawpha County; but he uses his power with restraint and fidelity, and for a life lived as closely as possible to the source of his moral energy. It is what he gains from that source that makes the life possible and makes Ike what he is: a Christ-like person with some ineradicable southern biases. It is a dimensional increase of perception, and through this also Ike is uniquely capable of reading the past correctly. The total change at work in *The Bear* may thus, in these various respects, be compared to the transition from the pagan to the Christian era, if not from the Old to the New Testament.

History became readable, according to most apologists, when meaning was put into it at the moment of the Incarnation. Now what has been most striking in Faulkner's earlier novels has been just that endless, hopeless fumbling in the past, that obsessive struggle for its meaning by constant re-arrangements of its content: which seem the only resource of a person or a people from whom the gift of illumination has been so far withheld. From this point of view, the repeated attacks of Quentin Compson on the history of his country may be fruitfully contrasted with the disciplined exposition of Isaac McCaslin, and Quentin's suicide with Ike's honorable long career. This is not to say that Ike is intended to represent Christ in a second coming, but only that Ike moves in a world of light—a light still meagre but definite; a new world in which values have been confirmed by being raised to a higher power; not the new world beyond the frontier—that is precisely what is transcended —but a world so perpetually new that Ike sometimes seems to be its only living inhabitant. It is worth insisting that the life of Christ is not under any circumstances a subject for fiction: not at all because it would be irreverent, but because within the limits of literature it would be impossible. But *The Bear* does as much as literature may with propriety try to do: it enacts for us, by means of human individuals in a local habitation, the miracle of moral regeneration.

Ike McCaslin and the Second Fall of Man

Lewis P. Simpson

The source of William Faulkner's powerful vision of the American South, duly allowing for his innate genius, was fundamentally not the accident of birth which made him a Southerner but the accident of birth which made him a modern. Unlike Southerners of the last century and, unfortunately, many of this century, Faulkner knew that the history of American Southern culture is an integral part of the crisis of modern Western civilization. This crisis—which by now seems to have assumed total proportions—announced itself in one significant way in 1751, when Jean-Jacques Rousseau won a prize from the Academy of Dijon for his essay asserting that the arts and sciences have done more to corrupt than to aid human beings. Rousseau's attitude prophesied the aftermath of the Enlightenment, indicating that in the very midst of the century which coined the word "civilization" a profound discontent with civilization had begun to arise. From that time until the present the existence of this element of dissatisfaction has been a major characteristic of the literary and artistic expression of Western culture. Indeed Western literature may be said to have become modern only when this virulent discontent began to get into the central nervous systems of its writers. "It seems to me," Lionel Trilling observes, "that the characteristic element of modern literature, or at least of the most highly developed modern literature, is the bitter line of hostility to civilization which runs through it."

Why did a deep unhappiness with civilization become manifest at the moment when Voltaire thought that Europe, in spite of all its political and religious differences, had achieved intellectual unity; and when the French Encyclopedists believed that the advancement of human knowledge was going to create an almost perfect world? Many answers have been ventured, one of the least satisfactory being the oversimplified notion of "the rise of romanticism." Romanticism was only superficially a cause. Basically it was a symptom of a drastic historical displacement of the individual in relation to the world. This dislocation occurred, Hannah Arendt argues in her brilliant work entitled *The Human Condition,* when the ancient distinction between the "public realm" (the realm of the *polis* in Greece and of the *res publica* in Rome

Reprinted from Donald E. Stanford, ed., *Nine Essays in Modern Literature,* by permission of Louisiana State University Press. Originally titled "Isaac McCaslin and Temple Drake: The Fall of New World Man."

—the realm in which the individual person could be seen and heard and through his actions and words achieve a kind of permanence) and the "private realm" (the realm of the family—the undisclosed, impermanent area dominated by the sustenance of the physical life process) began to be reversed and finally more or less erased by "the rise of society." By the twentieth century, society—a great, utilitarian mass world dominated by abstract scientific and technological processes—has absorbed the realms through which Western man traditionally ordered his existence and maintained his world. "What makes mass society so difficult to bear," Professor Arendt points out, "is not the number of people involved, at least not primarily, but the fact that the world between them has lost its power to gather them together, to relate and to separate them."

As the traditional world was replaced by modern society, a typical response of the sensitive mind to the loss of order was "romantic individualism." This emphatic, introspective individualism tended to center on a longing to discover or to rediscover the primal, instinctual sources of life. If mankind could begin over again! The translation of this impulse into possibility was no more than a wishful hope in the congested European metropolis. But out on what Walter Prescott Webb calls "the great frontier," especially on that portion of it existing in what is now the continental United States, modern man could express his frustration with the civilized condition in an actual search for new ways of defining and ordering his existence to be developed out of a vitalizing new relationship between the individual and nature in a virgin wilderness.

Lewis Mumford has an interesting theory in this regard that, I think, can be adapted to the argument I am attempting to set forth here. According to this theory, Old World man began in the eighteenth century to try "to find a new way out from the repetitive impasses of 'civilization' by making a fresh start on a more primitive basis. This effort, imposed by the very need to survive in the raw American wilderness, brought modern man face to face with the ancient realities of paleolithic and neolithic culture, on which the life of the indigenous Indian was based: in the New World modern man turned to . . . pre-civilized existence . . . and lived on this older level with a new intensity, as a conscious *release* from civilization—though fortified both with many civilized skills and with infiltrations of . . . Christian morality." But New World man had in a sense too many civilized skills, in particular his rapidly increasing mechanical ones. The opening of the New World, Mumford remarks, was accomplished with the help of many technological innovations—the navigation chart, the chronometer, the rifle, the railroad. In his desire to conquer the land, New World man destroyed the possibility of making a truly fresh beginning in mankind's social and moral history by allowing his mechanical side to take precedence over his romantic inclinations. He did not, in other words, effect a "synthesis of the romantic and utilitarian elements." He did not keep "alive the new values that he had experienced" in his contact with a virgin world. Instead "once he had conquered the wilderness he surrendered abjectly to the instruments that had made his conquest so swift—and his life so rootless. . . ." Mumford declares, "Properly interpreted the rise and fall of New World man is a more significant drama than anyone has yet portrayed, though the pioneer himself was doubtless only partly aware of the significance of his actions and the implied goal of his efforts." . . .

II

[In the] complicated and difficult story [of "The Bear"] Isaac McCaslin comes closer than any of Faulkner's characters to realizing the idea of the development in the New World of a new version of man. Tutored by the old half Indian, half Negro, Sam Fathers, he enters into a relationship with the wilderness which clearly suggests Mumford's notion of modern man returning in the New World to a more primitive level of existence and living on this "older level with a new intensity, as a *conscious* release from civilization," although deriving support both from civilized skills and Christian morality.

Following his initiation into manhood when he kills his first deer and Sam Fathers ritualistically smears his face with the blood, Ike completes his induction into not only the skills but the mystique of the hunter when he first sees Old Ben, the great bear, who is a kind of primal god. To see the bear Ike has to divest himself, Sam Fathers tells him, of his gun—the gun being of course a prime symbol of civilized man's technological domination of the woods. "You will have to choose," Sam tells him. Ike makes his choice one morning before daylight and leaves the hunting camp without his gun and enters the forest. He takes with him nonetheless two major devices of modern civilization: a compass and a watch. After nine hours during which he goes far deeper into the wild country than he has ever gone before, he still has not seen Old Ben. And he thinks: "It was the watch and the compass. He was still tainted." "A child, alien and lost in the green and soaring gloom of the markless wilderness," Ike brings himself to relinquish "completely to it."

Having abandoned the watch and the compass and even a stick he has carried along for protection against the numerous snakes, the boy loses all sense of direction. But he does not panic. "He did . . . as Sam had coached and drilled him: made this next circle in the opposite direction and much larger, so that the pattern of the two of them would bisect his track somewhere. . . ." At the same moment he discovers the bush on which he had hung his compass and watch, he sees the fresh tracks of the bear. Then he sees the animal itself:

> It did not emerge, appear: it was just there, immobile, fixed in the green and windless noon's hot dappling, not as big as he had dreamed it but as big as he had expected, bigger, dimensionless against the dappled obscurity, looking at him. Then it moved. It crossed the glade without haste, walking for an instant into the sun's full glare and out of it, and stopped again and looked back at him across one shoulder. Then it was gone. It didn't walk into the woods. It faded, sank back into the wilderness without any motion as he had watched a fish, a huge old bass, sink back into the dark depths of its pool and vanish without even any movement of its fins.

Having thus "released" himself from civilization and having entered with proper respect and humility into a living relationship with the wilderness, Ike has achieved newness of life. He has won for himself the right to moral freedom. Now he can use his gun throughout a long career as a hunter in Yoknapatawpha County prudently and wisely. In his hands mechanical power will not destroy the great values of the human heart: "courage and honor and pride, and pity and love of justice and liberty." Is, then, Ike the New World man redeemed from the impasses of civilization?

One distinguished student of modern literature, R. W. B. Lewis, attempts in an essay on "The Bear" to prove that Ike becomes something like a new man in a new world, that he is a key to salvation. In a long and arresting argument which I cannot reproduce in the limited space of this essay, Lewis contends that Ike is "the hero of the New World" and that in his "honorable long career" he "moves in a world of light—a light still meagre but definite; a new world in which values have been confirmed by being raised to a higher power; not the new world beyond the frontier—that is precisely what is transcended—but a world so perpetually new that Ike sometimes seems to be its only living inhabitant." Lewis carries the parallel between Jesus and McCaslin far enough to suggest that the Yoknapatawpha hunter possibly is a new incarnation, "a miracle of moral regeneration."

This is hardly so. Although Ike voluntarily gives up his title to the property of his family because the land has been cursed by slavery, he is, I would agree with Robert D. Jacobs, in his total aspect "a pathetic figure, slightly comic, certainly ineffectual." He represents only the nostalgic possibility of modern man rising in the guise of New World man to a new and better moral condition. In reality New World man in his effort to follow Rousseauesque discontent into a new condition was creating another Fall of Man and binding himself more securely by the fetters of society than ever before. In Faulkner's works Ike serves not, I believe, as a hero. He is a witness, the primary witness in Faulkner, to what Stephen Spender has described as the "Second Fall of Man." The English poet, commenting on theories of modern culture like Eliot's famous idea of a "dissociation of sensibility," says:

> In all these theories there is perhaps concealed the idea of a Second Fall of Man in the industrial age. The operative cause of this Second Fall was the concept of individualism [in contrast, Spender apparently means, to the feudal concept of community], which led from the Renaissance onward, to the scientific era. Knowledge of science and industry here plays the role of eating of the tree of knowledge. The Second Fall is considered so much worse than the first one that Original Sin can be looked back on as the sign of man's comparative innocence, whilst it is precisely the loss of the sense of Original Sin which is the peculiar worse-than-damned condition of men in the period of exile which is the Second Fall. For the sense of Original Sin offers man the possibility of redemption whereas the loss of this sense condemns him to a life deprived of all moral significance.

When I say that Ike is Faulkner's chief witness to the Second Fall, I do not mean to suggest that he is a fully aware witness. I mean that through his perspective as a kind of moral philosopher he affords us an ironic and dramatic commentary on the Second Fall. About God's intention in revealing the New World to mankind Ike theorizes:

> Dispossessed of Eden, Dispossessed of Canaan, and those who dispossessed him dispossessed him dispossessed, and the five hundred years of absentee landlords in the Roman bagnios, and the thousand years of wild men from the northern woods who dispossessed them and devoured their ravished substance ravished in turn again and then snarled in what you call the old world's worthless twilight over the world's gnawed bones, blasphemous in His name until He used a simple egg to discover to them a new world where a nation of people could be founded in humility and pity and sufferance and pride of one to another.

But the spiritual redemption of the New World was prevented by greed and pride. These sins inspired the effort to possess and to exploit the virgin land by means of chattel slavery, which is the subject of the fourth section of "The Bear," and by the ever-increasing use of the instruments invented by the technological-industrial revolution. More especially by the last. For—and I state what I think Faulkner implies—slavery was a curse, but a curse bears a moral significance rooted in man's original sinfulness. Technology masks greed and pride in the amorality of scientific and industrial "progress." It separates man from both his sense of involvement with his fellow man and with nature and dehumanizes him.

Do we not see this in the last section of "The Bear"? Did not Faulkner choose, among other reasons, to place the story of the eighteen-year-old Ike's return to the wilderness rather than that of the twenty-one-year-old Ike's meditation on slavery in the plantation commissary at the end of "The Bear" for the sake of emphasis? In any event in the final section Ike sees with his own eyes the coming doom of the wilderness after the end of slavery in the form of a new planing mill. He sees the mill already half completed, covering two or three acres of what had been untouched forest land. He sees "what looked like miles and miles of stacked steel rails red with the light bright rust of newness and of piled cross ties sharp with creosote, and wire corrals and feeding-troughs for two hundred mules at least and the tents for the men who drove them. . . ." This irrepressible attack on the wilderness had been preceded by the work of an insignificant little locomotive used for several years in a small logging operation:

> It had been harmless then. They would hear the passing log-train sometimes from the camp . . . They would hear it going out, loaded . . . flinging its bitten laboring miniature puffing into the immemorial woods-face with frantic and bootless vainglory, empty and noisy and puerile, carrying to no destination or purpose sticks which left nowhere any scar or stump. . . . But it was different now. . . . It was as though the train (and not only the train but himself, not only his vision which had seen it and his memory which remembered it but his clothes too, as garments carry back into the clean edgeless blowing of air the lingering effluvium of a sickroom or of death) had brought with it into the doomed wilderness, even before the actual axe, the shadow and portent of the new mill not even finished yet and the rails and ties which were not even laid; and he knew now . . . why Major de Spain had not come back, and that after this time he himself, who had had to see it one time other, would return no more.

At the conclusion of "The Bear" Ike is walking through the woods when he comes upon a large rattlesnake. Not only does he see the snake, but with the acute sensory perception of the woodsman he smells him: "the thin sick smell of rotting cucumbers and something else which had no name, evocative of all knowledge and of pariah-hood and of death." As the snake glides away, Ike addresses him in the primal tongue he had heard Sam Fathers use six years ago when they had confronted a large buck deer in the wilderness: "Chief," he said: "Grandfather." Shortly after this mystical moment with the snake, Ike hears "a sound as though someone were hammering a gunbarrel against a piece of railroad iron, a sound loud and heavy and not rapid yet with something frenzied about it, as the hammerer were not only a strong man and an earnest one but a little hysterical too." He comes upon a gum tree where he is to meet Boon Hogganbeck, the more or less irresponsible hunter who two years earlier had finally put an end to the legendary bear, Old Ben, and had thereby, as Robert D. Jacobs says, symbolized "the abrogation of the old relationship between man and nature." In the years before,

Major de Spain and the others had hunted Old Ben each year as a ritual rather than as an act of depredation. Ike witnesses this scene:

> At first glance the tree seemed to be alive with frantic squirrels. There appeared to be forty or fifty of them leaping and darting from branch to branch until the whole tree had become one green maelstrom of mad leaves, while from time to time, singly or in twos and threes, squirrels would dart down the trunk and then whirl without stopping and rush back up again as though sucked violently back by the vacuum of their fellows' frenzied vortex. Then he saw Boon, sitting, his back against the trunk, his head bent, hammering furiously at something on his lap. What he hammered with was the barrel of his dismembered gun, what he hammered at was the breech of it. The rest of the gun lay scattered about him in a half-dozen pieces while he bent over the piece on his lap his scarlet and streaming walnut-face, hammering the disjointed barrel against the gun-breech with the frantic abandon of a madman. He didn't even look up to see who it was. Still hammering, he merely shouted back at the boy in a hoarse strangled voice: "Get out of here! Dont touch them! Dont touch one of them! They're mine."

We remember the story of Eli Whitney, the inventor of the cotton gin: how he sent the rifles the Army had ordered from him—a box of barrels, a box of triggers, etc.—and thus announced the invention of interchangeable parts. Or we may remember this story. Whether or not Boon's confounding is linked specifically with the history of technology, it effectively symbolizes the combination of greed and mechanical power which destroyed the wilderness and its creatures. That the power has momentarily failed only makes Boon a more striking example of the Second Fall.

In "Delta Autumn," a tale about Ike in his old age, he is a witness to one of the ultimate results of the Second Fall, the creation of a wasteland out of the great Delta forests of Mississippi:

> Now a man drove two hundred miles from Jefferson before he found wilderness to hunt in. Now the land lay open from the cradling hills on the east to the rampart levee on the west, standing horseman-tall with cotton for the world's looms . . . —the land in which neon flashed past them from the little countless towns, and countless shining this-year's automobiles sped past them on the broad plumb-ruled highway, yet in which the only permanent mark of man's occupation seemed to be the tremendous gins, constructed in sections of sheet iron and in a week's time . . . —the land across which there came no scream of panther but instead the long hooting locomotives; trains of incredible length and drawn by a single engine, since there was no gradient anywhere and no elevation save those raised by forgotten aboriginal hands as refuges from the yearly water and used by their Indian successors to sepulchre

their fathers' bones, and all that remained of that old time were Indian names on the little towns. . . .

Lying in his tent alone, old Ike conceives of the judgment upon the Second Fall of man:

> This Delta. *This land which man has deswamped and denuded and derivered in two generations so that white men can own plantations and commute every night to Memphis and black men own plantations and ride in Jim Crow cars to Chicago to live in millionaire's mansions on Lake Shore Drive; where white men rent farms and live like niggers and niggers crop on shares and live like animals.* . . . No wonder the ruined woods I used to know don't cry for retribution! . . . The people who have destroyed it will accomplish its revenge.

Ike's bitterness assumes that the Second Fall has not completely obliterated the element of Rousseauesque discontent that drove modern man to seek to return to nature. It may be, however, that Faulkner is one of the last writers to experience fully the Rousseauesque tradition of discontent—that is to say, a writer who really feels what it means for modern man to have lost the chance to enter into a living, instead of a bull-dozing, relationship with nature. We may now be entering the age of "post-modern man." A major characteristic of this age will be the full acceptance of a mass-technological society as the one and only way of existence. No doubt the people who live in the post-modern world will accomplish the revenge of "the ruined woods," but will they realize it? Punishment is meaningless when the punished have no moral norm to which they can relate their punishment, and nature as a moral or ethical norm has become almost meaningless. . . .

God's Moral Order and the Problem of Ike's Redemption

Olga W. Vickery

Of central importance . . . is the significance of Isaac's renunciation. On one side of him is Cass Edmonds representing the plantation world and its tradition. On the other is Sam Fathers, scion of a "vanished and forgotten people," who is linked to the plantation only through that drop of blood which had been the blood of slaves. For Isaac, it is scarcely a matter of choosing between the two traditions as represented by Sam and Cass. His long midnight conversation with Cass in the commissary represents his effort to explain a decision already made inevitable by

Reprinted from Olga W. Vickery, *The Novels of William Faulkner: A Critical Interpretation*, by permission of Louisiana State University Press.

and encompassed in the ritual of the hunt. Significantly enough, his explanation of the eternal consists of juxtaposing the McCaslin ledger, symbol of the history of the South, against the Bible and its expression of the eternal verities of the heart.

Isaac's interpretation of history is Biblical and, more specifically, Miltonic in its poetic emphasis on the hierarchy and the contractual agreement between man and God: "He made the earth first and peopled it with dumb creatures, and then He created man to be His overseer on the earth and to hold suzerainty over the earth and the animals on it in His name." Man's happiness consists in recognizing the greatness and the limitations of his position in the divine order. By forgetting, even momentarily, that he is at once the ruler and the ruled, man destroys that order and with it his proper relationship to God and to nature. Nor does it matter whether he sinks below or attempts to rise above his divinely ordained position. Since animal and demi-god are both foreign to his nature, both constitute a threat to his distinctive humanity. It is only by recognizing and accepting his place in the hierarchy that man fully realizes his moral nature.

The fact that men will destroy the hierarchy and deny God is foreknown though not foredoomed: " 'I will give him his chance. I will give him warning and foreknowledge too, along with the desire to follow and the power to slay.' " Since man is created sufficient to stand, though free to fall, the responsibility for the destruction of the moral order and the consequent corruption of his own nature, must be his alone. His sin is pride and the lust for power, the one perverting his relationship to God, the other to nature and other men. In either case, the overseer becomes the tyrant, seeing himself as the measure of all things and replacing God's laws with his own. His punishment is increasing blindness to his own corruption until the game he hunts and kills becomes human.

The original sin, repeated by each successive generation, spreads through time and place. Even the new world with its promise of a new beginning serves only to confirm the old error. Out of it, however, there slowly emerges the reverse pattern of redemption. The actual enslavement of man by man marks the final horrifying destruction of the moral order. But ironically, his bondage prevents the Negro from learning how to forget God. Barred from possessing land or exercising authority over other men, he is forced into " 'the communal anonymity of brotherhood' " where he pays God's fee of " 'pity and humility and sufferance and endurance and the sweat of his face for bread.' " In his chains lies the assurance of his salvation. And he is not alone. In the midst of the fallen world there is still the individual who can resist the way of the world and say " '*I am just against the weak because they are niggers being held in bondage by the strong just because they are white.*' " This gesture of protest prepares the way for Isaac's repudiation of his patrimony and the more active engagement of Chick Mallison. That such gestures are made indicates God's continued presence in the fallen world and gives earnest of His final forgiveness. Each is a preparation for and an anticipation of the triumph of Christ as a man. Thus, what begins as an explanation of Isaac's decision to relinquish the land becomes an impassioned poetic effort to "justify God's ways to man."

Isaac's repudiation of the wrong and the shame, symbolized for him by Eunice's suicide, is made possible by the fact that Sam Fathers has provided him with the wilderness and the code of the hunter as an alternative to the plantation world. In the forest Isaac can be one of a group of men "not white nor black nor red but men, hunters, with the will and hardihood to endure and the humility and skill to survive." From this vantage point Isaac can examine the history of his people and although he cannot change it, he can at least refuse to condone it and to contribute to it. The gesture of protest too can become part of recorded time. His rejection of the McCaslin tradition and his subsequent life together constitute a transcendence of public morality. But the significance of that rejection depends on whether it is juxtaposed against the wilderness or the tamed land. Isaac's moral and spiritual stature is not only derived from but, in a sense, dependent on the existence of the wilderness and the ritual of the hunt. He becomes literally one of the "Old People" who have vanished and been forgotten by invoking the past until "those old times would cease to be old times and would become a part of the boy's present, not only as if they had happened yesterday but as if they were still happening." What is an annual vacation for Major de Spain and his friends becomes Isaac's life.

This pastoral form of existence in which the hunter and the hunted share immortality and eternal youth constitutes Isaac's dream of escape from the McCaslin world. Because it is an escape and a desire to find personal salvation, his gesture of relinquishment is only superficially an atonement for the sin of his forefathers. He shows his own awareness of this when he calls himself " 'an Isaac born into a later life than Abraham's and repudiating immolation: fatherless and therefore safe declining the altar because maybe this time the exasperated Hand might not supply the kid.' " Accordingly, Isaac's withdrawal is in reality an attempt to evade both the guilt of his forefathers and his own responsibilities. Thus, while his daily life is a humble imitation of Christ's, it also denies the spirit of Christ who did not hesitate to share in the life of men, to accept guilt, and to suffer immolation. In rejecting sin, Isaac also rejects humanity. Significantly, he holds himself aloof from close human ties; though he is uncle to half the county, he is father to no-one and husband solely to the wilderness. Having confused the wilderness with the Garden of Eden, he not only dedicates but sacrifices his life to it. Man must leave the Garden in order to discover his humanity and whatever the reason, Isaac does not do so; his knowledge stops just short of the paradox of the fortunate fall.

When he is outside the wilderness, Isaac is virtuous but ineffective. His is essentially "a fugitive and cloistered virtue, unexercised and unbreathed." The measure of this lies in the fact that nothing happens to him between his twenty-first and seventieth year. We know that he married and that his wife failed to draw him back into history, failed even to give him a son who might have provided the crucial test of his withdrawal from life. And we know that he retreated into his dream while excluding his wife from it. The magnificent ritual of the hunt holds a promise which is never fulfilled by Isaac's life. The significance of any ritual must lie in its power to create order and to establish a sense of continuity with the past for the individual. Isaac, however, confuses the ritual with the life it orders. The qualities he learned under the tutelage of Sam Fathers, the fyce, and Old Ben should have been asserted within the context of civilization, whereas he forever applies them solely to the hunt itself, until he finally presides over a group of city vacationers who find sport in slaying a doe. Thus, as the wilderness retreats and shrinks in size, Isaac seems to lose stature even as his gesture of dissent loses significance.

Ike McCaslin, Cop-Out

David H. Stewart

I propose to re-examine the one Faulkner character, Isaac McCaslin, who has been most favorably and generously received by the critics, and to examine him as briefly as possible both within the larger context of Faulkner's Southern cycle and within the largest context of all, the social and ideological world outside Faulkner's fiction which Ike was evidently devised to influence. I shall try to describe what Ike's life and thought actually mean once the fine patina, provided by the critics, is removed.

Of the many aristocratic families whose chronicles Faulkner has detailed, the McCaslins, except for their founder, appear to follow a path quite different from those of the others, though as I shall show this is only the surface impression. What is striking about the McCaslins is that from the day of old Carothers' death in 1837, the second generation set out in a curious direction. The twin brothers, Buck and Buddy, conceived a sort of rural cooperative, a Mississippian New Harmony, slaveless yet solvent because it could compete with big planters. It was to be so constituted that the coercive features of patriarchal aristocracy could be avoided as

Reprinted from David H. Stewart, "The Purpose of Faulkner's Ike," *Criticism*, III: 4 (Fall 1961), 333–342, by permission of the Wayne State University Press. Title supplied by the editors.

easily as the equally coercive features of the radical Yankee alternative which meant black insurrection and, later on, carpetbag domination. But the entire program vanished over the precipice of civil war.

Then comes Isaac, the most fascinating McCaslin of all—and perhaps Faulkner's most fascinating character for the simple reason that he seems to be his creator's favorite standard-bearer, a forthright "positive hero." This is not to call him unique in the Faulkner canon. He is, indeed, a spiritual brother to the gentlemen who function as central consciousnesses in Faulkner's earlier novels: Quentin Compson, Gail Hightower, Bayard Sartoris (narrator of *The Unvanquished*), and Vladimir Ratliff. Like Quentin and Bayard, he is acutely conscious of the overriding importance of social form, evidenced by his formal gesture of repudiating his patrimony when he cannot actually "cure the wrong and eradicate the shame" of his heritage. Similarly he denies that his young fourth cousin, Roth, would actually promise to contract a legal marriage with a woman whom he loved illicitly. More important, he too believes in the efficacy of that abiding Faulknerian virtue, announced already in *Sartoris*, "spitting in deestruction's [sic] face"; he learned it first from a mongrel and later from the great bear. It is supposed to explain not only the Southern performance in the Civil War but human behavior in general.

Ike's trouble with time is exactly like that of his precursors: they all desire to elude it, to resist distinguishing what actually happened from what they had been told, hence to prolong or postpone things past into the present or even the future. In addition, the impulse which seems to animate Ike and give him direction—as it does Quentin and Bayard and Gail Hightower—is a need for peace and escape. He shares even the superficial characteristic of shaking and trembling when excited or confronted with difficulty.

The only differences between him and every other Faulknerian central consciousness are first, his freedom from feminine influence, though even he had to struggle against an Amazonian wife comparable in some ways to Drusilla, who disturbed Bayard so violently, or Eula Varner Snopes and her daughter, who confounded Gavin Stevens. Ike had no grandmother to mold his character nor a mother or sister to betray the old sacred code for him. Instead he has Sam Fathers who, of course, seems comparable to Teiresias, hence probably combines female qualities with his primitive masculinity. The second difference is his singular inheritance from his father and uncle, who were not cavaliers like Colonel John Sartoris or generals and governors like Quentin's forbears. Slightly similar to the first Ratliff (Ratcliffe), Uncle Buck and Buddy disapproved slavery and hence alleviated for their progeny the burden imposed by this social crime.

Differences notwithstanding, Ike is a creation essentially similar to Faulkner's earlier central consciousnesses: he feels what they feel, fails where they fail. Born after the Civil War (1867), he has escaped exposure to its violence, which helps explain the estrangement, emphasized frequently by Faulkner, between him and his substitute-father, cousin McCaslin Edmonds. It is the period in which he lives, together with his heritage, which defines the problems he must confront and delimits the range and manner in which he responds. He seems to be involved in three things: reaching maturity, expiating the original sin of miscegenation and incest committed by Carothers, and reconciling or achieving a viable position with regard to the dilemmas of property ownership. Restitution for inherited guilt plus self-justification are fundamental, the latter taking precedence as Ike lives further into the twentieth century.

Ike's approaches to his problems are as varied and devious as they are revealing. As we learn in "The Old People" and "The Bear," he comes to maturity in three stages. After a belated infant baptism in the blood of the deer he killed as a nine-year-old boy, he reaches age twelve (the Protestant "age of responsibility") and under Sam's tutelage passes through a ritual, comparable perhaps to the confirmation. The rite is curious: his task is to go forth into the wilderness, like the Indian boys of an earlier age, and to see a vision, vouchsafed only after he has stripped off all the accoutrements of civilization and reduced himself to the level of an animal. Then he sees Old Ben, the wilderness symbol, and returns home purified. More than this, he is ostensibly prepared to face the world on its own terms so that when he realizes the next year that Old Ben must die, he knows "that he would not grieve." Of course, he cannot play the role of priestly executioner. Twice he had the opportunity but, like his mentor, declined it despite his eminent worthiness. For him decisive action is difficult; and he waits until the plebeian, Boon Hogganbeck, who is as much animal as man (Faulkner's plebeians often are), commits the final deed and thus absolves Ike of responsibility so that he can assist with pure hands at Sam Fathers' funeral. What Ike achieves through this sequence of events is not only a degree of maturity but sanctity: he emerges incorruptible, a kind of consecrated altar boy, who can in time develop into the wise prophet and judge which he is destined to become, without losing the "young boy's high and selfless innocence."

But before his position is secure, he must pass through another ritual, comparable to the venerable Protestant practice of making an adult Decision for Christ, a mature reaffirmation of the childhood commitment. This Ike does when he is twenty-one by renouncing the things of this world, adopting the kenotic idea, becoming a carpenter "because if the Nazarene had found carpentering good for the life and ends He had assumed and elected to serve, it would be all right too for Isaac McCaslin. . . ." Thus he becomes a man.

The solution of Ike's second problem, expiating the old sin of his heritage, is not very imaginative. His grandfather's will has imposed upon him the legal duty of transferring a cash forfeit to the colored descendants of the McCaslin line. The thousand dollars, bequeathed for this purpose by Carothers, has been increased by Buck and Buddy to three thousand, one for each of the children of the black man begot incestuously by the old patriarch.

Now the "pay-off," softened and rendered a little more palatable by Ike's kindly ruminations and the clouds of rhetoric in which he and his cousin love to indulge, stands before Ike as a solemn obligation, harsh, mechanical, and brutal. And he discharges his duty. Bearing up nobly beneath the weight of his white burden, he arranges for Fonsiba's security, protecting her from her own silly illusion of freedom and from her ridiculous negro husband whose very skin exuded "that rank stink of baseless and imbecile delusion, that boundless rapacity and folly, of the carpet-bagger followers of victorious armies." The youngest son, Lucas, claims his own third: the oldest, Jim, vanishes in 1885 so that Ike has to wait forty-five years until he can pay the final third to Jim's grand-daughter whom he rewards additionally with the old hunting horn given him by General Compson and with the consoling admonition that "*We* will have to wait" for racial equality. Although Ike might disagree, one may fairly consider that his solution was a good bargain: three thousand dollars of someone else's money and a horn discharge a century of guilt.

His solution to the land problem is also easy—indeed almost pathetic beside Buck's and Buddy's earlier attempt. In the first place Ike ponders the ingenious possibility that he personally does not own any land at all, on the ground that buying or bequeathing land is impossible by divine edict. Cousin McCaslin Edmonds puts an end to this notion by insisting that in practice at any rate old Carothers did own land and did hand it on to his descendants. Later on, McCaslin suggests that even if Carothers never owned the land, it must then have passed from Ikkemotubbe to Sam Fathers, and "who inherited from Sam Fathers if not you? co-heir perhaps with Boon . . . ?" Whichever way Ike may try to look at it, he does own or "hold suzerainty" over the family plantation fifteen miles from Jefferson, and he is obsessed with the desire to free himself from this land which he believes contaminates him morally (because of Carothers' wickedness) and spiritually (because property-owning is unchristian or at least un-Christ-like).

What he does is simple: after all the talk and theorizing, he gives all of his property to his cousin, fastidiously and successfully evading the entire problem of social position and power. He remains inviolable and pure—and is on two occasions judged rather severely for it: Faulkner, thinking about such rugged individuals as Lucas Beauchamp, Buck and Buddy, says that "old Isaac . . . in a sense, say what a man would, had turned apostate to his name and lineage by weakly relinquishing the land which was rightfully his. . . ." Later on, when Ike is an old man, the colored girl, remotely his kin and pregnant with Roth Edmonds' child, tells him that she could have made a man of Roth, but Isaac had spoiled him before birth by transferring the McCaslin land to the Edmonds family, hence weakening or emasculating them just to save himself.

So much for Ike's attempts to solve his problems. What he achieves is little more than cheap self-satisfaction, cheap because his basic urge is to gain peace and to escape, which prevents him from finding solutions that really satisfy or that are really meaningful. To reach a clear estimate of his character and behavior is, therefore, difficult. What is one to say of a person presented by his creator as a Christ-figure, yet whose entire performance is negative? He repudiates land, writes off the guilt of slavery with three thousand dollars and a horn, proclaims for the black race a theory of "wait and endure," constantly evades responsibility to his fellow men, lives alone, isolated, impotent, ineffectual, and childless, and appears finally to have more in common with the pathetic Reverend Hightower than with Christ. He is a mere passive consciousness whose meager gestures at activity, far from contradicting, serve to emphasize his passivity.

Yet he is portrayed for the most part so sympathetically that instead of judging him immediately, one is inclined to attempt a closer examination in order to ascertain exactly what his habitual attitudes are, what he stands for. His mind focuses again and again on three things, the nature and role of mankind, the "ways of God," and the nature and meaning of the Southern order. His view of man seems to rest on a pair of complementary theorems: that man is "puny" and that total irrationality is man's proper condition. His insignificance is seen in relation to the wilderness which, in the seventies of the nineteenth century, appeared to scorn the traces "of man's puny gnawing at the immemorial flank." The wilderness was "a phantom, epitome and apotheosis of the old wild life which the little puny humans swarmed and hacked at in a fury of abhorrence and fear like pygmies about the ankles of a drowsy elephant." Even as an old man nearing eighty when, in order to reach the receding remnant of wilderness, Ike had to travel two hundred miles, he still thought it a "tremendous, primeval, looming" thing looking down upon the camp (and perhaps every human habitation) and considering it "the puny evanescent clutter of human sojourn which after a single brief week would vanish and in another week would be completely healed, traceless in the unmarked solitude."

This would be an unpleasant or at least uncomfortable judgment against man if it were true. But man in time triumphed over the wilderness, hacked the "drowsy elephant" to pieces, an exasperating fact which Ike cannot ignore. He must extricate himself from a curious predicament. Ike, after all, is a man whose theory ought to have led him to join the local conservation club in order to preserve his beloved forests. Instead, all his life he has been a member of rich men's hunting parties which can afford to penetrate deeper and deeper into the virgin lands and leave a "clutter" each time which, despite Ike's assurance, is not "healed" or "traceless" in two weeks (a bottle, for example, does not decay quickly). Thus Ike feels at last a need to justify himself and tells us that "suddenly he knew why he had never wanted to own any of it, arrest at least that much of what people called progress, measure his longevity at least against that much of its ultimate fate. It was because there was just exactly enough of it." That is, there is just enough wilderness to last out Ike's lifetime. With extraordinary selfishness he explains that the "two spans"—he himself and the wilderness—will run out together, "not toward oblivion, nothingness, but into a dimension free of both time and space." In short, Ike and the virgin land will be born again in heaven. And the moral of the story seems to be: man may live out his years doing what he pleases with no sense of responsibility, but with the assurance that he is doing only and always what fate has destined him to do, and with the guarantee that paradise is a comfortable Eldorado where everything is restored to its happy youthful state.

The natural corollary to this is Ike's other theorem about man, namely that he is irrational. When cousin McCaslin objects to Ike's highly subjective interpretation of the Bible, Ike silences him with the explanation that there is no possibility of contradictory interpretations because "the heart already knows." Biblical scribes themselves sometimes lied because they could not make truth simple enough, but this does not matter because the pure-in-heart know truth instinctively. Ike's truth is *the* truth, if only men would stop using their minds long enough to recognize it.

This brings Ike to confront the deity and to answer the obvious question about how he managed to establish direct contact with Him. Ike's God is a predestinator who first gave men Europe and then, when they spoiled it, He gave them America "founded in humility and pity and sufferance and pride. . . ." But then (Ike's dialectic is a little obscure here). He found that even in the New World there was corrupt blood because the Indians too tried to possess and bequeath land; hence, to accomplish His purpose, He "voided" the Indian blood with White blood, which in turn raised "the white man's curse," that is, Black blood. God did all this and more: He created the beautiful South, watched wicked men destroy it, collaborated with John Brown though disapproving his methods, kept His blessed face turned toward His special people because the Southern ladies fed jelly to niggers and nursed them, and finally made the Rebels unite and fight against hopeless odds, which was far more significant than their having somehow lost the war. God, in short, "must accept responsibility for what He Himself had done in order to live with Himself in His lonely and paramount heaven." But in Ike's view, God does not mind this responsibility at all for He has already appointed a Divine Emissary whose duty it is to begin the long task of leading mankind away from the path of darkness. Who is this Emissary? Ike! "Chosen," says McCaslin Edmonds, "out of all your time by Him. . . ."

God is a great comfort to Isaac, who has lived directly under His sanctifying hand since he was twelve—whence, I suppose, his confidence in the future. Guided by God Almighty, he has done nothing to protect his beloved wilderness, nothing to save Old Ben. But this is all right, since the divine powers "would give [Old Ben] his paw back even, certainly they would give him his paw back." Here, then, is Ike's Calvinist God, a private and personal friend who doubtless has a special salvation prepared for Isaac just as He had a special reason for creating him.

Ike's handling of the Southern order stems logically from his view of God and man. If men (except Ike). are puny runts, and if Ike's beneficent Creator alone is responsible for what happens, then the South, past, present, or future, is the best of all possible worlds because it is the only possible world. "Submit!" becomes the catchword. And the world to which one is invited to submit is really no worse than any other. The true Southern lady is, after all, an angel. The ugliest features of Southern life, for example the Ku Klux Klan lynchings, are not, after all, authentically Southern but direct products of vile Yankee abolitionist or carpet-bagger meddling. The racial problem, while at times vexing, is at least bearable. Witness Isaac himself who became as vexed as he could be but learned to bear up at the cost of three thousand dollars—which he had not earned. He treats the black race exactly as he treats the wilderness, perhaps a little less kindly. The woods will last until Ike is gone, and he is satisfied; the colored people will keep their subordinate place until Ike is gone, but he is not quite satisfied and suggests that they stay down for an additional thousand years or two which of course is no time at all, a mere wink to God's benevolent eye, especially for people who above all else love to be patient and to endure. In the last analysis, the one thing Ike, like his grandfather before him, cannot tolerate is recognition of racial cross-breeds. To acknowledge the product of miscegenation is the ultimate outrage as Ike explicitly says: "No wonder the ruined woods I used to know don't cry for retribution! . . . The people have destroyed it and will accomplish its revenge." And who are the people? Precisely "*Chinese and African and Aryan and Jew,* [who] *all breed and spawn together until no man has time to say which one is which nor cares.*"

Although he has stirred many American critics to sympathy, Isaac is in many ways an unattractive creature. Whether his creator willed it or not, he turns out to be a more eloquent and persuasive apologist for the Old Order than the Vardamans and Bilbos whom Faulkner at times detests so much. Like Hightower's personality, Ike's is so perfectly divided between the will to preserve and perpetuate intact his heritage and the will to escape responsibility for the iniquities which his heritage places upon him that he continually approaches a futile and agonized passivity. His acts are usually inconclusive, his ideas always autocathartic.

Just as Faulkner twice registered objections against Ike's ineffectuality, so at the end of "The Bear," Ike's biggest story, Faulkner relates an incident which may be taken as his final negative judgment upon Ike. Clearly imitating his Indian-negro preceptor, Sam Fathers, Ike salutes a child of the wilderness in Sam's own tongue. But Sam's salutation was addressed to a handsome deer, Ike's to a rattlesnake—the one a symbol of life, the other a symbol of death. Thus it appears that Faulkner recognizes the failure of Ike to achieve a vision of reality in any way more profound or satisfying than Quentin's or Bayard's. His subjective effusions bring a viable conclusion no closer. He remains selfish, self-satisfied, and alone, retaining nevertheless a certain seductive charm.

Ike McCaslin surpasses his earlier spiritual brethren in three ways. His unique heritage of purity permits him to walk safely the thin line between guilt and expiation, and it prepares him for his special role as savior, while his predecessors were only executors of the regional conscience. His supreme egotism saves him from the evil consequences of isolation which destroyed Quentin and Hightower because it insulates him against the sense of futility and defeat which beset them. He survives as old Bayard survived, though his abdication from the office of "The McCaslin" preserves him from active engagement in the social organism and permits him to play the kindly sage like Will Fall in *Sartoris*. As a central consciousness, therefore, he is admirably equipped to tell us (or rather refract for us) the Southern story. Indeed, he is a far more persuasive narrator than the Stevens-Mallison team in *Intruder in the Dust* or than Faulkner himself in the entr'actes of *Requiem for a Nun*, though the argument remains the same. Even the shrewd tale-teller, V. K. Ratliff, who informs us in *The Hamlet* that the color-line still exists beyond the grave, is no match for Ike. Like William Jennings Bryan at the monkey trial, Ike can readily evoke in the jurors a kindly disposition toward himself because he is the authentic, sterling example and product (impurities notwithstanding) of the righteous Cause which he advocates.

To conclude with the assertion that Faulkner is echoing Yeats's famous lines in "The Second Coming" would be attractive but unjustified:

> The best lack all conviction, while the worst
> Are full of passionate intensity.

By refusing to decide the issue, by declining Yeats's aristocratic solution, Faulkner induces a condition of paralysis and in this way perpetuates the status quo. It is his frenzied meditations that many critics have mistaken for actual commitment, negative or positive, when in fact Mr. Faulkner provides little more than consolation for the suspended intellect.

Two Brief Commentaries

*On Method and Theme in Faulkner**

MALCOLM COWLEY

Faulkner's novels have the quality of being lived, absorbed, remembered rather than merely observed. And they have what is rare in the novels of our time, a warmth of family affection, brother for brother and sister, the father for his children—a love so warm and proud that it tries to shut out the rest of the world. Compared with that affection, married love is presented as something calculating, and illicit love as a consuming fire. And because the blood relationship is central in his novels, Faulkner finds it hard to create sympathetic characters between the ages of twenty and forty. He is better with children, Negro and white, and incomparably good with older people who preserve the standards that have come down to them "out of the old time, the old days." (1946)

Primitivism and "The Bear"†

HARRY MODEAN CAMPBELL and RUEL E. FOSTER

Primitivism—or what might be called "conceptual primitivism"—has to do with the impingement of the "nature as norm" concept on the fields of philosophy, religion, literature, sociology, ethics, politics, and economics. This phase of primitivism, which has received a detailed and scholarly treatment in rceent studies by George Boas and Arthur O.

* Reprinted from Malcolm Cowley, ed., *The Portable Faulkner*, by permission of the Viking Press, Inc. Copyright 1946 by The Viking Press, Inc.

† Reprinted from Harry Modean Campbell and Ruel E. Foster, *William Faulkner: A Critical Appraisal*, by permission of the University of Oklahoma Press. Copyright © 1951 by the University of Oklahoma Press.

Lovejoy,[1] goes back at least to Greco-Roman antiquity. Its primary technique in art has been that of regression: the artist regresses in time to a far-off primal golden age (chronological primitivism); or regresses in culture to a simple, primitive savage stage (cultural primitivism); or regresses to childhood or to the domain of the subconscious (psychic primitivism)....

In terms of allegory, this story might be interpreted thus. It would seem there are two worlds: the primitive world of the old free fathers—the first world—the wilderness and the animals of the wilderness and the men who live by and in and through the wilderness; and the civilized world of contemporary man who has insulated himself against the primitive world by interposing houses, societies, and material values between himself and the land, the earth, nature. Ike is born into this latter world but soon learns the existence of the primitive world. Through the ritual of the hunt, he is initiated into the primitive world, prefers it, and decides that, although he cannot completely escape the civilized world, he will repudiate its values and live in terms of primitive values. His problem is how to live by the rules of the wilderness when the wilderness no longer exists—how to be a primitive while living in a small Southern town. What happens to Ike is what would happen to any true primitive caught in our present society. The curse of Ike is that familiar one of other moderns who are caught between two worlds and spread-eagled. . . . (1951)

[1] The reference is to *Primitivism and Related Ideas in Antiquity,* Vol. I of *A Documentary History of Primitivism and Related Ideas* (Baltimore: John Hopkins Press, 1935). No other volume in the series was completed. See also George Boas, *Essays in Primitivism and Related Ideas in the Middle Ages* (Baltimore: Johns Hopkins Press, 1948) and Arthur O. Lovejoy, *Essays in the History of Ideas* (Baltimore: Johns Hopkins, 1948).—Eds.

"The Bear" in Relation to *Go Down, Moses*

The first edition of this book suggested some relationship of the stories in Go Down, Moses*—as Faulkner himself insisted—by inviting speculation on "Delta Autumn" alongside "The Bear." Since that time, more critics have come to comment on the connections between these and other stories (or "chapters") in* Go Down, Moses.

The Unity of Go Down, Moses

MICHAEL MILLGATE

The publication of *Go Down, Moses* in May 1942 appears in retrospect as a moment of culmination in Faulkner's career. It marked the end of that supremely creative period which had begun with the writing of *The Sound and the Fury;* it was followed by six years of virtual silence during which Faulkner published only four short stories, none of them among his best. These were not years of inactivity for Faulkner, since he spent a good deal of time in Hollywood and was largely engaged with the writing of *A Fable,* but they were years during which his reputation reached a low ebb, and from which he emerged, with the publication in 1948 of *Intruder in the Dust,* as apparently a different kind of novelist, much more ready to commit himself to specific statements on contemporary issues. But *Go Down, Moses* also represented a culmination in thematic terms, as the book in which Faulkner finally achieved the conjunction, and in some measure the fusion, of a number of apparently disparate ideas which had long occupied his imagination. The exploration of the history and society of his own region had been one of Faulkner's major concerns in books like *Sartoris, Light in August, Absalom, Absalom!* and *The Unvanquished,* and in the last three of these he had in different degrees engaged the problem of white-Negro relationships. *The Hamlet,* foreshadowed in this respect by *Sartoris* and other early works, had revealed Faulkner's deep and almost religious sense of the permanence and richness of the land and his preoccupation with the problem of its ownership, while a number of short stories, from "Red Leaves" (1930) onwards, had demonstrated his fascination with the wilderness and with the narrative and symbolic potentialities of the hunt.

It is not altogether clear in what way or at what moment Faulkner first clearly recognised the possibility of treating these ideas in terms of a single work, a single novelistic structure, but the conception must in some way have involved the realisation that he would need a central character whose combination of sensitivity and long life would afford scope for the two complementary strategies of innocent childhood and retrospective old age, and that he would also need to create a new family, or greatly extend an existing one, in order to provide sufficient genealogical complications to allow a full exploitation of the white-Negro theme. His answers to these needs were Isaac (Ike) McCaslin and the numerous other members, black and white, of the McCaslin family; and the fact that there exists a McCaslin family tree, drawn by Faulkner himself, is perhaps suggestive of the degree to which the family was created for a specific purpose, not evolved slowly from Faulkner's original conception of the world of Yoknapatawpha County.[1]

Because its crucial importance as an expression of Faulkner's ideas has been generally recognised, *Go Down, Moses* has attracted an unusual amount of critical attention. More often than not, however, this attention has been focused not on the book itself, but on "The Bear," a single segment of the whole. Again and again the five sections of "The Bear" as it appears in *Go Down, Moses* have been reprinted, anthologised, and discussed as if they constituted an independent entity, capable of being considered in isolation from the context of the whole book. The story, "The Bear," which appeared in the *Saturday Evening Post* a few days before the publication of the book, obviously possesses independent existence, as does the earlier story "Lion," from which "The Bear" must be considered to have grown, but Faulkner himself several times made it plain that

[1] For the genealogy, see James Meriwether, *The Literary Career of William Faulkner,* p. 31; Faulkner, however, says that the genealogy "developed itself" (*Faulkner in the University,* p. 97).

he considered *Go Down, Moses* to be a novel, and that the five-section version of "The Bear" was essentially "part of the novel, just as a chapter in the novel," to be neither printed nor discussed out of that context:

> That story was part of a novel. It was—the pursuit of the bear was simply what you might call a dangling clause in the description of that man when he was a young boy. When it was taken from the book and printed as a short story, the publisher, who is very considerate, has a great respect for all work and for mine in particular, he would not have altered one word of that without asking me, and he didn't ask me. If he had told me he was going to print it separately, I would have said, Take this [i.e., section four] out, this doesn't belong in this as a short story, it's a part of the novel but not part of the story. But rather than to go ahead and do that without asking me—and I wasn't available at that time—he printed it as it was. It [section four] doesn't belong with the short story. The way to read that is to skip that when you come to it.[2]

Many critics intent on interpreting "The Bear" have nevertheless persisted in the assumption that *Go Down, Moses* is simply a collection of short stories, lacking even the narrative consistency of *The Unvanquished,* and apparent support for this position might be derived from the fact that in the first printing of the first edition (May 1942) the book was entitled *Go Down, Moses and Other Stories.* Although the English edition still retains this title, the last three words were removed from later printings of the first American edition and from the Modern Library issue (from the plates of the first edition) of 1955. The alteration was made at Faulkner's request,[3] and there are grounds for believing that the original title may not have been entirely of his own choosing. Some light is thrown on the problem by the typescript setting copy of *Go Down, Moses,* now in the Alderman Library, from which it is clear that the fly-titles for the various chapters were not only inserted after the original preparation of the typescript but written and inserted not by Faulkner but by one of his editors. The title page itself is in a hand other than Faulkner's and it seems that the so-called "chapters" of "The Fire and the Hearth" were also an editorial innovation: Faulkner had distinguished them by Roman numerals with sub-divisions headed by Arabic numerals, and it was an editorial hand which altered the I, II, and III to Chapter One, Chapter Two, and Chapter Three. It is possible, of course, that the editor was acting on Faulkner's instructions, but some evidence to the contrary is provided by a copy of an unsigned letter from Random House which is now among Faulkner's papers at Charlottesville. Dated January 10, 1949, it mentions plans for re-issuing *Go Down, Moses,*

[2] *Faulkner in the University,* pp. 4, 273.

[3] Mr. Albert Erskine of Random House (letter, November 6, 1963) recalls Faulkner telling him that the book was a novel and that the words "and Other Stories" should never have appeared.

recalls that Faulkner had emphasised in conversation the fact that he considered it a novel rather than a group of stories, and asks whether, when the book was re-issued, he would like to insert chapter numbers in addition to the titles of the individual sections. That Faulkner did not accept this suggestion may have been due in part to his familiar reluctance to return to work which was behind him, preferring always to move forward with the work he had in hand or in prospect; but he may also have recognised the force of the observation, also made in the letter, that it might be a mistake to eliminate the section titles altogether because of the way in which they had become accepted as part of the text.[4]

To establish that Faulkner thought of *Go Down, Moses* as a novel is not, of course, to resolve the critical problem of whether the book *is* a novel, whether it possesses the organic unity we are accustomed to require of the books we agree to call novels. The fact that the volume consists largely of apparently separable units, and that versions of several of these had previously been published in the form of short stories, undoubtedly encourages the assumption that it is simply a short story collection or, at most, a sequence of related short stories. And some of the shifts in period, setting, theme, and personnel which occur in the course of the book may seem disturbing at a first reading: for example, the abrupt transition between the end of "Pantaloon in Black" and the beginning of "The Old People," the first of the hunting stories; the gulf dividing the grotesquely comic presentation of Miss Sophonsiba in "Was" from our subsequent realisation that she is Ike McCaslin's mother; the apparent inconsistency between the characterisation of Roth Edmonds in "Delta Autumn" and in "The Fire and the Hearth"; and, again in "The Fire and the Hearth," the placing of the crucial confrontation between Lucas Beauchamp and Zack Edmonds, Roth's father, within a context of primarily comic incident.

Difficulties of this kind tend to disappear with a closer reading. The introduction of the hunting episodes at the beginning of "The Old People" has already been ironically foreshadowed in "Was" by the pursuit of old Carothers McCaslin's Negro son, Tomey's Turl, by his white half-brother, Buck McCaslin, and this episode, together with the whole theme of white-Negro relationships, is further called to mind in "The Old People," as in "The Bear," by the presence of Tennie's Jim, child of Tomey's Turl and Tennie Beauchamp, brother of Lucas and Fonsiba, grandfather of the girl in "Delta Autumn," himself a concrete embodiment of the McCaslin miscegenation. One of the important factors in

[4] Mr. Erskine, loc. cit., states that the letter must have been from Robert Haas, who had brought Faulkner to Random House when the firm of Smith and Haas was taken over and had retained some editorial responsibility for his work; according to Mr. Erskine, Faulkner replied to the letter towards the end of January, confirming the suggestions but saying that he saw no necessity for adding numbers to the chapter titles.

Ike's upbringing is precisely his remoteness from his parents and the degree to which he is consequently "many-fathered" by his cousin McCaslin (Cass) Edmonds and by Sam Fathers, as well as by that real father, Theophilus (Buck) *McCaslin*, whom he had never known. In "Delta Autumn" it is the very uneasiness of Roth Edmonds, the savageness of a man whom we have previously seen as quick-tempered but essentially well-meaning, which points to the guilt from which he is suffering, while the presentation of Lucas in his relationship with Roth Edmonds in the comic episodes of "The Fire and the Hearth" does help to establish the pride and independence of Lucas's character, and this relationship, dominated by the fact that Lucas is a McCaslin and by the outcome of Lucas's fight with Zack many years previously, has important implications for Roth's own attitudes and actions.

Throughout *Go Down, Moses*, indeed, the various narrative strands are rarely treated in isolation, and there are few characters who are not related in some way to more than one of the major themes. The chief and most obvious themes are those which centre upon white-Negro relationships and upon the destruction of the wilderness. It is primarily in terms of the former that the episode entitled "Pantaloon in Black" is satisfactorily integrated into the novel, despite its lack of narrative links with other chapters: indeed, Faulkner's refusal to make the few minor changes in names and relationships which would have made Rider a McCaslin has the effect not of isolating the episode in which Rider is the major character but actually of expanding, beyond the limits of the single McCaslin family, the whole scope and relevance of the book. Related to these major themes, however, are a number of minor ones, of which the most fundamental is that of love. In the hunting episodes the love is mainly that of the man for the beast he hunts and kills, and for the animal which assists and accompanies him in the hunt: Faulkner insists repeatedly, for example, on the utter selflessness of Boon's love for Lion. Elsewhere in the novel the theme is explored partly in terms of the brotherly love between successive generations of white and Negro children, especially between Lucas and Zack and between their sons, Henry and Roth, but primarily through the presentation of a series of marriages. In "Pantaloon in Black," Rider's agony at the death of his wife is immediately contrasted with the meaninglessness of the deputy's marriage, making it plain that the deputy's incomprehension of Rider's actions springs in part from his utter unfamiliarity with the kind of love which Rider had known. But these marriages connect thematically with others in the novel, principally with that of Lucas and Molly, a union sustained over long years by loyalty and by love and itself contrasted with the marriage of Ike McCaslin, a union begun in love and passion but allowed to founder on a question of principle. The materialism of Ike's wife, her greed for possession of the plantation, is the root cause of the failure of their marriage, but Ike's refusal to compromise in this matter contrasts unfavourably with Lucas's decision to abandon the search for gold when his activities provoke Molly to seek a divorce. In this as in so many other ways the opposition between Ike and Lucas, who are first cousins, supplies a focus for the whole pattern and meaning of the book.

A number of symbols also run through the novel, and several of these are especially associated with Ike: the hunt, General Compson's hunting horn, the tainted legacy, the commissary books, with their record of "the slow outward trickle of food and supplies and equipment which returned each fall as cotton made and ginned and sold (two threads frail as truth and impalpable as equators yet cable-strong to bind for life them who made the cotton to the land their sweat fell on)." [p. 44] It is, however, through Lucas and the account of his marriage that one of the novel's most positive symbols, that of the fire on the hearth, is first established. When Lucas marries Molly he lights a fire "which was to burn on the hearth until neither he nor Molly were left to feed it," (p. 47) and it is by this fire that he sits alone during the months which Molly spends in Zack Edmonds's house. At the very depth of his despair Lucas suddenly catches himself standing over the fire, "furious, bursting, blind, the cedar water bucket already poised until he caught himself and set the bucket back on the shelf, still shaking, unable to remember taking the bucket up even." (p. 47) The crisis of Lucas's fears is here expressed in concrete terms, and the fact that he stops short of extinguishing the fire is a clear indication that he does not intend passively to accept the destruction of his marriage. The symbol recurs in "Pantaloon in Black," where there is a specific reference to the fire which Lucas Beauchamp had lit on his wedding night, and it is hinted at in the final chapter, "Go Down, Moses," when Gavin Stevens goes to Miss Worsham's house and finds Molly grieving for her grandson "beside the hearth on which even tonight a few ashes smoldered faintly." (p. 379) Molly's concern for a murderer's burial may have its comic side, but it is another aspect of that intensity and longevity of family loyalty and love in which the Negroes of the novel show themselves to be so much the superiors of their white relatives and neighbours. And it is, in part, this contrast between the two races which brings to bear such a weight of anguish and bitter irony upon the moment when Roth's Negro mistress speaks to Ike the terrible words which underline more clearly than anything else the ultimate failure of his life and his endeavour: " 'Old man,' she said, 'have you lived so long and forgotten so much that you dont remember anything you ever knew or felt or even heard about love?' " (p. 363)

Ike's failure as a man is in question here, not simply his failure as a white man, but it is with this encounter between Ike and the granddaughter of Tennie's Jim that Faulkner gives the final twist to that tragic interrelationship between the white and Negro branches of the McCaslin family which he deploys as the chief vehicle for his exploration of the racial theme. The revelation of the nature and full extent of this interrelationship has been delayed until the fourth section of "The Bear," that portion of the novel which not only contains, in the discussion between Ike and Cass, the most extended account of Ike's reasons for repudiating his inheritance, but which also displays, in Ike's recollections of his inspection of the commissary books, what Malcolm Cowley rightly seizes upon as an extreme instance of Faulkner's exhaustive exploration of a moment of time held suspended within a single extended sentence.[5] Undoubtedly the fourth section of "The Bear" is a *locus classicus* for an understanding of Faulkner's views on man and society, but the fact that these views have been given such widely divergent interpretations by different critics seems to be due not only to the inherent difficulty of the ideas themselves and of the language in which they are expressed but to the frequency with which "The Bear," in its five-section version, has been printed and discussed in isolation from the rest of the novel.

Even when critics have offered to consider *Go Down, Moses* as a whole their fascination with "The Bear" has often led them to ignore or underestimate the extent to which a proper understanding of that chapter depends upon its being read in the context not only of the other hunting episodes but of the novel as a whole. A recent critic who seizes on several important aspects of the book—notably, its enactment of successive variations on the concepts of freedom and bondage—nevertheless allows his interpretation of the discussion in the fourth section of "The Bear" to lead him into an obvious misreading of the conclusion of "The Old People," where, he says, Cass refuses to believe Ike's account of the encounter with the buck:

> He dismisses the incident as merely a buck-fever hallucination on Isaac's part. But the reader, given no previous or subsequent hints which cast doubt on the actuality of that salute, is inclined to feel that Cass is thus represented as becoming more and more blinded by and enslaved to practical matters, even while Isaac is becoming liberated from the merely practical, by Sam Fathers.[6]

Such an interpretation seems not to take into account the chapter's final paragraphs:

> "But I saw it!" the boy cried. "I saw him!"
>
> "Steady," McCaslin said. For an instant his hand touched the boy's flank beneath the covers. "Steady. I know you did. So did I. Sam took me in there once after I killed my first deer." (p. 187)

[5] *Portable Faulkner*, p. 226.

[6] Lawrance Thompson, *William Faulkner: An Introduction and Interpretation*, p. 87.

The point about the argument between Cass and Ike is precisely that they are so alike in so many ways, virtually two sides of the same Southern coin. The closeness of Ike's personal relationship to Cass—"rather his brother than cousin and rather his father than either" (p. 4)—is insisted upon at the very beginning of the book, and reiterated on many subsequent occasions. Cass, Sam Fathers, and the wilderness itself are the main sources of Ike's education, and Cass, as the conclusion of "The Old People" makes clear, has himself, in his earlier day, learned from Sam Fathers and from the woods. It was Cass who interpreted for Ike the reasons why he had refrained from killing Old Ben, concluding with the words which are of central significance for an understanding of the whole novel:

> *'Courage and honor and pride, and pity and love of justice and of liberty. They all touch the heart, and what the heart holds to becomes truth, as far as we know truth. Do you see now?'* [p. 68]

The extent to which Ike accepts Cass's views appears during the conversation in the commissary, when he repeats, almost word for word, several of Cass's earlier statements about the nature of truth, and indeed their discussion is for the most part not so much an argument as a joint exploration of possible approaches to certain crucial issues which face them both as Southerners, as landowners, and as heirs of old Carothers McCaslin.

It is of the utmost importance, here as throughout Faulkner's work, not to regard any single character as a mouthpiece for the author's own views: Faulkner never expresses himself directly in this way but only in terms of a book's total pattern. Thus Cass is not present simply as a foil to Ike; his position is no less firmly based than Ike's and in certain ways it is he who gets the better of the discussion. Ike's emphasis throughout is on "pity and love of justice and of liberty," his attempt is to expiate through repudiation of his inheritance the sins of his grandfather, old Carothers McCaslin, and of the whole history of the South. Cass, while not denying the existence or importance of the qualities on which Ike insists, nevertheless lays greater stress on "Courage and honor and pride," qualities which also "touch the heart" and hence constitute some part of "truth." There is dignity in Ike's position, but it clearly represents a withdrawal from the realities and the difficulties of life not unlike that displayed by Horace Benbow and Quentin Compson. It is a position grounded in pathetic compromise—the monthly pension which Ike accepts from Cass as a "loan"—and involving, in Ike's relationship with his wife, an insistence on principle which ultimately emerges as sterile and life-denying, somewhat in the manner of Charlotte Rittenmeyer's inflexible demand for an abortion in *The Wild Palms*.

A certain toughness and hard-headedness is essential to Cass's whole nature, and he is not always an attractive character, but his determination to run the plantation, to eschew what he regards as the luxury of repudiation, is rooted in reality and in life in a way that Ike's solution is not. When Ike declares himself to be "free," Cass retorts that the Southern white man will never be free of the Negro, nor the Negro of the Southern white man, and goes on to assert that he himself could never take any other position: "Even you can see that I could do no else. I am what I am; I will be always what I was born and have always been. And more than me." [p. 70] The conversation ends with the two positions unreconciled but neatly in balance: Ike has idealism on his side, but by his act of repudiation, of withdrawal, he disqualifies himself from making any effective contribution to the developing historical situation, so that even Roth Edmonds, whom Ike so bitterly condemns in "Delta Autumn," has previously won at least some measure of our sympathy by his unimaginative but not insincere or inhumane attempts to cope with the difficult practical situations presented to him as the present owner of the McCaslin plantation in "The Fire and the Hearth"—situations such as Ike himself has never been called upon to confront.

There is a revealing interchange in an interview which Faulkner gave in 1955. Having learned from the interviewer that Isaac McCaslin was her favourite among his characters, Faulkner asked her why she admired him:

> INT: Because he underwent the baptism in the forest, because he rejected his inheritance.
>
> WF: And do you think it's a good thing for a man to reject an inheritance?
>
> INT: Yes, in McCaslin's case, he wanted to reject a tainted inheritance. You don't think it's a good thing for him to have done so?
>
> WF: Well, I think a man ought to do more than just repudiate. He should have been more affirmative instead of shunning people.[7]

Ike's life is a failure, primarily because he allows himself to rest in negation, in repudiation, and rejects all opportunities for affirmation. And so the fourth section of "The Bear" draws to a close with the comic story of Hubert Beauchamp's "legacy"—an ironic counterpoint to Ike's rejection of his McCaslin inheritance—and with the details of Ike's compromise over the loan and of the agony and waste of his relationship with his wife.

Yet this is not in the least to deny Ike's essential goodness, nor the quality of his idealism. "Sam Fathers set me free," [p. 70] Ike declares at the end of his long debate with Cass, and the invocation of Sam's name at this crucial point reminds us that the context of this section, which is almost entirely concerned with slavery and miscegenation and

[7] Grenier, "The Art of Fiction," p. 175. Cf. *Faulkner in the University*, p. 246.

McCaslin family history, is an account of the hunting of an old bear and of the gradual disappearance of the wilderness in which he lived. Ike's experience as a hunter has played a vital part in his education, in the process of his becoming the man capable of renouncing his inheritance. In the other sections of "The Bear," Ike's skill as a woodsman and hunter is repeatedly insisted upon, and it is also made plain that he has learned thoroughly all that Sam Fathers has had to teach him about the proper rituals of the hunt, about loving and respecting the creatures who are pursued and killed. Faulkner's most direct attempt to link Ike's experience in the wilderness with his repudiation of the plantation occurs in "Delta Autumn," as Ike, an old man, lies in his tent and recalls his past life, beginning with the moment (recorded in "The Old People") when he shot his first buck:

> Old Sam Fathers was alive then, born in slavery, son of a Negro slave and a Chickasaw chief, who had taught him how to shoot, not only when to shoot but when not to; such a November dawn as tomorrow would be and the old man led him straight to the great cypress and he had known the buck would pass exactly there because there was something running in Sam Fathers' veins which ran in the veins of the buck too, and they stood there against the tremendous trunk, the old man of seventy and the boy of twelve, and there was nothing save the dawn until suddenly the buck was there, smoke-colored out of nothing, magnificent with speed: and Sam Fathers said, 'Now. Shoot quick and shoot slow:' and the gun levelled rapidly without haste and crashed and he walked to the buck lying still intact and still in the shape of that magnificent speed and bled it with Sam's knife and Sam dipped his hands into the hot blood and marked his face forever while he stood trying not to tremble, humbly and with pride too though the boy of twelve had been unable to phrase it then: *I slew you; my bearing must not shame your quitting life. My conduct forever onward must become your death;* marking him for that and for more than that: that day and himself and McCaslin juxtaposed not against the wilderness but against the tamed land, the old wrong and shame itself, in repudiation and denial at least of the land and the wrong and shame even if he couldn't cure the wrong and eradicate the shame, who at fourteen when he learned of it had believed he could do both when he became competent and when at twenty-one he became competent he knew that he could do neither but at least he could repudiate the wrong and shame, at least in principle, and at least the land itself in fact, for his son at least: and did, thought he had: then (married then) in a rented cubicle in a back-street stock-traders' boardinghouse, the first and last time he ever saw her naked body, himself and his wife juxtaposed in their turn against that same land, that same wrong and shame from whose regret and grief he would at least save and free his son, and saving and freeing his son, lost him. (pp. 350–351)

If Ike has achieved any kind of freedom, it is only that of loss itself; at best, it is the quasi-freedom of withdrawal and escape, such as Cass had accused him of seeking and such as Sam Fathers himself would surely not have approved. In *Go Down, Moses* the linking of the wilderness material with the themes of white-Negro relationships and of the ownership of the land is sometimes thought to be rather forced; but the tenuousness of the connection between the hunting episodes and the rest of the novel may be in some measure a direct and deliberate reflection of Faulkner's conception of Ike and of Ike's idealism. There seem to be some grounds for arguing that Ike's attempt to carry over into the practical workaday world the lessons Sam Fathers taught him in the wilderness was bound to fail, that the values he had learned from Sam Fathers, though fine in themselves, were already outmoded, and became steadily more obsolescent with the passing of the years. Certainly Ike's declaration that Sam Fathers had set him free has a hollow ring in the context of other examinations of the meaning of "freedom"[8] which Faulkner offers in the fourth section of "The Bear": the other character who declares herself to be free is Fonsiba, hopelessly enslaved though she is by appalling poverty and by the delusions of her husband, and we come to see, though Ike does not, that the husband himself, reading with his lensless spectacles and relying on his pension cheque while his farm stagnates, is not so many steps removed from Ike himself.

Although it is obviously an over-simplification, there is a sense in which it is true of Ike that what he *says* is right, but what he *does* is wrong. Nowhere is this distinction more valid than in "Delta Autumn," the one chapter of the novel in which the various themes merge and fuse not solely in terms of argument but also, and with profoundly moving effect, in terms of action, situation, and naturally invoked symbol. Roth's killing of the doe at the end of the chapter offers a wholly satisfying image of the white-Negro theme in the terms of the wilderness and hunting themes, and suggests at the same time that Ike has failed to pass on to younger men even the practical training he received from Sam Fathers. But the point at which all the threads of the novel seem to cross, at which the whole pattern of the book emerges with final and absolute clarity, is that of Ike's encounter with Roth's mistress. At the moment when we see the completion of the terrible circle initiated by old Carothers McCaslin—"the gnarled, bloodless, bone-light bone-dry old man's fingers touching for a second the smooth young flesh where the strong old blood ran after its long lost journey back to home" (p. 362)—we realise that not even Ike himself has succeeded in breaking out of that circle. For all his fine statements about love earlier in the chapter, Ike fails to recognise it in the young Negress. For all his admiration for the Negro, his hatred of his grandfather's sin, his repudiation of his inheritance, Ike at this moment

[8] Cf. Thompson, *op. cit.*, p. 81.

of confrontation can only muster the traditional reactions: in effect he ratifies the solution offered by Roth Edmonds, the man he has affected to despise, by passing on the money to the girl; he can suggest no course of action other than her going North with the child and marrying "a black man . . . who would ask nothing of you and expect less and get even still less than that, if it's revenge you want." (p. 363) Ike's use of the word "revenge" indicates his own failure to recognise the strength and quality of the girl's love and points to the dignity of the Negro refusal to take revenge. It also shows a kind of muddled thinking on his part, since it should presumably be on a white man that she would seek revenge, and this confusion in its turn perhaps reveals the degree to which Ike is still trapped within traditional patterns of thought: he apparently sees revenge as a gesture against the world in general, and, in effect, he recommends the girl to hurt someone who is racially her inferior (Ike says, "a black man," and we already know that the girl is almost white) as a means of making good the hurt she has received from someone racially, and socially, her superior.

In the light of Ike's advice to the girl to go North, his presentation to the child of General Compson's hunting horn, a symbol of the wilderness and its values, becomes an almost meaningless gesture, while in the book's final chapter, "Go Down, Moses," the point is underlined that going North, with its consequent deracination, is unlikely to provide a satisfactory solution to any Negro's problems. From "Go Down, Moses" it appears that Ike's advice to the girl represents a further ratification of action previously taken by Roth, since Roth had first been responsible for sending Lucas and Molly's grandson away: "Roth Edmonds sold my Benjamin," Molly cries. (p. 380) The last chapter thus has its thematic function in relation to the whole work; it also has a structural importance, as a kind of epilogue, functionally linked with the somewhat detached prologue provided by "Was" and with the similarly detached yet immensely powerful central episode of "Pantaloon in Black." Gavin Stevens in "Go Down, Moses" occupies a role as uncomprehending outsider to the Negro way of life, thought, and feeling which is somewhat similar to that occupied by the deputy in "Pantaloon in Black." Stevens, unlike the deputy, is sympathetic, within his limits as a white man, and he is certainly well-meaning: indeed, he appears in a better light than Ike McCaslin, for all of Ike's advantages, at least to the extent that he takes positive action to help one particular Negro. At the same time, he completely fails to understand, or seriously to affect, either the situation or old Molly herself: "I wants hit all in de paper. All of hit," (p. 383) she insists, and nowhere in the whole of Faulkner's work is there a more persuasive dramatisation of the gulf dividing the white man's mind from the Negro's than the scene in which Stevens, confronted by Molly's grief, flees from the house in a kind of terror. In all this Stevens compares unfavourably with Cass, the man who had been fully committed to the practical situation, and the last words of the book seem to suggest that Stevens would have been better advised to confine himself to the job which he is paid, and presumably competent, to perform: " 'Come on,' he said. 'Let's get back to town. I haven't seen my desk in two days.' " (p. 383)

Considered in abstract terms, the two major themes of white-Negro relationships and of the destruction of the wilderness are inextricably linked: the wilderness disappears to make way for a system based on physical or economic slavery, and Ike's education in the wilderness fosters a sense of values which prompts him to a repudiation of that system and of the concept of land-ownership upon which it is based. Faulkner's expression of this dialectic is far richer than such an abstraction would suggest; in part this is because Ike's actions and assumptions are questioned and explored, not simply endorsed, because the technical scope of the book permits of great variety in the selection and presentation of characters and episodes, and because the novel possesses, despite its disrupted chronology, a firm underlying framework of historical continuity. One of the chief functions of "Was" is to supply historical perspective in terms of a superbly imagined vignette of a certain stratum of Mississippi society in the year 1859, while in subsequent chapters, and above all through the evocative device of the commissary books in the fourth section of "The Bear," Faulkner builds up—obliquely, by implication and slow accretion of detail, rather than by direct statement—a rich contextual presentation of a land and a society undergoing a process of slow but inevitable change. Faulkner spoke of his attitude towards this process in answer to a questioner at the University of Virginia:

> What the writer's asking is compassion, understanding, that change must alter, must happen, and change is going to alter what was. That no matter how fine anything seems, it can't endure, because once it stops, abandons motion, it is dead. It's to have compassion for the anguish that the wilderness itself may have felt by being ruthlessly destroyed by axes, by men who simply wanted to make that earth grow something they could sell for a profit, which brought into it a condition based on an evil like human bondage. It's not to choose sides at all—just to compassionate the good splendid things which change must destroy, the splendid fine things which are part of man's past too, part of man's heritage too, but they were obsolete and had to go. But that's no need to not feel compassion for them simply because they were obsolete.[9]

This combination of regret for a vanishing past with a clear recognition of the necessity for change is a fundamental source of that internal tension and conflict which characterises the whole of *Go Down, Moses,* and

[9] *Faulkner in the University,* p. 277.

which is reflected most obviously in the structure of the novel and in its constant interplay of comic and tragic elements. . . .

Faulkner and the Possibilities for Heroism

ARTHUR F. KINNEY

In Faulkner's evolving achievement, the trilogy composed of "The Old People," "The Bear," and "Delta Autumn" which constitutes the fundamental portion of *Go Down, Moses,* his last major novel, remains the repository of his most significant ideas and attitudes. The reconstruction of a Southern history which Isaac McCaslin and McCaslin Edmonds create together in a dialectic of cryptic ledger notes and expansive imaginations in Part IV of "The Bear" is Faulkner's last chief formulation of the rise and fall of an antebellum South marred by the economic strategies of slavery. The necessary complications and refinement come in the two stories which frame "The Bear." The Indians, whites, and blacks who populate "The Old People" insinuate in their mixed attitudes and ancestral biases precisely those intellectual and emotional failings which for Faulkner gave to the South the twin legacies of hope and pride and so caused a double portion of despair. In "Delta Autumn" the grandeur of the hunt for a monolithic king of beasts is displaced by the interminable noise of planing mills, the mechanically destructive inroad of the locomotive, and the reduction of the wilderness to muddy flatlands which together chart pettiness and loss. Caught up as it is not only with Ike but with Ike's historic, economic, social, natural, and ethical milieus—with human nature and with the South generally—the trilogy repeatedly asks of us what we are to make of a diminished thing.

The writer's own response comes in the final movement, in "Delta Autumn." But the conclusions there result from the conflict of ideas and episodes, of events and metaphors in the two earlier stories of the trilogy: true to the developmental mode which fashions his finest fiction, Faulkner is able in the last story to resolve the forces of courage, freedom, intellectualization, and experience which had charged his own speculations and consciousness since *Sartoris* and served to focus his attention in all the major novels. Ike gathers up the problems of all the Faulknerian heroes in his attempts to accommodate himself to principles which transcend a fluid and mutable social history: he surmounts time and place by choosing

Revised from *The Southern Review,* Vol. VI, N. S. (Autumn 1970), 1110–1125.

The author is grateful to David Williams, Deidre Ryan Lannon, Charles Dean, and John Cooley for suggestions.

experience over concept, act before word, thereby acquiring, if with limited insight, what Faulkner submits as man's single claim to nobility.

I

Many of the subtleties of Faulkner's thought are made clear in the explicit series of contrasts with which "Delta Autumn" opens. Subsequent to "The Bear," Ike's world is marked by change. More than a half-century has passed: it is November 1940 now, and Ike is seventy-three. He is again on a hunting party, but he is no longer awed by the countryside nor by sensing the threshold of life in a hunter's cabin while preparing for a sacrament of initiation and rebirth. Instead he comes not thirty but more than two hundred miles to a tent in the rain, a tent located not in a "big woods" but in the wet delta. He arrives by truck, not horse and wagon; and now the game is scarce. Reduction is underlined by loss. Major deSpain is now dead, his cabin gone. Large bear are no longer to be found. Does must not be shot, since they are needed to stretch out the thinning population of the delta and so prolong the annual hunting parties. The hunters themselves are no longer filled with wonder for the woods, respect for the rituals of hunting, or even admiration for each other. Instead they quarrel: Will Legate taunts Roth Edmonds, while Roth himself is defensive, nervous, self-deprecating. There is no longer fraternity among the hunters; and together they condescend to Ike. They suffer his presence with silence, out of pity; his stories arouse resentment and even his inactivity is occasion for slight contempt. The generation gap is showing, but a disjunction now thematic and rich in Faulknerian overtones.

Yet warning came for Ike as early as his trip into the woods in Part V of "The Bear": "he had forewarning and had believed himself prepared." The sawmills and the railroad were extirpating the woods, and slowly he had to accept this as the maddened Boon, isolated by his sense of loss and his recognition of waste, could not. Kierkegaard has warned us that "the specific character of despair is precisely this: it is unaware of being despair." So the sawmills are followed by dust and then by highways, and Ike has failed to see this; not until "Delta Autumn" does he observe that degeneration and death are concomitants of life and eradication and even then his imagination embroiders it with fiction, a deliberate but temporary stay against mortality. Now "he seemed to see the two of them—himself and the wilderness—as coevals." He lessens the danger by making "this land which man has deswamped and denuded and derivered in two generations" a concrete representation of himself, and thus witnessing it, can see it "not being conquered, destroyed, so much as retreating since its purpose was served now and its time an outmoded time." Ike thus repeats Roth's reaction of internalizing events and so weakening them all but disposing of them. This autumn seems at once something less, yet something more mellow than the cold bitter Novembers of the former grand hunts for Old Ben.

Part of this slackening of tension is directly attributable to the distinction between the core elements in the two works. In "The Bear" the chief confrontation (in Part IV) is what Karl Jaspers calls a "boundary-situation"; that is, a personal crisis (here one of guilt and suffering) seen in relation to its historically determining features (the past actions of the McCaslin family). "Delta Autumn" deals not with this personal-extra-personal interstice but with the meeting of Ike and the octoroon mistress of Roth, and though this shares an element of eschatology with the earlier confrontation, it is in this instance also apocalyptic. The mistress issues her prophetic disclosure and then invites Ike to examine his own soul, quite apart from the weight of history and society.

This recognition of his failure is for Ike even more dramatic than the realization of his legacy in "The Bear." For Ike responded to his earlier knowledge with an act of repudiation: the voluntary relinquishment of land, wife, and paternity, and the free acceptance of a life of austerity and insistent moral commitment. Translated into the terms of the annual hunt, this act has not been costly; he has charged his new life with the inherited energy of the simple pursuits of Old Ben, displacing his own father with the surrogate father Sam and projecting on later hunts the imaginative, vivid, and ritualistic adventures of an earlier day, making of all the years a single continuum, precious, pure, elemental, and even visionary. He has fashioned of his carpentry and his hunts in the delta—of his life generally—a singular existence of faith and hope. That he has not faced up to the fact that the sawmills, the locomotive, and the dissension of the hunters—the slow decay of the hunt—has no ritual value clearly indicates his increasing inability to cope with change and marks the slow dry-rot which constitutes his own form of a tragic fall. His life once based on freedom—" 'I am free' " he tells Cass in the commissary—leads to an unresolved dialectic, life-long, of pride and humility and restrains his capacity to think and act more than he comprehends. By surrendering to a ritual of the hunt and a singular model in Christ, Ike has chosen bondage of will and has blinded his own imagination. He is no longer the *eiron* of the Old South, for he has not found in emulating Christ a successful mask by which to serve or influence humanity. So this would-be *eiron* has turned *alazon,* betraying the South and himself by finding an alternative means of getting along with an outmoded system.

That he has betrayed both the South and himself is shown in his single sharp image of horror in "Delta Autumn." Ike, now a shivering old man, reaches for the octoroon, his "gnarled, bloodless, bone-light bone-dry old man's fingers touching for a second the smooth young flesh where the strong old blood ran." The blood is blood again guilty of incest and miscegenation; the crime Ike has served a lifetime of penance for has come full circle upon him. His asceticism, his intentions, his resignation from life cannot prevent his conditioned response against incest and miscegenation, hence against total freedom to love. Suddenly Ike McCaslin is both old and ineffectual. *Eiron* turned *alazon* he figures forth through the ignorance of his own limitations, a victim as well as a perpetrator of McCaslin (and Old Southern) tragedy.

II

Faulkner's trilogy is a work of indirection; "Delta Autumn" carries forward this technique. The bantering of the first part of the story, accomplished with sharp jests, and the bargaining of the second part, done with a mounting desperation, alike provide for but do not state Ike's need and demand for the appropriate measure of heroism.

Ike's first response is to explain the loss. He does this through a salvational theory based on communal atonement. When Roth cynically defines patriotism as barroom singing and "dime-store flags in our lapels," Ike recalls the patriotism of the Civil War which helped sustain the best motives and efforts of man. He counters with " 'This country is a little mite stronger than any one man or group of men, outside of it or even inside of it either. I reckon, when the time comes and some of you have done got tired of hollering we are whipped if we dont go to war and some more are hollering we are whipped if we do, it will cope with one Austrian paper-hanger, no matter what he will be calling himself.' " The conclusion is axiomatic given Ike's own premise: most men are a little better than their circumstances give them a chance to be. It is also consistent: war is welcome, because it is not only divine punishment but in its anguish provides a bequest of salvation.

The other hunters counter Ike, for they are realists; they do not see an Edenic past as Ike does. Wyatt tries again to torment Roth, but he really answers Uncle Ike. " 'Meaning that it's only because folks happen to be watching him that a man behaves at all,' " and Roth, as realistic as anyone in "Delta Autumn" by this point, agrees and is not annoyed: " 'Yes,' Edmonds said. 'A man in a blue coat, with a badge on it, watching him.' " The attack is on Ike; he argues concisely, firmly, but it is evident that all his lessons—the expanding railroad, the commissary ledgers—support Wyatt and Roth. Ike appears to them to see too simply; he does not accept what is now established fact: that if the Civil War sets a precedent and allows communal atonement, that process has failed. By analogy World War II—the present generally—can do no better for the Negro. Nothing yet has rubbed out the sins of slavery and miscegenation (as "sin") so deeply imbedded in Southern and personal historic fact.

Against them Ike is shorn of thought; only an indomitable will to salvage the South and through it mankind preserves his hope and his integrity. Still Ike's position is not altogether futile nor his gestures useless; throughout the bickering in the truck and at the camp, alongside the increasing sense of despair that overtakes the hunters, his repetition of ethical responses, his role as guardian of the moral tag, underscores the genuineness of his stance and the generosity of his perspective. "God said *'This is enough'* "; *"Apparently they can learn nothing save through suffering, remember nothing save when underlined in blood."*

Ike is more successful in substituting a private mythology: God " 'created man to be His overseer on the earth and to hold suzerainty over the earth and the animals on it in His name, not to hold for himself and his descendants inviolable title for ever, generation after generation, to the oblongs and squares of earth, but to hold the earth mutual and intact in the communal anonymity of brotherhood, and all the fee He asked was pity and humility and sufferance and endurance and the sweat of his face for bread.' " The logical shift here is delicate and oblique, but Ike manages to build a case for himself, evading responsibility for the land which has taxed his family so dearly and exercised his own conscience in anguish. Instead he continues: ownership of land has encouraged a plantation economy, ownership of man, " 'that whole edifice intricate and complex and founded upon injustice and erected by ruthless rapacity.' " Then there is another subtle shift of the *daemon* inside Ike and the private myth suffers again from hybris. He alone can free the McCaslins and by extension the South. " 'Chosen, I suppose (I will concede it),' " agrees Cass, " 'out of all your time by Him as you say Buck and Buddy were from theirs. And it took Him a bear and an old man [Sam Fathers] and four years just for you.' "

As he privately reviews his life, Ike realizes that the inheritance of the land is a sin compounded by the Indians; slavery was practiced by the Indians and McCaslins both. What is uniquely McCaslin, however—and therefore what allows and constitutes the basis for his own personal renunciation and his vocation as a Christ-like carpenter—is the denial of humanity by his great-grandfather: Ike's first substantial bid for heroism is his open reaffirmation of his ancestry. For he is appalled in the final analysis not so much by incest (which he does not mention) nor by miscegenation (which he knows also produced Sam Fathers) but by the betrayal of one's kin in denying any relationship. This is the unforgivable crime of Lucius McCaslin, causing the thousand dollar legacy *"That was cheaper than saying My son to a nigger."* The crime was repeated but in knowledge in Zack's duel on the bed with Lucas. Concerning it, Ike is most bitter: *"My son wasn't but just two words."* Lucius left money, but he knew he would die before it was due; his ancestors would even need to suffer the shame of passing on the inheritance. Buck and Buddy, in allowing the Negroes to move into the white owner's house, paid their allegiance to the freedom of the Negro, but they also refused to recognize their own kin. They merely tripled the cash legacy. That they did not perceive the horror—and the genuine dishonor—of denying their own flesh and blood is our realization, for Ike does not tell us directly that they could not admit that Uncle Hubert himself took a Negro mistress when Sophonsiba left home and Uncle Buck moved the Negroes out of the slaveowner's house so he could return there. That silence underscores Ike's own measure of despair.

Ike's sense of outraged humanity as well as his comprehension of the McCaslin legacy are what require him to repair the damage by attempting personally to pay the thousand dollars to each of Lucius's heirs. There is more than a modicum of stature in this act; and it too is underscored when Tennie's Jim dismisses him, and Fonsiba—whom he nearly calls his own until her husband dismisses him rudely—shows her own refusal to recognize their blood relationship. " 'I am free,' " she announces proudly, although Ike is not certain whether she feels she is free from work, from suffering ("Canaan"), or from himself. It is a pathetic moment. When her husband had asked to marry Fonsiba, he recognized Ike's relationship—" 'I acknowledge your authority only so far as you admit your responsibility toward her as a female member of the family of which you are the head' "—but this is no longer true: " 'The curse you whites brought into this land has been lifted,' " he tells Ike and in "you whites" he withdraws any possibility of clan. Given such a response Ike knows any admission of their relationship would be futile, would even detract from his purpose, and he pursues instead his offer of material welfare. But this bearing of gifts is not repudiation: it is reparation; and it is not sufficient reparation until it becomes a public proclamation of kinship. Ike continues to fail in part, then; and his failure is twofold: the world will not present him with the possibility of self-redemption, and he is incapable of forging for himself that opportunity.

Against this somewhat lengthy background, the Isaac McCaslin of "Delta Autumn" once again faces the problem of recognizing and proclaiming his relationship to a partly black woman. The pattern should by now be familiar to a McCaslin: an envelope of money discharges guilt, shame, and responsibility. But Ike has learned from his previous experiences that cash is not enough—as the octoroon says, " 'That's just money.' " So Ike adds his own highly significant portion, the hunting horn, "the one which General Compson had left him in his will, covered with the sunbroken skin from a buck's shank and bound with silver." In itself such an object is useless to the girl. But Ike's point is that he is not making payment, providing legacy; rather he is fashioning a present out of a family heirloom. It is his indirect but clear gesture to her that she is a member of his family, entitled to its more valuable properties. Because it is a symbol of the good and meaningful old times when half-Negroes such as Sam Fathers were respected and loved for their tutelage to the young, the gift, given to a mulatto mother, takes on greater meaning and poignance. Because it also heralds death as well as life, the death of the girl's affair with Roth and (quite clearly) Ike's own death, the gift is one of regeneration, passing on to the child of mixed blood the old wilderness which he cannot know at first hand. The horn is from the good past, not the bad; it is significantly generous. Ike's present recognition stands as pointed corrective to past denials: Lucius of Eunice and her daughter, Buck and Buddy of Tomey's Turl and Hubert Beauchamp's mistress, Roth of the woman.

Such an act is more than heroic; it is cathartic. For Ike is at last able—as he was not with Cass, with his wife, and with Roth—to link his concept of honor with his concept of the hunt. By telescoping the man's honor with the hunter's cherished object, he finds temporarily a fixed center to his own being, a coherent and cohesive unity of will that allows him to sustain himself, directing his beliefs and containing and guiding the diversity and disposal of his desires. Although generally ineffective even on a personal level, Ike McCaslin is not without his flash of insight and his moment of triumph in "Delta Autumn."

III

That Ike thinks of honor conceptually rather than practically, and that his response to the wilderness is based on his belief in it rather than the reality of its loss is not new for the McCaslins nor for Faulkner himself. Throughout his work a chief means of definition for Faulkner has been his use of landscape as metaphor: in this way, too, the trilogy serves as a climax to Faulkner's achievement. Earlier Haiti in *Absalom, Absalom!* functioned as Sutpen's only geography of success because there races lived and intermarried in natural bonds of love and trust, such simple goodness later made antithetical to the fighting of blacks and whites in the barn at Sutpen's Hundred, the estate significantly raised out of slime. *Sanctuary* is perhaps best understood as a Southern triptych in which Faulkner pictures forth the Old Frenchman Place as the natural jungle of earth, bounded by the Hades imagery of the brothel in Memphis and the "heaven tree" making of Jefferson a paradise. That Horace Benbow cannot find love or justice in Jefferson—that in fact Faulkner can find no modern analogue for paradise in Yoknapatawpha—constitutes the awful judgment which *Sanctuary* renders on the South generally and for Faulkner on the modern age as well. Likewise in this trilogy of Isaac McCaslin, the plantation, especially as it casts shapes and values in the minds of various characters, must be taken metaphorically, if we are to explore past the surface of Faulkner's art. The plantation, in encouraging a social and ethical life grounded in possessiveness (of both land and slaves) and materialism (basing success on accumulation of wealth), controls Ike's instincts even to the point of creating his horror in touching the octoroon to whom he would give General Compson's hunting horn.

For both the *idea* of plantation and the *ideas* of white superiority and Negro sexuality have controlled the thoughts and psyches of the McCaslins through three generations. The concept of plantation has lent to the McCaslins a social position which insures their prestige and security and feels their pride at the expense of stifling their better impulses. Even Buck and Buddy are motivated by a false sense of charity. The treatment of Negroes is seen by us as despicable because we are not conditioned as the McCaslins to a treatment of black people that supports and sustains an economy in which servitude and racial superiority are not only feasible but vital. Ike's problem, like that of his forbears, is that he tends to turn realities into metaphorical concepts, and thereby assigns to them stereotyped (and fossilized) values.

Conceptually speaking, Ike at first escapes his family's tendency to forge out of abstract squares of land a social, political, and ethical entity which is self-perpetuating. He escapes because he rejects the plantation totally for an alternative commitment to the wilderness. Yet his substitute identification is also total; and it is this which proves a fatal weakness to his understanding of his accomplishments and of his nature. For Ike is able to accommodate new meaning given the wilderness only until the death of Old Ben; at that point his definition is fixed: Ike freezes his picture of the woods in memory willed kinetic; he simultaneously turns a solitary moment of wilderness existence into an eternal refuge, a personal and private sanctuary. The "big woods" offers him "an unforgettable sense . . . not a quality dangerous or particularly inimical, but profound, sentiment, gigantic and brooding." He continues to see "the faces of the old men he had known and loved for a little while outlived, moving again among the shades of tall unaxed trees and sightless brakes where the wild strong immortal game ran for ever before the tireless belling immortal hounds, falling and rising phoenix-like to the soundless guns."

In "The Bear" this idealization of the woods is contrasted to the commissary, to Cass, and to the profits measured in "that slow trickle of molasses and meal and meat, of shoes and straw hats and overalls, of plough-lines and collars and heel-bolts and buckheads and clevises, which returned each fall as cotton"—a life of bartering and economic gain. In "Delta Autumn" Ike is contrasted to Roth who treats people as properties and his mistress as an overdue account. We learn Roth has given her money (not love) before; it is little wonder that she disposes of it quickly as if it were dirty, as if she were dirty if "bought off." Roth punishes himself like other Southern Puritans in Faulkner—Horace and young Bayard —and consequently seeks self-mortification. In this he is a slower-witted yet more frenzied Uncle Ike.

Indeed, it is when we range the plantation and the commissary alongside the white McCaslins, and freedom of mind and movement alongside the mulatto McCaslins, that we develop the proper equation and see how

Faulkner has used landscape and race—and also vocation—as metaphor to assert both meaning and point. Both Ike and Roth are, like Buck and Buddy and Lucius, caught up in the stratified values of a past economy; they are unable to change attitudes and so free themselves from the past which Faulkner in "Delta Autumn" labels "outmoded." Meanwhile Cass does accept change insofar as he accepts the business of the commissary; he is freed insofar as he is able to turn a profit from a new business, that of the small merchant class which has succeeded the landed aristocracy in the South. The girl of "Delta Autumn" also accepts change, as Ike's wife could not. Adaptability in Faulkner presages the only meaningful liberty.

The world of this trilogy admits a diptych—the wilderness juxtaposed to civilization. Rather than struggle, Ike submits himself totally to the wilderness, changing it into Eden; Fonsiba's husband surrenders totally to a new freedom of self-reliance in Canaan. Both are chained to their landscapes. Yet neither is any worse off than Roth who in committing himself to the plantation is unable to allow his mulatto mistress-cousin any public acknowledgment of stature or kinship.

It is precisely such outmoded racial bondage which the mulatto attempts to destroy by transcending it: her risk, prompted by love rather than advancement or self-justification, is that Roth will respond not to the Old Order of justice but to a New Order of love. It is crucial that he does not and that Ike does not see the immediacy (though perhaps by giving her the horn he recognizes the validity) of her attempt; yet he maintains the old code: it is important that he thinks of the woman as Negro when she tells him she takes in washing, his mind as ever contracted and perverted by the values of a plantation economy.

IV

Single words in shifting contexts as well as geographical metaphors and character analogies serve to define heroism for Faulkner in this culminating trilogy on the South. Like the other portions of *Go Down, Moses,* "Delta Autumn" is about a hunt; but it combines the narrative lines of such segments as "Was" and "The Old People" by making both men and animals the objects of pursuit. This unexpected fusion is prepared for in "The Bear," where Sam Fathers feels his life span at one with that of Old Ben. In "Delta Autumn" the word "doe" is from the outset possessed with twin meanings and is consistently reduplicative and reflexive. " 'Oh, Roth's coming. . . . If it was just a buck he was coming all this distance for, now. But he's got a doe in here. Of course an old man like Uncle Ike cant be interested in no doe, not one that walks on two legs—when she's standing up, that is. Pretty light-colored, too. The one he was after them nights last fall when he said he was coon-hunting, Uncle Ike. The one I figured maybe he was still running when he was gone all that month last

January.' " The language of sport is thus heightened by "light-colored," "coon-hunting," each with its double allusion: since Roth appears to kill a doe at the conclusion of the story, serving to complete the traditional narrative line of a hunting story and also underlining Roth's gesture of futility alongside his obvious cynicism and his apparent self-contempt, Roth himself reflects back on Ike, and so seals his futility as well. The act of doe-killing destroys man and woman together in love, a moment Ike has likened to divinity. The shooting functions as a kind of self-damnation for Roth; and the act redounds as well on Ike, though here not so much an act of blasphemy as, once again, an act of resignation and despair.

Faulkner frequently comes to comprehend a situation through words which are consistently modified in the course of an account: witness the use of "glory" in *Sartoris*, "vengeance" in *The Unvanquished*, "confession" in *Requiem for a Nun.* In this triology the "sight" emphasized in "The Old People," insinuating a metamorphosis into "insight," is succeeded by the "pride" and "humility" of "The Bear" which together conceive it; and these in turn give way in "Delta Autumn" to "code" and "honor," the social and personal dimensions of actions caused by the two respected social virtues.

These two concepts of "code" and "honor" are introduced explicitly by Roth's mistress when she tells Ike she did not expect marriage. But her application is not in the proud, aristocratic sense which assumes unquestioned value, but in the new twisted shapes into which Roth and Ike have helped to change them. Thus "code" has for her now become the communal laws which fail to take the individual into account, while "honor" has come to mean pride. Ike is especially guilty: his theory of communal atonement has been displaced by the "code" of the South which preaches the superiority of the white man and the purity of racial bloods while "honor" now emphasizes respectability instead of responsibility. For the McCaslins both were first embodied in Lucius when he raped his black servant Eunice.

This final observation is the most important. The words "code" and "honor" look backward on the trilogy, reorganizing its contours so as to provide a reinterpretation of the three stories taken as a single unit. Both words now become restrictive in their force, frozen in their signification. They insist on a fundamentally stratified society. "Code" is grounded in position, enforced through "caste" and "clan" and social superiority: Faulkner's extensions in this trilogy are always pointed, sometimes surprising, and usually ironic. So Sam Fathers sees himself as fated to hunt down " 'the head bear. He's the man' " largely because he is himself the leader of the hunters. Boon is described in "The Bear" as a "plebeian strain"; he is enslaved by the ideals and orders of Sam yet shifts into a position of authority with the young boy Isaac. That Sam remains quite naturally a product of the wilderness while the adult Ike is never even potentially one of its own is also comprehensible in terms of civilization's social positionings and hence of code; for Sam is also a product of miscegenation, the son of a quadroon slave woman and a Chickasaw chief, and elsewhere in "The Old People," is the son of a quadroon and a Chickasaw, mixing in his veins white, black and red blood; he is seen "in the battered and faded overalls and the frayed five-cent straw hat which had been the badge of the negro's slavery and was now regalia of his freedom." That this undercuts Sam's self-proclaimed roles of priest and mentor is indicative of Faulkner's method of suggesting that Sam, too, is marked by his racial caste and like Ike is sternly limited in tragic ways he does not perceive.

Classification of men by caste is reflexive of classification by clan and race; it is the confusion of these in the instance of the McCaslins that so confounds Ike and causes him to respond irrationally. He knows an assortment of codes—the code of the hunter, the code of the landed gentry, the code of the white man—but because these are no longer discrete (Sam in his way combining all three), Ike is unable to establish clear premises for action. Thus his logic gives way to desire and vision, hope and memory. By catching at an image of Christ, he can be all-inclusive yet deny evil; he can embody all humanity in a particular model for behavior. Yet Ike fails to see that in accepting Christ he ought to give his allegiance to a code of behavior considerably different from that fostered by the McCaslin plantation and the traditions characteristic of the Old South.

Ike also turns to Christ as an exemplar of "honor" (a virtue frequently assigned to the medieval Christ as chivalric knight). For Faulkner honor was traditionally that characteristic defined and defended by an act in which man stakes his claim to nobility, an act accorded public recognition for affirming man's individual and corporate dignity. It is based in principle, not pride, an investment made at some personal cost: Byron Bunch's devotion to Lena Grove, Henry Sutpen's murder of his half-brother, and Bayard's refusal to avenge his father's death are early exempla. Ike stakes his honor on his relinquishment of property and his acceptance of carpentry as a vocation. In terms of his responsibility to his forbears, this is an act of evasion; and the act, like his identification with Christ, strains our credibility. It is at once too simple and too spectacular. Christ as exemplum for Ike is neither attainable nor altogether natural despite Ike's leaning toward asceticism; and the irony of Faulkner's concluding emphasis makes this clear: "if the Nazarene had found carpentering good for the life and ends He had assumed and elected to serve, it would be all right too for Isaac McCaslin even though Isaac McCaslin's ends, although simple enough in their apparent motivation, were and would be always incomprehensible to him." There is further irony in Ike's desire to be, as Christ, a carpenter—to abet the lumber mills and to fashion artificial objects out of the natural wilderness of the "big woods."

Honor is an unconscious art, not a conscious design: Christ is to be emulated according to Faulkner not as God incarnate, agent of justice and power, but as men Godlike, limited in human activity yet reaching toward infinite capacities of responsibility and love. Ike tends to fashion himself after the ineffable, as he tends to translate his own profane time into the sacred time of God's intervention in human affairs and to transform his own private moments of ecstasy and vision into moments of anagogic truth. Influenced by Dostoevsky's use of the *doppelgänger*, a character functioning as partial alter-ego of the protagonist, Faulkner makes Sam Fathers a limited "double" of Ike. For Ike yearns to be like Sam: simple, natural, part of the cyclic rhythm of the woods. He is not Sam; Sam's simplicity and absolute devotion to nature cause him to die with the death of Old Ben. Ike's real double—and this is the basis for the shock entailed in his tragic *peripeteia*—is with Roth's mistress. She provides the key to his atonement in the third important word in "Delta Autumn," "love." " 'Old man,' " she asks with the simplicity and clarity Ike now needs, " 'have you lived so long and forgotten so much that you dont remember anything you ever knew or felt or even heard about love?' " It is the answer of the savior turned messiah; and it is the answer for which Ike has been searching. It is typical of Faulkner that such an answer comes from a woman, from a black, and involves the primacy of the heart—and it is not surprising that for Ike, with his confused public and private mythologies serving him as facts, that it comes relatively late.

V

Ike's failure to succeed as Christ is adumbrated when in "The Bear" he fails as simply one of the Christian Magi. His response to the octoroon is likewise adumbrated in his remark to Fonsiba's husband fifty years previously: " 'This whole land, the whole South, is cursed, and all of us who derive from it, whom it ever suckled, white and black both, lie under the curse? Granted that my people brought this curse on to the land: maybe for that reason their descendants alone can—not resist it, not combat it—maybe just endure and outlast it until the curse is lifted. Then your people's turn will come because we have forfeited ours. But not now. Not yet. Dont you see?' " Ike's attitudinal development stopped when Old Ben died; his intellectual discernment stopped at the age of twenty-one, in the commissary with Cass. Ike as all of Faulkner's tragic heroes—Quentin Compson, Thomas Sutpen, and young Bayard Sartoris among them—fails because at one moment in life he stopped growing. As Part III of "The Bear" shows us that Boon cannot function properly outside the woods, "Delta Autumn" shows Ike as an isolate with no proper landscape left. The geography of circumstances provides no geography acceptable to his mind. Although he had been trained to respond to the wilderness by Sam—even to the point of voluntarily surrendering his watch and compass—his intuitive responses are also conditioned by the plantation; once both are transformed into commissary and muddy flatlands, Ike is homeless, rootless. He lives beyond the time and space that could have accommodated him.

Ike's tragedy along with his bid for heroism goes beyond self-recognition of loss, waste, and limitation: he must now find a way to realize the ineffable, to recapture and transmit the epiphany of love he has felt for Sam, Old Ben, and the wilderness generally. For his sense of the hunt was not one of pursuing game for the kill, but of transcending ritual into a moment of mysticism; his need, that of communicating the ineffable. To this predicament the octoroon does not respond for her acknowledgment of human respect and dignity contains her love in the human arena. She expects less because she accepts a greater degree of reality, yet her recognition is also a diminished thing. She cannot fully conceive of Ike's grand design nor calculate the dimensions of his gamble.

Faulkner can. Throughout his fiction Faulkner sees the antebellum South as out of joint—and more pointedly as never having existed except in the romantic memories of passionate and sorrowing men. Ike pays homage to an economy based in selfishness and acquisitiveness; he serves a false vision. In matters of ethics and religion, Ike can be more seriously faulted. Ethically he pursues a separate peace. His actions appear as monkish withdrawal, as if he were rejecting the intersecting lines of kinship and history which he sees it as his duty to accept. Such willed delusion can only be temporary yet it is not unexpected in a man of obsessive imagination, a man who recognizes Eden and corruption but who cannot comprehend the paradox of the fortunate fall. For Faulkner Ike's problem is that he does not assess love properly. Ike cannot appreciate the octoroon's comments because she speaks of experience outside the appropriate social and moral sanctions: her extraordinary acts reveal his extraordinary failure of sensibility. In advising the girl to seek vengeance he betrays his own self-righteousness and displays the tawdry moral superiority to which he had pledged allegiance.

Thus Roth's nervousness in "Delta Autumn" in deciding at first not to attend the hunt, in stopping on the way to camp, in rising early is an outward manifestation of Ike's intellectual frenzy. Although outwardly Ike cannot appreciate light skin and mixed blood, basically he cannot cope with the compromises which love demands—in his wife or in Roth's mistress. His breeding as a plantation owner has awarded him human separateness which he can conquer only in dream and memory. It is significant therefore that Ike lies in his cot as if it were a coffin, exhausted as Sam was exhausted in "The Bear": "childless, kinless, peopleless—motionless, his eyes open but no longer looking at any of them." He is a relic, superannuated; he ignores the "skeleton cotton- and corn-fields [which] would flow away on either hand, gaunt, and motionless beneath the grey rain." His posture resembles an effigy, inviting us to reexamine his sighting of the buck when he was twelve (at the close of "The Old People"): perhaps this was not vision, after all, but mirage. For instead of Christ Ike now resembles Prufrock; his inflexible will and his tenacious hold on the past make this example of living death more profound than Faulkner's earlier draft, the reporter of *Pylon*.

Then how is it possible to see Ike as even a limited hero? How can Faulkner admit heroism in a restrictive environment where historic, social, and economic forces press in on a vulnerable human community? Faulkner's final answer, in this relatively late work, lies both in the admission of man's awful limitations and in his courageous desire to take the necessary risks of living. In this Faulkner came to appreciate similar responses from other writers, notably Camus. Perhaps to the traditional readers and critics of Faulkner, who have insisted in reading his work as Christian theology, his eulogy subscribed to Camus came as something of a surprise. It should not be unsettling to the readers of this trilogy, however. Faulkner writes,

> Camus said that the only true function of man, born into an absurd world, is to live, be aware of one's life, one's revolt, one's freedom. He said that if the only solution to the human dilemma is death, then we are on the wrong road. The right track is the one that leads to life, to the sunlight. One cannot unceasingly suffer from the cold.
>
> So he did revolt. He did refuse to suffer from the unceasing cold. He did refuse to follow a track which led only to death. The track he followed was the only possible one which could not lead only to death. The track he followed led into the sunlight in being that one devoted to making something which had not existed in life until we made it. . . .
>
> At the very instant he struck the tree [and died], he was still searching and demanding of himself; I do not believe in that bright instant he found them. I do not believe they [answers only God knows] are to be found. I believe they are only to be searched for, constantly, always by some fragile member of the human absurdity. Of which there are never many, but always somewhere at least one, and one will always be enough.

The gesture of risk is thus a gesture of faith; and it gives the lie to Ike.

Ike of course does not know this, disclaiming one life and taking up another. But Faulkner underscores Ike's limited understanding by the suggestiveness of his name. The Biblical Abraham was willing to sacrifice the very life of Isaac to his faith and trust in God; Ike McCaslin rather than risking his life pleads for a separate peace by sacrificing land, land already tainted. He is " 'an Isaac born into a later life than Abraham's and repudiating immolation . . . declining the altar because maybe this time the exasperated Hand might not supply the kid.' " Ike's substitution of stained land for his own potentially stained life is as significant as the lack of trust Faulkner here ascribes to him.

Faulkner liked best in Camus the understanding of the necessity for risk and the denial of death. But he also incorporates into his thought the outlook of Unamuno who argues in *The Tragic Sense of Life* that man is a sick animal and that the wages of life consist in risking a search for a cure. Yoknapatawpha County resembles a hospital more than anything else, a land of Andersonian grotesques. *The Sound and the Fury* is a detailed study in the variety of social and personal illnesses; and only the patience of Dilsey and the love of Benjy hint at anything like a possible remedy. In *Go Down, Moses* there is not even this modicum of hope. Ike's grand risk is reactionary; he looks back to former societies—the antebellum Southern and the Christian—which Faulkner, through the apposition of Ike and the octoroon in "Delta Autumn," suggests are incompatible and self-defeating. Ike does not say "No to death" either; by breaking off his marriage and escaping the McCaslin inheritance he embraces a fiction. And like Sam who escapes to Jobaker's cabin or Sophonsiba, Ike's mother, who imposes on a rotting house the grand title of Warwick (in "Was"), Ike surrenders to the dead past thus corrupting the living present.

In his prefatory note to *The Mansion* Faulkner comments that " 'living' is motion, and 'motion' is change and alteration and therefore the only alternative to motion is un-motion, stasis, death." Man must act conditionally, must be adaptive. In the language of "The Bear," man must examine the Grecian urn, acknowledge the truth and beauty of its depictions, and then transcend the static moments captured there. He cannot transport himself into a bygone frieze, into an historic moment like the past hunt for Old Ben or into a conscious artistic design like the Nazarene of messianic teaching. It is important that Old Ben in death "almost resembled a piece of statuary" for he resembles both beauty and non-life. Any fixed moment or grand design is contrived, a kind of death rather than eternal life (which is God's gift); life for Faulkner is in becoming rather than being; ripeness is all. That is why truth for Faulkner embodies intuition as well as intellect and why conceptualization must ultimately give way to the primacy of the heart.

Thus Faulkner discerns saving hope in Ike's indomitable will, in his attendance at the "yearly pageant-rite" no longer furious nor immortal, yet still invested with partial meaning due to the power of Ike's vision and the strength of his hope. This comes at last remarkably close to immortality, to "saying No to death." Ike can recapture his childhood vision and so capitalize on its thrusting energies of mind and spirit. For Ike "was born knowing" what the "Sartorises and Edmondses invented farms and banks to keep . . . from having to find out": the moral content of manliness, the ceremonial and sacramental value of ethically oriented experience. At the conclusion of "Delta Autumn," it is Ike alone who is aware of the paradoxes of life.

To clarify his understanding of human epistemology, Faulkner ranges about Ike certain other characters who serve in some but not in all features as analogues: the hopeful but simple-minded hunters, the loving octoroon, the uneasy Roth. The Ike of "Delta Autumn" is even strangely reminiscent of Old Ben, "an anachronism indomitable and invincible out of an old dead time, a phantom . . .—old Priam reft of his old wife and outlived all his sons." The verbal shadings here hover between respect and futility, admiration and condemnation, a double-edged regret. Ike's posture is also partially defined by his surrender to a new ritual, the ritual of death: "he had accepted not a gambit, not a choice, but a condition in which not only the bear's heretofore inviolable anonymity but all the ancient rules and balances of hunter and hunted had been abrogated." His uneasy exhaustion in "Delta Autumn" resembles the earlier spent condition of Sam Fathers, for like Sam "*He had no children, no people, none of his blood anywhere above earth that he would ever meet again. And even if he were to, he could not have touched it, spoken to it, because for seventy years now he had had to be a negro* [substitute *white McCaslin*]. *It was almost over now and he was glad.*" Ike's despair is always bifocal as a corrupted primitive; he cannot see the purity of emotion as the octoroon can because he is too cognizant of social conditioning.

Ike McCaslin illustrates that for Faulkner heroism lies not in the vision of a new Canaan nor even in the sacrifice of a corrupted heritage, but in an ability to suffer, in Ike's remarkable capacity to grieve. Ike's life enacts Addie Bundren's preference for action over words; it enacts Hightower's mere theorizing on " 'Poor man. Poor mankind.' " Ike's honor in refusing to deny the values of the plantation insofar as they initiate pride and patience, his acceptance of the woods so long as it teaches him humility and vision: all these combine to make of Ike not only an honorable man but a hero.

Ike learns the fundamental incompatibility of human truth and the demands of organized society. He pays for understanding in an increased sense of futility, for his forbears' social mistakes by his own social ineffectuality: Ike's rationalized puritanism and the octoroon's inspired messianic love are finally seen by him as alike insufficient. Both Ike and the octoroon end their stories without disciples, yet both offer alternatives to the baby in the blanket, significantly a baby of mixed blood. If Faulkner's trilogy—his final comprehensive and, I think, basic statement—is not a verification of man's potentiality as found in the romantic adjectivizing of Ike and Cass in the commissary and of Faulkner himself later at Stockholm, still Isaac emerges as more human, more valid—and more profoundly tragic. Ike admits at the close of "Delta Autumn" that "the time is not yet." But the man who is fallen is still free to choose, capable of the powers of cognition, will, passion, and dream. In one like Ike who can feel guilt and pain and understand responsibility and freedom (especially as Faulkner understands Camus' appreciation of it), there is both sentience and reason. Because of this, there always remains in Faulkner's difficult but passionately honest art the possibility of joy.

Land Ownership in Go Down, Moses

Ursula Brumm

. . . Ownership of the land is the basic theme of the stories in *Go Down, Moses.* The book relates the story of a family, the McCaslins, their white and their black branch, narrated not in novel form but in more or less long short stories (the most substantial being "The Bear") which are focused on various members and events in the family history. This is their common background: Old Carothers McCaslin bought his land "with white man's money" from the Indian chief Ikkemotubbe, who in turn possessed it by treachery. (There is no sentimentalizing about the Indians here; they share the guilt.) McCaslin "tamed and ordered or believed he had tamed and ordered (the wilderness) for the reason that the human beings he held in bondage and in the power of life and death had removed the forest from it and in their sweat scratched the surface of it to a depth of perhaps fourteen inches in order to grow something out of it which had not been there before and which could be translated back into money. . . ." The ownership of the land through money as well as its use for money and profit-making are part of the guilt, because God created the earth to hold it "mutual and intact in the communal anonymity of brotherhood."

Two of McCaslin's grandsons figure prominently in these stories: Isaac McCaslin, the only white descendant in the male line, and the Negro Lucas Beauchamp, son of McCaslin's son by a black mistress. Isaac, who was initiated to the wilderness, and manhood and huntership, by Sam Fathers, inherits the land but relinquishes it to his cousin Edmonds, a son of old McCaslin's daughter (it seems all good heroes of Faulkner have to give up their inheritance):

> "I can't repudiate it. It was never mine to repudiate. It was never Father's and Uncle Buddy's to bequeath me to repudiate because it was

Reprinted from Ursula Brumm, "Wilderness and Civilization: A Note on William Faulkner," *Partisan Review,* XXII:3 (Summer 1955), 340–350, by permission of *Partisan Review* and the author.

> never Grandfather's . . . because on the instant when Ikkemotubbe discovered, realized that he could sell it for money, on that instant it ceased ever to have been his forever, father to father to father, and the man who bought it bought nothing."

Isaac McCaslin pays back, and increases, to his black cousins the money intended for them by his grandfather in atonement of his guilt. After he has given up the land, he possesses "but one object more than he could wear and carry in his pockets and his hands at one time and that was an iron cot and the stained lean mattress which he used camping in the woods for deer and bear or for fishing or simply because he loved the woods." He takes up the trade of a carpenter, "because if the Nazarene had found carpenting good for the life and end He had assumed and elected to serve, it would be all right too for Isaac McCaslin." Isaac, who renounces the rapacity and guilt of property is in that sense a forerunner of the Corporal in *A Fable,* though without quite realizing as yet that this is a renunciation of civilization and all it implies. However, we find him in such close communion with the wilderness that this in itself is already a repudiation of civilization; and he rejects the responsibility of keeping the farm, which his wife demands of him. But like the Corporal, he only establishes an example of refusal; he saves nobody but himself perhaps.

The McCaslin saga is another of Faulkner's representations of the story of the South: the ownership of the land by one man (the white man) under exclusion of another (his black cousin) results in tension and guilt, and this is the famous "curse" of the South. But not only of the South. Already in *Go Down, Moses* allusion is made to the rapacity of the westward expansion, and the plantation is made symbol of exploitation on world-historic scale: ". . . on down through the tedious and shabby chronicle of His chosen sprung from Abraham, and of the sons of them who dispossessed Abraham, and of the five hundred years during which half the known world and all it contained was chattel to one city as this plantation and all the life it contained was chattel and revokeless thrall to this commissary store and those ledgers yonder. . . ." The plantation and its system symbolizes Roman imperialism. . . .

Faulkner and the Blacks

During the last ten years of his life Faulkner made a number of public remarks concerning racial relations in Mississippi and elsewhere. Many of the events and attitudes defined in "The Bear" and "Delta Autumn" foreshadowed fact and came to be tested by historic experience. The following opinions represent all shades of response: objective and subjective, white and black, liberal and conservative, Northern and Southern. To aid in following the debate which emerges here, selections are arranged chronologically and dated in parentheses at the end.

The American Dream

William Faulkner

This was the American Dream: a sanctuary on the earth for individual man: a condition in which he could be free not only of the old established closed-corporation hierarchies of arbitrary power which had oppressed him as a mass, but free of that mass into which the hierarchies of church and state had compressed and held him individually thralled and individually impotent.

A dream simultaneous among the separate individuals of men so asunder and scattered as to have no contact to match dreams and hopes among the old nations of the Old World which existed as nations not on citizenship but subjectship, which endured only on the premise of size and docility of the subject mass; the individual men and women who said as with one simultaneous voice: 'We will establish a new land where man can assume that every individual man—not the mass of men but individual men—has inalienable right to individual dignity and freedom within a fabric of individual courage and honorable work and mutual responsibility.'

Not just an idea, but a condition: a living human condition designed to be coeval with the birth of America itself, engendered created and simultaneous with the very air and word America, which at that one stroke, one instant, should cover the whole earth with one simultaneous suspiration like air or light. And it was, it did: radiating outward to cover even the old weary repudiated still-thralled nations, until individual men everywhere, who had no more than heard the name, let alone knew where America was, could respond to it, lifting up not only their hearts but the hopes too which until now they did not know—or anyway dared not remember—that they possessed.

A condition in which every man would not only not be a king, he wouldn't even want to be one. He wouldn't even need to bother to need to be the equal of kings because now he was free of kings and all their similar congeries; free not only of the symbols but of the old arbitrary hierarchies themselves which the puppet-symbols represented—courts and cabinets and churches and schools—to which he had been valuable not as an individual but only as that integer, his value compounded in that immutable ratio to his sheer mindless numbers, that animal increase of his will-less and docile mass.

The dream, the hope, the condition which our forefathers did not bequeath to us, their heirs and assigns, but rather bequeathed us, their successors, to the dream and the hope. We were not even given the chance then to accept or decline the dream, for the reason that the dream already owned and possessed us at birth. It was not our heritage because we were its, we ourselves heired in our successive generations to the dream by the idea of the dream. And not only we, their sons born and bred in America, but men born and bred in the old alien repudiated lands, also felt that breath, that air, heard that promise, that proffer that there was such a thing as hope for individual man. And the old nations themselves, so old and so long-fixed in the old concepts of man as to have thought themselves beyond all hope of change, making oblation to that new dream of that new concept of man by gifts of monuments and devices to mark the portals of that inalienable right and hope: 'There is room for you here from about the earth, for all ye individually homeless, individually oppressed, individually unindividualised.' . . .

. . . That dream was man's aspiration in the true meaning of the word aspiration. It was not merely the blind and voiceless hope of his heart: it was the actual inbreathe of his lungs, his lights, his living and unsleeping metabolism, so that we actually lived the Dream. We did not live *in* the dream: we lived the Dream itself, just as we do not merely live *in* air and climate, but we live Air and Climate; we ourselves individually representative of the Dream, the Dream itself actually audible in the strong uninhibited voices which were not afraid to speak *cliché* at the very top of them, giving to the *cliché*-avatars of 'Give me liberty or give me death' or 'This to be self-evident that all individual men were created equal in one mutual right to freedom' which had never lacked for truth anyway, assuming that hope and dignity are truth, a validity and immediacy absolving them even of *cliché*.

That was the Dream: not man created equal in the sense that he was created black or white or brown or yellow and hence doomed irrevocably to that for the remainder of his days—or rather, not doomed with equality but blessed with equality, himself lifting no hand but instead lying curled and drowsing in the warm and airless bath of it like the yet-wombed embryo; but liberty in which to have an equal start at equality with all other men, and freedom in which to defend and preserve that equality by means of the individual courage and the honorable work and the mutual responsibility. Then we lost it. It abandoned us, which had supported and protected and defended us while our new nation of new concepts of human existence got a firm enough foothold to stand erect among the nations of the earth, demanding nothing of us in return save to remember always that, being alive, it was therefore perishable and so must be held always in the unceasing responsibility and vigilance of courage and honor and pride and humility. It is gone now. We dozed, slept, and it abandoned us. And in that vacuum now there sound no longer the strong loud voices not merely unafraid but not even aware that fear existed, speaking in mutual unification of one mutual hope and will. Because now what we hear is a cacophony of terror and conciliation and compromise babbling only the mouthsounds; the loud and empty words which we have emasculated of all meaning whatever—freedom, democracy, patriotism—with which, awakened at last, we try in desperation to hide from ourselves that loss. . . . (1955)

A Talk with William Faulkner

Russell Warren Howe

New York, February 27, 1956.

William Faulkner said in an exclusive interview this week that he believed there was a grave danger of civil war in the South.

The Nobel Prizewinning author, who runs a cotton plantation near Oxford, Mississippi, the state where tension runs highest, said he had "always been on the side of the Negroes" but that if shooting started he would "fight for Mississippi against the United States."

Commenting on the incidents which have made the battle for Negro equality the main home affairs issue in the 1956 presidential election campaign, Faulkner said:

"The Northerner doesn't understand what's going on down there. He doesn't realize that most people in Alabama, Mississippi or Tennessee will go to any lengths. They will even accept another civil war. If the National Association for the Advancement of Colored People and the liberal opposition push this thing, the South will go to its guns.

"The NAACP have done a very fine job. Now they should stop. They have got us off balance. They should let us try to regain balance, not put us in a position that makes us feel like an underdog with regard to the rest of America.

"My position is this. My people owned slaves and the very obligation we have to take care of these people is morally bad. It is a position which is completely untenable. But I would wish now that the liberals would stop—they should let us sweat in our own fears for a little while. If we are pushed by the government we shall become an underdog people fighting back because we can do nothing else. Our position is wrong and untenable but it is not wise to keep an emotional people off balance.

"The Negroes have had 90 years of that sort of life and now they are winning it would take a lot of wisdom to say 'Go slow.' Perhaps it is too much to ask of them but it is for their own sake. I have known Negroes all my life and Negroes work my land for me. I know how they feel. But now I have people who say they are Negroes writing

On February 21, 1956, Russell Warren Howe, then New York correspondent for the London *Sunday Times,* interviewed Faulkner. On February 27 he filed a story to London that was later (March 22) reprinted in the United States in *The Reporter* magazine (pp. 18–20). Both publications had edited down a controversial interview, and Mr. Howe has therefore kindly supplied the present editors with the original copy he submitted for publication. This is the first printing anywhere of the original text.

to me and saying 'You mean well for us but please hush. You mean good but you do harm.' "

Asked if a "go slow" would not cause ground already gained to be lost, Faulkner said:

"I don't know. I try to think of this in the longterm view. Now, I grant you that it is bad that there should be a minority people who because of their color don't have a right to social equality or to justice. But it is bad that Americans should be fighting Americans. That is what will happen because the Southern whites are back in the spirit of 1860. There could easily be another civil war and the South will be whipped again. My brother's son's a fairly intelligent man and he says 'If I have to die I'll die shooting niggrahs trying to get into a white school.' He's typical.

"In the long view, the Negro race will vanish in 300 years by intermarriage. It's happened to every racial minority everywhere and it will happen here."

Q. What would be the best strategy for the liberals?

A. "Let the people stop a while. If that girl Autherine Lucy goes back to Alabama University on March 1st she will be killed. The NAACP should forget about Alabama University. They should send people now to the Universities of Georgia, Mississippi and South Carolina and let them be thrown out of each of those places too, until the white people of the South get so sick and tired of being harassed and worried they will have to do something about it. If they send that girl back to Tuscaloosa on March 1st she will be killed."

Q. Have you heard the reports of the arms buying in Tuscaloosa?

A. "Yes. If that girl dies, two or three white men will be killed, then eight or nine Negroes. Then the troops will come in. You know, we've never had race riots in the South before. They've had race riots in the North but in the South we just have persecution.

"The South is armed for revolt. After the Supreme Court decision (of May 17, 1954 on school integration) you couldn't get as much as a few rounds for a deer rifle in Mississippi. The gunsmiths were sold out. These white people will accept another civil war knowing they're going to lose. If the North knew the South they would know that this is not a theory or a moral convention which they are up against but a simple fact. I know people who've never fired a gun in their lives but who've bought rifles and ammunition."

Q. How long do you think it will be before the concrete aspects of discrimination—housing, employment, enfranchisement, education, social contacts—will have disappeared?

A. "In the Deep South, I don't know. As it was, in 15 years, the Negroes would have had good schools. Then came the decision of the Supreme Court and that will mean probably 20 years of trouble. I think that decision put the position of the Negro in the South back five years."

Q. Does that mean that you disapprove of the Court decree?

A. "I don't disapprove of it. It had to be promulgated and it just repeated what was said on January 3, 1863. If the white folks had given Negroes proper schools there would have been no need for the Court's decision."

Faulkner then restated the opinion which has divided him against the other Southern liberal writers:

"The Negro in the Deep South doesn't want to mix with the white man. He likes his own school, his own church. Segregation doesn't have to imply inferiority."

Asked "When your tenants tell you they prefer segregation, how do you know if they are talking to you as man to man and not as Southern Negro tenant to Southern white landlord?" Faulkner smiled and closed his eyes in thought but did not answer.

Q. How would you re-educate the Southern white to a different way of thinking?

A. "First of all, take off the pressure. Let him see just how untenable his position is. Let him see that people laugh at him. Just let him see how silly and foolish he looks. Give him time—don't force us. If that girl goes back to Tuscaloosa she will die: then the top will blow off. The government will send in its troops and we shall be back at 1860. They must stop pushing these people. The trouble is the North doesn't know that country. They don't know the South will go to war.

"Things have been getting better slowly for a long time. Only six Negroes were killed by whites in Mississippi last year, according to the police figures. The Supreme Court decree came 90 years too late. In 1863 it was a victory. In 1954 it was a tragedy. The same thing is happening in South Africa, in Algeria. People were too ignorant of their fellow-man and they realized his equality too late. This whole thing is not a confrontation of ideologies but of white folks against folks not white. It is worldwide. We must win the Indians, the Malayans, the 16 million Negro Americans and the rest to the white camp, make it worth their while."

Q. Apart from your advice to promising Southerners, white and black, to get their education out of the South, what would your advice to an ambitious Negro be?—To get out of the South altogether?

A. "No, he should stay in the South, where we need promising people, and be patient. Now is a time for calm, but that time will pass. The Negro has a right to equality. His equality is inevitable, an irresistible force, but as I see it you've got to take into consideration human nature which at times has nothing to do with moral truths. Truth says this and the fact says that. A wise person says 'Let's use this fact. Let's obliterate this fact first.' To oppose a material fact with a moral truth is silly."

Q. The Negroes of Montgomery, the capital of Alabama, have been boycotting the city's buses since December 5. Do you think this sort of passive resistance is a good idea?

A. "Yes, anything they do is good as long as they don't carry it too far. Today the white women of Montgomery have to go and fetch their Negro cooks by car. It is a good step, to let the white folks see that the world is looking on and laughing at them.

"But I don't like enforced integration any more than I like enforced segregation. If I have to choose between the United States government and Mississippi, then I'll choose Mississippi. What I'm trying to do now is not have to make that decision. As long as there's a middle road, all right, I'll be on it. But if it came to fighting I'd fight for Mississippi against the United States even if it meant going out into the street and shooting Negroes. After all I'm not going out to shoot Mississippians."

Q. You mean white Mississippians?

A. "No, I said Mississippians—in Mississippi the problem isn't racial. Ninety per cent of the Negroes are on one side with the whites, against a handful like me who believe that equality is important."

Q. Some of your remarks could be interpreted as disapproval of the existence of militant Negro defense organizations. How do you feel about the NAACP?

A. "That organization is necessary, but it must know when to let the opponent make the next move. Ninety years of oppression and injustice are there, but it is a lot for the white man to have to admit. It takes an extremely intelligent man to stop dead after 90 years of wrongdoing and the Southerner isn't that intelligent. He has to feel that what he is doing (when he reforms) is not being forced on him but is spontaneous. We have to make it so that he feels that he is being not just honest but generous. Give him time—right now it's emotional and he'll fight because the country's against him."

Q. In the European Press, "go slow" is criticized on the grounds that the susceptibilities of the persecuted deserve more consideration than the susceptibilities of the persecutor. How would you answer that criticism?

A. "The European critics are right, morally, but there is something stronger in man than a moral condition. Man will do certain things whether they be right or wrong. We know that racial discrimination is morally bad, that it stinks, that it shouldn't exist, but it does. Should we obliterate the persecutor by acting in a way that we know will send him to his guns, or should we compromise and let it work out in time and save whatever good remains in those white people?"

Q. If the position in the South was reversed and the Negroes formed a majority which had been persecuting and murdering a white minority for 90 years would you still say "Go slow" on reform?

A. "Yes. Yes, I would. But the way we see it in the South, the way I see it, is that the Negro is in a majority, because he has the country behind him. He could have the support of the federal army."

Q. Then you don't advise delays as an expedient because the Negro is numerically outnumbered by over two to one in the South?

A. "No. Take the case of Autherine Lucy. I say she shouldn't go back to Tuscaloosa not because she'll be one against a mob of 2000—there'll be a hundred million Americans behind her—but because she'll be killed.

"The Negroes are right, make sure you've got that, they're right. But March 1st at Tuscaloosa is not a moral condition, it's a question of fact. I've always been on their (the Negroes') side, but if there's no middle ground, if people like me have got to choose then I'm on the side of Mississippi.

"I will go on saying that the Southerners are wrong and that their position is untenable but if I have to make the same choice Robert E. Lee made then I'll make it. My grandfather had slaves and he must have known that it was wrong but he fought in one of the first regiments raised by the Confederate Army, not in defense of his ethical position but to protect his native land from being invaded."

Q. Do you believe regional loyalty is a good quality?

A. "Well, you must believe in something."

Q. What about your belief in the principles expressed in your books?

A. "I shouldn't be betraying them. My Negro boys down on the plantation would fight against the North with me. If I say to them 'Go get your shotguns, boys,' they'll come."

Q. The churches are segregated in the South. Don't you think the churches could do much to improve the South by sticking to Christian principles?

A. "They could do much more but they are afraid to open their mouths. The Catholics have made a few moves. It is easier for the Catholics because they are Catholics first and members of the human race second."

Q. Is the basic cause of race prejudice economic, in your opinion?

A. "Absolutely. To produce cotton we have to have a system of peonage. That is absolutely what is at the bottom of the situation."

Q. Are the psychological rationalizations for prejudice something grafted on to the economic root?

A. "Yes. I would say that a planter who has a thousand acres wants to keep the Negro in a position of debt-peonage and in order to do it he is going to tell the poor class of white folks that the Negro is going to violate his daughter. But all he wants at the back of it is a system of peonage to produce his cotton at the highest rate of profit."

Q. Do you see the basic problem as one of re-education?

A. "Yes, whites and Negroes must be re-educated to the issue. The most important thing is good schools. The trouble is that Southern white people are not interested in schools. Only the Negro cares about education. If we had good schools we could get good teachers."

Q. Isn't it Utopian to hope for a high standard of schools in a rural community?

A. "Yes, it's a Utopian dream, but it must be a good dream because there's always been someone to dream it."

Q. Do you agree that the ambition-spur provided by persecution has made the Negro the potentially more capable of the two "races" in the South?

A. "Certainly. He's calmer, wiser, more stable than the white man. To have put up with this situation so long with so little violence shows a sort of greatness. Suppose two Negroes had murdered a white Emmett Till—there would have been a flood of emotionalism. The Negro rose above his anger. He knows that the problem (of his equality) will be solved because it must be. But these ignorant white people have got to be let alone so that they can think that they arc changing on their own initiative.

"The poor white man knows that although the Negro can only buy the worst land, has bad tools and inferior livestock he can make a living better than white men could. With a little more social, economic and educational equality the Negro will often be the landlord and the white man will be working for him. And the Negro won't come out on top because of anything to do with the race but because he has always gotten by without scope—when they are given scope they use it fully. The Negro is trained to do more than a white man can with the same limitations.

"The vices that the Negro has have been created in him by the white man, by the system. He will make his own contribution to our society. Already his music and poetry have passed to the white man and what the white man has done with them is not Negro any more but something else.

"There is no such thing as an 'Anglo-Saxon' heritage and an African heritage. There is the heritage of man. Nothing is extinct in any race, only dormant. You are brave and tough when you have to be. You are intelligent when the age demands it. There are all things in like degree in all races."

Q. How is it for a man like you to live in Mississippi?

A. "I get a lot of insulting and threatening letters and telephone calls, since I established my position (on this issue). The tragic thing is that some of them come from Negroes, at least they say they're Negroes: it isn't just a solidarity of race—you get doctors and lawyers and preachers and newspaper editors and some Negroes too, all grouped against a few liberals like me. People phone me up to threaten my life at three or four in the morning—they're usually drunk by then."

Q. Do you carry a gun?

A. "No. My friends say I ought to carry a pistol. But I don't think anyone will shoot me, it would cause too much of a stink. But the other liberals in my part of the country carry guns all the time." (1956)

The South in Labor

William Faulkner

Immediately after the Supreme Court decision abolishing segregation in schools, the talk began in Mississippi of ways and means to increase taxes to raise the standard of the Negro schools to match the white ones. I wrote the following letter to the open forum page of our most widely-read Memphis paper:

> We Mississippians already know that our present schools are not good enough. Our young men and women themselves prove that to us every year by the fact, that, when the best of them want the best of education which they are entitled to and competent for, not only in the humanities but in the professions and crafts—law and medicine and engineering—too, they must go out of the state to get it. And quite often, too often, they don't come back.
>
> So our present schools are not even good enough for white people; our present State reservoir of education is not of high enough quality to assuage the thirst of even our white young men and women. In which case, how can it possibly assuage the thirst and need of the Negro, who obviously is thirstier, needs it worse, else the Federal Government would not have had to pass a law compelling Mississippi (among others of course) to make the best of our education available to him.
>
> That is, our present schools are not even good enough for white people. So what do we do? make them good enough, improve them to the best possible? No. We beat the bushes, rake and scrape to raise additional taxes to establish another system at best only equal to that one which is already not good enough, which therefore wont be good enough for Negroes either; we will have two identical systems neither of which are good enough for anybody.

Reprinted from James B. Meriwether, ed., "On Fear: The South in Labor," *Essays, Speeches and Public Letters of William Faulkner*, by permission of Random House, Inc., the Author's Literary Estate, and Chatto & Windus Ltd. Copyright © 1965 by Random House, Inc.

A few days after my letter was printed in the paper, I received by post the carbon copy of a letter addressed to the same forum page of the Memphis paper. It read as follows: 'When Weeping Willie Faulkner splashes his tears about the inadequacy of Mississippi schools . . . we question his gumption in these respects' etc. From there it went on to cite certain facts of which all Southerners are justly proud: that the seed-stock of education in our land was preserved through the evil times following the Civil War when our land was a defeated and occupied country, by dedicated teachers who got little in return for their dedication. Then, after a brief sneer at the quality of my writing and the profit motive which was the obvious reason why I was a writer, he closed by saying: 'I suggest that Weeping Willie dry his tears and work up a little thirst for knowledge about the basic economy of his state.'

Later, after this letter was printed in the Memphis paper in its turn, I received from the writer of it a letter addressed to him by a correspondent in another small Mississippi town, consisting in general of a sneer at the Nobel Prize which was awarded me, and commending the Weeping Willie writer for his promptness in taking to task anyone traitorous enough to hold education more important than the color of the educatee's skin. Attached to it was the Weeping Willie writer's reply. It said in effect: 'In my opinion Faulkner is the most capable commentator on Southern facts of life to date. . . . If we could insult him into acquiring an insight into the basic economy of our region, he could (sic) do us a hell of a lot of good in our fight against integration.'

My answer was that I didn't believe that insult is a very sound method of teaching anybody anything, of persuading anyone to think or act as the insulter believes they should. I repeated that what we needed in Mississippi was the best possible schools, to make the best possible use of the men and women we produced, regardless of what color they were. And even if we could not have a school system which would do that, at least let us have one which would make no distinction among pupils except that of simple ability, since our principal and perhaps desperate need in America today was that all Americans at least should be on the side of America; that if all Americans were on the same side, we would not need to fear that other nations and ideologies would doubt us when we talked of human freedom.

But this is beside the point. The point is, what is behind this. The tragedy is not the impasse, but what is behind the impasse—the impasse of the two apparently irreconcilable facts which we are faced with in the South: the one being the decree of our national government that there be absolute equality in education among all citizens, the other being the white people in the South who say that white and Negro pupils shall never sit in the same classroom. Only apparently irreconcilable, because they must be reconciled since the only alternative to change is death.

In fact, there are people in the South, Southerners born, who not only believe they can be reconciled but who love our land—not love white people specifically nor love Negroes specifically, but our land, our country: our climate and geography, the qualities in our people, white and Negro too, for honesty and fairness, the splendors in our traditions, the glories in our past—enough to try to reconcile them, even at the cost of displeasing both sides: the contempt of the Northern radicals who believe we dont do enough, the contumely and threats of our own Southern reactionaries who are convinced that anything we do is already too much.

The tragedy is, the reason behind the fact, the fear behind the fact that some of the white people in the South—people who otherwise are rational, cultured, gentle, generous and kindly—will—must—fight against every inch which the Negro gains in social betterment; the fear behind the desperation which could drive rational and successful men (my correspondent, the Weeping Willie one, is a banker, perhaps president of a—perhaps the—bank in another small Mississippi town like my own) to grasp at such straws for weapons as contumely and threat and insult to change the views or anyway the voice which dares to suggest that betterment of the Negro's condition does not necessarily presage the doom of the white race. Nor is the tragedy the fear so much as the tawdry quality of the fear—fear not of the Negro as an individual Negro nor even as a race, but as an economic class or stratum or factor, since what the Negro threatens is not the Southern white man's social system but the Southern white man's economic system—that economic system which the white man knows and dares not admit to himself is established on an obsolescence—the artificial inequality of man—and so is itself already obsolete and hence doomed. . . .

. . . The Church, which is the strongest unified force in our Southern life since all Southerners are not white and are not democrats, but all Southerners are religious and all religions serve the same single God, no matter by what name He is called. . . .

Where is that voice now, which should have propounded perhaps two but certainly one of these still-unanswered questions?

1. The Constitution of the U.S. says: Before the law, there shall be no artificial inequality—race creed or money—among citizens of the United States.
2. Morality says: Do unto others as you would have others do unto you.
3. Christianity says: I am the only distinction among men since whosoever believeth in Me, shall never die.

Where is this voice now, in our time of trouble and indecision? Is it trying by its silence to tell us that it has no validity and wants none outside the sanctuary behind its symbolical spire?

* * *

If the facts as stated in the *Look* magazine account of the Till affair are correct, this remains: two adults, armed, in the dark, kidnap a fourteen-year-old boy and take him away to frighten him. Instead of which, the fourteen-year-old boy not only refuses to be frightened, but, unarmed, alone, in the dark, so frightens the two armed adults that they must destroy him.

What are we Mississippians afraid of? Why do we have so low an opinion of ourselves that we are afraid of people who by all our standards are our inferiors?—economically: i.e., they have so much less than we have that they must work for us not on their terms but on ours; educationally: i.e., their schools are so much worse than ours that the Federal Government has to threaten to intervene to give them equal conditions; politically: i.e., they have no recourse in law for protection from nor restitution for injustice and violence.

Why do we have so low an opinion of our blood and traditions as to fear that, as soon as the Negro enters our house by the front door, he will propose marriage to our daughter and she will immediately accept him?

Our ancestors were not afraid like this—our grandfathers who fought at First and Second Manassas and Sharpsburg and Shiloh and Franklin and Chickamauga and Chancellorsville and the Wilderness; let alone those who survived that and had the additional and even greater courage and endurance to resist and survive Reconstruction, and so preserved to us something of our present heritage. Why are we, descendants of that blood and inheritors of that courage, afraid? What are we afraid of? What has happened to us in only a hundred years? . . .

Because it makes a glib and simple picture, we like to think of the world situation today as a precarious and explosive balance of two irreconcilable ideologies confronting each other: which precarious balance, once it totters, will drag the whole universe into the abyss along with it. That's not so. Only one of the opposed forces is an ideology. The other one is that simple fact of Man: that simple belief of individual man that he can and should and will be free. And if we who are still free want to continue so, all of us who are still free had better confederate and confederate fast with all others who still have a choice to be free—confederate not as black people nor white people nor blue or pink or green people, but as people who still are free, with all other people who are still free; confederate together and stick together too, if we want a world or even a part of a world in which individual man can be free, to continue to endure.

And we had better take in with us as many as we can get of the nonwhite peoples of the earth who are not completely free yet but who want and intend to be, before that other force which is opposed to individual freedom, befools and gets them. Time was when the nonwhite man was content to—anyway, did—accept his instinct for freedom as an unrealisable dream. But not anymore; the white man himself taught him different with that phase of his—the white man's—own culture which took the form of colonial expansion and exploitation based and morally condoned on the premise of inequality not because of individual incompetence but of mass race or color. As a result of which, in only ten years we have watched the nonwhite peoples expel, by bloody violence when necessary, the white man from all the portions of the Middle East and Asia which he once dominated, into which vacuum has already begun to move that other and inimical power which people who believe in freedom are at war with—that power which says to the nonwhite man: 'We dont offer you freedom because there is no such thing as freedom; your white overlords whom you have just thrown out have already proved that to you. But we offer you equality, at least equality in slavedom; if you are to be slaves, at least you can be slaves to your own color and race and religion.'

We, the western white man who does believe that there exists an individual freedom above and beyond this mere equality of slavedom, must teach the nonwhite peoples this while there is yet a little time left. We, America, who are the strongest national force opposing communism and monolithicism, must teach all other peoples, white and nonwhite, slave or (for a little while yet) still free. We, America, have the best opportunity to do this because we can begin here, at home; we will not need to send costly freedom task-forces into alien and inimical nonwhite places already convinced that there is no such thing as freedom and liberty and equality and peace for nonwhite people too, or we would practice it at home. Because our nonwhite minority is already on our side; we dont need to sell the Negro on America and freedom because he is already sold; even when ignorant from inferior or no education, even despite the record of his history of inequality, he still believes in our concepts of freedom and democracy. . . .

Soon now all of us—not just Southerners nor even just Americans, but all people who are still free and want to remain so—are going to have to make a choice, lest the next (and last) confrontation we face will be, not communists against anti-communists, but simply the remaining handful of white people against the massed myriads of all the people on earth who are not white. We will have to choose not between color nor race nor religion nor between East and West either, but simply between being slaves and being free. And we will have to choose completely and for good; the time is already past now when we can choose a little of each, a little of both. We can choose a state of slavedom, and if we are powerful enough to be among the top two or three or ten, we can have a certain amount of license—until someone more powerful rises and has us machine-gunned against a cellar wall. But we cannot choose freedom established on a hierarchy of degrees of freedom, on a caste system of equality like military rank. We must be free not because we claim freedom, but because we practice it; our freedom must be buttressed by a homogeny equally and unchallengeably free, no matter what color they are, so that all the other inimical forces everywhere—systems political or religious or racial or national—will not just respect us because we practice freedom, they will fear us because we do. (June 1956)

Faulkner and Desegregation

James Baldwin

Any real change implies the breakup of the world as one has always known it, the loss of all that gave one an identity, the end of safety. And at such a moment, unable to see and not daring to imagine what the future will now bring forth, one clings to what one knew, or thought one knew; to what one possessed or dreamed that one possessed. Yet, it is only when a man is able, without bitterness or self-pity, to surrender a dream he has long cherished or a privilege he has long possessed that he is set free—he has set himself free—for higher dreams, for greater privileges. All men have gone through this, go through it, each according to his degree, throughout their lives. It is one of the irreducible facts of life. And remembering this, especially since I am a Negro, affords me almost my only means of understanding what is happening in the minds and hearts of white Southerners today.

For the arguments with which the bulk of relatively articulate white Southerners of good will have met the necessity of desegregation have no value whatever as arguments, being almost entirely and helplessly dishonest, when not, indeed, insane. After more than two hundred years in slavery and ninety years of quasi-freedom, it is hard to think very highly of William Faulkner's advice to "go slow." "They don't mean go slow," Thurgood Marshall is reported to have said, "they mean don't go." Nor is the squire of Oxford very persuasive when he suggests that white Southerners, left to their own devices, will realize that their own social structure looks silly to the rest of the world and correct it of their own accord. It has looked silly, to use Faulkner's rather strange adjective, for a long time; so far from trying to correct it, Southerners, who seem to be characterized by a species of defiance most perverse when it is most despairing, have clung to it, at incalculable cost to themselves, as the only conceivable and as an absolutely sacrosanct way of life. They have never seriously conceded that their social structure was mad. They have insisted, on the contrary, that everyone who criticized it was mad.

Faulkner goes further. He concedes the madness and moral wrongness of the South but at the same time he raises it to the level of a mystique which makes it somehow unjust to discuss Southern society in the same terms in which one would discuss any other society. "Our position is wrong and untenable," says Faulkner, "but it is not wise to keep an emotional people off balance." This, if it means anything, can only mean that this "emotional people" have been swept "off balance" by the pressure of recent events, that is, the Supreme Court decision outlawing segregation. When the pressure is taken off—and not an instant before—this "emotional people" will presumably find themselves once again on balance and will then be able to free themselves of an "obsolescence in [their] own land" in their own way and, of course, in their own time. The question left begging is what, in their history to date, affords any evidence that they have any desire or capacity to do this. And it is, I suppose, impertinent to ask just what Negroes are supposed to do while the South works out what, in Faulkner's rhetoric, becomes something very closely resembling a high and noble tragedy.

The sad truth is that whatever modifications have been effected in the social structure of the South since the Reconstruction, and any alleviations of the Negro's lot within it, are due to great and incessant pressure, very little of it indeed from within the South. That the North has been guilty of Pharisaism in its dealing with the South does not negate the fact that much of this pressure has come from the North. That some—not nearly as many as Faulkner would like to believe—Southern Negroes prefer, or are afraid of changing, the status quo does not negate the fact that it is the Southern Negro himself who, year upon year, and generation upon generation, has kept the Southern waters troubled. As far as the Negro's life in the South is concerned, the NAACP is the only organization which has struggled, with admirable single-mindedness and skill, to raise him to the level of citizen. For this reason alone, and quite apart from the individual heroism of many of its Southern members, it cannot be equated, as Faulkner equates it, with the pathological Citizen's Council. One organization is working within the law and the other is working against and outside it. Faulkner's threat to leave the "middle of the road" where he has, presumably, all these years, been working for the benefit of Negroes, reduces itself to a more or less up-to-date version of the Southern threat to secede from the Union.

Faulkner—among so many others!—is so plaintive concerning this "middle of the road" from which "extremist" elements of both races are driving him that it does not seem unfair to ask just what he has been doing there until now. Where is the evidence of the struggle he has been carrying on there on behalf of the Negro? Why, if he and his enlightened confreres in the South have been boring from within to destroy segregation, do they react with such panic when the walls show any signs of falling? Why—and how—does one move from the middle of the road where one was aiding Negroes into the streets—to shoot them?

Now it is easy enough to state flatly that Faulkner's middle of the road does not—cannot—exist and that he is guilty of great emotional and intellectual dishonesty in pretending that it does. I think this is why he clings to his fantasy. It is easy enough to accuse him of hypocrisy when he speaks of man being "indestructible because of his simple will to freedom." But he is not being hypocritical; he means it. It is only that Man is one thing—a rather unlucky abstraction in this case—and the Negroes he has always known, so fatally tied up in his mind with his grandfather's slaves, are quite another. He is at his best, and is perfectly sincere, when he declares, in *Harpers*, "To live anywhere in the world today and be against equality because of race or color is like living in Alaska and being against snow. We have already got snow. And as with the Alaskan, merely to live in armistice with it is not enough. Like the Alaskan, we had better use it." And though this seems to be flatly opposed to his statement (in an interview printed in *The Reporter*) that, if it came to a contest between the federal government and Mississippi, he would fight for Mississippi, "even if it meant going out into the streets and shooting Negroes," he means that, too. Faulkner means everything he says, means them all at once, and with very nearly the same intensity. This is why his statements demand our attention. He has perhaps never before more concretely expressed what it means to be a Southerner.

What seems to define the Southerner, in his own mind at any rate, is his relationship to the North, that is to the rest of the Republic, a relationship which can at the very best be described as uneasy. It is apparently very difficult to be at once a Southerner and an American; so difficult that many of the South's most independent minds are forced into the American exile; which is not, of course, without its aggravating, circular effect on the interior and public life of the South. A Bostonian, say, who leaves Boston is not regarded by the citizenry he has abandoned with the same venomous distrust as is the Southerner who leaves the South. The citizenry of Boston do not consider that they have been abandoned, much less betrayed. It is only the American Southerner who seems to be fighting, in his own entrails, a peculiar, ghastly, and perpetual war with all the rest of the country. ("Didn't you say," demanded a Southern woman of Robert Penn Warren, "that you was born down here, used to live right near here?" And when he agreed that this was so: "Yes . . . but you never said where you living now!")

The difficulty, perhaps, is that the Southerner clings to two entirely antithetical doctrines, two legends, two histories. Like all other Americans, he must subscribe, and is to some extent controlled by the beliefs and the principles expressed in the Constitution; at the same time, these beliefs and principles seem determined to destroy the South. He is, on the one hand, the proud citizen of a free society and, on the other, is committed to a society which has not yet dared to free itself of the necessity of naked and brutal oppression. He is part of a country which boasts that it has never lost a war; but he is also the representative of a conquered nation. I have not seen a single statement of Faulkner's concerning desegregation which does not inform us that his family has lived in the same part of Mississippi for generations, that his great-grandfather owned slaves, and that his ancestors fought and died in the Civil War. And so compelling is the image of ruin, gallantry and death thus evoked that it demands a positive effort of the imagination to remember that slaveholding Southerners were not the only people who perished in that war. Negroes and Northerners were also blown to bits. American history, as opposed to Southern history, proves that Southerners were not the only slaveholders, Negroes were not even the only slaves. And the segregation which Faulkner sanctifies by references to Shiloh, Chickamauga, and Gettysburg does not extend back that far, is in fact scarcely as old as the century. The "racial condition" which Faulkner will not have changed by "mere force of law or economic threat" was imposed by precisely these means. The Southern tradition, which is, after all, all that Faulkner is talking about, is not a tradition at all: when Faulkner evokes it, he is simply evoking a legend which contains an accusation. And that accusation, stated far more simply than it should be, is that the North, in winning the war, left the South only one means of asserting its identity and that means was the Negro.

"My people owned slaves," says Faulkner, "and the very obligation we have to take care of these people is morally bad." "This problem is . . . far beyond the moral one it is and still was a hundred years ago, in 1860, when many Southerners, including Robert Lee, recognized it as a moral one at the very instant they in turn elected to champion the underdog because that underdog was blood and kin and home." But the North escaped scot-free. For one thing, in freeing the slave, it established a moral superiority over the South which the South has not learned to live with until today; and this despite—or possibly because of—the fact that this moral superiority was bought, after all, rather cheaply. The North was no better prepared than the South, as it turned out, to make citizens of former slaves, but it was able, as the South was not, to wash its hands of the matter. Men who knew that slavery was wrong were forced, nevertheless, to fight to perpetuate it because they were unable to turn against "blood and kin and home." And when blood and kin and home were defeated, they found themselves, more than ever, committed: committed, in effect, to a way of life which was as unjust and crippling as it was inescapable. In sum, the North, by freeing the slaves of their masters, robbed the masters of any possibility of freeing themselves of the slaves.

When Faulkner speaks, then, of the "middle of the road," he is simply speaking of the hope—which was always unrealistic and is now all but smashed—that the white Southerner, with no coercion from the rest of the nation, will lift himself above his ancient, crippling bitterness and refuse to add to his already intolerable burden of blood-guiltiness. But this hope would seem to be absolutely dependent on a social and psychological stasis which simply does not exist. "Things have been getting better," Faulkner tells us, "for a long time. Only six Negroes were killed by whites in Mississippi last year, according to police figures." Faulkner surely knows how little consolation this offers a Negro and he also knows something about "police figures" in the Deep South. And he knows, too, that murder is not the worst thing that can happen to a man, black or white. But murder may be the worst thing a man can do. Faulkner is not trying to save Negroes, who are, in his view, already saved; who, having refused to be destroyed by terror, are far stronger than the terrified white populace; and who have, moreover, fatally, from his point of view, the weight of the federal government behind them. He is trying to save "whatever good remains in those white people." The time he pleads for is the time in which the Southerner will come to terms with himself, will cease fleeing from his conscience, and achieve, in the words of Robert Penn Warren, "moral identity." And he surely believes, with Warren, that "Then in a country where moral identity is hard to come by, the South, because it has had to deal concretely with a moral problem, may offer some leadership. And we need any we can get. If we are to break out of the national rhythm, the rhythm between complacency and panic."

But the time Faulkner asks for does not exist—and he is not the only Southerner who knows it. There is never time in the future in which we will work out our salvation. The challenge is in the moment, the time is always now. (1956)

A Letter to the Leaders in the Negro Race

William Faulkner

Recently I was quoted in several magazines with the statement that 'I . . . between the United States and Mississippi . . . would choose Mississippi . . . even (at the price or if it meant) shooting down Negroes in the

Reprinted from James B. Meriwether, ed., "A Letter to the Leaders of the Negro Race," *Essays, Speeches and Public Letters of William Faulkner*, by permission of Random House, Inc., the Author's Literary Estate, and Chatto & Windus Ltd. Originally published in the September 1956 issue of *Ebony* magazine under the title "If I Were a Negro."

street.' Each time I saw this statement, I corrected it by letter, to this effect: That is a statement which no sober man would make nor any sane man believe, for the reason that it is not only foolish, but dangerous, since the moment for that choice and that subsequent act will never arise, but even to suggest it would only further inflame the few (I believe) people in the United States who might still believe such a moment could occur.

I quote the following from a piece of mine printed in *Life*, March 5th last, entitled "A Letter to the North," this part of the "Letter" addressed specifically to the NAACP and the other organizations working actively for the abolishment of segregation: 'Go slow now. Stop now for a time, a moment. You have the power now; you can afford to withhold for a moment the use of it as a force. You have done a good job, you have jolted your opponent off-balance and he is now vulnerable. But stop there for a moment; dont give him the advantage of a chance to cloud the issue by that purely automatic sympathy for the underdog simply because he is under . . . You have shown the Southerner what you can do and what you will do if necessary; give him a space in which to get his breath and assimilate that knowledge; to look about and see that (1) Nobody is going to force integration on him from the outside; (2) That he himself faces an obsolescence in his own land which only he can cure; a moral condition which not only must be cured but a physical condition which has got to be cured if he, the white Southerner, is to have any peace, is not to be faced with another legal process or maneuver every year, year after year, for the rest of his life.'

By 'Go slow, pause for a moment', I meant, 'Be flexible'. When I wrote the letter and then used every means I knew to get it printed in time, Autherine Lucy had just been compelled to withdraw temporarily from the University of Alabama by a local violence already of dangerous proportions. I believed that when the judge validated her claim to be re-admitted, which he would have to do, that the forces supporting her would send her back for re-admission, and that when that happened she would probably lose her life. That didn't happen. I want to believe that the forces supporting Miss Lucy were wise enough themselves not to send her back—not merely wise enough to save her life, but wise enough to foresee that even her martyrdom would in the long run be less effective than the simple, prolonged, endless nuisance-value of her threat, which was what I meant by '. . . a physical condition which has got to be cured if he, the white Southerner, is to have any peace, is not to be faced with another (sic) Miss Lucy every year . . . for the rest of his life.'

Not the individual Negro to abandon or lower one jot his hope and will for equality, but his leaders and organizations to be always flexible and adaptable to circumstance and locality in their methods of gaining it. If I were a Negro in America today, that is the course I would advise the leaders of my race to follow: to send every day to the white school to which he was entitled by his ability and capacity to go, a student of my race, fresh and cleanly dressed, courteous, without threat or violence, to seek admission; when he was refused I would forget about him as an individual, but tomorrow I would send another one, still fresh and clean and courteous, to be refused in his turn, until at last the white man himself must recognise that there will be no peace for himself until he himself has solved the dilemma.

This was Gandhi's way. If I were a Negro, I would advise our elders and leaders to make this our undeviating and inflexible course—a course of inflexible and unviolent flexibility directed against not just the schools but against all the public institutions from which we are interdict, as is being done against the Montgomery, Alabama, bus lines. But always with flexibility: inflexible and undeviable only in hope and will but flexible always to adapt to time and place and circumstance. I would be a member of NAACP, since nothing else in our U.S. culture has yet held out to my race that much of hope. But I would remain only under conditions: That it recognise the most serious quantity in our problem which, so far as I know, it has not publicly recognised yet; That it make the same flexibility the watchword of its methods. I would say to others of my race that we must never curb our hopes and demands for equal rights, but merely to curb with flexibility our methods of demanding them. I would say to other members of my race that I do not know how long 'slow' will take, but if you will grant me to mean by 'going slow', being flexible, I do not believe that anything else save 'going slow' will advance our hopes. I would say to my race, The watchword of our flexibility must be decency, quietness, courtesy, dignity; if violence and unreason come, it must not be from us. I would say that all the Negroes in Montgomery should support the busline boycott, but never that all of them *must*, since by that *must*, we will descend to the same methods which those opposing us are using to oppress us, and our victory will be worth nothing until it is willed and not compelled. I would say that our race must adjust itself psychologically, not to an indefinite continuation of a segregated society, but rather to a continuation as long as necessary of that inflexible unflagging flexibility which in the end will make the white man himself sick and tired of fighting it.

It is easy enough to say glibly, 'If I were a Negro, I would do this or that.' But a white man can only imagine himself for the moment a Negro; he cannot be that man of another race and griefs and problems. So there are some questions he can put to himself but cannot answer, for instance: Q. Would you lower your sights on your life's goals and reduce your aspirations for reasons of realism? A. No. I would impose flexibility on the methods. Q. Would this apply to your children? A. I would teach them both the aspirations and the flexibility. But here is hope, since life itself is hope in simply being alive since living is change and change must be either advancement or death. Q. How would you conduct yourself so as to avoid controversy and hostility and make friends for your people instead of enemies? A. By decency, dignity, moral and social responsibility. Q. How would you pray to God for human justice and racial salvation? A. I dont believe man prays to God for human justice and racial salvation. I believe he affirms to God that immortal individual human dignity which has always outlasted injustice and before which families and clans and tribes talking of themselves as a race of men and not the race of Man, rise and pass and vanish like so much dust. He merely affirms his own belief in the grace and dignity and immortality of individual man, as Dostoievsky's Ivan did when he repudiated any heaven whose order was founded on the anguished cry of one single child. Q. Surrounded by antagonistic white people, would you find it hard not to hate them? A. I would repeat to myself Booker T. Washington's words when he said: 'I will let no man, no matter what his color, ever make me hate him.'

So if I were a Negro, I would say to my people: 'Let us be always unflaggingly and inflexibly flexible. But always decently, quietly, courteously, with dignity and without violence. And above all, with patience. The white man has devoted three hundred years to teaching us to be patient; that is one thing at least in which we are his superiors. Let us turn it into a weapon against him. Let us use this patience not as a passive quality, but as an active weapon. But always, let us practise cleanliness and decency and courtesy and dignity in our contacts with him. He has already taught us to be more patient and courteous with him than he is with us; let us be his superior in the others too.'

But above all, I would say this to the leaders of our race: 'We must learn to deserve equality so that we can hold and keep it after we get it. We must learn reponsibility, the responsibility of equality. We must learn that there is no such thing as a 'right' without any ties to it, since anything given to one free for nothing is worth exactly that: nothing. We must learn that our inalienable right to equality, to freedom and liberty and the pursuit of happiness, means exactly what our founding fathers meant by it: the right to *opportunity* to be free and equal, provided one is worthy of it, will work to gain it and then work to keep it. And not only the right to that opportunity, but the willingness and the capacity to accept the responsibility of that opportunity—the responsibilities of physical cleanliness and of moral rectitude, of a conscience capable of choosing between right and wrong and a will capable of obeying it, of reliability toward other men, the pride of independence of charity or relief.

'The white man has not taught us that. He taught us only patience and courtesy. He did not even see that we had the environment in which we could teach ourselves cleanliness and independence and rectitude and reliability. So we must teach ourselves that. Our leaders must teach us that. We as a race must lift ourselves by our own bootstraps to where we are competent for the responsibilities of equality, so that we can hold on to it when we get it. Our tragedy is that these virtues of responsibility are the white man's virtues of which he boasts, yet we, the Negro, must be his superior in them. Our hope is that, having beaten him in patience and courtesy, we can probably beat him in these others too.' (September 1956)

Faulkner's Fictional Negroes

Ralph Ellison

. . . In Faulkner most of the relationships we have pointed out between the Negro and contemporary writing come to focus: the social and the personal, the moral and the technical, the nineteenth-century emphasis upon morality and the modern accent upon the personal myth. And on the strictly literary level he is prolific and complex enough to speak for those Southern writers who are aggressively anti-Negro and for those younger writers who appear most sincerely interested in depicting the Negro as a rounded human being. What is more, he is the greatest artist the South has produced. While too complex to be given more than a glance in these notes, even a glance is more revealing of what lies back of the distortion of the Negro in modern writing than any attempt at a group survey might be.

Faulkner's attitude is mixed. Taking his cue from the Southern mentality in which the Negro is often dissociated into a malignant stereotype (the bad nigger) on the one hand and a benign stereotype (the good nigger) on the other, most often Faulkner presents characters embodying both. The dual function of this dissociation seems to be that of avoiding moral pain and thus to justify the South's racial code. But since such a social order harms whites no less than blacks, the sensitive Southerner, the artist, is apt to feel its effects acutely—and within the deepest levels of his personality. For not only is the social division forced upon the Negro by the ritualized ethic of discrimination, but upon the white man by the strictly enforced set of anti-Negro taboos. The conflict is always with him. Indeed, so rigidly has the recognition of Negro humanity been tabooed that the white Southerner is apt to associate any form of personal rebellion with the Negro. So that for the Southern artist the Negro becomes a symbol of his personal rebellion, his guilt and his repression of it. The Negro is thus a compelling object of fascination, and this we see very clearly in Faulkner.

Sometimes in Faulkner the Negro is simply a villain, but by an unconsciously ironic transvaluation his villainy consists, as with Loosh in

The Unvanquished, of desiring his freedom. Or again the Negro appears benign, as with Ringo, of the same novel, who uses his talent not to seek personal freedom but to remain the loyal and resourceful retainer. Not that I criticize loyalty in itself, but that loyalty given where one's humanity is unrecognized seems a bit obscene. And yet in Faulkner's story, "The Bear," he brings us as close to the moral implication of the Negro as Twain or Melville. In the famous "difficult" fourth section, which Malcolm Cowley advises us to skip very much as Hemingway would have us skip the end of *Huckleberry Finn,* we find an argument in progress in which one voice (that of a Southern abolitionist) seeks to define Negro humanity against the other's enumeration of those stereotypes which many Southerners believe to be the Negro's basic traits. Significantly the mentor of the young hero of this story, a man of great moral stature, is socially a Negro.

Indeed, through his many novels and short stories, Faulkner fights out the moral problem which was repressed after the nineteenth century, and it was shocking for some to discover that for all his concern with the South, Faulkner was actually seeking out the nature of man. Thus we must turn to him for that continuity of moral purpose which made for the greatest of our classics. As for the Negro minority, he has been more willing perhaps than any other artist to start with the stereotype, accept it as true, and then seek out the human truth which it hides. Perhaps his is the example for our writers to follow, for in his work technique has been put once more to the task of creating value. . . . (1964)

William Faulkner and the Southern Negro

NANCY M. TISCHLER

The travesty on justice recently played out in Mississippi courts has led the Northerners—liberals and conservatives alike—to look with amazement on the aberrations of the Southern mind, finding themselves confounded by the psychology of their own countrymen. At such a time, it seems simple contrariness to turn to the words of redneck politicians rather than to the eloquent and probing explanations by the late William Faulkner, a Mississippian who spent his life trying to understand himself and his neighbors, both black and white.

Faulkner was obsessed with the plight of the Southern Negro. Part of his concern grew from his own inability as a white man to understand

Reprinted from Nancy M. Tischler, "William Faulkner and the Southern Negro," *Susquehanna University Studies,* VII: 4 (June 1965), 261–265, by permission of Susquehanna University Press, Selinsgrove, Pennsylvania.

the workings of the Negro mind. He never felt able to delve into the psychology of his Negro characters; only when they had white blood as well did he dare make the attempt. Unlike the egalitarians, Faulkner started from the premise that the Negro is basically different from the white man—his color, his customs, his food, even his smell—so certainly his mind must be different. The white man is severely restricted in his understanding of this alien world impinging on his own; this is one of the reasons Faulkner limited his own depiction of the Negro to his relations with the white community.

Even greater concern for Faulkner the moralist, however, lay in the guilt of slavery. He sensed an evil in slavery and in the rape of the land as well as of the people—an evil that had evoked a curse on the South, which the South had yet to expiate. The curse is not a matter of guilt simply for the white man's enslavement of the Negro in the antebellum South. A later sin has been the Southern white man's unwillingness to prepare the slaves for the responsibilities of freedom. For example, the northern Negro who is given a farm in Arkansas after the Civil War, but who understands nothing about farming or providing for his family's needs is Faulkner's symbol of the Negro's radical ignorance of the facts of life. A white benefactor, Ike McCaslin, finds this man sitting in a cabin without firewood on a farm without fences; he is reading a book, wearing glasses without lenses, and waiting for the spring before he starts to work. Ike, Faulkner's spokesman, looking at the desolation and at the Negro sitting in his ministerial clothing with pretentious dignity, cries that this is proof that the land is cursed. The Negro replies calmly that Ike is wrong, the curse has been lifted: "We are seeing a new era," he pontificates in the rhetoric of the modern idealist, "an era dedicated, as our founders intended it, to freedom, liberty and equality for all, to which this country will be a new Canaan—"

Ike can only reply, "Freedom from what? From work?" The Negro cannot understand the meaning of liberty until either his fellow man or brutal experience educates him.

Faulkner, in exploring the reason for this ignorance, shows that the Negro was treated like a child (or an animal) and then given the responsibilities of an adult. He shows the emancipated Negroes after the Civil War: marching and singing their way to the River Jordan (which they assume to be the nearest creek), becoming part of the jerry-built Reconstruction governments, telling their white masters that they are free—or as Ringo says [in *The Unvanquished*], Negroes have been abolished. This time it is the intrepid Miss Rosa who serves as Faulkner's spokesman to enunciate the problem of responsibility that goes with freedom—she wishes, she says, that she could be free. Milton distinguished the ideas Faulkner is dramatizing by calling one *liberty* and the other *license*. The Negro, according to Faulkner, interpreted his emancipation as license.

This confusion, Faulkner feels, was largely the fault of the white man. He gave the Negro, not his virtues, but his vices: promiscuity, violence, instability, lack of control, inability to distinguish between thine and mine. The Negroes learned to ape these white vices, transforming them into Negro vices and adding to them a slyness that is part of the Negro's method of accommodating himself to a dominant white world. He has learned to hide his resentment with the proper response to the white man, and he has learned improvidence and intemperance and evasion—not laziness: evasion. This has been the black man's passive resistance to white tyranny for a century or more. And, in a sense, the white man has not only taught the black his vices and encouraged him to new ones, he has also revelled in the sense of superiority that these vices allow him, the white man, to assume. The ability to look down on his Negro associates with paternal indulgence has been an inestimable boost to the Southern white man's ego.

Faulkner sees the virtues of the Negro as far more impressive than his vices. Over and over, the really admirable Faulkner character is the Negro, frequently the Mammy. "They are better than we are," he says. "Stronger than we are." Their virtues are: endurance and pity and tolerance and forbearance and fidelity and love of children—whether their own or not or black or not. Nor significantly, does Faulkner ever make a pure-blooded Negro the villain of his books.

The most nearly villainous negroid type is the mixed-blooded figure. For such men, Faulkner feels overwhelming sympathy. In such decent men as Sam Fathers, part Indian, part Negro, the blood mixture serves as a barrier to any of the three worlds of the South. Several of the Faulkner characters are doomed to loneliness because their mixed blood alienates them from all communities. But more sinister is the mixture that brings the antagonism of black and white into a man, making his being the horrible battlefield for a never-ceasing civil war. The attraction-revulsion pattern between the black and white communities is violently exaggerated when compressed into the grotesque mulatto brain of a Joe Christmas [*Light in August*].

All of this would seem to suggest that Faulkner sees no future for the Negro—either in moving from the South, in mixing with whites, or in overcoming his vices. In spite of the fact that the South is a socially conservative area, where the Peabodys are traditionally the doctors, the Stevenses the lawyers, Snopses the small businessmen, and where the Negroes are historically laborers and servants, there is no reason that there cannot be change. The two wars in this century have, in fact, already brought changes to the Southern Negro. Faulkner pictures Caspey returning from World War I proud of having dressed like the white soldiers. Having served as a dock-worker, he had no opportunity to fight beside the whites in that war, but he did learn pride in his race. By the Second World

War, that pride was clearly justified. One of the Faulkner characters, Major Devries, risks his life to save a Negro under his command, and is in turn saved by another Negro—on whom he pins his own medal. Thus, the Negro is now a character with opportunities as well as capacity for heroism, opportunities that earlier had been restricted primarily to the white man. The heroism had been there all along in the quiet gestures of the inevitable family retainers. Wit and wisdom were also there all along in the Faulkner Negroes, but were recognized only by a few of the landed aristocrats. Now these virtues are becoming obvious even to the rodent-like Snopes clan.

By the end of his life, Faulkner saw the Negro's evolution into a more dignified role in the community. Many of the old virtues have consequently disappeared; the process of deterioration works in white and Negro families of Yoknapatawpha County alike. But these were, by and large, the virtues of a servile race; they had to drop off to allow for new virtues. By the end, Faulkner's Negroes, preferring to find salvation for themselves, are not interested in the services of white Lady Bountifuls. The *noblesse oblige* of the aristocrat has proven impotent for the betterment of the Negroes' position; the Negroes themselves reject the subsequent self-righteous philanthropy of the liberal. When Linda Snopes, a Communist enthusiast temporarily fascinated with the Negro's plight, tries to interfere with the Negro schools, the Negro principal explains why he does not want the fumbling ministrations of inept white reformers:

> . . . we have got to make the white people need us first. In the old days your people did need us, in your economy if not in your culture, to make your cotton and tobacco and indigo. But that was the wrong need, bad and evil in itself. So it couldn't last. It had to go. So now you don't need us. There is no place for us now in your culture or economy either. We both buy the same installment-plan automobiles to burn up the same gasoline in, and the same radios to listen to the same music and the same iceboxes to keep the same beer in, but that's all. So we have got to make a place of our own in your culture and economy too. Not you to make a place for us just to get us out from under your feet, as in the South here, or to get our votes for the aggrandisement of your political perquisites, as in the North, but *us*. You cannot do without us because nobody but us can fill that place in your economy and culture which only we can fill and so that place will have to be ours. So that you will not just say Please to us, you will need to say Please to us. . . . (*The Mansion*, pp. 224–225)

Herein lies the seed of Faulkner's solution. He recognizes the injustice, the daily brutality, as the white man degrades the black. He also realized that cruelty is learned—children mix easily with Negroes; the initiation into hatred comes with adolescence. But black and white alike in his novels insist that the injustice cannot be abolished overnight by legislating it out of existence—any more than the Negroes themselves could be legislated out of existence by a Reconstruction government. Evolution, not revolution, is Faulkner's answer. To the outraged cry that evolution is too slow, that the need for reparation is immediate, Faulkner replies, in the *persona* of Gavin Stevens, that haste will harm the Negro himself. "Outlanders" who hope to help the Negro, says Stevens, "will fling him back decades, back not merely into injustice but into grief and agony and violence too by forcing on us laws based on the idea that man's injustice to man can be abolished overnight by police."

> Sambo will suffer it of course; there are not enough of him yet to do anything else. And he will endure it, absorb it and survive because he is Sambo and has that capacity; he will even beat us there because he has the capacity to endure and survive but he will be thrown back decades and what he survives to may not be worth having because by that time divided we may have lost America. (*Intruder in the Dust*, pp. 203–204)

The answer of the reformer is not Faulkner's answer any more than it is Stevens's. He explains that he is not excusing injustice. "I only say that the injustice is ours, the South's. We must expiate and abolish it ourselves, alone and without help nor even (with thanks) advice."

In keeping with this philosophy, he said in 1956, that it was clear that segregation was going, "whether we like it or not." Since the South had already lost the initiative on that decision, Faulkner told an Alabama University student, "I vote that we ourselves choose to abolish it. . . ." His vote was also for law and order, so that when the dust of the race conflict had settled, there would be something worth having.

Faulkner may not have been a typical Southerner, or a typical Mississippian, but in his disgust with red-necks and lynch mobs, his reverence for due process of the law, his sense of responsibility for his ancestor's sins, and his brooding love of his native South, he does speak for the best of Southern conservatism. (June 1965)

Faulkner's Negroes

Robert Penn Warren

. . . Most of the Negroes in Faulkner—certainly those (including the problematical [Joe] Christmas [of *Light in August*]) who have significant roles—are of mixed blood. Waiving the fact that, even in the period treated

Reprinted from Robert Penn Warren, "Faulkner: The South and the Negro," *The Southern Review*, I:3 (Summer 1965), 501–529, by permission of William Morris Agency, Inc.

by Faulkner, the infusion of white blood among Negroes was marked, there remains the fact that Faulkner's theme of the rejected "brother," is at the very center of his drama: the character of mixed blood is mandatory, the mixture of blood is, in one sense, the story. Second, if the "mulatto" character suffers, Faulkner can scarcely be said to be avenging himself because of "an inherited fear of blood mixture"—the mulatto being the living symbol of that. The world and society—not Faulkner, the writer—"make" the character suffer; and in those works like *Light in August*, "Pantaloon in Black," "The Fire and the Hearth," "The Bear," and *Intruder in the Dust*, where Negroes have central or important roles, what Faulkner does is to make the character transcend his sufferings *qua* Negro to emerge to us not as Negro but as man. It may even be said that the final story is never one of social injustice, however important that element may be, but of an existential struggle against fate, for identity, a demonstration of the human will to affirm itself. . . .

With the characters of mixed blood another question arises. There is the not uncommon view of Faulkner's characters of mixed blood (and of those in real life) that when dignity and intelligence appear the white strain is to be credited. Lucas is cited in support of this view, for he himself finds in the blood of the ruthless old Carothers McCaslin a point of pride and dignity. When he goes to Zack Edmonds to demand his wife back, he says: "I'm a nigger. But I'm a man too. I'm more than just a man. The same thing [the blood of old Carothers] made my pappy that made your grandmaw." And later in the duel with Zack it is the blood of old Carothers that is a central fact.

Does this mean that Lucas has spiritually, if not actually, "passed," has repudiated his Negro blood? I do not think so. But the key point is whether this is to be taken as evidence that Faulkner holds the Negro strain in contempt. In the same story, the next Edmonds, the son of old Zack, looking into the "absolutely blank, impenetrable" face of the now old Lucas, as they talk about a still, thinks: "I am not only looking at a face older than mine . . . but at a man most of whose blood was pure ten thousand years when my own anonymous beginnings became mixed enough to produce me."

As for Sam Fathers (whose very name tells us something) he is, as Faulkner says in "The Old People," the "old dark man sired on both sides by savage kings." If McCaslin Edmonds emphasizes the blood of the Chickasaw chief Ikkemotubbe, he can also say, in the same story: "He was a wild man. When he was born, all his blood on both sides, except the little white part, knew things that had been tamed out of our blood so long ago that we have not only forgotten them, we have to live together in herds to protect ourselves from our own sources." And if Sam Fathers is, after the time of the "savage kings," an inheritor "on the one hand of the long chronicle of a people who had learned humility through suffering and learned pride through the endurance which survived the suffering," that merely makes him the appropriate teacher for the young Isaac, who must learn those things in order to become fully a man. And it is Isaac, who, when he reaches twenty-one and decides to order his life by the mystic lesson of Sam Fathers and repudiate his inherited land, will say of the Negroes: ". . . they will endure. They are better than we are. Stronger than we are." And in the same famous passage he says: "What they got not only not from white people but not even despite white people because they had it already from the old free fathers a longer time free than us because we have never been free." And with this Isaac echoes the notion we often find in Faulkner's work of a world of the right relation to nature that has long since been lost through the violations and destructions of modernity—and we may add, "white modernity."

I am not saying that we should take the word of Isaac, Carothers Edmonds, Gavin Stevens, or any other single character in Faulkner. We know, in fact, that Lucas regards the repudiation of the inheritance by Isaac as an act of weakness, and that Faulkner later, at the University of Virginia, implied that the withdrawal and self-purgation of Isaac are related to weakness. But such characters do lie within the circumference of Faulkner's special sympathy and their utterances demand respect. Their utterances do bear relation to the context of the utterances in Faulkner's own voice or of the dramatic context of his work.

For instance, Isaac's view of the Civil War is, when shorn of Ike's theology, very like Faulkner's own. Slavery, the curse against "the communal anonymity of brotherhood," was in the South, and there were not enough men like Uncle Buck and Uncle Bud (two of Faulkner's Southern emancipationists who moved out of their inherited houses built by the hands of slaves); so God decreed the Civil War, decreed that the valor and skill of men like Lee and Jackson should scare the Yankees into unity; and decreed defeat, not because He wished to turn His face away from the South, but because He "still intended to save" the South, which was able to "learn nothing save through suffering." Isaac, at the age of twenty-one, identifies himself with his own kind, defeated and impoverished, and not with the outside world of comfort and success.

But let us return to Isaac. Long after he has repudiated his patrimony to avoid any share in the inherited evil of slavery, we find a significant scene in "Delta Autumn." A young woman with an infant turns up when Isaac is alone in the hunting camp. He learns that the child is by his kinsman Roth Edmonds (of "The Fire and the Hearth"), and that the young woman, a descendant of Eunice, the slave of old Carothers McCaslin, has Negro blood. Roth is trying to buy her off; and so the family curse reappears in another rejection.

But another point emerges here. The girl, hunting Roth, confronts Isaac in his tent and flings down on his cot the money the lover had left her, instead of a message. "Take it out of my tent," Isaac commands her, in some complex outrage, one element of which is certainly at the fact that Roth had tried to settle such an obligation for money. We realize, however, that this act of Roth's is, in its way, a parallel to Isaac's old act of trying to buy out of responsibility by refusing his inheritance. In other words, the consequence of the crime cannot be commuted by money.

But there is another stage. Isaac, touched by her clarity and integrity, gives her the hunting horn, his most prized possession, the symbol of the old white order as well as of the old truth he had learned from the wilderness and from Sam Fathers. But as she takes the horn he says, "Go back North. Marry: a man of your own race. That's the only salvation for you. . . . We will have to wait."

To which she replies: "Old man, have you lived so long and forgotten so much that you don't remember anything you ever knew or felt or even heard about love?" Again, we have it: the consequences of the crime against love—i.e. against the "communal anonymity of brotherhood"—cannot be commuted: no more by the sentimentality of the past or a promise of the distant future, than by money.

She leaves the old man lying on the cot, shaking with the horror of his vision of the wilderness ruined to make room for a world of "*usury and mortgage and bankruptcy and measureless wealth,*" where "*Chinese and African and Aryan and Jew all breed and spawn together until no man has time to say which one is which nor cares.*" But out of what amounts to a racist nightmare Isaac is awakened by the news that Roth has killed a deer—but "nothing extra." By this phrase, Isaac knows it is a doe his kinsman has killed, and with this he swings from his generalized nightmare back to the other pole of his feelings, to the pathos of that particular human event: Roth, in a double sense, has killed a "doe" and has violated honor.

Before the perilously balanced resolution of the episode, Isaac's bosom is a battleground for all the conflicting needs, loyalties, terrors, phobias, sympathies, loves, and hopes, that revolve around the question of race. Is he to be equated with Faulkner? Clearly not—however much Faulkner may have known of such conflicts. For Faulkner stands outside Isaac and criticizes him for weakness. At the same time Faulkner presents him with sympathy, respect, and tenderness. Isaac, a man of an older generation, born in 1867, is caught in his own moment of time, struggling to clear his mind and feelings, and up to that last moment lies impotent and shaking in horror at which, *for him,* is the unresolvable issue.[1] Lying on the cot in

[1] "He used 'a thousand or two thousand years' in his despair. He had seen a condition which was intolerable, which shouldn't be but it was, and he was saying in effect that this must be changed, this cannot go on, but I'm too old to do anything about it, that maybe in a thousand years somebody will be young enough and strong enough to do something about it. That was all he meant by the numbers. But I think that he saw, as everybody that thinks, that a condition like that is intolerable, not so

the ruined wilderness, with "the constant and grieving rain" on the canvas of the tent, he is the image of the anguishing tale of time.

. . . James Joyce went forth from Ireland to forge, as he put it in the words of his hero Stephen Dedalus, the conscience of his race. Faulkner did a more difficult thing. To forge the conscience of his race, he stayed in his native spot and, in his soul, in images of vice and of virtue, reenacted the history of that race. (Summer 1965)

William Faulkner, James Baldwin, and the South

M. E. Bradford[1]

"Why—and how—does one move from the middle of the road where one was aiding Negroes—into the streets—to shoot them?" Thus responds James Baldwin, in an essay entitled "Faulkner and Desegregation," to William Faulkner's complex reactions to racial revolution in the twentieth-century South. Baldwin can make no sense out of the combination of concern and warning which animates most of Faulkner's discussion of the problems of a multiracial society; and he is especially provoked by an interview with Faulkner which appeared in a March, 1956, issue of *Reporter*—the interview in which the Mississippi novelist supposedly spoke of the possibility of an ultimate recourse to arms. In fairness we must admit that we had no reason to expect the Negro novelist to be particularly perceptive in his comments on the squire of Oxford. His fictions and essays, in their suffocating narcissism, have augured no such marvel of judgment. But he is remarkably revealing in the contradiction he imagines he has found in Faulkner's logic. For although Faulkner is (in this writer's opinion) neither miraculously wise nor representative of the thinking of his fellow Southerners on what form a future racial accommodation should assume, he is absolutely representative and realistic in his insistence on the organic and communal framework within which any real adjustment must occur. And it is to his credit that (contrary to much

---

much intolerable to man's sense of justice, but maybe intolerable to the condition, that any country has reached the point where if it is to endure, it must have no inner conflicts based on a wrong, a basic human wrong." *Faulkner in the University*, p. 46.

Reprinted from M. E. Bradford, "Faulkner, James Baldwin, and the South," *The Georgia Review*, XX:4 (Winter 1966), 431–441, by permission of the *Georgia Review*, Copyright © by the University of Georgia.

[1] Professor Bradford has also written the following criticism on *Go Down, Moses:* "Brotherhood in 'The Bear': An Exemplum for Critics," *Modern Age*, X (Summer 1966), 278–281; "The Gum Tree Scene: Observations on the Structure of 'The Bear,'" *Southern Humanities Review*, I (Summer 1967), 141–150; "All the Daughter's of Eve: 'Was' and the Unity of *Go Down, Moses*," *Arlington Quarterly*, I (Autumn 1967), 27–28—Eds.

published misrepresentation) from that insistence he never deviated—except in making rhetorical concessions for the purpose of argument, and even then not much.

Community—as we have known it in the South and as it persists in traditional cultures abroad, in New England, and in the rural Middle West—pre-supposes certain attitudes and axioms of behavior. One of these is commitment to a place and to the location of family or clan in that place. Out of the experience of the family in the place grows the communal society. Like the English Constitution as Burke conceived of it, it is the product of a collective experience. Its authority is historical, the result of a dialectic of trial and error and of the test of time. The society is dynamic, and the process which creates it is continual. The values which govern prescriptively the behavior of those who live within it we might call (again thinking of Burke) "prejudice." With the pedigree of wide distribution and long establishment, these collective reactions to significant experiences need no discussion among those who are agreed upon them. Their status is assured by their experimental origin and constant reapplication. In function they " . . . [render] a man's virtue his habit: and not a series of unconnected acts. Through just prejudice, his duty becomes part of his nature."

The very survival of this type of community depends upon both its constant restoration and renewal through adjustment to new circumstances and its resistance against any and all attempts to pull it up from the roots, to break off utterly from the past and start afresh. It depends upon the primacy of its members' sense of obligation to its smallest units, to the family and the clan which are its archetype and miniature. And that sense of obligation, these members must understand, often precludes their loving everything and everyone in the same way or to the same degree—the indiscriminate confusion of lesser and greater goods which the theologians used to call (before they forgot the distinction) cupidity. Community is inveterately provincial (rooted in space and therefore not adrift in time) and has no excessive confidence in self-appointed social prophets or the untested judgment of individual men or even generations of men who would arbitrarily explain or "adjust" it (from within or without). The defenders of such a society could say with Burke:

> We are afraid to put men to live and trade each on his own private stock of reason; because we suspect that this stock in each man is small, and that the individuals would do better to avail themselves of the general bank and capital of nations and of ages.

Like Swift they assume man to be *animal rationis capax*, a creature capable of reason and not *animal rationale*, a creature of reason. They are suspicious of intellectual pride; but they are not irrationalists and have faith in the *consensus gentium* they live by, the end product of a piously reverenced and organic historical process.

There is nothing in this Burkean conception of community that allows for any but restorative reform. Such reform, as Burke put it, must come not of love but of hatred for innovation; and it must come from within the communal framework and be a natural outgrowth of some new stage in the community's experience. Its object is to preserve the integrity of community. It is *never* imposed from without, *never* comes quickly, and is *never* the product of a few men, or even of a single generation. Indeed it must grow out of the society's past; if it is genuine reform, it will appear to the inheritors of its adoption as unsurprising as the renewal of life with the passage of the seasons. . . .

There can be little question about Faulkner's affinity for most aspects of the communal idea described above. His identity with Mississippi was almost absolute; it was, in fact, so strong that he was unwilling that even animals belonging to him should give birth to their young elsewhere; and for that reason, in a somewhat quixotic gesture, he gave up a profitable script-writing job in California to take his mare home to foal. Unlike so many American men of letters (but like quite a few Southern writers) Faulkner was most at home where he was born. His homeland was both the location and the subject of most of his writings. As his brother John Faulkner wrote, there can be no doubt of his proprietary devotion to it. The anachronism of his piety as well as the anachronism of its object secured him from the peculiarly virulent affliction of the modern mind, the "New Provincialism" (ignorance of history) identified over twenty years ago by Allen Tate as the poison within our received intellectual systems.

Nor can there be any question concerning the importance which Faulkner attached to the history of his world. He brooded upon it continually; for in it he found both the explanation of what his people were and some suggestion as to what they might be. Even when he chose to be critical of the South, he spoke from within a Southern framework, as a Mississippian. Whenever he was asked to "explain" the South, he began with history—and not the formal history of the textbook apologist for the world as it is, but the history of communal memory, within which present and past come together and link in mysterious covenant the living with the dead and with the yet unborn. That much of this communal memory was of suffering and disappointment did not disturb Faulkner; for as he told a group of Japanese students, " . . . it's hard believing, but disaster seems to be good for people. But if they are too successful too long, something dies. . . ."

He was well aware of how much the future of his people depended upon their ability to meet and endure new circumstances—and their determination to frustrate any and all attempts from the outside to direct their response to these circumstances. It was perhaps because he feared for the integrity of his culture, because he feared a new era of internecine conflict within the Southern community that he urged his fellow Southerners, white and black, to renegotiate their differences. But even his strongest statements in favor of the abolition of some formal barriers between coexistent racial societies in the South are directed principally to his fellow Southerners as persuasion and cannot be taken as advocacy of any externally imposed solution. . . .

Faulkner's insistence that the responsibility for the stewardship of the Southern community must ultimately fall upon the white Southerner is nothing more or less than a recognition of fact. It is not a defense of the status quo, not a reflection upon the Southern Negro. On the contrary, it is an acknowledgement of the irrevocability of history, of the necessity to work from what is and not from what one imagines ought to be. . . .

Most of Faulkner's responsible and enduring characters realize, as he does, that "there is no such thing as equality *per se*." Rather than troubling over inequities, they fulfill themselves through their commitment to some social unit, such as the family, or the implementation of a patriarchal design (which is not "just Sartoris") on behalf of the larger family which is the community. In contrast Faulkner condemns the abnegation of place which the much admired and much misunderstood hero of "The Bear," Ike McCaslin, makes in behalf of what he calls the "communal anonymity of brotherhood" (*Faulkner in the University*, pp. 245–46, 276). As Faulkner knew very well, there can be no such thing as "communal anonymity" or "anonymous brotherhood." The word "brother" presupposes the family structure, which Ike rejects when he turns away from the problems which his father and his uncle, Buck and Buddy McCaslin, and his cousin McCaslin Edmonds had dealt with manfully. Ike imagines that he will escape from community into freedom and thereby free others from the "curse" that is on his family's plantation, that he will open to them a better life. Yet in the world of Faulkner's fiction there is no escape and only a precarious existence outside of community; and it is certainly not through flight from patriarchal responsibility that one may best help others rise to a station in accordance with their worth and ability. . . .

When he is not playing the role of the militant Negro intellectual or proving his social relevance, and especially when he is not writing about the United States, James Baldwin is willing to recognize the importance of status and place and of a reasonable degree of hierarchy in an orderly and civilized society. He remarks approvingly that Europeans have lived with the idea of status for a long time:

> A man can be as proud of being a good waiter as of being a good actor, and, in neither case, feel threatened. And this means that the actor and the waiter can have a freer and more genuinely friendly relationship in Europe than they are likely to have here. The waiter does not feel with obscure resentment, that the actor has "made it," and the actor is not tormented by the fear that he may find himself, tomorrow, once again a waiter. (*Nobody Knows My Name*, pp. 7–8)

He is also well aware that "every society" is "governed by hidden laws, by unspoken but profound assumptions" which constitute its communal memory and direct its behavior (*Nobody Knows My Name*, pp. 11–12). But when he speaks of America, he insists that the past has no relevance, that the heritage of Western civilization is of questionable value, that what we have in this country must be utterly new and unrelated to any past scheme of social order. Baldwin pictures the Southern gentleman as something like the autocrat, Thomas Sutpen, of *Absalom, Absalom!* And he imagines paternalism means nothing but being completely in someone's power—when in fact it should properly mean being able to depend on the people in whose power we inevitably are (*Nobody Knows My Name*, p. 110). He is, as we might expect, suspicious or even resentful of Faulkner's identification with the place Mississippi—which makes it all the more interesting and ironic that Mr. Baldwin's own best work is the result of his marked (if unwilling) identification with Harlem.

But Harlem is not community, as Baldwin himself convinces us. As an angry Southern Negro educator told him in reaction to the alternative which he, a Northern Negro, represented, "Negroes in the South form a *community*" (*Nobody Knows My Name*, p. 85). Because of where and how Baldwin grew up, because of the violent eschatologies (religious and political) he allowed his mind to feed upon, it would seem most unlikely that he would understand community or the difference between change and progress within a communal framework; and indeed at the very heart of much of his writing, in the midst of solipsistic rambling on the tragedy of poor colored boys, stands an impious attitude toward his own father, an attitude which makes it impossible for him to have the vaguest understanding of the truly communal life.

Baldwin rejects the world that produced him and is filled with self-hatred for his recollected boyhood self and for everything about the older Negroes who surrounded him in his youth. He is the victim of all those who taught him to do so and created in him (and his kind) expectations that cannot be fulfilled.

We in the South (or at least most of us) are too much aware of how self-dividing and psychotic would be the consequence of our submission to the proposition that our fathers were entirely mistaken and malicious in their approach to the problems of a multiracial society to reject in toto the value of their experience. We will bide our time and allow the enthusiasm (and the rhetoric) of the moment to founder upon the rock of fact. Regardless of whatever laws are made by an intimidated Congress, whatever decisions are handed down by a sociological court, or whatever directives are issued from the bureaucratic catacombs of the Leviathan's "angelic" minions, we will consider carefully their precept and example; and we will apply them, as (and when) we are able, to the cataclysmic world we inhabit. Baldwin himself, in his prolonged literary quarrel with the image of his father, is a telling argument against the total impiety in whose behalf he speaks; for he seems to have made of it nothing but rhetoric and despair.

In truth it is Baldwin (and the white liberals North and South who helped create him) who is monstrously inconsistent. In *The Fire Next Time* he writes, "The only thing that white people have that black people need or should want is power," and then comes back to tell us that an unqualified, make-believe love can conquer all. Elsewhere in the same book he says of the white man that it is impossible to love him (p. 116). Baldwin's is a voice now heard nightly (in this summer of 1966) crying love-in-hate on a thousand darkened streets. Out of a desire to avoid this kind of chaos-breeding double-think and schizophrenia Faulkner (and the South he spoke prophetically for) says to the "new" Negro, to the makers and shapers *and* to the proponents of "black power": we would help you, but we will oppose you if we must—even, if necessary, to the point of force. And in his allegiance to an age-old and well-proven ideal of community, the intelligent Southerner (or genuinely conservative non-Southern American) can take no other position. (1966)

The Relation of Style and Form to Meaning in Faulkner's Work

Literary style is increasingly recognized both as form and semantics. The selections below often deal with both concepts of style.

Faulkner's Concepts of Time

FREDERICK J. HOFFMAN

[One of the major thematic concerns in Faulkner's work is his] treatment of time (including historical time, tradition, as well as narrative rhythm and pace) . . . it is probably the most important approach one may make to Faulkner. While a literal, lineal time has no place of appreciable significance in Faulkner's work, the pressure of past upon present is seen in a variety of complex and interesting ways as affecting the psychology and morality of individual actions.

I shall begin by offering a diagram of the several time patterns in Faulkner's work. It is an oversimplification, but it should help. . . .

This sketch demands several preliminary observations. The "Edenic time" (A) is a pre-historical or a non-historical time, or a non-temporal existence, a point before or beyond time, when active moral criteria either have not yet entered human history or are not really contained within the

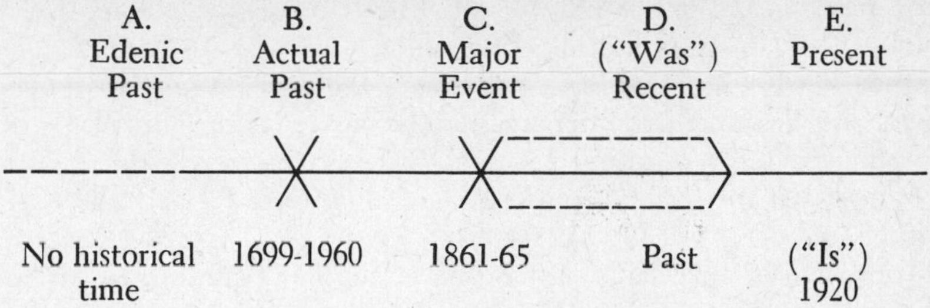

human consciousness. The "actual past" (B) means the beginning of recorded history—that is, within Faulkner's record; the earliest specific date mentioned by him is 1699, a date given in the 1946 appendix of *The Sound and the Fury.* But the developing time is largely emphasized as within the nineteenth century, leading toward and away from the Major Event (C), the Civil War, in which the accumulated tensions and moral crises received a catastrophic and a significantly violent expression. This does not mean that Faulkner is an "historical novelist," nor that he gives the Civil War much specific attention. . . . The most important use of time in Faulkner is the pattern or movement of it—largely in the consciousness of his characters, not in terms of narrative exposition—from this major event through the Recent Past (D) to the Present (E). This movement is reciprocal, and it alternates in terms of symbol and forms of psychological reaction. . . .

There is, of course, an historical pattern in Faulkner's work, but it has to be picked up from here and there in the novels and stories; it is not presented as a straightforward chronology. . . .

Faulkner sees time in a complex of human tensions and as fully absorbed in and integrated with rhetoric, style, and narrative pace and rhythm. The reader is almost never aware of a pure present . . . nor is a *specific past* very often exclusively given. There are two important, typical uses of time in the novels: the slow, gradual, painstaking reconstruction of the past by narrators who exist in the present or existed in the recent past (as in *Absalom*); and the pattern of movement from past to present to past, or within points in the past (*The Sound and the Fury* is a good example). In either case, one almost never sees the present as a pure or separate time; it is infused with the past, it has meaning only in terms of it, and its complex nature results from the fusion of the two.

One may describe Faulknerian time as a continuum time flowing from past into present and from present into past. Reality is not so much objective existence but what past and present have made of an object or an event within a given set of psychological conditions. . . .

Besides this very important view of time, there is the idea of an "Edenic past" (A of the above diagram). This may be called pure stasis or a timeless vision or an unhistorical condition existing before and transcending human complication. In various ways it is described (and glimpsed briefly) in "The Bear," *Absalom, Light in August, Requiem for a Nun,* and in numerous brief images elsewhere. Irving Howe calls it "a past removed from historical time, an Eden coexisting with society yet never mistaken for society by those who come to it for refreshment and purification." . . .

The vision of an Edenic past is one of the more substantial in American literature. The "state of innocence" which ante-dates or ignores or avoids experience is in one way or another expressed as a point of reference for a major journey of the American personality from innocence to experience. As Henry Nash Smith has abundantly proved in *The Virgin Land* (1950), it was one of the most frequently employed images on the frontier. Its many literary variations include James Fenimore Cooper's Leather-Stocking tales, Mark Twain's *The Adventures of Huckleberry Finn,* the Nick Adams of Hemingway's *In Our Time* and stories of other volumes, and such cruder uses of it as Sherwood Anderson's *Dark Laughter* and Waldo Frank's *Holiday.*

In Faulkner's novels, the figure of the Edenic past is symbolized variously in the wilderness of "The Bear"; in the state of pre-historical innocence described in *Absalom;* and in the vision of the arrested, static, still reality of the road to Jefferson in the first chapter of *Light in August* and of the landscape of the farm beyond Jefferson in *Intruder in the Dust.*

Faulkner's language also has an especial relevance to this kind of "still moment": the words *motionless, arrested, frozen, suspended, immobile, soporific,* and others define the condition of static innocence. The following passage, from *Intruder in the Dust,* illustrates the effect upon Faulkner's rhetoric:

> . . . there should have been fixed in monotonous repetition the land's living symbol—a formal group of ritual almost mystic significance identical and monotonous as milestones tying the county-seat to the county's ultimate rim as milestones would: the beast the plow and the man integrated in one foundationed into the frozen wave of their furrow tremendous with effort yet at the same same [sic] vacant of progress, ponderable immovable and immobile like groups of wrestling statuary set against the land's immensity . . .

This rhetoric, and many figures like it, is used to define an arrest of consciousness, a state of suspension; in many cases it also suggests an "ideal" state of nature which precedes the onrushing of time, the beginning of "progress" and decay in human affairs. In most examples, there is an implicit criticism of the nature of human evil or vileness or sheer moral insensibility. But it would be a serious mistake to assume from this that Faulkner is a "primitivist": that he counsels a retreat from the present to an ideal, undefiled state of nature.

In many respects, the quality of Edenic stillness is also a matter of characterization and description; the hero in Faulkner frequently matches stillness against violence. He is sometimes badly mistaken in so doing. . . . The Edenic past is a form of representing a state of nature, both a descriptive and a normative means of defining the role and the effect of man's effect upon it and upon history. . . .

. . . perhaps the most obvious [of the human attempts to fix time] is the cliché reaction or stock response to human event. Men and women give labels to events unthinkingly and irresponsibly, and this tendency is an example of meeting evasively the moral burden of the past. Faulkner most successfully contrasts this cliché with the problem of man himself: the abstraction "nigger" is forced to meet the test of the vitality of "man." . . .

Besides [this manipulation] of time as abstract versus time as "real," there are five other ways in which Faulkner describes the relationship of the individual to the past. On occasions, the Faulkner character assumes the burden of the past in an obsessive way. . . .

In another example, the Faulkner hero drives relentlessly toward the accomplishment of an abstract "design." . . .

In a third example of the individual's reaction to time, we have the hero who is "trapped in history"—immobilized because of a fixation in the past. . . .

The fourth kind of available reaction to time is to deny that the past exists. The reverse of assuming that only it exists, it is a psychological variant upon the obsessed figure who tries to order the world in his own image. . . .

Finally, the Faulkner character may adopt a simple vision of the past, setting aside its extreme aberrations and resting trustfully upon its promise of stability and endurance. This fifth class of response to time is truly complex, and it involves many variants. There is the "Edenic vision," discussed above; there is the steady, balanced "acceptance" of time and its erosive effect upon man . . . There are many such characters in Faulkner's works who often seem his "reserve" of stability: . . . Sam Fathers and Ike McCaslin of "The Bear"; and many of the Negroes throughout his fiction.

Rhetoric in Southern Writing: Faulkner

William Van O'Connor

Faulkner's rhetoric has several sources: it is indebted to Tennyson and to Swinburne, to the elegance of *la fin de siècle,* to the Ciceronian periods of Southern oratory, and to a Southern folk tradition that is anti-grammat-

Reprinted from William Van O'Connor, "Rhetoric in Southern Writing: Faulkner," *Georgia Review,* XII:1 (Spring 1958), 83–86, by permission of the *Georgia Review.*

ical and colorful. Perhaps his major styles can be classified as "high rhetoric" and as "folk language." The two styles meet in *The Hamlet*, and there are varieties of the folk language in most of his books. When people speak of Faulkner's rhetoric, however, they commonly mean the "high rhetoric."

Millar MacLure, writing in the *Queen's Quarterly* (Autumn, 1956), says: "Faulkner's prose has an archaic sound, like a hunter's horn." This is the best characterization of it I have read. Faulkner's prose has a nineteenth century quality, it belongs to a different world from the present.

Perhaps the simplest way of examining the high rhetoric is to read and then analyze a characteristic sentence. The sentence is from "The Bear":

> It was as if the boy had already divined what his senses and intellect had not encompassed yet: that doomed wilderness whose edges were being constantly and punily gnawed at by men with plows and axes who feared it because it was wilderness, men myriad and nameless even to one another in the land where the old bear had earned a name, and through which ran not even a mortal beast but an anachronism indomitable and invincible out of an old dead time, a phantom, epitome and apotheosis of the old life which the little puny humans swarmed and hacked at in fury of abhorrence and fear like pygmies about the ankles of a drowsing elephant;—the old bear, solitary, indomitable, and alone; widowered, childless and absolved of mortality—old Priam reft of his old wife and outlived all his sons.

First, there is the suspension of meaning in the long sentence, there are colons, semicolons, and dashes (sometimes there are parentheses); the sentence is a small self-contained world. Second, there is the now famous vocabulary: *divined, encompassed, doomed, myriad, nameless, anachronism, indomitable, invincible, phantom, apotheosis, abhorrence, absolved* —words that evoke an older morality and recall an older order. Third, there is a reference to a tragic or noble event in an older romantic literature —"old Priam." Fourth, there is the negative followed by a positive, usually, not this nor this but this; in this sentence it is "and through which ran *not* even a mortal beast *but* an anachronism indomitable and invincible . . ." Fifth, there is repetition: "*solitary*, indomitable, and *alone*." Sixth, there is poetic extension of meaning brought about by an unexpected word, "absolved of mortality," whereas one expected "freed from" or "escaped from." Seventh, there is the metaphor the vehicle of which is foreign to the subject under discussion, but which sheds a light on that subject: thus the relationship of the man to the bear is likened to pygmies troubling a drowsy elephant. And lastly, there is Faulkner's indifference to standard structures—"reft of his old wife and outlived all his sons."

There are several other characteristic devices which are not found in this passage; the use of paradox, as in the oxymoron "roaring silence"; the piling up of adjectives as in the phrase "passionate tragic ephemeral loves of adolescence" (leaving out of commas of course adds to the dreamlike quality, the being above time and space that the true work of art sometimes achieves); the running of two words together (after the manner of Joyce and Cummings), such as "allembracing"and "eunuchmountebank"; and the liking for hyphenated words, as with "rodent-scavengered tomb," "smoke-colored twilight," or better, this sentence: "It (the talking, the telling) seemed (to him, to Quentin) to partake of that logic- and reason-flouting quality upon which it must depend to move the dreamer (verisimilitude) to credulity—horror or pleasure or amazement—depends as completely upon a formal recognition of an acceptance of elapsed and yet-elapsing time as music or a printed tale."

What do we have thus far in the way of devices? We have

1. the long sentence, with colons, semicolons, dashes, and parentheses
2. the vocabulary that evokes an older morality and a realm of high romance
3. the allusions to romantic episodes in history and in literature
4. the sentence that employs a negative or series of negatives followed by a positive
5. the use of synonyms for the purpose of repetition
6. a symbolist or poetic extension of the meaning of words
7. the reaching out for a metaphor or a simile the "vehicle" of which is foreign to the subject being discussed
8. breaking with standard grammatical forms; sometimes solecisms
9. the use of paradox
10. the piling up of adjectives
11. the merging of two words into one word
12. the use of hyphenated words

For many writers the paragraph, or the chapter, or even the over-all argument or thesis is the chief unit of composition. For Faulkner the chief unit is the sentence. His ideal, as certain sections in *Requiem for a Nun* suggest, would be a booklength sentence. His public statements and short speeches show that Faulkner is not a gifted expository writer, and he seems incapable of developing a thesis slowly or subtly. Faulkner's sentences evoke, they do not state. Perhaps I should qualify this argument to the extent of saying the sentence is the chief unit in those books that most depend upon the high style. The parallel phrases, the repetitions, the circling of the subject, or the piling up of adjectives—everything contributes to a self-contained and static world. Faulkner's sentences are spatial rather than analytical. . . .

Ratliff's speech is probably the purest example of the folk style. This is a passage from *The Hamlet:*

> I did, that is, because Ab was laying out in the wagin bed by then, flat on his back with the rain popping him in the face and me on this

slat driving now and watchin' the whiny black horse just turning into a bay horse. Because I was just eight then, and me and Ab had done all our horse trading up and down that lane that run past his lot. So I just drove under the first roof I come to and shaken Ab awake.

Many of Faulkner's characters talk a variety of folk language, including some, like Gavin Stevens, with university degrees. Sometimes they shift from standard to folk usages and back again in a single conversation.

Although they are far from fully accounting for Faulkner's success as a fiction writer, these styles, the high style and the folk style, do account for much of his greatness. There are innumerable passages that would serve very well as set pieces for anthologies. He has always been able to use language as a virtuoso—but if this helps to account for his genius it also helps to account for his failures, especially his more recent failures, *The Fable* and *The Town*. In the former, the high style creates a world out of words, a world that seems hypnotized and bemused by the sounds that went into its making. In the latter, each of the narrators is a cracker-barrel philosopher, pleased as all hell with his shrewd and comic folk idiom. In each book character and dramatized incident have been sacrificed to Faulkner's style, to the voice of high rhetoric, and to the color of the folk language.

Faulkner: The Rhetoric and the Agony

Alfred Kazin

. . . The problem that faces every student of Faulkner's writing is its lack of a center, the gap between his power and its source, that curious abstract magnificence (not only a magnificence of verbal resources alone), which holds his books together, yet seems to arise from debasement or perplexity or a calculating terror. It is the gap between the deliberation of his effects, the intensity of his every conception, and the besetting and depressing looseness, the almost sick passivity, of his basic meaning and purpose. No writer, least of all a novelist so remarkably inventive and robust of imagination, works in problems of pure technique alone; and though it is possible to see in his books, as Conrad Aiken has shown, the marks of a writer devoted to elaboration and wizardry of form, who has deliberately sought to delay and obscure his readers so that the work may have a final and devastating effect, Faulkner's "persistent offering of

Reprinted from Alfred Kazin, "Faulkner: The Rhetoric and the Agony," *Virginia Quarterly Review*, XVIII:3 (Summer 1942), 393–395, 399–400, by permission of the *Virginia Quarterly Review* and the author. Mr. Kazin's views have changed since this was written, and readers should therefore consult as well such essays as "The Stillness of *Light in August*," in *Twelve Original Essays on Great American Novels*, ed. Charles Shapiro (Detroit: Wayne State University Press, 1958), pp. 257–283.

obstacles, a calculated system of screens and obtrusions, of confusions and ambiguous interpolations and delays," seems to spring from an obscure and profligate confusion, a manifest absence of purpose, rather than from an elaborate, coherent aim.

For while Faulkner has brought back into the novel a density of perception and elaboration of means unparalleled since Henry James, his passion for form has not been, like James's, the tortuous expression of an unusual and subtle point of view; it has been a register of too many points of view, and in its way a substitute for a point of view. It is precisely because his technical energy and what must be called a tonal suggestiveness are so profound, precisely because Faulkner's rhetoric is so portentous, that it has been possible to read every point of view into his work and to prove them all. To a certain type of social or moralist critic, his work seems at once the product of some ineffable decadence and a reluctant commentary upon it; to certain sympathetic Southern readers, notably George M. O'Donnell, Faulkner has even seemed a traditional moralist, not to say a belated neo-Humanist, devoted to the "Southern social-economic-ethical tradition which [he] possessed naturally as part of his sensibility"; to many critics and graduate students (no novelist has ever been so rich in citations), he has even seemed a new and distinctive philosophical voice in the novel. For Faulkner's fluency, even his astounding fecundity, has been such that it is almost impossible not to take his improvisations for social philosophy, his turgidity for complexity, and even his passivity for a wise and reflective detachment. It is not strange that he has appeared to be all things to all men, and often simultaneously—a leading exponent of the cult of violence and a subtle philosophical force in the novel; a calculating terrorist and (as in "Sartoris") a slick-magazine sentimentalist of the gladiola South; the most meticulous and misanthropic historian of the South's degeneration and a country-store humorist; an Edgar Allan Poe undecided whether to play Bret Harte or Oswald Spengler. He has been all things to himself. Like Tolstoy at Yasnaya Polyana, he has in one sense been a provincial fastening upon universality, a provincial whose roots are so deep that the very depth and intensity of his immersion have made for a submarine cosmopolitanism of the spirit; his imagination is of itself so extraordinarily rich and uncontrolled, his conscious conceptions so few and indifferent, that he has been able to create an irony of a higher order than he himself shares. For his imagination is not merely creative in the familiar sense; it is devastatingly brilliant, and at the same time impure; it is a kind of higher ventriloquism, a capriciousness at once almost too self-conscious in its trickery and inventiveness, yet not conscious enough, not even direct or responsible enough, in its scope and deliberation. . . .

In the end one must always return to Faulkner's language and his conception of style, for his every character and observation are lost in the spool of his rhetoric, and no more than they can he ever wind himself free. That rhetoric—the most elaborate, intermittently incoherent and ungrammatical, thunderous, polyphonic rhetoric in all American writing—explains why he always plays as great a rôle in his novels as any of his characters, to the point of acting out *their* characters in himself; why he has so often appeared to be a Laocoön writhing in all the outrageous confusions of the ineffable; why he has been able, correlating the South with every imagined principle and criticism of existence, writing in many styles, to project every possible point of view, every shade or extremity of character, and to persuade us of none. In one sense, of course, Faulkner has sought to express the inexpressible, to attain that which is basically incoherent in the novel and analogous only in the most intense mysticism in poetry, where sensations contract and expand like tropical flowers. Yet his novels are not poetry or even "poetic"; they are linked together by a sensational lyricism, itself forever in extremis and gasping for breath that, as Yeats said of rhetoric, is "an attempt of the will to do the work of the imagination." For what one sees always in Faulkner's mountainous rhetoric, with its fantastic pseudo-classical epithets and invertebrate grandeur, its merely verbal intensity and inherent motor violence, is the effort of a writer to impose himself upon that which he cannot create simply and evocatingly. It is the articulation of confusion rather than an evasion of it, mere force passing for directed energy. With all its occasional felicity and stabbing appropriateness of phrase, Faulkner's style is a discursive fog, and it is not strange—so clever and ready is his style the advantage taken *over* confusion—that his extremities should seem intimations of grandeur and the darkness within which his characters move an atmosphere of genuine tragedy. . . .

The Function of Form in The Bear, *Section IV*

WILLIAM V. NESTRICK

In Section IV of *The Bear,* Faulkner, like Joyce, experiments in the deformalization of the novel. Although the variety of stylistic forms of language resembles Joyce's techniques, nothing could be further from Joyce than that authorial-universalist voice connecting the different styles. Almost alone among Joyce's followers, Faulkner violates the literary "rules" of tone and speech style and permits a boy at one time to say

Reprinted from William V. Nestrick, "The Function of Form in *The Bear,* Section IV," *Twentieth Century Literature,* XII:3 (October 1966), 131–137, by permission of *Twentieth Century Literature* and the author.

"I aint never been to the big bottom before" [p. 11 above] and at another time to preach in the involuted and syntactically complex style of Faulkner's voice. In the fourth section, Faulkner flaunts the dramatic form of the dialogue by writing like a formal epic poet. Ike and McCaslin speak with the same voice. Even Ike's preconscious thinking takes on the authorial stance. By keeping spatial and punctuation conventions to a minimum, Faulkner deliberately foils the analytical, rational reader who, in the middle of a paragraph, suddenly stops and wonders just who is doing the talking. The writer enforces the connection and continuity between speakers by placing the "and he" phrases in the "wrong" places. In an age when criticism has cut the ties between the author and the narrator, between the author and his characters, Faulkner ostentatiously projects his authorial voice into his main character. Ike suddenly uses this voice, not because the author crudely identifies with him, but because he is seeking in Ike's response to history the justification for a form of language.

Faulkner juxtaposes Isaac and his cousin "not against the wilderness but against the tamed land" [p. 43]. He focuses, not upon the contrast of the primitive wilderness and the urban sterility of a Memphis, as he does in the hunting story, but rather upon the similarity of the problems that Ike resolves in each story. The opening phrase in this section, "then he was twenty-one," implies that the whole hunting story precedes as a "given." The hunting story formally becomes a kind of dependent clause: "then he was twenty-one" serves as a conclusion and an epitome of the first three sections. Grammatically Ike inherits the hunt at the moment he comes into his social inheritance. Faulkner translates the essential bonds that tie man to the land into those that tie man to man through time. A heritage of land becomes a heritage of history—the history of mankind, of the races, of one Southern family, and of a single individual. Each of these histories is written in a specific form: the Bible, the ledgers, the documents of the Civil War, and the IOU's placed in an unstained tin coffee pot. By transforming each of these histories into "a Legacy, a Thing, possessing weight to the hand and bulk to the eye," Faulkner recreates for history the dilemma of the land in the hunting story. Having learned that he cannot really possess the land, Ike learns that history, too, may become a possession, a property inherited as a socially dead convention. Ike tries to relinquish history as object and to come into a relationship with it in the vital and somewhat primitive way in which he inherited the wilderness from Sam Fathers.

In the hunting story, Ike sees the bear only after he has relinquished his compass, watch and gun. Mythic identity depends upon a sacrifice of social conventions. Sam Fathers substitutes rituals for these conventions. In the fourth section, the Faulknerian voice assumes ritual's function of returning a fluidity to social institutions. As Ike develops this voice, he relinquishes history as object. Freeing himself from dead history, he inherits it in a new way. Both Faulkner and Ike recreate an original fluidity by freeing language from conventional forms. Paradoxically, by freeing language, they give it the special form of the authorial voice. Ike defines his voice against a variety of linguistic styles. In this linguistic spectrum, Section IV reveals the artist conscious of style and capable of imitating forms of language. Ike's own approach to language provides the means of justifying the form of the Faulknerian voice.

Sophonsiba's husband shows in his language, as in his lensless spectacles, that he has taken over the white man's vices:

> "I have a few groceries in the house from my credit account with the merchant in Midnight who banks my pension check for me. I have executed to him a power of attorney to handle it for me as a matter of mutual—" [p. 58]

Instead of freeing himself, he has only imbedded himself more deeply in the lifeless social institutions of the white man. His stilted, grammatically clear speech contrasts the primitive speech of Ike's spiritual father: "He do it every year" (p. 198) or "Maybe he aint nowhere" (p. 201). For Sophonsiba's husband, language expresses only class and social position. The abstract terms of his speech, derived from the kind of conventions Ike relinquished in the woods, draw him away from the primitive conflicts of the psyche, the sense of original sin that Isaac tries to expiate. He falls into the same category as the politicians "to whom the outrage and the injustice were as much abstractions as Tariff or Silver or Immortality . . ." [p. 60].

Faulkner's authorial voice hardly lacks abstraction, but Ike develops this voice only through an immediate experience of the concrete:

> ". . . He had done so much with woods for game and streams for fish and deep rich soil for seed and lush springs to sprout it and long summers to mature it and serene falls to harvest it . . ." [p. 60]

The immediate experience arises from the natural land. Ike feels the modern man's alienation from the spiritual purposefulness the Romantics found. The imagery contributes a sense of richness, fertility contrasted with the sterility of Sophonsiba's husband's conventional language. Ike's speech has a very real simplicity in the nonlatinate, monosyllabic diction and in the rhetorical repetition of constructions. The natural subject confers upon the rhythms and the syntax the positive connotations that Faulkner associates with the wilderness.

The same author who measures the intensity of experience by the grandeur of rhetoric also sets limits to the poetic techniques available for prose. Rhetoric always simplifies because it orders experience; rich language usually tends to become artificial (just as for Spenser evil converted the beautiful into the garish). Its unnatural quality suits a civilization abstracted from real bonds with the natural wilderness and natural man. The poetic technique of alliteration expresses the basic insincerity of the politicians "to whom outrage and injustice were . . . abstractions":

> The other beer and banners . . . and sleight-of-hand and musical handsaws: and the whirling wheels which manufactured for a profit the pristine replacements of the shackles and shoddy garments . . . [p. 60]

Having suggested dramatically the positive and negative connotations of the wilderness and civilization in the hunting story, Faulkner gives examples of the styles that correspond to those connotations. Form and style become means of morally evaluating different kinds of human experience.

Ike learns that simplicity and concreteness are not enough. The form and style of the ledgers and the IOU's of Herbert Beauchamp teach him the necessity of a voice like Faulkner's. In the ledger he reads his father's handwriting "almost completely innocent now even of any sort of spelling as well as punctuation":

> *Miss sophonsiba b dtr t t @ t 1869* [p. 54]

The ledgers are fading just like the footprint of the bear. They have distilled too much. Only a person who can believe that the truth covers all things that touch the heart can infuse this "shorthand hieroglyphic of truth" with the proper understanding. Innocence and compression are inadequate for people who may only bring the rational mind to language and literature. Isaac responds to the crucial entries about Eunice's suicide [pp. 50–51] with the deepest parts of his unconscious. He reads the archaic dialogue in the ledgers:

> *Drownd herself . . .*
> *Who in hell ever heard of a niger drownding him self*
> *Drownd herself*

And he wonders, "*But why?*" Gradually he reconstructs the incestuous act that laid a curse on his family. Innocence merely represses knowledge of this act. By internalizing this historic act in his consciousness, Isaac takes responsibility for it. Consciousness is the prerequisite of conscience. Faulkner pictures in the history of the McCaslin family the incestuous sin that each one of us accrues from his earliest wishes. The ledgers, like the defense mechanisms of the governing conscience, obscure in the distilled innocence of language the original crime.

The last of the scraps of ledger papers in Hubert Beauchamp's tin coffee pot reads "*One silver cup. Hubert Beauchamp*" [p. 74]. The compression expresses an amazed innocence, refusing to believe the fact of dishonesty. Hubert Beauchamp kept his innocence and projected it in the dignified phrasing of his IOU's. McCaslin only sees the copper coins and the dishonesty. Isaac understands the huge irony between the innocence of the language and the coffee pot that gives evidence of the guilty act. He recognizes the meaning that the notes, in their "simplicity not of resignation but merely of amazement," epitomize and distill. "*One silver cup*" is an inadequate form of language: such totally concrete language becomes meaningless unless it is expounded. Its truth is too simple. The ledgers take on a "shadowy life with their passions and complexities" [p. 49] only when the reader adds both knowledge of the 'facts' and a basic sympathy. The writers of the Bible have "to write down the heart's truth out of the heart's driving complexity." "What they were trying to tell, what He wanted said, was too simple . . . It had to be expounded" [p. 46]. Expounding completes Isaac's education; it is the last step in his development of the Faulknerian voice. He learns that the ledgers' distillation needs expounding; he realizes that his own decision not to act, not to inherit, not to pass on a heritage, in order to expiate, to take on himself the whole history of doomed man, to become the third Adam, needs expounding. Perhaps he remembered Compson's admitting that it looked like he just quit [p. 39]. Without expounding, this relinquishment of history as property would seem like quitting. The purpose of the dialogue in Section IV *is* for Isaac to expound to McCaslin his decision to repudiate an external and artificial history:

> "I'm trying to explain to the head of my family something which I have got to do which I don't quite understand myself, not in justification of it but to explain it if I can." [p. 63]

The ledgers fade because they reveal a too simple truth; Isaac briefly redeems them from "the anonymous communal original dust" [p. 47] by bringing to them the "complexities" of the human heart. He expounds them for us just as the writers of the Bible expounded God's truth. The reading of the ledgers, that exercise in Puritan hermeneutics, marks Ike as one of "the doomed and lowly of the earth who have nothing else to read with but the heart" [p. 46]. By "heart," Faulkner does not simply mean emotional responses: he also refers to the deeper responses of the personality: "You don't need to choose [between truths]. The heart already knows" [p. 46]. The most archaic and primitive aspect of the psyche, the childlike conscience, chooses absolutely between moral right and wrong.

This technique of expounding, of amplifying, is the final quality of Faulkner's authorial voice and style. Without the rolling, involuting prose, without its rhetorical rhythms, its consciousness and conscience, *The Bear* would be a simple hunting story. By expounding and meditating upon the concrete elements in the story, Faulkner magnifies the proportion of the story. The *expounding* makes the story archetypal. The bear itself does not fire the imagination until Faulkner links it to our earliest childhood dreams, until he seizes upon our primitive fear and admiration of phallic objects and then makes us see the same quality in the bear:

> he saw the bear, half erect, strike one of the hounds . . . and then, rising and rising as though it would never stop, stand erect again . . . [p. 35]

It is a truism that mythology is psychology, but this definition does not attempt to explain the process of transforming a simple story into myth. The bear hunt may be in itself archetypal. Yet Faulkner undeniably stimulates a more immediate response to this mythic quality by expounding the psychological and anthropological aspects of the story. The expansive style, the "over-writing," the technique of claiming that language is too limited ("it was *more* than justice . . . *more* than vengeance")—all magnify the story into gigantic, even grotesque, proportions.

Section IV itself stretches the narrative to include all of time, the totality of the universe in a sentence fragment. Through this totality there persists a sense of unity, just as the rhythmic simplicity of Faulkner's rhetoric underlies the syntactical complexities of the expounding. Faulkner extends the authorial voice from the deepest psychological thinking to the consciousness of God:

> He had seen how in individual cases they were capable of anything any height or depth . . . and therefore must accept responsibility for what He Himself had done in order to live with Himself. [p. 59]

Unconsciously Ike repeats the words of God when he explains to McCaslin, "I have got myself to have to live with" [p. 63]. Faulkner connects the thought of God with that of Ike when God considers the brotherhood men establish in suffering:

> so that He said . . . *Apparently they can learn nothing save through suffering, remember nothing save when underlined in blood.* [p. 61]

Verbal parallels reveal that Ike is continuing this thought within his own preconscious when he considers the Negro's misuse of freedom:

> so that he thought *Apparently there is a wisdom beyond even that learned through suffering necessary for a man to distinguish between liberty and license.* [p. 64]

Probably no writer since the Renaissance has shown such an ability to bind together the human, the natural and the divine orders. In Faulkner's literary universe, the form of the authorial voice of a responsible conscience links the orders.

By putting the totality of the world into the fourth section, Faulkner translates his thematic concerns into formal novelistic techniques. God, according to Ike's explanation, gave men suzerainty over the earth "to hold the earth mutual and intact in the communal anonymity of brotherhood" [p. 44]. For a thousand years "men fought over the fragments of that collapse until at last even the fragments were exhausted" [p. 45].

Even the wilderness, which Major de Spain bought from Thomas Sutpen, is only a fragment [p. 43]. The memory, however, can keep a totality intact, through the medium of language. Ike still hears the words McCaslin spoke about truth, "intact in this twilight as in that one seven years ago, no louder still because they did not need to be because they would endure" [p. 68]. The ledgers too have managed to keep a totality intact, "as the stereopticon condenses into one instantaneous field the myriad minutia of its scope" [p. 69]. Ike *internalizes* the ledgers in order to keep the totality intact in a single instant. The yellow pages become "a part of his consciousness" [p. 53]. Ike can only expiate the doom of man by making the totality of man *endure intact* in the internal self: he relinquishes only the temporal fragmentary part that his individual life would play in the course of history. Faulkner demands that the reader make the same internalization of everything that has gone before. He continually plays on the phrase "and that was all" [pp. 52, 53, 59] to refer to everything that has happened before in the section. He translates the suspense of the hunting story into the formalistic suspension of Section IV. By stretching out the syntax, Faulkner requires the reader to hold the elements in a state of fluidity. The internal suspension keeps the totality of history intact. By giving up the fragmentation of punctuation and logical grammar, the reader makes a relinquishment of lifeness conventions, a relinquishment that parallels Ike's.

Faulkner's omniscience of a totality has the perspective of time. His vision coalesces in the present both the past and the future: he speaks of the white race "which for two hundred years had held them [the Negroes] in bondage and from which for another two hundred years not even a bloody civil war would have set them free." This technique corresponds to Ike's internalization of all past history and his preconscious thought which foreknows that he will never shoot the bear and that Sam will die. This looking forward and backward parallels the stylistic technique of repeating linguistic elements in order to suggest the unending continuum of time. Each step further into the past necessitates another turn of language upon itself:

> It was never Father's and Uncle Buddy's to bequeath me to repudiate because it was never Grandfather's to bequeath them to bequeath me to repudiate because it was never old Ikkemotubbe's to sell to Grandfather for bequeathment and repudiation. But it was never Ikkemotubbe's father's father's to bequeath Ikkemotubbe to sell . . . [p. 44]

The language retrogresses before it moves ahead. Repetition reproduces sequences of time: "Dispossessed of Canaan, and those who dispossessed him dispossessed him dispossessed" [p. 45]. In the cyclic development of the repetitions, it is no longer possible to tell whether the dispossessed man came first or the dispossessing. Cause and effect are confused as "dispossessed" is used as a verb and as an adjective. By leaving the cycle unfinished (without a final "him"), Faulkner suggests a process infinitely extending into the future. Temporality in language reaches toward the infinite past and the infinite future. The form of Section IV trails off at the beginning and end to include everything that precedes and follows. This view of past and future explains why Ike, sacrificing himself to expiate the sinful past, not only has to give up the external historical legacies but also has to step out of the eternal procession of generations, "uncle to half a county and still father to none" [p. 70]. Ike repudiates the history of the ledgers and legacy as property and the future as a means of passing on the curse of fragmentary property. At the same time, however, he internalizes both the spiritual past and the future of all the races he has inherited from the paternal Sam Fathers. Ike paradoxically unites the totality of human experience in the conscious and preconscious processes of his personality. By means of this internalization, he coalesces all time in an instant of the present. Paradoxically, too, Section IV unites, in its form, the totality of time in a single phrase, an instantaneous suspension which the reader must hold in mind at one time. In form, the section is a fragment, a fragment, nevertheless, that remains spatially intact. Stylistically, the rhetoric combines a simplicity of repetition and rhythm with a grandeur of sustained and periodic expounding. The style mediates between a "too simple" truth and "the driving complexity" of the human heart. Faulkner's voice fulfills the classical criterion of harmony: its difficult balance of simplicity and grandeur imitates the dramatic tension of unity and totality in Ike's internalization of history. The final effect is formative, for the style and form require the reader to imitate Ike's relinquishment of dead conventions. Accompanying this deformalization, Faulkner's authorial voice infuses the newly freed materials with a moral consciousness, and stylistically imitates Ike's definition of a truth covering all things that touch the heart. The style becomes functional, for it reproduces in the reader's response to the artistic work the process of Ike's response to history. This integrating harmony ultimately justifies Faulkner's artistic uses of form in *The Bear.*

The Saxon Beauty and the Three Black Bears

MARTHA BENNETT STILES

Once in the middle, center of the Okeyouchokee Forest lived three black bears where Father Bear (a tall, silent, but not overly silent, either; speaking up when Mother Bear had the porridge too hot or someone had

Reprinted from Martha Bennett Stiles, "The Saxon Beauty and the Three Black Bears," *Generation* (Spring 1958), pp. 29–30, by permission of the author.

rumpled the cushions on his pet chair: chair made by his grandfather who had been part red bear, part black zoo captive, in those days when the black bear's position had been less desirable perhaps, perhaps more circumscribed but possibly not, but less equivocal too than now, now that a bear was free but had to keep to the woods or get shot by men; bear) had built them a house, with window boxes and such; where they could be bears and never see any men to remind them that they were, after all, bears, not men.

It (the sanctuary) housed (sheltered) in addition to this tall proud male bear Mother Bear and Baby Bear, tall too, for his years, but not so tall as his father; black, too, as all black bears are in some degree, but not so black as his mother, who was (she, Mother Bear, was) blacker. Mother Bear had not been born in captivity but her mother had, whose mother had danced for gypsies, or rather for the audiences these gypsies gathered but were not well paid by, or appreciated by, indeed were even feared, loathed, looked down upon by.

One day Mother Bear made porridge, a kind of pottage but they didn't know that, had forgotten that; had forgotten it came from *pot* a pot, lost it from their memories before they were born even; boiling the (some) leguminous or perhaps farinaceous substance in water, or milk (in a liquid, then) stirring and waiting waiting and watching watching and stirring until it was done, finished, ready to eat

but not quite ready either, it (the porridge) being still steaming, exhalation of warm hot (milk, liquid) vapor curling reaching winding groping wriggling toward the ceiling when Mother Bear took it from the stove which was electric now, now that even the bears themselves no longer chopped wood, carried ashes, stirred the fire, Montgomery Ward having become, one might almost say, handyman to the whole bear community, who named their sons Gomry or Ward, or even Roebuck if some forgotten taint of *droit du seigneur* left in them some nonconformist streak, ability, tendency, pride.

Steaming then it (the porridge) was placed on the table—oh, yes, there was a table too, in the bear's (Father Bear's) house to cool until it was edible, could be eaten without burning the tongue throat gullet gut of Father Bear, and Mother Bear and Baby Bear too, who all picked up malacca canes (they had those too, even then) and went for a walk in the Forest, immemorial, static, immemorial.

That was when Goldy Snocks, like her tribe tow headed blue eyed fair skinned (Goldy Snocks) not very bright came tripping or wandering or blundering or anyhow coming up the path to the bear's house even though she had been told by Missis Snocks, Uncle Sickly Snocks' distant cousin by marriage with the Jukes (Kalikaks?) and married to his nephew too, so there was a double relationship, not to go into the Forest, immemorial, timeless, immemorial. "What uh purty house" said Little

Goldy Snocks, scratching, or not so much scratching as currying, her head and went inside without knocking because that too was like her tribe and saw there the table with the steaming, but not steaming so much now since time—time that had brought Goldy Snocks into the world as surely as it would take her out or at least would help and who would miss her?—had passed and the porridge was cooler; bowls of porridge, and she

decided to taste some whom by her appearance and, yes, behaviour, no Snocks could say was not a true Snocks, although paternities were not their surest points, and grabbed a spoon (Little Goldy Snocks never picked up something without seeming to seize, capture, it) grabbed a spoon and tasted the first bowlful. "Crawlin Hawg Waller, thet porrdge is too hot" exclaimed (cried) Goldy Snocks, and moved to the next bowl, basin, tureen, or whatever Mother Bear liked to call it now that her bear talk was taking on a thin and sometimes treacherous (because deceptive) veneer of men's talk. "Phth-h-h-h-t" spit Goldy Snocks, "thet'n's too cole" and she took up the third bowl, who was determined to eat something since she was hungry, always—and why not Baby Bear's porridge, since she had as much right to it as anything she (the Snockses) ate? She was a Snocks (one of them) and she ate it all up.

Feeling full, replete, sated, packed, satiated, surfeited, glutted, gorged, surfeit-gorged, fed to the gills or neck, overfed, she—Goldy Snocks now—sat down in the nearest chair or even throne and leaned back, not tilting, for it was too big a chair or throne for that, but leaning until her back —Goldy Snocks'—touched its back, but not for long, because the chair (or throne) was too hard, not soft enough. Into the next one then, not knowing it was a bear's chair, a bear's house she had entered, she sat and, because it was she found too old, too sag-bottomed, like Mother Bear herself, got up once more, still seeking questing perfection finding it at last but for a brief moment only in Baby Bear's seat. Brief because, with scarcely a warning creak cry give crackle it, the baby bear's seat, split from under her, Goldy Snocks, dumping her, Goldy Snocks still, on the floor hard, harder than even Father Bear's—whose great-grandfather the red bear never sat in chairs—chair, or throne.

"Good Gawd Ah reckon!" shrieked, cried protesting, yelled Goldy Snocks—to express disapprobation, discontent—and leapt up, or anyhow got up, since those of her—large—family or clan or even race or nation were not noted for precipitate action, or even action, as a rule.

Rubbing not currying this time that portion of her which was (it was) bruised Little Goldy Snocks ascended muttering the stairs—not knowing whither they led, but ascending nonetheless—who had been bruised—Goldy Snocks—and came at length (short or long) to the bedroom, sleeping quarters (they slept there) (the bears) of Father, Mother, and, not to hold anything back, Baby Bear. This time she was unable to sample the first, nearest, bed because it was too high, far off the ground for her (she was a Snocks) to reach and turning to the (relatively) lower one next to it she sank luxuriously but too luxuriously since she right away got up again, not liking it, into Mother Bear's bed.

No, she didn't like it, it was too yielding, not sufficiently rejecting of her (Snocks) weight, too immersing in bedclothes—quilts and sheets and coverlets and blankets, and yes, even a spread now, in a bear's house —so she, getting impatient now, wanting to go to bed, as what girl —what Snocks—in particular, what Snocks girl—didn't, she, who was a girl, and a Snocks, a Snocks girl even, transferred or shifted if you like herself to Baby Bear's bed. Who wasn't there then, any more than he had been when she busted up his chair.

There she slept (nor woke) finding perfection at last, in that form of narcosis, in oblivion, in peace or if you like simply in digestive processes. There she was sleeping, still, when the bears, all of them, came home and proud-silent, voluble-murmurous, eager-excited, according to their natures, ages, followed her trail, her spoor (for she *was* a *Snocks*) from porridge to chairs, upstairs, knowing all the time and fearing too maybe but without being afraid and she

what course would—could—dared Goldy Snocks take when awakening she beheld (not dreamt, beheld) Father Bear, and Mother Bear and Baby Bear too, coming in the door? Not saying anything, coming into the room; a bear's room, that she, a human, had entered, walked into, uninvited; though they could not have come into her, Snocks, home, and she knew that; knew that and leapt, this time leapt unequivocally, out of that bed, Baby Bear's bed, and fled through the window through the forest (immemorial, immutable, immemorial), called the Okeyouchokee Forest by the people who lived there, called it anything (nobody else ever called it anything, ever thought of it even) to her own home house dwelling domicile, nor did she tell the truth, whatever that is, about where she had been to Uncle Sickly Snocks' niece by marriage, who was, after all, her mother [and curiously enough that was by marriage too, but that (curiosity) is another story, tale, legend].

Appendixes

Included here are materials which provide additional information about the McCaslin genealogy and the chronology of "The Bear." The annotated bibliography of published commentary and the listing of Faulkner's canon (based on the latest scholarship) should enable the reader to explore further material relevant to "The Bear" and Faulkner's other work.

The McCaslin Genealogy

DOROTHY TUCK

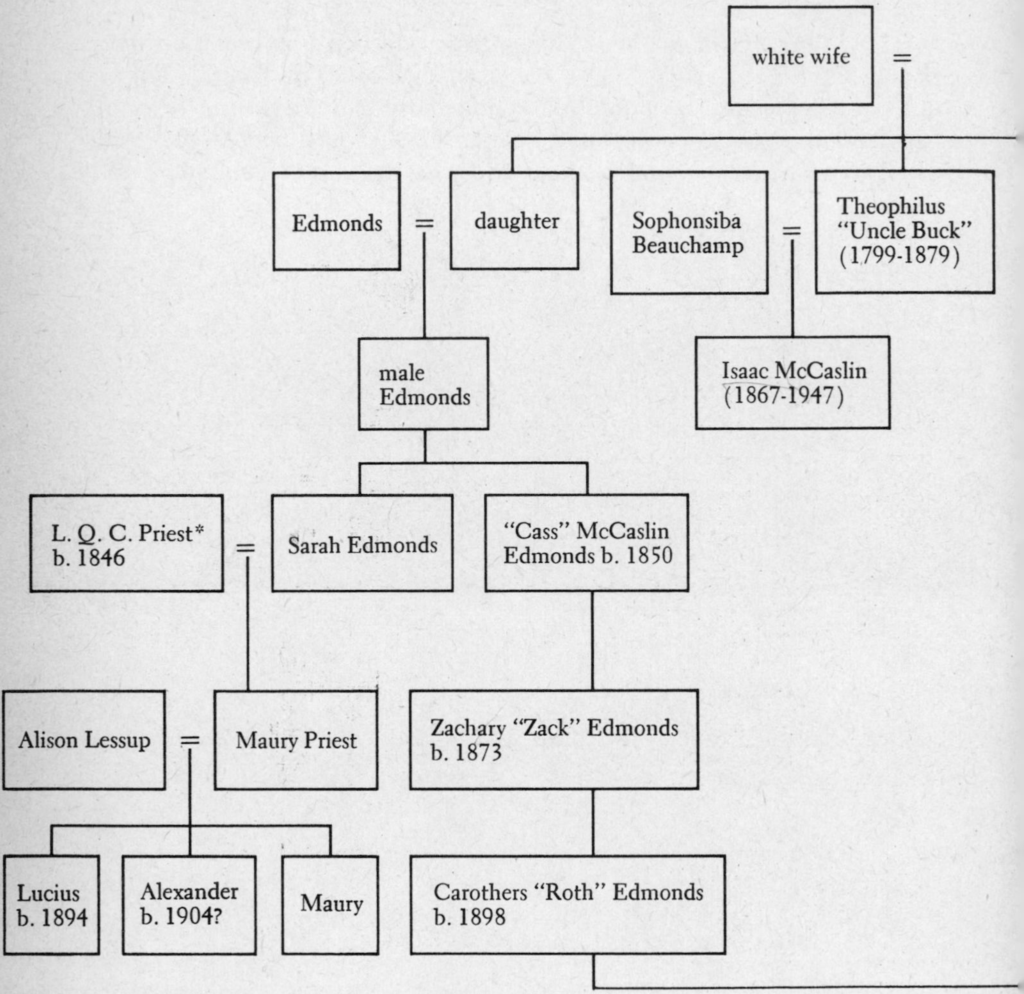

*distant kinsman of L. Q. C McCaslin

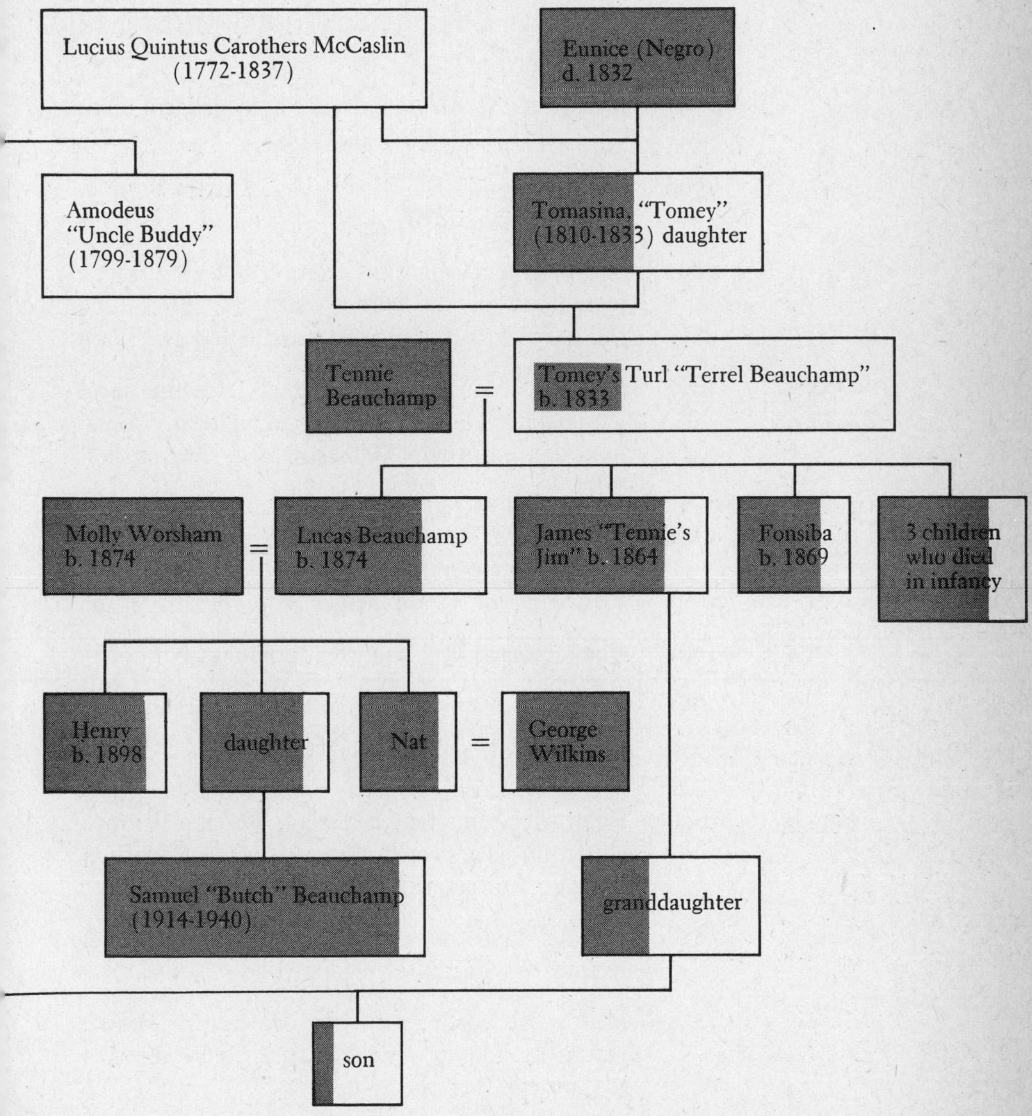
Lucius Quintus Carothers McCaslin
(1772-1837)
Eunice (Negro)
d. 1832
Amodeus
"Uncle Buddy"
(1799-1879)
Tomasina, "Tomey"
(1810-1833) daughter
Tennie
Beauchamp
=
Tomey's Turl "Terrel Beauchamp"
b. 1833
Molly Worsham
b. 1874
=
Lucas Beauchamp
b. 1874
James "Tennie's
Jim" b. 1864
Fonsiba
b. 1869
3 children
who died
in infancy
Henry
b. 1898
daughter
Nat
=
George
Wilkins
Samuel "Butch" Beauchamp
(1914-1940)
granddaughter
son

The Chronicle of Ike McCaslin

THOMAS J. WERTENBAKER, JR.

	1772	Lucius Quintus CAROTHERS McCASLIN born
	1787?	Carothers McCaslin buys land for a farm from Chickasaw Chief Ikkemotubbe
	1799?	"BUCK" and "BUDDY" McCASLIN born to Carothers McCaslin
	1809?	Sam Fathers, son of Ikkemotubbe and black woman, born and traded with his mother by the chief to Carothers McCaslin for a gelding
Dec. 25,	1832	Eunice, a slave married to McCaslin slave Thucydides, learns that her daughter is pregnant by Carothers McCaslin and drowns herself
June 27,	1837	Carothers McCaslin dies. Buck and Buddy McCaslin, now running the farm, build a log cabin to live in, move the slaves into the big house
	1843?	Boon Hogganbeck, quarter-Indian, is born
	1851?	Carothers McCASLIN EDMONDS ("Cass") is born, a grandson of the sister of Buck and Buddy
March 3,	1856	Buck McCaslin buys the slave Percival Brownlee from slave dealer (later General) Nathan Bedford Forrest at Cold Water for $265
Oct. 3,	1856	Having done $100 damage, Brownlee is freed, refuses to leave, later disappears
	1859	Buddy McCaslin wins the slave girl Tennie (Beauchamp) in a poker game, to be married to Tomey's Terrel
	1862	Brownlee reappears, conducts revival meetings on McCaslin farm

Adapted by the editors from Thomas J. Wertenbaker, Jr., "Faulkner's Point of View and the Chronicle of Ike McCaslin," *College English*, XXIV:3 (December 1962), 169–178. Adapted and reprinted with the permission of the National Council of Teachers of English and the author.

	Dec. 29,	1864	"Tennie's Jim" born to Terrel and Tennie
		1865	Civil War ends. Buck McCaslin returns to the farm, marries Sophonsiba Beauchamp ("Sibbey"); they move to big house on McCaslin farm. Hunting parties begin on Tallahatchie River bottom land bought by Major de Spain from Thomas Sutpen. Logging train makes its first trip to Big Bottom, frightens a bear in a tree
IKE'S AGE			
0	Oct./Nov.	1867	ISAAC Beauchamp McCASLIN ("Ike") born to Buck and Sibbey McCaslin
0		1867	Hubert Beauchamp, Ike's uncle and godfather, seals 50 gold pieces in a silver cup as a legacy for Ike at age 21
1½		1869	Sophonsiba ("Fonsiba") is born to Terrel and Tennie
5		1873?	Buck and Buddy McCaslin die; management of farm passes to McCaslin Edmonds
6	March 17,	1874	LUCIUS ("Lucas") BEAUCHAMP is born to Terrel and Tennie
6		1874?	Silver cup, wrapped in burlap in closet, changes shape overnight
7		1875?	Young Ike McCaslin shoots rabbits near McCaslin farm
9	March	1877	Sam Fathers goes to live on Major de Spain's land in Big Bottom
9		1877?	Ike's mother dies
10	Nov.	1877	Ike McCaslin is taken to the Big Bottom on his first deer-bear hunt
10½	June	1878	Ike goes alone into the woods, discards his gun, watch, and compass, sees Old Ben
11	Nov.	1878	With Sam Fathers Ike kills his first buck
12	Nov.	1879	Ike kills his first bear; kills a buck; sees Old Ben
12½	June	1880?	With Sam, Ike and the "fyce" corner Old Ben but let him escape

13	March	1881	A doe and fawn, and later a colt, are found killed: Old Ben suspected
13½	June	1881	Sam captures the killer, a wild mongrel Airedale dog, "Lion"
15	Nov.	1882	With Lion the hunters twice corner Old Ben. Boon shoots 5 times and misses. General Compson "draws blood"
16	Dec.	1883	Ike accompanies Boon to Memphis for whiskey. The hunters close in on Old Ben. With Lion, Boon kills the bear. Lion dies. Sam Fathers "quits" and dies, probably with Boon's help
16	Dec.	1883?	Ike reads the ledgers in commissary on McCaslin farm
17	Nov.	1884	The hunters (without Major de Spain) go farther into the woods to hunt
17	Dec.	1884	Major de Spain leases the timber rights on his land
17½	June	1885	Ike revisits de Spain's land, visits the graves of Sam and Lion, finds Boon under a gum tree
18	Dec. 29,	1885	Tennie's Jim disappears on his 21st birthday. Ike traces him to Tennessee to give him his $1000, but loses him
18½	Summer	1886	A Negro man takes Fonsiba to Arkansas to be his wife
19	Dec.	1886	Ike takes Fonsiba's $1000 to a bank at Midnight, Arkansas; orders her paid $3 a month
		1886	Cass hears Brownlee is proprietor of a New Orleans brothel
21	Oct./Nov.	1888	In the commissary on his 21st birthday, in conversation with his cousin McCaslin Edmonds, Ike relinquishes his title to the McCaslin farm. Finds Uncle Hubert's "legacy" to be a tin coffee pot stuffed with coppers and I.O.U.'s. Accepts as a loan a "pension" of $30 a month from McCaslin Edmonds
21½	June	1889	Ike, now a carpenter, repays his "loan"

22		1890?	Ike marries a girl who has been living on a farm where he and his partner have rebuilt the barn
27	March 17,	1895	Lucas, on his 21st birthday, appears at Jefferson and asks Ike for the rest of Carothers McCaslin's legacy
73		1941	Ike hunts the delta with descendants of his former companions, meets a granddaughter of Tennie's Jim and her child by Roth
80		1947?	Projected year of Ike McCaslin's death

*Bibliography**

GENERAL

BASSO, HAMILTON *et al.* "William Faulkner: Man and Writer," *Saturday Review,* XLV:29 (July 28, 1962), 10–26. A collection of critical remarks and essays, photographs and cartoons of Faulkner which provided an assessment of his career at the time of his death.

BLOTNER, JOSEPH. *William Faulkner's Library—A Catalogue.* Charlottesville: University Press of Virginia, 1964. A listing of Faulkner's personal library emphasizing books he consulted and his reactions to them; this work is important in tracing Faulkner's sources and influences on his work.

BUCKLEY, G. T. "Is Oxford the Original of Jefferson in William Faulkner's Novels?" *PMLA,* LXXVI:4, Part 1 (September 1961), 447–454. Faulkner's fictional locales are "a composite or abstraction of a half dozen small county seat towns of North Mississippi."

FAULKNER, WILLIAM. *Essays, Speeches, and Public Letters,* ed. James B. Meriwether. New York: Random House, 1965. An anthology, usually from the author's own typescripts, of essays, introductions, book reviews, speeches, and his public letters which, in his later years, showed increasing concern with national and international events.

HARVARD ADVOCATE, CXXXV:2 (November 1951). This special issue devoted to commentary on Faulkner has contributions on his style by Alfred

* Comments of four pages and fewer have been omitted because of limitations in space.

Kazin, his retelling of stories by Leonard Doran and further remarks by Conrad Aiken, John Crowe Ransom, Archibald MacLeish, and Albert Camus.

Massey, Linton R. *"Man Working," 1919–1962: William Faulkner. A Catalogue of the William Faulkner Collections at the University of Virginia.* Charlottesville: Bibliographical Society of the University of Virginia, 1968. A complete listing of Faulkner's writings, including manuscripts and (correted) galley proofs; there are separate sections listing works related to Faulkner and his estate. Illustrated.

Meriwether, James B. *The Literary Career of William Faulkner: A Bibliographic Study.* Princeton: Princeton University Library, 1961. Based on the Faulkner exhibition held at Princeton Library in 1957 this indexed bibliography describes the manuscript papers now at Virginia (see above), descriptions of English editions, a check list of translations, a list of motion pictures on which Faulkner worked or which were adapted from his work, and a record of Faulkner's schedule of sending his early stories to prospective publishers. Well indexed.

Millgate, Michael. *The Achievement of William Faulkner.* London: Constable and Company, Ltd., and New York: Random House, 1965. The most detailed and authorized biography preceding that of Joseph Blotner is followed here by a rich textual and critical study of each of Faulkner's works. Unlike most critical studies, Millgate turns repeatedly to letters, interviews, manuscripts, typescripts and corrected proofs of Faulkner's work.

Sleeth, Irene Lynn. "William Faulkner: A Bibliography of Criticism," *Twentieth Century Literature,* VIII:1 (April 1962), 18–43. A comprehensive bibliography of American criticism of Faulkner from the early 1920s to early 1961 and selected foreign criticism.

Warren, Robert Penn. "William Faulkner," from *Selected Essays.* New York: Random House, 1958, pp. 59–79. Faulkner defines the moral confusion of today by contrasting it with a traditional order; his work is a "backward-looking" for a moral center. Slavery, not the Negro, is the curse of the South and the black cross is for Faulkner the chief white man's burden.

"THE BEAR" IN RELATION TO FAULKNER'S OTHER WORKS

Adam, Percy G. "The Franco-American Faulkner," *Tennessee Studies in Literature,* V (1960), 1–11. French and American critics of Faulkner agree, among other things, that he can create real people and that his work has technical virtuosity and intellectual appeal.

Adams, Richard P. "Faulkner and the Myth of the South," *Mississippi Quarterly,* XIV:3 (Summer 1961), 131–137. Faulkner deals primarily with man in motion, and in fluid (not fixed) time.

Beck, Warren. "Faulkner and the South," *The Antioch Review*, I:1 (March 1941), 82–94. In an early attempt to recognize Faulkner's stature and genius, Beck argues that Faulkner is not overly romantic about the aristocratic past but is melancholic in his concern for man as sinning and needing redemption (as with the Sartorises). The blacks' patience combats the white man's sins.

Beja, Morris. "A Flash, A Glare: Faulkner and Time," *Renascence*, XVI:3 (Spring 1964), 133–141, 145. Faulkner's characters have insights coming as "sudden revelations" based on confrontations with "evanescent trivia." His intention is " 'to arrest for a believable moment' the experience of life."

Brien, Dolores E. "William Faulkner and the Myth of Woman," *Research Studies*, XXXV:2 (June 1967), 132–140. The ambiguity or unreality of the myth of Southern woman, chaste and devoted, causes Faulkner's men to reconstitute her in new and different unrealistic terms or to remain estranged. His women are "seldom individualized human beings, but shadowy, enigmatic creatures. . . ."

Brown, Calvin S. "Faulkner's Geography and Topography," *PMLA*, LXXVII:5 (December 1962), 652–659. Faulkner bases his settings on Lafayette County, Mississippi, sometimes distorting facts to suggest universal meaning.

Doyle, Charles. "The Moral World of Faulkner," *Renascence*, XIX:1 (Fall 1966), 3–12. Faulkner's major work, his life, and his remarks all suggest he is a humanist, rather than a believer in orthodox religion, portraying man's deep awareness of good and evil and dramatizing stoicism. He transforms the aesthetic consciousness into a moral consciousness.

Faulkner, William. *Big Woods*. New York: Random House, 1955. This collection reprints "The Bear" (without Part IV), "The Old People," and "A Bear Hunt" [a tall tale from *The Saturday Evening Post*, CCVI (February 10, 1934), 8ff.]. "Race at Morning" is new. Interchapters tell the history of the wilderness and are drawn from "Red Leaves," "Delta Autumn," and Part IV of "The Bear."

———. "A Courtship," from *Collected Stories*. New York: Random House, 1950, pp. 361–380. The most comic of Faulkner's wilderness tales in the tradition of the tall tale; here Boon Hogganbeck's father Dave, a captain of a steamboat used in the slave trade, and Doom (before he becomes the Chief) compete in extravagant contests for the Indian Herman Basket's sister. An opening passage discusses the whites' apportionment of land to the Indians and how the Indians came to possess what Ike will call unpossessable.

———. "The Fire and the Hearth," from *Go Down, Moses*. New York: Random House, 1942. The first story of Lucas Beauchamp, modern black survivor of the McCaslin miscegenation, and his defense of mixed blood as well as his foolish hunt for gold. Important for flashbacks on Ike's and Lucius' heritage; see especially Chapter III, Part 1.

———. "Red Leaves," from *These Thirteen*. New York: J. Cape and H. Smith, 1931, pp. 127–166. Sam Fathers' ancestor, the Choctaw Indian chief Doom, is corrupted through miscegenation and slavery; through ownership of land he becomes "burgher-like": already slavery breeds indolence in the slave owner.

Glicksberg, Charles I. "The World of William Faulkner," *Arizona Quarterly*, V:1 (Spring 1949), 46–58, 85–88. Faulkner's works are nihilistic, nightmarish representations of evil and sin showing Faulkner's philosophy of naturalistic pessimism.

Guerard, Albert. "Justice in Yoknapatawpha County: Some Symbolic Motifs in Faulkner's Later Writing," *Faulkner Studies*, II:4 (Winter 1954), 49–57. Faulkner's early works do not simply present an apocalyptic doom; his later works show the Northern Snopeses punishing the South for slavery by exploiting it.

Hoffman, Frederick J., and Olga W. Vickery. *William Faulkner: Three Decades of Criticism*. East Lansing: Michigan State University Press, 1960. A fine collection of significant critical essays on various works by Faulkner, including one on "The Bear" by William Van O'Connor, prefaced by a concise survey of Faulkner criticism. [This is a revision of the editors' *William Faulkner: Two Decades of Criticism* (East Lansing: Michigan State College Press, 1951).]

Holman, C. Hugh. "William Faulkner: The Anguished Dream of Time," in *Three Modes of Modern Southern Fiction*. Athens: University of Georgia Press, 1966, pp. 27–47. Faulkner borrows from earlier Southern and Southwestern writing a sense of frontier humor, local color, and romance which he raises to high tragedy through rhetoric and an emphasis on the cosmic nature of events.

Jackson, James Turner. "Delta Cycle: A Study of William Faulkner," *Chimera*, V:1 (Autumn 1946), 3–14. A somewhat personal description of Faulkner's Mississippi fiction as illustrative of a seasonal and an historical cycle.

Litz, Walton. "William Faulkner's Moral Vision," *Southwest Review*, XXXVII:3 (Summer 1952), 200–209. A single moral vision pervades Faulkner's works from 1929 to 1952; he sees man as having inner moral freedom "to endure and expatiate the evils which he inherits from the past," as having received the earth in trust but having "of his own free will . . . violated the conditions of stewardship." Thus Faulkner's man has broken "the foreordained pattern of respect between man and nature" in the South and left "a fragmented and loveless society suffering under the curse of its past history."

McGrew, Julia. "Faulkner and the Icelanders," *Scandinavian Studies,* XXXI:1 (February 1959), 1–14. Faulkner's interest in the nature of the epic hero and heroic choice stems from an artist's recognition of an historic situation that illustrates "the total disruption of a social and moral order and a resulting conflict between the dying and the newer order."

Rinaldi, Nicholas M. "Game Imagery and Game-Consciousness in Faulkner's Fiction," *Twentieth Century Literature,* X:3 (October 1964), 108–118. Game imagery in Faulkner suggests his characters see experience as a contest, but they are dehumanized in their "game" relationships which are racial, sexual, legal, military, and personal. Only in "The Bear" does a central figure decline to follow the "rules of the game" pursuing a life of sacrifice instead.

Robb, Mary Cooper. *William Faulkner: An Estimate of His Contribution to the American Novel.* Pittsburgh: University of Pittsburgh Press, 1957. An eclectic study which, among other things, sees Faulkner as a writer concerned with nature (what is right) opposed to custom (what is done); as a man reacts to nature so he reacts to man. Faulkner's characters face essentially Christian ethical choices.

Roth, Russell. "William Faulkner: The Pattern of Pilgrimage," *Perspective,* II:4 (Summer 1949), 246–254. *Go Down, Moses* effectively summarizes Faulkner's work through 1942. Ike tries to avoid Snopesism by gaining "intuitive strength and humility" from Southern aristocracy and humanist motivations and the ability to act from the Sartoris perspective.

Rubin, Louis. "The South and the Faraway Country," *Virginia Quarterly Review,* XXXVIII:3 (Summer 1962), 444–459. Southern writers, aware of their allegiance to a community which existed before industrialism, have generally left the South; only Faulkner remained. But he, too, felt alienated and his work is morally centered, a direct reaction to the disruptive forces of present social change.

Sartre, Jean-Paul. "American Novelists in French Eyes," *Atlantic Monthly,* CLXXVIII (August 1946), 114–118. Europeans are more responsive than Americans to Faulkner and other American novelists, seeing them as "manifestations of American liberty" commenting on universal conditions. American writers have influenced Camus, deBeauvoir, and others.

Stewart, Randall. "Poetically the Most Accurate Man Alive," *Modern Age,* VI:1 (Winter 1961–1962), 81–90. Faulkner's poetic accuracy depends upon (1) his understanding of community, (2) his portrayal of the mythic struggle between humanism and naturalism, (3) his sense of place, and (4) his relation to Southern writing, especially with Gothic horror tales and frontier humor.

TURNER, ARLIN. "William Faulkner, Southern Novelist," *Mississippi Quarterly*, XIV:3 (Summer 1961), 117–130. Faulkner is not as traditional as some have argued, for he is skeptical of the benefits of plantation life, he creates subtle and successful characters of low life, and his views of nature and the black are more complex. His originality in characterization makes him a great writer.

VICKERY, OLGA W. *The Novels of William Faulkner: A Critical Interpretation.* Baton Rouge: Louisiana State University Press, 1959. Part II is a perceptive and philosophically oriented attempt to summarize many of Faulkner's views after the exhaustive examination of each novel in Part I. Faulkner's use of memory, legend, and point of view allow him to achieve a fresh sense of reality; and his language as both technique and theme. Faulkner sees man as a social being who has been disappointed by law and religion and finds salvation in his individual consciousness.

WATKINS, FLOYD C. "The Gentle Reader and Mr. Faulkner's Morals," *The Georgia Review*, III:1 (Spring 1959), 68–75. Faulkner's characters are not depraved and immoral but, rather, lifelike. Faulkner is honest but too immediate and realistic to be accepted easily as a classical author.

FAULKNER ON FAULKNER

BURGER, NASH K. "A Story to Tell: Agee, Wolfe, Faulkner," *The South Atlantic Quarterly*, LXIII:1 (Winter 1964), 32–43. James Agee, Thomas Wolfe, and Faulkner, in different ways, illustrate that the Southern writer true to his material is regional, historical, and universal. Only Faulkner of these three never left the South for any extended period; he transformed his own county into a myth.

CANTWELL, ROBERT. "The Faulkners: Recollections of a Gifted Family," *New World Writing*. New York: New American Library, 1952, pp. 300–315. A reporter for *Time* visits Faulkner's home and describes the author, his conversation, his house, and his use of his ancestors.

CARTER, HODDING. "The Forgiven Faulkner," *Journal of Inter-American Studies*, VII:2 (April 1965), 137–147. An informal and occasionally ironic account of Faulkner's peculiar "genius" of mind and character; includes references to his various opinions on the blacks.

COINDREAU, MAURICE EDGAR. "The Faulkner I Knew," *Shenandoah* XVII:2 (Winter 1965), 27–35. An affectionate, honest account of Faulkner by his chief French translator and their association of more than twenty years.

Coughlan, Robert. *The Private World of William Faulkner*. New York: Harper and Bros., 1954. A biography emphasizing Faulkner's Southern culture and environment as related to his life and writing. Next to *Old Times in the Faulkner Country* this is the most anecdotal book on Faulkner.

Falkner, Murry C. *The Falkners of Mississippi*. Baton Rouge: Louisiana State University Press, 1962. A brother's nostalgic and usually affectionate memoir of Faulkner and their family.

Green, A. Wigfall. "William Faulkner at Home," *The Sewanee Review*, XL:3 (Summer 1932), 294–306. A detailed description of the town and county on which Faulkner based his work and a highly personal summary of the early novels.

Jelliffe, Robert A., ed. *Faulkner at Nagano*. Tokyo: Kenkyusha, Ltd., 1956. The transcription of discussions between Faulkner and Japanese teachers of literature in Japan in August 1955. Recurring topics are Faulkner's opinion of his own craftsmanship and works, and his impressions of Japanese literature and character.

Richardson, H. Edward. "The Ways That Faulkner Walked: A Pilgrimage," *Arizona Quarterly*, XXI:2 (Summer 1965), 133–145. A brief description of Oxford, Mississippi, and its relationship to Faulkner's Jefferson. An interview with Faulkner's closest friend and early editor, Phil Stone, is also drawn on.

Shaw, Joe C. "Sociological Aspects of Faulkner's Writing," *Mississippi Quarterly*, XIV:3 (Summer 1961), 148–152. Faulkner's theory of plantation economy and the necessary evil of slavery, his studies of social stratification, and his special pleading for the South reveal that he is a product of his Southern culture rather than a shaper of it.

Stein, Jean. "William Faulkner" in *Writers at Work: The 'Paris Review' Interviews*, ed. Malcolm Cowley. New York: Viking Compass editions, 1960, pp. 119–141. This memorable conversation of 1956 includes Faulkner's comments on art, criticism, his own works and techniques, the writer and his needs, Sherwood Anderson, Freud, the Bible, the movies, and the future of the novel.

Watkins, Floyd C. "William Faulkner in His Own Country," *The Emory University Quarterly*, XV:4 (December 1959), 228–239. With some exceptions, most Mississippians and their newspapers strongly disliked Faulkner's picture of a decaying, immoral society, for they felt it untruthful, embarrassing, and even malicious.

THE CULTURAL ROOTS OF "THE BEAR"

ARTHOS, JOHN. "Ritual and Humor in the Writing of William Faulkner," *Accent*, IX:1 (Autumn 1948), 17–30. Faulkner's concern with man's corrupt nature is symbolized by the ghostlike figures and the sense of the past which haunt his characters of the present. They try to expiate this sense of evil, guilt, and foreboding through a formalized ritual, and Faulkner attempts to treat it both by ritual and by comic scenes and incidents. But his heart-driving emotions are at odds with his basic nature (that of a gifted comic writer) and his comedy usually does not succeed well.

BALDWIN, JOSEPH G. *The Flush Times of Alabama and Mississippi.* New York, 1853. Southeast tales closer to home.

BLAIR, WALTER. *Native American Humor (1800–1900).* New York: American Book Company, 1937. The basic collection of such humor, including Thorpe's "Big Bear."

CHAPMAN, ARNOLD. "Pampas and Big Woods: Heroic Initiation in Guiraldes and Faulkner," *Comparative Literature*, XI:1 (Winter 1959), 61–77. "The Bear" and Ricardo Guiraldes' *Don Segundo Sombra* are allegorical stories of initiation rites told in part through local color and dialect. Both heroes are boys who achieve death and resurrection through slaying a sacrificial animal only to learn they are not free because they possess land; despite their passage through a puberty ritual, they still seek their liberty.

COLLINS, CARVEL. "Faulkner and Certain Earlier Southern Fiction," *College English*, XVI (November 1954), 92–97. Flamboyant humor, violence, and various folklore traditions are characteristic of Southern regional literature, and are manifested in Thorpe's "Big Bear of Arkansas" and Faulkner's "The Bear."

DRIVER, HAROLD E. *Indians of North America.* Chicago: University of Chicago Press, 1961. A convenient study in the cultural anthropology of American tribes.

HARRIS, GEORGE W. *Sut Lovingood*, ed. Brom Weber. New York: Grove Press, 1954 (original edition 1867). A novel of especially boisterous Southwestern humor.

KERN, ALEXANDER C. "Myth and Symbol in Criticism of Faulkner's 'The Bear,'" in *Myth and Symbol: Critical Approaches and Applications*, ed. Bernice Slote. Lincoln: University of Nebraska Press, 1963, pp. 152–161. Parts I, II, III, and V of "The Bear" depend to some extent on Chickasaw myth and the Indian idea of totem, while Part V and especially Part IV draw on the Christian myth, and the whole work draws on the American myth of innocence, the destruction of the wilderness Eden "and the fate of the Adamic hero." Faulkner sees the doom of both man and wilderness as inevitable.

LONGSTREET, AUGUSTUS B. *Georgia Scenes.* New York: Harper and Bros., 1897 (reprint of 1835). A collection of Southeastern tales.

RONALD, R. A. "William Faulkner's South: Three Degrees of Myth," *Landfall: A New Zealand Quarterly,* XVIII:4 (December 1964), 329–338. Faulkner's art is best understood when it is seen as relying on myth. Faulkner eschews the first level of myth—distorted reality, dramatizing what is desirable—for the second level of patterns and the third of Christian allegory.

ROURKE, CONSTANCE. *The Roots of American Culture,* ed. Van Wyck Brooks. New York: Harcourt, Brace and World, 1942. The classic analysis of American folk humor and folk culture.

SWANTON, JOHN R. *Myths and Tales of the Southeastern Indians.* Bureau of American Ethnology: Bulletin 88. Washington, 1929. Creek, Hitchiti, Alabama, Koasati, and Natchez stories.

CRITICAL INTERPRETATIONS OF "THE BEAR"

ADAMS, RICHARD P. *Faulkner: Myth and Motion.* Princeton: Princeton University Press, 1968, pp. 137–154. Ike McCaslin, in assigning moral value to a neutral wilderness, and in abdicating social responsibility by becoming a carpenter, fixes on static ideas and so fails. *Go Down, Moses* informs us that "we must go on with change, whether we like it or not."

ALTENBERND, LYNN. "A Suspended Moment: The Irony of History in William Faulkner's 'The Bear,'" *Modern Language Notes,* LXXV:7 (November 1960), 572–582. A detailed and thorough explication of "The Bear," which interprets Part IV as Ike's résumé of American and world history from the Creation onward. Faulkner develops the paradox that those who love the land destroy it in their love.

BRADFORD, M. E. "Faulkner's 'Tall Men,'" *South Atlantic Quarterly,* LXI:1 (Winter 1962), 29–39. Faulkner admires yeoman farmers who resist capitalism and industrialization in the South and whose values the young Ike shares. The values of the "tall men" are a subtle counterpoint and moral alternative to withdrawn passivity and ruthless aggressiveness in others of Faulkner's characters.

———. "The Gum Tree Scene: Observations on the Structure of 'The Bear,'" *Southern Humanities Review,* I:2 (Summer 1967), 141–150. The concluding scene in "The Bear" summarizes and judges earlier actions in the story and dramatizes the consequences of those who fail to practice endurance.

BREADEN, DALE G. "William Faulkner and the Land," *American Quarterly,* X:3 (Fall 1958), 344–357. The Southerner's economy, history, and mythology are based on the land. Faulkner, like Locke, the Physiocrats, and Henry George, argues that the evils plaguing man result from his false possession of the land.

BROOKS, CLEANTH. *William Faulkner: The Yoknapatawpha Country.* New Haven: Yale University Press, 1963, esp. pp. 261–268. A detailed reading of Part IV suggests that the structure of "The Bear" is based on associative psychology, not logic.

FISHER, RICHARD E. "The Wilderness, the Commissary, and the Bedroom: Faulkner's Ike McCaslin as Hero in a Vacuum," *English Studies,* XLIV:1 (1963), 19–28. Ike becomes a hero when he relinquishes his land and learns to trust nature as a guide. But the self-assertion of Ike's wife poisons his own charity and he becomes isolated, no longer tragic hero but merely tragic figure.

GILLEY, LEONARD. "The Wilderness Theme in Faulkner's 'The Bear,'" *The Midwest Quarterly,* VI:4 (Summer 1965), 379–385. Like Old Ben, Ike has a violent relationship to the wilderness; he destroys it instead of using it properly. The snake's manlike, erect head represents the possibility of self-transcendence, the best man can aim for in a harsh universe. But Ike doesn't achieve it.

GOLD, JOSEPH. *William Faulkner: A Study in Humanism From Metaphor to Discourse.* Norman: University of Oklahoma Press, 1966, esp. pp. 49–75. Some of "The Bear" verges on allegory. The wilderness is merely metaphor for the past and none of the characters except Ike ever becomes real. Ike himself is pathetically, not tragically, ineffectual, more like Pontius Pilate than Christ.

HUNT, JOHN W. "Morality with Passion: A Study of 'The Bear,'" in *William Faulkner: Art in Theological Tension.* Syracuse: Syracuse University Press, 1965. Ike's romantic and Christian reading of his experience is countered by both the realism of Cass Edmonds' interpretation in the commissary and the narrator's stoicism. Together realism and stoicism point up the inadequacy of feeling; but Faulkner offers only the alternative of morality ("recognizing the guilt which makes the past a living present") aligned with passion ("grieving at the loss").

LONGLEY, JOHN LEWIS, JR. *The Tragic Mask: A Study of Faulkner's Heroes.* Chapel Hill: The University of North Carolina Press, 1963, esp. pp. 79–101. In "The Bear" Ike realizes the most Christian of paradoxes: he who loses his life shall gain it. Yet paradoxically in "Delta Autumn" Ike realizes that "he who saves himself cannot save others."

MACLURE, MILLAR. "William Faulkner," *Queen's Quarterly*, LXIII:3 (Autumn 1956), 334–343. Faulkner's canon is historically a microcosm of the developing South, poetically an epic of the ravaging of land and its vengeance. His world integrates an ancient period under Indians, its medieval period of chivalric white settlers, and its modern period of economic and political parasites: nigger-mule-land is the bass chord throughout.

MALIN, IRVING. *William Faulkner: An Interpretation.* Stanford: Stanford University Press, 1957. A psychoanalytic study stressing the father-son relationship in Faulkner's work. See especially the discussion of the Abraham and Isaac motif in "The Bear," pp. 26–28, and in Faulkner's use of the Bible (Chapter 5) the idea of covenant, pp. 70–73.

MACLEAN, HUGH. "Conservatism in Modern American Fiction," *College English*, XV:6 (March 1954), 315–325. "The Bear" represents Faulkner's conservatism in its approval of order, tradition, ritual, and class, and in its primary concern with God's purpose and grace for man.

MOSES, W. R. "Where History Crosses Myth: Another Reading of 'The Bear,'" *Accent*, XIII:1 (Winter 1953), 21–33. Reared in a mythic world, Ike as a man sees reality destroy mythic perspective; as a result, he forsakes history and retreats into myth, "remain[ing] a myth-man all his life."

O'CONNOR, WILLIAM VAN. *The Tangled Fire of William Faulkner.* Minneapolis: University of Minnesota Press, 1954, pp. 125–134 [originally "The Wilderness Theme in Faulkner's 'The Bear,'" *Accent*, XIII:1 (Winter 1953), 12–20]. Faulkner's attempt in "The Bear" and "Delta Autumn" to combine the themes of man's proper relationship to nature as learned from the wilderness and his injustice to the Negro is largely unsuccessful; in "Delta Autumn" Ike, tutored by the wilderness, can acknowledge but not "materially modify" the injustice.

PERLUCK, HERBERT A. "The Heart's Driving Complexity: An Unromantic Reading of Faulkner's *The Bear*," *Accent*, XX:1 (Winter 1961), 23–42. "The Bear" is ironic, Parts IV and V showing the discrepancy between what Ike thought he achieved in the woods and what in fact he did.

RICHARDSON, KENNETH E. *Force and Faith in the Novels of William Faulkner.* The Hague and Paris: Mouton and Co., 1947, pp. 45–61. Ike learns of the wilderness through his spiritual father, Sam Fathers, who sees life in a cyclic progressive unity. Private ownership, slavery, or any unnatural and rigid design is evil. Nurtured by the creative force of the wilderness, Ike, through his "stewardship," undoes evil and becomes a selfless, enduring man.

ROLLINS, RONALD G. "Ike McCaslin and Chick Mallison: Faulkner's Emerging Southern Hero," *West Virginia University Bulletin Philological Papers*, XIV (October 1963), 74–79. "The Bear" and *Intruder in the Dust* are similar in theme, structure, and symbolic situations; both portray 16-year-old boys suddenly embarrassed by the injustice of the South who, with the help of surrogate fathers, learn and manifest "an acute moral sensitivity," withdraw from and partially reject society, and finally reemerge with "a radically reconstructed and enlarged moral vision."

STONESIFER, RICHARD J. "Faulkner's 'The Bear': A Note on Structure," *College English*, XXIII:3 (December 1961), 219–223. Each part of "The Bear" has a sevenfold structure which is a significant clue to its meaning.

WAGGONER, HYATT H. *William Faulkner: From Jefferson to the World*. Lexington: University of Kentucky Press, 1959, esp. pp. 206–211. "The Bear" results from a "double vision" in which no man is free of a world where good and evil are inseparable. Thus nature presents these: the wilderness, Old Ben, Lion—or the good, the bad, and both in combination—and Faulkner finds man's proper answer in community, his evil in acts of exploitation. The story stops short of allegory, however, since nothing is totally good or bad and since it locates an immanent but not a transcendent God.

WOODRUFF, NEAL, JR. " 'The Bear' and Faulkner's Moral Vision," *Studies in Faulkner*, in Carnegie Series in English VI. Pittsburgh: Department of English, Carnegie Institute of Technology, 1961, pp. 43–67. Faulkner's fiction contains many polarities of situation, theme, and character; such polarities invite readers to see human frustration and failure when men and nature are exploited and become ends rather than means to human fulfillment.

"THE BEAR" IN RELATION TO *GO DOWN, MOSES*

BRYLOWSKI, WALTER. *Faulkner's Olympian Laugh: Myth in the Novels*. Detroit: Wayne State University Press, 1968, esp. pp. 150–168. In capturing a "religious-ethical mode of consciousness" which transcends materiality, Faulkner eliminates the distance between object and subject and the self attempts to merge with the infinite. This act is illustrated by the initiation rites in "The Old People," and "The Bear," and Ike's failure in "Delta Autumn."

MUSTE, JOHN M. "The Failure of Love in *Go Down, Moses*," *Modern Fiction Studies*, X:4 (Winter 1964–1965), 366–378. Although the stories in *Go Down, Moses* "vary widely both in tone and in intention" (p. 367), central to all of them is the love relationship, characterized between the races as "mutual tolerance" (p. 369). Love unifies man and nature, white and black; but it also heightens Ike's inability to love in marriage or to comprehend love among the Negroes. The mulatto in "Delta Autumn" rightly accuses him and his failure is underlined by juxtaposing it to the love Molly Beauchamp has for the whites who kill her black son, since Molly knows that love involves forgiveness.

Sultan, Stanley. "Call Me Ishmael: The Hagiography of Isaac McCaslin," *Texas Studies in Literature and Language*, III:1 (Spring 1961), 50–66. *Go Down, Moses* is an integrated single unit; Ike's life in "The Old People," "The Bear," and "Delta Autumn" is the paradigm of Faulkner's indictment of civilization. Ike's redemption is a principal question in "The Bear," but "Delta Autumn" reveals that although "the wilderness had given him spiritual guidance and a way of life . . . [it] had not become his own heritage." Both the story "Go Down, Moses" and the book are "a plea for a deliverer."

Swiggart, Peter. *The Art of Faulkner's Novels*. Austin: University of Texas Press, 1962, pp. 175–179. In "Delta Autumn" Faulkner divorces himself from Ike, whom he sees as "an hysterical and self-deceiving old man." Yet in "The Bear" and elsewhere in "Delta Autumn" Ike can recognize the symbolic relation of the wilderness to life generally and to himself, and he is redeemed "by his awareness of the alienation between social man and primitive nature."

Taylor, Walter F., Jr. "Let My People Go: The White Man's Heritage in *Go Down, Moses*," *South Atlantic Quarterly*, LVIII:1 (Winter 1959), 20–32. The McCaslins are characterized by their mistaken attitude toward land and slaves, using both for their own aggrandizement; all except Ike are blind and selfish.

Thompson, Lawrance. "*Go Down, Moses*," in *William Faulkner: An Introduction and Interpretation*. New York: Barnes and Noble, 1967, pp. 81–98. The seven stories of *Go Down, Moses* dramatize various concepts of "freedom" and "bondage."

Tick, Stanley. "The Unity of *Go Down, Moses*," *Twentieth Century Literature*, VIII:2 (July 1962), 67–73. Except for "Pantaloon in Black," *Go Down, Moses* is a unified six-part novel compellingly integrated by "the continuum of time and the consequent growth of moral consciousness" and by the theme of hunter-hunted and the theme of the hunted-brought-home.

FAULKNER AND THE BLACKS

Backman, Melvin. "The Wilderness and the Negro in Faulkner's 'The Bear,' " *PMLA*, LXXVI (December 1961), 595–600. Through his treatment of the black and the wilderness in "The Bear," Faulkner shows how "mankind, driven by rapacity, has destroyed God's wilderness and enslaved His black creatures." The burden of guilt is on the South and on mankind and is reflected in Ike McCaslin's behavior; for Ike tries to "atone for the sin against the Negro" and to escape the Southern dilemma.

CARTER, HODDING. "Faulkner and His Folk," *Princeton University Library Chronicle*, XVIII:3 (Spring 1957), 95–107. Faulkner pricked the Southern conscience by advocating integration and was condemned by the Southern white majority for his liberal views, despite the fact that Faulkner "is Southern in his pride in the past . . . in his clannishness; in his unposed love of the land; and in the ambivalent love and outrage with which he confronts the South."

DANIEL, BRADFORD. "William Faulkner and the Southern Quest for Freedom," in *Black, White and Gray: Twenty-one Points of View on the Race Question*, ed. Bradford Daniel. New York: Sheed and Ward, 1964, pp. 291–308. In trying to understand Faulkner's position on the blacks, this study draws on his letters to the Memphis *Commercial Appeal* and on reactions from other Southerners.

FAULKNER, WILLIAM. "Address to the Raven, Jefferson, and ODK Societies of the University of Virginia," *University of Virginia Magazine* (Spring 1958). Virginia should lead the way in matters of civil rights; no one can afford any longer to ignore the black 10 per cent of the American population.

———. "Address to the Southern Historical Association," Memphis *Commercial Appeal*, November 11, 1955; expanded in *Three Views of Segregation Decisions*. Atlanta: Southern Regional Council, 1956. Faulkner argues the moral right of integration and stresses its importance to self-preservation.

THE RELATION OF STYLE AND FORM TO MEANING IN FAULKNER'S WORK

AIKEN, CONRAD. "William Faulkner: The Novel as Form," *Atlantic Monthly*, CLXIV:5 (November 1939), 650–654. An historically important analysis of Faulkner's style, including observations on his technique which deliberately withholds meaning.

ANTRIM, HARRY T. "Faulkner's Suspended Style," *The University Review*, XXXII:2 (December 1965), 122–128. "Faulkner's 'suspended style' is a way of showing the possibility inherent in any given instant, and the style's parentheses, negations, recapitulations, and qualifications are indicative of an attempt to show how the past, continually shifting and changing in the re-creation, nonetheless proceeds inexorably to a qualification and conditioning of the present." This style is "a necessary accompaniment to his concern to bridge the gap between word and deed, between the person thinking and the thing thought about."

BALDANZA, FRANK. "Faulkner and Stein: A Study in Stylistic Intransigence," *Georgia Review*, XIII:3 (Fall 1959), 274–286. A fruitful analysis of Faulkner's use of repetition, stasis, periodicity of sentence structure, and rhythm through free syntax and lack of concrete detail by an examination of Faulkner's *Absalom, Absalom!* and Gertrude Stein's *The Making of Americans*.

BECK, WARREN. "William Faulkner's Style," *American Prefaces*, IV (Spring 1941), 195–211. Faulkner's style is "progressive" because it synthesizes many past styles.

BERINGAUSE, A. F. "Faulkner's Yoknapatawpha Register," *Bucknell Review*, XI:3 (May 1963), 71–82. Onomatology is indispensable in studying Faulkner; "Names permit [him] to create an Existentialist present, to universalize his tales, to symbolize and radiate meanings historically, geographically, and psychologically. . . ."

CAMPBELL, HARRY MODEAN, and RUEL E. FOSTER. *William Faulkner: A Critical Appraisal*. Norman: University of Oklahoma Press, 1951, esp. pp. 40, 111. Generally Faulkner's symbolism is limited to developing tones through ironies or pathetic fallacies, introducing antecedent action, describing characters, advancing the narrative, unifying the narrative through refrains, relating chaotic appearances to cosmic chaos, and embodying satire. Humor, which may be cruel, sadistic, genial, or anecdotal, often mingles tones, offsetting romance or horror as in the laconic ledger entries announcing Eunice's death.

FLANAGAN, JOHN T. "Faulkner's Favorite Word ["implacable"]," *Georgia Review*, XVII:4 (Winter 1963), 429–434. Faulkner turns repeatedly to Latinisms, neologistic compounds (formed by telescoping words), idiomatic language, and strongly negative adjectives. He especially liked to accumulate epithets for a single noun.

GREEN, MARTIN. *Re-Appraisals: Some commonsense readings in American literature*. London: Hugh Evelyn, 1963; New York: W. W. Norton Co., 1967, pp. 167–194. Faulkner's rhetoric has "gone crazy with unlimited power, betraying itself . . . in demonstrable absurdities, infelicities, and errors" by means of tautologies, elaborate similes at odds with their referents, and "strained and unnatural narration." Faulkner does not know what he is talking about and believes only in "the consciously ambiguous or the aggressively inadequate."

HARRISON, ROBERT. "Faulkner's 'The Bear': Some Notes on Form," *Georgia Review*, XX:3 (Fall 1966), 318–327. Harrison views the story three ways—as myth (archetypal material underlines "The Bear"), art (Faulkner replaces chronological time with an epicycle of interpenetrating *times*), and idea (the story alternates between sentence and example, idea and allegory).

HOVDE, CARL F. "Faulkner's Democratic Rhetoric," *South Atlantic Quarterly*, LXIII:4 (Autumn 1964), 530–541. The exultant style, extravagant "linguistic pyrotechnics," and passionate generalities of Faulkner's style are derived from American political oratory.

LEAVER, FLORENCE. "Faulkner: The Word as Principle and Power," *South Atlantic Quarterly*, LVII:4 (Autumn 1958), 464–476. Faulkner's key mood of intensity comes from making words serve dual and polar purposes rather than from long, involuted sentences. He characteristically uses negative words, coined compounds, and repetition.

LEHAN, RICHARD. "Faulkner's Poetic Prose: Style and Meaning in *The Bear*," *College English*, XXVII:3 (December 1965), 243–247. Much of the story's meaning derives from descriptive detail and verbal associations "which interrelate the characters and extend the theme of the novel imagistically," as if it were a poem. Through mechanistic imagery and other details Faulkner connects Boon with Lion.

MAYOUX, JEAN-JACQUES. "The Creation of the Real in William Faulkner," *Études Anglaises* (February 1952), 25–39; trans. Frederick Hoffman in F. J. Hoffman and O. W. Vickery, *William Faulkner: Three Decades of Criticism*, pp. 156–172. An examination of Faulkner's style of immediacy, through the observing, narrating character and the listener character, which allows him to juxtapose the interior consciousness against the exterior action and to approach reality as the materialization of events, the "psycho-drama of the present," the Platonic symbol for the eternal truth.

O'FAOLAIN, SEAN. *The Vanishing Hero*. London: Eyre and Spottiswoode, 1956, esp. pp. 99–134. Faulkner is a "maimed genius" who "cannot write plain English." He uses extravagant tropes and large, meaningless abstractions to write with "passionate provincialism" only of Mississippi.

POIRIER, RICHARD. *A World Elsewhere: The Place of Style in American Literature*. New York: Oxford University Press, 1966, esp. pp. 78–83. Faulkner's style insists we reject our assumptions and "in the very grammar of refutation [giving up] all that we might conventionally expect about the events he is narrating, his alternative version of them necessarily [exciting] our attention and consent."

SLATOFF, WALTER J. "The Edge of Order: The Pattern of Faulkner's Rhetoric," *Twentieth Century Literature*, III:3 (October 1957), 107–127 [later incorporated in *Quest for Failure* (Ithaca, N.Y.: Cornell University Press, 1960)]. Faulkner presents many things in conflicting terms; thus he writes of events in ways which simultaneously "suggest motion and immobility."

SWIGGART, PETER. *The Art of Faulkner's Novels*. Austin: University of Texas Press, 1962. In the first part of his study Swiggart examines Faulkner's "stylized characterization" and isolates "various techniques by which he establishes moral and social themes without sacrificing crucial elements of narrative realism"; Faulkner's "social mythology" and contrasts between rational-"puritan" and primitive-natural characters; and Faulkner's point-of-view techniques. In the rest of the book he analyzes Faulkner's canon in detail, emphasizing language, structure, theme, and characterization.

THOMPSON, LAWRANCE. "A Defense of Difficulties in William Faulkner's Art," *The Carrell,* IV:2 (December 1963), 7–19. The apparent obscurities and repetitions in Faulkner's narratives are deliberate means by which he implies meanings and invites readers to act out some important part of the relationships he is portraying, often so the reader may better understand the moral dimensions of those relationships.

TRITSCHLER, DONALD. "The Unity of Faulkner's Shaping Vision," *Modern Fiction Studies,* V:4 (Winter 1959–1960), 337–343. In trying to discover the essence of any moment, Faulkner approaches it from past, present, and future, often mixed and submerged; he sacrifices time to do so.

TURNER, ARLIN. "William Faulkner and the Literary Flowering in the American South," *Durham* [England] *University Journal,* LX:1 [n.s. XXIX:2] (March 1968), 109–118. Faulkner's work draws on many older literary traditions in the South but departs from them in using symbols and advanced narrative techniques; and in unremittingly pursuing an understanding (although a skeptical and unpopular one) of human nature. His use of fantasy, horror and humor, and his emphasis on decay and the grotesque, have had a broad and deep influence on later Southern writers.

William Faulkner's Canon

This is a listing of published volumes only; all books are novels unless otherwise indicated. For a listing of articles by and interviews of Faulkner, as well as foreign editions of his books, see reference to Meriwether, p. 318.

THE MARBLE FAUN (Poetry). Boston, 1924.

SOLDIERS' PAY. New York, 1926. London, 1930, 1931.

MOSQUITOES. New York, 1927.

SARTORIS. New York, 1929, 1951. London, 1932, 1954.

THE SOUND AND THE FURY. New York, 1929; with *As I Lay Dying*, in Modern Library, 1946.

AS I LAY DYING. New York, 1930; Modern Library, 1946.

THESE THIRTEEN (Short stories). New York, 1931. See also *The Collected Stories of William Faulkner*.

IDYLL IN THE DESERT (Short fiction). New York, 1931.

SANCTUARY. New York, 1931.

MISS ZILPHIA GANT (Short fiction). Dallas, 1932.

SALMAGUNDI (Newspaper sketches), ed. (with intro.) Paul Romaine. Milwaukee, 1932.

LIGHT IN AUGUST. New York, 1932; Norfolk, Conn., 1947.

A GREEN BOUGH (Poetry). New York, 1933.

DOCTOR MARTINO AND OTHER STORIES (Short stories). New York, 1934. See also *The Collected Stories of William Faulkner*.

PYLON. New York, 1935, 1951.

ABSALOM, ABSALOM! New York, 1936, 1951.

THE UNVANQUISHED. New York, 1938. 1952.

THE WILD PALMS. New York, 1939.

THE HAMLET. New York, 1940, 1956.

GO DOWN, MOSES. New York, 1942, 1945.

INTRUDER IN THE DUST. New York, 1948.

KNIGHT'S GAMBIT (Short stories). New York, 1949.

COLLECTED STORIES OF WILLIAM FAULKNER (Short stories). New York, 1950.

NOTES ON A HORSETHIEF (Novella). Greenville, Miss., 1951.

REQUIEM FOR A NUN (Drama). New York, 1951.

A FABLE. New York, 1954.

BIG WOODS (Short stories). New York, 1955.

THE TOWN. New York, 1957.

NEW ORLEANS SKETCHES (Newspaper sketches from *Salmagundi*), ed. (with intro.) Carvell Collins. New Brunswick, N.J., 1958.

THE MANSION. New York, 1959.

THE REIVERS. New York, 1962.

ESSAYS, SPEECHES, AND PUBLIC LETTERS, ed. James B. Meriwether. New York, 1965.

5.00
132